The Paraglyph Mission

This book you've purchased is a collaborative creation involving the work of many hands, from authors to editors to designers and to technical reviewers. At Paraglyph Press, we like to think that everything we create, develop, and publish is the result of one form creating another. And as this cycle continues on, we believe that your suggestions, ideas, feedback, and comments on how you've used our books is an important part of the process for us and our authors.

We've created Paraglyph Press with the sole mission of producing and publishing books that make a difference. The last thing we all need is yet another tech book on the same tired, old topic. So we ask our authors and all of the many creative hands who touch our publications to do a little extra, dig a little deeper, think a little harder, and create a better book. The founders of Paraglyph are dedicated to finding the best authors, developing the best books, and helping you find the solutions you need.

As you use this book, please take a moment to drop us a line at **feedback@paraglyphpress.com** and let us know how we are doing - and how we can keep producing and publishing the kinds of books that you can't live without.

Sincerely,

Keith Weiskamp & Jeff Duntemann
Paraglyph Press Founders

Paraglyph Press
4015 N. 78th Street #115
Scottsdale, Arizona 85251

email: **feedback@paraglyphpress.com**
Web: **www.paraglyphpress.com**
Phone: 602-749-8787

Recently Published by Paraglyph Press:

Degunking Windows

By Joli Ballew and Jeff Duntemann

Mac® OS X 10.3 Panther Little Black Book

By Gene Steinberg

Windows XP Professional: The Ultimate User's Guide, Second Edition

By Joli Ballew

Visual Basic .NET Black Book

By Steven Holzner

The SQL Server 2000 Book

By Anthony Sequeira
And Brian Alderman

The Mac OS X.2 Power User's Book

By Gene Steinberg and Pieter Paulson

Mac OS X v.2 Jaguar Little Black Book

By Gene Steinberg

The Mac OS X.2 Jaguar Book

By Mark R. Bell

Game Coding Complete

By Mike McShaffry

Monster Gaming

By Ben Sawyer

Looking Good in Print, 5th Edition

By Roger C. Parker

Jeff Duntemann's
Wi-Fi Guide

2nd Edition

Jeff Duntemann

PARAGLYPH™
PRESS

President
Keith Weiskamp

Editor-at-Large
Jeff Duntemann

Vice President, Sales, Marketing, and Distribution
Steve Sayre

Vice President, International Sales and Marketing
Cynthia Caldwell

Production Manager
Kim Eoff

Cover Designer
Kris Sotelo

Jeff Duntemann's Wi-Fi Guide 2nd Edition

Limits of Liability and Disclaimer of Warranty

The author and publisher of this book have used their best efforts in preparing the book and the programs contained in it. These efforts include the development, research, and testing of the theories and programs to determine their effectiveness. The author and publisher make no warranty of any kind, expressed or implied, with regard to these programs or the documentation contained in this book.

The author and publisher shall not be liable in the event of incidental or consequential damages in connection with, or arising out of, the furnishing, performance, or use of the programs, associated instructions, and/or claims of productivity gains.

Trademarks

Trademarked names appear throughout this book. Rather than list the names and entities that own the trademarks or insert a trademark symbol with each mention of the trademarked name, the publisher states that it is using the names for editorial purposes only and to the benefit of the trademark owner, with no intention of infringing upon that trademark.

Paraglyph Press, Inc.
4015 N. 78th Street, #115
Scottsdale, Arizona 85251
Phone: 602-749-8787
www.paraglyphpress.com

Paraglyph Press ISBN: 1-932111-88-3

Printed in the United States of America
10 9 8 7 6 5 4 3 2 1

To the Eternal Memory of
Victoria A. Duntemann
1924-2000

Who pulled my life from the void,
Named the stars for me,
And always had a dollar
For one more pipe fitting!

About the Author

Jeff Duntemann's career as technology author/editor spans almost thirty years, since his first technical articles began appearing in 1974. After six years as programmer/analyst for Xerox Corporation, Jeff served as Technical Editor for Ziff-Davis' *PC Tech Journal* and founding editor of Borland International's *Turbo Technix*. He is the sole author of ten books on computer technology and has collaborated with others on almost twenty more. His book *Assembly Language Step By Step* has been in print continuously since 1989 and is probably the best-selling title on Intel assembly language ever. He wrote the "Structured Programming" column at *Dr. Dobb's Journal* for four years. His books and magazine articles have won several awards from the Society for Technical Communication and the Arizona Book Publishing Association, including the STC's coveted Distinguished Technical Communication award, presented to him in 1993.

Jeff co-founded The Coriolis Group in 1989 with publishing entrepreneur Keith Weiskamp, and edited the firm's journal *PC Techniques* (later *Visual Developer*) throughout its ten-year life. Most recently, Jeff helped establish Paraglyph Press, at which he now holds the position of Editor at Large. He is an accomplished teacher and public speaker, and has given numerous presentations on the technology industry at conferences and conventions in the US, Canada, and the U.K.

At home, Jeff writes science fiction, and tinkers with electronics, robotics, astronomy, amateur radio (as K7JPD) and (of course) wireless networking. He lives with Carol, his wife of 28 years, in Colorado Springs, Colorado. Readers may contact him via email at wifiguy@duntemann.com, and are encouraged to see his Web site at www.duntemann.com. For more information on Wi-Fi, see his site www.drivebywifiguide.com.

Acknowledgments

Abundant thanks are due to many parties:

- My informal review board: David Beers, Eric Brombaugh, Michael Covington, Bill Leininger, and Jim Mischel.

- The guys on the NetStumbler forums, particularly Blackwave, Thorn, and Lincomatic. You didn't hear much from me because I was too busy hitting the "Search" button.

- Jacco Tunnissen, for maintaining wardrive.net, from which I learned a *lot*.

- Vendors Pacific Wireless, Linksys, and D-Link, for product photos. Note that no "review products" were used in writing this book. I chose them for their merits and paid for them all.

- The whole Paraglyph gang: Keith Weiskamp, Steve Sayre, Cynthia Caldwell, Ben Sawyer, Kris Sotelo, and Kim Eoff. The magic is back—let it always be so!

- Carol, my spouse and best friend, for listening to me say, "It's almost done!" for the last three months, before it finally was.

Contents at a Glance

Contents

Chapter 6
Access Points and Gateways 113

Chapter 7
Wi-Fi Client Adapters 145

Chapter 8
Antennas, Cables, and Connectors 173

Chapter 9
Putting It Together and Testing It Out 209

Making Connections by Cutting the Cables

When the infamous tech bubble burst in early 2000, the computer products industry went into a miles-deep funk from which it is only now beginning to emerge. Nobody was buying computers or printers and nobody was buying add-in memory or hard drives. However, people *were* buying something—a new and remarkable technology that kept selling through the worst of the tech recession, and continues to sell briskly to this day. That technology is "wireless Ethernet," better known as Wi-Fi. It was hot in 2003, when the first edition of this book was published. It's even hotter today.

Why? Wi-Fi neatly and cheaply solves a number of problems that no other earlier technology could address:

- It allows home network users to transfer files among all computers in the home, and back up crucial files to a central backup location—without pulling wires through the walls.

- It allows people to share a single broadband Internet connection among all the computers in their homes—without pulling wires through the walls.

- It allows people to sit with their laptops wherever they want and read email and do their online work. They can now work on the porch, by the pool, or at the picnic table in the yard. Computing is no longer something chained to a desk.

- It allows business travelers to connect to the Net while on the road, simply by opening a laptop computer at a "hotspot" located at a coffee shop or hotel lobby.

- It allows people to use their networked laptops in company conference rooms, for comparing notes or making presentations.

- It allows a "media server" computer in the home to stream music and video to computers and digital media receivers throughout the home, without pulling wires or physically playing CDs or DVDs.

- It allows high-speed data transfers between houses or business/college campus buildings where pulling wires between locations would be difficult or prohibitively expensive.

- It allows the mounting of security cameras where pulling wires would be difficult or impossible.

It seems like every month or so a new Wi-Fi product appears that solves yet another problem, and does it without adding to that ratsnest of wires under your desk.

I've had a Wi-Fi wireless network at home almost since the beginning of Wi-Fi time. For me, it was originally a way to dodge the work involved in networking a 30-year-old slump block house (drilling concrete—ugh!) but over time it went *way* beyond that. Using a high-gain add-on antenna, I learned how to use Web-based astronomy databases from my telescope out in the back of our very large yard, and on my tinkerer's bench a video-equipped "personal Mars crawler" robot is now taking shape, tied to my control computers by nothing more limiting than a Wi-Fi microwave beam.

It's amazing how just ditching the wires can change your life, even if you're not an incurable geek. Teaching you how to harness Wi-Fi—*especially* if you're not an incurable geek—is the primary mission of this book.

Getting through the Wi-Fi Confusion

The term "Wi-Fi" is an informal catchall for a whole family of wireless networking specifications with forbidding names like 802.11a, 802.11b, and 802.11g. (The oddly named Bluetooth is a distant cousin of Wi-Fi, as is HomeRF.) All Wi-Fi technologies are based on a fundamental 1997 specification called 802.11, created by the Institute for Electrical and Electronic Engineers, or IEEE. The "b" in "802.11b" means that this standard was the second "change request" submitted for the original 802.11 specification. The list currently goes out to the letter "n." If you think this is confusing, you're right. Unfortunately, a whole raft of 802.11 technical standards have been created and you can tell them apart only by their final, lower-case letter. (I'll summarize them all at the end of this book to help you sort through them.)

The word "wireless" is confusing too, since these days most people consider "wireless" to be technoslang for "cell phones," and wireless networking has nothing to do with cell phones. Furthermore, several different kinds of "wireless networking" technologies are in use, some obscure, some extinct, and none compatible with any of the others. Confusion, as usual, is rampant. Computer networking is not an easy business, and it has a great many moving parts. The rate of change in the networking world is breathtaking, and in the *wireless* networking world, things move even faster. Not only can't you step in the same river twice, you have to run as hard as you can just to find the river.

In this book, and especially in this first chapter, I want to set your bearings about the whole Wi-Fi concept. That way you can learn the basics properly so that you can teach yourself anything else that you might later need to know. This is not a "dummies" book; I have more respect for you as a reader than that. I will start at the beginning, but eventually the material will get fairly technical. There's no avoiding it, and it's made worse because I don't have the space to show you screen shots and provide completely unambiguous step-by-steps for every Wi-Fi device on every computing platform there is.

All of this is to say that you'll have to lay out some effort and study this stuff, try things, and take notes. *Do your damnedest to understand how it works.* When networking fails, it tends to fail *quietly*—that is, it doesn't necessarily put up error messages or do anything but sit there and ignore you. If you can't step back, think it through, gather information about what's going on, and then change something usefully, you will be lost.

Let's now take on the question of what Wi-Fi is in the simplest and briefest way possible.

The Essentials of Wi-Fi

Wi-Fi is a technology that connects computers (and other computerish devices like printers and game consoles) without wires, in a particular and standardized way. A Wi-Fi connection moves data files between devices precisely as a wired connection would, albeit not as quickly. From the perspective of your computer, there is no difference between a connection created with cables and a connection created with Wi-Fi equipment. To your PC's operating system, a network is a network. Your PC doesn't care how the hookup is accomplished.

Wi-Fi is a hardware solution even though it doesn't use cables. Each computer or other device that will connect to a Wi-Fi network requires a small device called a *client adapter*. This is usually a plug-in card of some kind (there are several different kinds) but can also be a USB (Universal Serial Bus) device. In addition to one client adapter for each connected device, a Wi-Fi network also requires a centrally located device called an *access point*. The access point is Grand Central Station for the wireless network and coordinates the connections among all the various wirelessly connected computers and other devices. To send data to one another, client adapters must transmit their data to the access point, which then relays it to the client adapters to which the data is addressed.

Client adapters do have the power to connect directly with one another (without having an access point in the middle as a radio relay station) but this feature is less useful than it sounds and few people in my acquaintance use it much.

Virtually all Wi-Fi networks are set up to work with an Internet connection, ideally a high-speed broadband connection like cable or DSL. Connecting a Wi-Fi network to the Internet requires some additional hardware, specifically something called a *router*. A router is a device that connects one network to another network, and the Internet is also a network. The router sits between your (small) network and the (huge) Internet, directing traffic and perhaps more importantly, limiting the sorts of connections that occur between your network and the Internet. There is a class of products that combine a router and a Wi-Fi access point into a single box. These are sometimes called *wireless gateways*, *wireless residential gateways*, or *wireless routers*. A gateway makes it very easy to share an Internet connection among several machines around your house or small office.

The connections between Wi-Fi adapters are accomplished with microwave-frequency radio waves. There is a small microwave transmitter and receiver in every client adapter and access point. This is obvious in some Wi-Fi devices, which come with small antennas. The strength of the microwave energy used is so minuscule as to not be any sort of health risk. Wi-Fi, in fact, uses much less powerful transmitters than the cellphones we mash up against our faces most of the livelong day, and its microwave energy is almost a million times less powerful than the microwave energy used in microwave ovens. (It's also helpful that Wi-Fi devices aren't held right up against the side of your head!)

The range of Wi-Fi devices is fairly short, no more than a couple hundred feet at very best, and usually less. (Within a building, it can be as little as 80 or 100 feet.) This range can be increased when necessary by using special antennas and by careful placement of access points. For larger homes and especially offices, it's possible to build Wi-Fi networks with multiple access points, connected by cables, allowing seamless *roaming* access anywhere in the building where one of the network's access points is within range. If designed and installed carefully, such a network can allow people to carry their laptops and PDAs (while their batteries hold out) anywhere in the building and never lose their connections to the network. Roaming is considered a "premium" feature and costs more (and requires more fussing) but it's there if you decide you need it.

Wi-Fi has been around for several years, but until fairly recently the gear was so expensive that consumers couldn't afford using Wi-Fi in home networks. That was then. These days, client adapters have a typical street price of $35 to $70, and access points can be had for $60 to $100. Wireless gateways cost in the neighborhood of $80 to $120. Rebates and sales—or buying used gear locally or on eBay—can bring prices down even further, and many people have equipped their home Wi-Fi networks for well under $200.

Among the most enthusiastic users of Wi-Fi networking are business travelers, who are taking advantage of the proliferation of Wi-Fi *hotspots* at coffee shops, hotels, conference centers, and even city parks, to connect their laptops to the Internet while on the road. A hotspot is simply a wireless access point that is connected to the Internet and available to the general public. Most of these hotspots are fee-based, but many are part of *community networks* and may be used for free.

Among computer enthusiasts, Wi-Fi has become a hobby with a vigor I haven't seen in computing for quite a few years. People are building Wi-Fi antennas out of coffee cans and potato chip cans, and modifying and enhancing Wi-Fi gear in a lot of really creative ways. I'll speak to that phenomenon later in this book as well.

Because Wi-Fi data is passed around the network on radio waves, it's possible for outsiders to listen in unless you take certain precautions like turning on Wi-Fi's built-in encryption system. Security is a very big issue in Wi-Fi, and I devote five whole chapters (Chapters 11 through 15) to security later in this book. Please read them *before* you install your Wi-Fi network!

Why Wi-Fi?

The curse of emerging technologies is "soft standards." Standards are supposed to ensure that devices made by different vendors can work with one another, but sometimes things don't work out, and subsequent chaos (and angry consumers) can sink a promising technology before it ever achieves critical mass. 802.11b, the major Wi-Fi networking standard, is fairly young (it was only finalized in 1999) and as communications standards go is relatively complex. Early in the life of 802.11b a group called the Wireless Ethernet Compatibility Alliance (WECA) created a logo-certification program for 802.11b devices. The 802.11b certification program was named "Wi-Fi," for "Wireless Fidelity," hearkening back to the Hi-Fi audio systems of the 1950s. WECA began testing vendor products for adherence to the 802.11b standard, and products that pass may display the Wi-Fi logo. Consumers are encouraged to see the Wi-Fi logo as indication that a product is fully compatible with the 802.11b standard. In this, it's directly comparable to the Microsoft Windows logo program that allows software vendors to indicate that their products have been tested for Windows compatibility.

> *As odd a term as it is, Wi-Fi was an unqualified success, with many millions of units now out there in the hands of consumers. For that reason, WECA changed its name to the Wi-Fi Alliance in mid-2002. The Wi-Fi Alliance has changed its Web address from* **www.weca.net** *to* **www.wi-fi.com,** *and the WECA acronym is now history.*

Although the "Wi-Fi" term and compatibility testing program began with the single 802.11b standard, as the two later (and related) wireless standards became popular, "Wi-Fi" was expanded to include the 802.11a and 802.11g technologies as well. As new 802.11-based technologies appear (like the 802.11n 108 Mbps standard, which we may see in 2005), I suspect that they will be incorporated into the overall Wi-Fi testing program by the Wi-Fi Alliance.

There are still weak spots and soft spots—and a few empty spots—in the three Wi-Fi standards: 802.11a, 802.11b, and 802.11g. Additional task groups have been convened by the standards-setting body (a group called the IEEE, for the Institute of Electrical and Electronic Engineers) to fill in the holes in the 802.11-based standards. Many of these task groups are still working, and thus the problems they are in the process of solving aren't quite solved yet. I'll be mentioning quite a few of these task groups later on in this book, and will summarize the whole lot of them in the IEEE Task Group Encyclopedia at the end of this book.

Finally, to avoid having to say "Eight Oh Two Dot Eleven" all the time (which is a clumsy mouthful), the terms *Wireless-A*, *Wireless-B*, and *Wireless-G* have become popular as synonyms for 802.11a, 802.11b, and 802.11g, respectively. I will be using these three shorter terms in preference to their more technical synonyms during the remainder of this book.

IEEE 802.11: How It Came About

Wireless networking has been around for some time. The University of Hawaii pioneered the wireless LAN idea with an experiment called ALOHANET way back in 1971. ALOHANET was an expensive, big-iron system solving a serious problem—trading data among university sites scattered across four islands—but the principles are the same as those that govern data-trading between the machine in your den and the ones in your kids' rooms. Sun Microsystems created a prescient hand-held mini-tablet computer called the Star 7 in 1992, which included 900 MHz wireless networking, but the poor Star 7 never made it to market. (Sun, like my alma mater Xerox, has a bad habit of pioneering technologies that it never markets, and then watching other companies make their fortunes doing the same things ten years later.)

The first wireless LAN technology I ever saw was a 900 MHz UHF ISM band WaveLAN system, which was demonstrated at a COMDEX trade show in 1994. The demo consisted of a laptop with a PCMCIA card (physically identical to today's Wi-Fi PCMCIA cards) networked to a PC about ten feet away. The data rate was 1.6 Mbps, which seemed mighty fast at the time. I wanted one but couldn't afford it—both ends of the connection together would have cost me almost $2,000!

The WaveLAN system worked, and worked well. It was expensive but the people who needed it needed it badly, and WaveLAN and numerous systems like it became a small and little-known sliver of the networking industry, mostly used by high-priced consultants to create proprietary solutions to specific problems, usually for big corporations. Everybody had a different scheme for bundling data into packets and spinning it off into the airwaves, and nobody's scheme talked to anybody else's scheme. That was the way all the vendors in that era wanted it; their customers had money and were willing to spend lots of it, so there was bottom-line value in keeping them captive to a proprietary system.

In 1997, the Institute of Electrical and Electronic Engineers (IEEE) released their 802.11 standard for wireless networking, and everything changed.

The Magic of (IEEE) Numbers

The IEEE is a large and influential body of engineers that does a great many things, but what they do that matters most (in my view) is develop and establish technology standards. Standards are important because they enlarge markets, and make it possible for technologies manufactured by different vendors to interoperate and communicate with one another. This is especially important in the area of computer communications, in which the whole idea is to get the machinery talking.

The IEEE has been doing this for a long time, and in many areas, some of them pretty far removed from computing. The process, however, happens in pretty much the same way: The IEEE establishes a "working group" to pursue a particular standards issue. The group meets and hashes out the issue, sometimes for several years, and eventually creates a document that defines or modifies a standard. The document is then sent out to interested IEEE members for a mail vote. Based on the results of that balloting, the document is either sent back for further work or is adopted as a new (or modified) standard.

Working groups are given numbers. When a working group is tasked with modifying an existing standard that already has a number, the group is given a new number that has either additional digits or else letters appended to the existing standard number.

The 802 Standard

The mother of all IEEE networking standards is the 802 standard, which was under discussion for most of ten years. This standard, which was finally adopted in 1990, governed the lowest level of networking functions: Physical and link control. (These are the bottom two layers of the Open Systems Interconnection model for networking. If you're reasonably technically inclined, the OSI model is worth some study, as it is enormously useful in keeping the countless network standards and mechanisms separated and correctly related. Unfortunately, it's a big subject, and I cannot cover it in detail in this book.)

The overall networking standard was numbered 802. Different standard areas within the greater 802 standard were given decimal qualifiers. The original Ethernet protocol invented by Xerox in the early 1970s was refined slightly and given the number 802.3 when it was standardized as part of the 802 definition. The Token Ring networking technology introduced by IBM in the mid-1980s was given the number 802.5.

In the mid-1990s, the IEEE created a working group to develop a standard for wireless networking. The working group was given the number 802.11 (which is the eleventh working group under the 802 standard, *not* a refinement of 802.1) and it was adopted in 1997.

The original 802.11 standard specified a frequency of 2.4 GHz with available data rates of 1 and 2 megabits per second (Mbps). 802.11 products were marketed almost immediately, but were slow to be accepted, at least in part because the data rates were so slow compared to contemporary wired networks. 802.3 wired Ethernet technology had gone from 10-Base-T (10 Mbps) to 100-Base-T (100 Mbps) at about the same time, and 2 Mbps looked pretty grim by comparison. Furthermore, radio hardware that could work effectively at 2.4 GHz frequencies was still pretty expensive at that time. The end result was that 802.11 networking did not exactly set the world on fire. The IEEE almost immediately created several task groups to begin work on improving 802.11, especially in the area of data rate.

The fire came in 1999 when the 802.11b amendment to 802.11 was accepted and published. The 802.11b standard was formerly known as "802.11 High Rate" because it added 5.5 Mbps and 11 Mbps data rates to the existing 1 and 2 Mbps rates. 802.11b was the right spec at the right time, and most manufacturers who had been selling 802.11 hardware wasted no time updating their products to adhere to the new 802.11b standard. Although still fairly expensive at that time (I paid $1,200 for an 802.11b access point in 1999!), the higher bit rates were enough to put 802.11b wireless networking on the radar screens of large and mid-sized companies that could afford it.

Apple Pioneers Consumer Wi-Fi

High prices kept 802.11b networking out of the hands of ordinary consumers (quite apart from technowhackos like me) until 2000, when Apple's AirPort wireless networking system took prices down into consumer territory. After that, it was *le deluge*, especially once an industry consortium called the Wireless Ethernet Compatibility Alliance (WECA) created the Wi-Fi compatibility testing program. (WECA changed its name in 2002 to the Wi-Fi Alliance.) These days, wireless access points can be had for under $100, and client adapters for as little as $50.

Until mid-2003, 802.11b was the most significant 802.11 standard extension, but others have now been released and still more are in process. 802.11a products reached the market late in 2001, with still-faster bit rates—and much higher prices. In early 2003, much faster 802.11g products hit the retail market, and will eventually push 802.11b products into obsolescence. (Note that the letters are assigned when a task group is *formed*, not when the eventual standard is finalized and adopted. The 802.11a and 802.11b task groups were formed at the same time, but the 802.11b folks had a less difficult job to do and finished first.)

Some 802.11 task groups are addressing only specific features of 802.11 networking, like encryption. Not all letters in the "alphabet soup" are full upgrades to the whole 802.11 idea. In fact, only four are full-fledged network technologies: 802.11a, 802.11b, 802.11g, and 802.11n.

Competing non-802.11 wireless network technologies are out there, but none have the same sense of destiny that 802.11 has. A technology called HomeRF hit the market early in 2000, and although slower than Wi-Fi, it was at its introduction much cheaper, and has arguably better security and built-in machinery for handling telephone calls. (In a sense, HomeRF merges wireless LANs and cordless phones.) However, HomeRF never achieved what 802.11 achieved: the magic of an IEEE standards designation.

The IEEE imprimatur, with its respect among major industry hardware vendors, is what makes the magic happen. Unless or until a directly competing technology gets that imprimatur, I don't see anything knocking 802.11 from its leadership position in wireless networking.

Internet Connection Sharing

Why buy Wi-Fi? I answered that question in the first paragraph of this chapter: The #1 reason people put wireless networks in place is to share an Internet connection among family members without knocking holes in the walls and pulling wires. In older times, families sometimes shared a single Internet dialup account, but it often required a second phone line, and only one family member could be logged in at once. This led to a lot of yelling down the halls of things like "Mike, dammit, are you still on that thing??!?" and fistfights among siblings.

Sharing Internet connections can be done with wires, of course. Creating a wired network using a cheap broadband router appliance like the famous Linksys BEFSR41 "blue box" has for years allowed several people to use the same Internet connection at the same time. The Internet connection cable was plugged into the back of the router, and all the computers wishing to share the connection were plugged into the router as well, all with cables.

Sharing an Internet connection seamlessly is possible because the Internet is a packet-based network. Files or data streams like text from a Web site are broken up into little chunks called *packets*, which are then routed individually to wherever they have to go. The router splits an Internet connection by looking at the packets entering the house single-file on the Internet connection, deciphering the addresses attached to all the packets, and then routing those packets individually to whichever computer in the house the packets are addressed to. The router works like a post office sorting mail: The mail comes into the post office on the back of a truck in one huge unsorted sack, and then the postal workers sort the pile into smaller piles, each of which is then delivered to a separate home or office.

If everybody in the house is bringing down MP3 music files or other large data files at the same time, the connection may seem to slow down. Still, because all the data is bundled into individually addressed packets, nothing in the data stream interferes with anything else, and each person in the house has the impression that he or she is the only one using the Internet connection.

This worked (and still works) beautifully. However, in those older times every computer in the house had to be connected to the router via a relatively fat wire called a "category 5" cable, "CAT5" for short. Wi-Fi put an end to the running of wires. More recently, the router and access point have been combined into a single appliance called a *wireless gateway*. This saves some space, some cable, and some complexity, and works just as well.

The router or gateway knows another trick that can be very useful: It limits how much the outside world can learn about the house's network. Some Internet Service Providers (ISPs) object to people sharing a single Internet connection among several computers, but the router makes it almost impossible for an ISP to determine how many computers are connected to the network. The router makes the network look like only *one* computer from the outside, no matter how many computers are in fact connected to the router. Most ISPs now cease to make a fuss over this, but some still do. Read the fine print of your ISP service agreement to see what the details are. There seems to be a general policy of "don't ask, don't tell" about this issue, and if you have trouble getting your home network to work, it's probably best *not* to ask your ISP for help. Their job is to get Internet packets into your home. What you do with the packets once they arrive is *your* challenge—and helping you with that challenge is what this book is about.

Sharing Printers and Other Wi-Fi Gadgetry

Internet connection sharing is probably the biggest single part of Wi-Fi's attraction for small office and home office users, but sharing printers can also be extremely useful. (Not everyone in the house needs his or her own laser printer!) You can buy a small device called a *wireless print server*, which connects to a printer via a parallel port or USB port and has a built-in Wi-Fi client adapter, complete with antenna. The new Linksys WPS-54GU2 is shown in Figure 1.1. It supports two printers, as do other similar devices like D-Link's DP-313, and its high-throughput Wireless-G connection allows graphics-intensive print jobs to move much more quickly over the network.

With its data cable connected to a wireless print server, your printer can be anywhere in your home or office where it's within range of a wireless access point. You don't need a computer nearby at all—whatever computing power is needed for the print server function is built into the wireless print server itself. Linksys also has a Wireless-B print server, the PPS1UW, with support for both a wired and wireless interface, making it compatible with almost any type of home office network.

Game consoles that allow Ethernet connections for multiplayer gaming can be connected to your Wi-Fi network through an *Ethernet wireless bridge* like the Linksys WGA-54G or the D-Link DWL-810. An Ethernet wireless bridge allows any Ethernet device to connect wirelessly to a Wi-Fi access point or gateway. Game consoles are the #1 use of such bridges, but they can also be used with Ethernet-equipped printers, scanners, and anything else that communicates through a standard Ethernet port.

Figure 1.1
The Linksys WPS-54GU2 Wireless-G Print Server. (Photo courtesy of Linksys.)

Other Wi-Fi gadgetry continues to show up on a regular basis, and some of it is very cool. One of my favorites is the D-Link DCS-1000W wireless network camera, shown in Figure 1.2. It can take both snapshot images and streaming video and send them over your Wi-Fi network. When used as a security camera, it has a motion detector feature that triggers transmission of images when something moves in its field of view. (It can actually email you when it "sees" something—with a snapshot attached!) It can stream video to hard disk or act as a Webcam with its integrated Web server. Unlike a lot of inexpensive wireless video baby monitors, it incorporates data encryption using Wired Equivalent Privacy (see Chapter 13) so that people outside your home can't use your own cameras to spy on you.

How Fast? Bit Rate vs. Throughput

There's a lot of confusion inherent in the common question: "How fast is Wi-Fi?" Well, that depends on what you mean by "fast." There is the rate at which bits move through the air, from one 802.11-family radio subsystem to another. This is commonly called the *bit rate*, and it is different for the three current members of the Wi-Fi family. For example, the top speed of an Wireless-B link is 11 Mbps, which means eleven million bits, or megabits, per second. When conditions get noisy or the two stations move too far apart to support that top speed, there are slower speeds that the link will automatically fall back to: 5.5 Mbps, 2 Mbps, and at the bottom 1 Mbps.

Figure 1.2
The D-Link DCS-1000W Wireless Network Camera. (Photo Courtesy of D-Link.)

Now, where you get in trouble is when you assume that if your bit rate is 11 megabits (million bits) per second, you can send an eleven-megabit file (which is about 1.37 mega*bytes*) in one second.

Not so. In fact, not even close.

The problem is that your file's bits aren't the only bits moving over the radio link. To move across the link, the file is broken up into *packets*, each of which is a kind of data container that is itself made out of bits that form headers and footers containing addresses and routing information. Without getting too technical right here, I'll simply say that there are multiple layers of containers, all of them made from bits. When your file is properly packetized and sent over the link, it's a *lot* bigger than it was when it was just a file on your hard drive. Think of packing something fragile for shipping cross-country. The final box, with all the bubble pack and foam peanuts inside, is *much* bigger than the glass brandy snifter it contains.

So even though your bit rate might be 11 Mbps, your *throughput* (that is, how many actual bits worth of data file you can transfer in a given time) is a lot less. Your actual maximum possible Wireless-B throughput, flat-out with no one else sharing the connection, will be under 7 megabits per second, and probably closer to 4 or perhaps 5 megabits per second. How much under 7 megabits per second (abbreviated Mbps) depends heavily on the manufacturer of your Wi-Fi access point and client adapter, and whether or not you have the security features enabled. On a Wireless-B link with an 11 Mbps bit rate, most of my throughput measurements have come in at about 5 Mbps with security disabled, and 4 Mbps with security enabled. That's still pretty fast, but be careful when doing bandwidth math in your head. Bit rate is not the same as throughput!

Your throughput will be *much* higher using Wireless-A or Wireless-G products, both of which have maximum bit rates of 54 Mbps. At their best, both the "A" and "G" standards both deliver a maximum throughput of about 20 Mbps—less than half their maximum bit rates.

 I'll explain how to test what your throughput actually is (using free software you can download from the Web) in Chapter 9, when we actually put some Wi-Fi networks together.

Roaming

Although most SOHO (Small Office/Home Office) Wi-Fi network users incorporate only one wireless access point (AP) in their networks, it's possible to create a network with multiple access points, each access point serving a zone within an area too large for a single AP to serve. Such a network, incorporating multiple access points, is called an *extended service set* (ESS). In an ESS, users with laptops and PDAs are able to roam about the entire area covered by the ESS and not lose their connections to the network. The several access points seamlessly "hand off" users who "roam" from place to place, just as the cells in our cellular telephone network do.

At least that's how it should work in theory.

The problem is that this is one of the several "soft spots" in the 802.11 family of Wi-Fi wireless networking specifications. 802.11 dictates that roaming is permitted, and explains what should happen when clients roam from the influence of one AP into the influence of another. Unfortunately, the specification doesn't say *how* this roaming should be accomplished. Roaming isn't trivial, and requires some pretty detailed communication among the various access points within the ESS. The numerous manufacturers of access points have all implemented the details of roaming in different ways, most of which are incompatible with all the others.

What this means is that for an ESS to implement roaming correctly, *all the access points in the ESS must be from the same manufacturer*—and, ideally, of the same model. In general, access points designed for corporate rather than residential service work best in roaming installations. Some of the lower-end residential access points and wireless gateways don't implement roaming at all.

An 802.11 task group was convened to work on the roaming problem, and the final draft of the 802.11f standard was approved in August 2003. When the 802.11f specification is implemented by the major manufacturers, access points from different manufacturers will be able to partake in an ESS that allows roaming across all access points. The 802.11f standard establishes a protocol called the *Inter-Access Point Protocol* (IAPP). Various flavors of IAPP exist among various manufacturers, but the 802.11f protocol, as it is adopted, will replace all the proprietary flavors with a single, universal protocol. Until 802.11f is implemented by all major wireless manufacturers, roaming will remain a single-vendor solution, and you should inquire closely of the vendor of an AP model under consideration to make sure that it supports 802.11f-compatible roaming among others of its own kind and those from other vendors.

Wi-Fi, PDAs, and Battery Life

PDAs (especially higher-end models running Windows CE and PocketPC) have been compatible with Wi-Fi for some time. There is, however, a catch: Using Wi-Fi will shorten your PDA's battery life radically. Wi-Fi cards are *not* low-power devices. The Linksys WCF11 Compact Flash Wireless-B adapter for PDAs draws 300 ma (milliamps) from the PDA battery. The Buffalo Airstation WLI-CB-G54A Wireless-G Cardbus card draws 550 ma on transmit and 250 ma even when idle. No wonder so few manufacturers actually post power consumption figures for their PC card and CF (Compact Flash) card products.

This will change to some degree in the near future. Chipset manufacturers including Phillips and Intel have begun producing Wi-Fi chipsets that incorporate *intelligent power management*, which drops the radio subsystem of the Wi-Fi card to low-power standby mode whenever data is not being passed. Keep in mind that if you're downloading large data files like MP3s or accessing Web sites continuously, the radio will not drop into standby, and the draw on your battery will remain high and charge life will be greatly shortened.

You have the option of buying an expansion sleeve (which is very common on high-end lines like HP's IPaq) for additional expansion cards and add-on batteries, but this bulks up the unit to a fist-sized lump that doesn't just slip into your shirt pocket. Many security consultants use sleeve-equipped PocketPC PDAs and the MiniStumbler wireless network auditing utility to perform "undercover" audits of corporate networks for the presence of rogue access points. However, for ordinary business-related PDA work, expansion sleeves and external battery packs are very awkward.

Some of the newer Wireless-G products (like D-Link's DWL-G650) draw relatively little power when in standby (only 2.4 ma for this product) and this will likely be a trend. You need to shop carefully and request power consumption information from manufacturers who do not post it. Whatever Wi-Fi product you choose for your PDA, you will have to be prepared to recharge it much more frequently than you did before you took it wireless. My own experiments with Wi-Fi installed in PDAs have not been good from a battery life standpoint, and I continue to recommend that you use a notebook computer instead of a PDA for portable Wi-Fi-connected computing.

*Interestingly, some newer PDAs come with built-in Bluetooth wireless connectivity. Bluetooth (a wireless technology related to but not compatible with Wi-Fi) has a much shorter range than Wi-Fi (typically 30-50 feet or so) and considerably lower power requirements. Bluetooth data rates are much lower than Wi-Fi data rates, but for tasks like downloading email it's more than fast enough. Unfortunately, while Bluetooth allows you to wirelessly synchronize your PDA with your PC, Bluetooth Internet hotspots are still extremely rare. Bluetooth will not help you read your email or surf the Web on business trips. The companies to watch for Bluetooth access points are Anycom (**www.anycom.com**) and Pico Communications (**www.pico.net**) but as best I know, there is no Web-based directory of public Bluetooth hotspots.*

Both Symbol (**www.symbol.com**) and Socket (**www.socketcom.com**) offer low-power Wireless-B adapters designed specifically for PDAs, in both Compact Flash and SDIO (Secure Digital Input/Output) form factors. These are worth watching, especially Socket's minuscule SDIO card. I'll have more to say about PDA-oriented Wi-Fi client adapters in Chapter 7. Some of them have gotten amazingly small (especially the SDIO format adapters) and once the power management problem is wrestled to the mat, Wi-Fi equipped PDAs will become *much* more popular and useful.

The 2.4 GHz ISM (Industrial, Scientific, & Medical) Band

Wi-Fi is a microwave technology, but that obscures the fact that it's a *radio* technology, and it has its place in the radio portion of the electromagnetic spectrum. Microwaves are just radio waves with very short wavelengths. The wavelength of your typical AM radio signal is a thousand feet. FM radio operates at a wavelength of a little under ten feet. Wi-Fi, by contrast, works at a wavelength of 12 centimeters—less than five inches. The frequency used by Wi-Fi gear is at a frequency of about 2.45 Gigahertz (GHz), which is 2.45 billion cycles per second. The key point to remember is that Wi-Fi isn't the only kid on that particular radio block.

The radio spectrum between 2.4 GHz and 2.4835 GHz was already a pretty busy place prior to 1997, when the 802.11 standard was first published, and it's gotten a lot busier with the ascendance of Wi-Fi. The band itself goes back some years before 1997, and it was originally set aside by the Federal Communications Commission (FCC) for the use of industrial machinery like induction heaters (including microwave ovens), cordless phones, and various arcane medical and scientific gadgetry gathered under the description "industrial, scientific, and medical." Licenses are not required for individuals to operate ISM equipment designed for use within the band. However, manufacturers must apply for and receive *type acceptance* from the FCC before they can manufacture products for the band, which must adhere to fairly strict FCC requirements for power output, band use, and purity of emissions.

Wi-Fi gear is, like ISM equipment, unlicensed, and it also must undergo FCC type acceptance. However, Wi-Fi gear is not considered ISM equipment and does not have any kind of priority on the frequencies it uses over ISM equipment. In fact, if a medical or industrial device causes interference to a Wi-Fi network, the network's owner has no legal recourse other than to move to a different Wi-Fi channel, of which (for American users) there are only 11.

Two other significant wireless networking technologies, Bluetooth and HomeRF, share space on this band. As with Wi-Fi, both are secondary uses to virtually all other uses of the band, parts of which are used by public safety (police and fire) communications, news gathering services, seaborne and airborne radar, and numerous other things. (More on this in Appendix B, where I speak in detail of Wi-Fi legalities.)

The allocation of the band to Wi-Fi equipment is complex. Figure 1.3 shows diagrammatically how the band is laid out. Perhaps the most important thing to notice is that other regions of the world have a larger Wi-Fi frequency allocation than American users do. The Japanese, in particular, have the use of a full 100 MHz between 2.4 and 2.5 GHz for 802.11b operation. American users have only the first 83.5 MHz of that space, with Europe falling somewhere in the middle. Parts of Europe have access only to limited subsets of the band, France being the most notable example.

Wi-Fi channels are spaced 5 MHz apart. However, the bandwidth of a Wi-Fi channel is 25 MHz. This means that individual channels overlap with two adjacent channels in either direction. Channel 6, for example, overlaps channels 4, 5, 7, and 8. For American users, at least, this means that only the three channels 1, 6, and 11 may be used simultaneously in the same general space without any channel interference. Channel 14 is something of an outlier and is set apart slightly from the first 13 channels. Channel 14, however, is used mostly in Japan and (along with channels 12 and 13) is not sanctioned by the FCC.

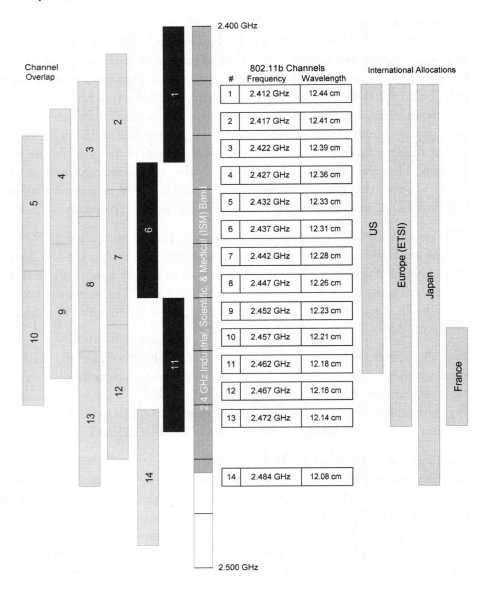

Figure 1.3
The 2.4 GHz Wi-Fi Channels, National Allocations, and Overlap.

How Products Become Wi-Fi Certified

The "Wi-Fi" logo is something like the "Intel Inside" stickers you used to see a lot on personal computers. (I think they dropped them eventually because nobody really cared what was inside as long as it ran Windows. "Windows Inside" would have made more sense.) The idea is that a product with the "Wi-Fi" logo on it could be trusted to "talk" to any other product bearing the Wi-Fi logo. Consumers wouldn't have to read technical specifications to gather parts for a wireless network. If it was all Wi-Fi, it would work. Thus the right to carry the Wi-Fi logo became something that no 802.11-family wireless networking manufacturer could do without.

Getting the logo means having a product tested for Wi-Fi compatibility and adherence to the Wi-Fi standard. To submit a product for testing, a vendor must first join the Wi-Fi Alliance, which used to be called WECA (Wireless Ethernet Compatibility Alliance). Membership fees are not cheap (currently $20,000 per year) and support the testing process and other Alliance overhead. Furthermore, it costs $15,000 per product to have a product tested for Wi-Fi logo compliance. Testing turnaround is fairly quick—currently about one month.

Products are tested using NetIQ's Windows-based Chariot network testing utility while connected to a standard Ethernet wired network under typical wireless operating conditions. Chariot emulates typical network application traffic, and records network throughput, errors, and other parameters. Products are given a pass/fail grade based on testing, which qualifies (or excludes) a product from using the Wi-Fi logo.

Growing the Wi-Fi Logo for the Growing Wi-Fi Family

The term "Wi-Fi" originally applied *only* to devices adhering to the 802.11b standard—Wireless-B—not 802.11a or any of the other flavors of 802.11. Early in 2002, the Wi-Fi Alliance had devised a separate logo program for 802.11a—Wireless-A—compatibility, and called it "WiFi5." The "5" indicated the 5 GHz band, where 802.11a wireless networking operates. By October 2002, after some focus group failures, the Wi-Fi Alliance decided that the term "Wi-Fi5" was confusing. You may still hear it from time to time and read it in publications written while it was current.

Once Wireless-G products began appearing in quantity in mid-2003, separate logos for *three* standards began to make less and less sense. Currently, the Alliance is treating all three 802.11-family wireless networking standards—802.11a, 802.11b, and 802.11g—as "Wi-Fi." Instead of a separate and distinctive logo for each standard, special annotations on a single, larger logo will indicate which of the three standards the equipment in the labeled box is compatible with. An example of this new, all-in-one logo is shown in Figure 1.4.

Figure 1.4
The New All-Standards Wi-Fi Logo.

Reading the Wi-Fi Logo

As you begin shopping for new Wi-Fi gear, it's important to know how to interpret the Wi-Fi certification logo on the product boxes you see. The new logo shown in Figure 1.4 has four checkable boxes, one for each of the Wi-Fi Alliance's four certification testing programs for 802.11-family gear. From top to bottom here's how you should read the logo:

1. The first box indicates that the device underwent and passed the compliance testing for Wireless-B (802.11b), which is the 11 Mbps technology operating on the 2.4 GHz band. This is by far the most common of the three Wi-Fi standards.

2. The second box indicates that the device underwent and passed the compliance testing for Wireless-G (802.11g), which is the 54 Mbps technology operating on the 2.4 GHz band.

 Although Wireless-G is required to be backward-compatible with Wireless-B, the Wi-Fi Alliance still requires that a Wireless-G device pass the Wireless-B test sequence separately.

3. The third box indicates that the device underwent and passed the compliance testing for Wireless-A (802.11a), which is the 54 Mbps technology operating on the 5 GHz band. I'll have more to say about Wireless-A (which never really caught on and is becoming increasingly uncommon) in Chapter 4.

4. The fourth box indicates that the device underwent and passed the compliance testing for Wi-Fi Protected Access (WPA), the new security technology

that addresses the serious security holes in the earlier Wired Equivalent Privacy (WEP) security system. Chapter 14 is devoted entirely to WPA, how it works, and how you can set it up on WPA-equipped Wi-Fi gear.

Multi-standard wireless networking products are available, which incorporate technology for two or even all three Wi-Fi standards. In those cases, all three boxes may be checked for a single product. However, in most cases, you'll have certification for either the 2.4 GHz technologies or the 5 GHz technology, but not both.

In reading the logo on Wireless-G product boxes, you may be puzzled to see that many Wireless-G products are certified as compatible with Wireless-B, but not Wireless-G itself. What happened here is that many of the larger Wi-Fi manufacturers (including D-Link and Linksys, the two largest) "jumped the gun" on Wireless-G, and released what they called "draft-G" gear before the IEEE formally completed and published the final Wireless-G technology specification, back in mid-2003. These draft-G products came close to the IEEE standard, but for small discrepancies were not able to pass the Wi-Fi Alliance's fairly rigorous Wireless-G testing sequence. Draft-G products are being revised to completely follow the 802.11g specification, and over time more and more of them will have the Wireless-G box checked in the Wi-Fi compliance logo.

Many of the later entrants, like Buffalo Technology (**www.buffalo-technology.com**) waited until the final 802.11g specification was published before submitting their products for testing, and thus the Buffalo Airstation Wireless-G product line was certified for Wireless-G from its first release.

How important Wi-Fi certification is in cases like these is hard to state in general terms. I always recommend that non-technical users buy all their Wi-Fi gear from the same vendor to be sure that no small incompatibilities will prevent their networks from working correctly or at peak efficiency.

It's About Connections

In just a few words, I've presented Wi-Fi from a height. Like all networking, Wi-Fi is about connecting things, and there is a very broad and very deep set of technologies that underlie all networking, wired and un-wired. You don't have to know a lot about networking to put together a good and (reasonably) secure Wi-Fi network—but you have to know *something*. So let's take a closer look at what computer networking is and how it has evolved to the current day, when it has come to embrace the entire world through the reach of the global Internet.

Networking, Ethernet-Style

The Networked Age began for me in mid-1980, when my building at Xerox Corporation's industrial campus in Webster, NY was wired for Ethernet. I watched, fascinated, as installers pulled these stiff yellow cables, as thick as my index finger—ThickNet, they called it—through the space above the suspended ceiling, and installed "vampire taps" (I'm not making this up!) periodically so that workstations could connect to the cable. Shortly afterward, I was taught how to access something called ARPANet, which I neither fully understood nor appreciated at the time. In the years that followed, ARPANet became the Internet—and Ethernet became the overwhelmingly dominant network technology in the world.

(A vampire tap, by the way, is a little clamp with one long tooth that you could tighten around a ThickNet cable. The tooth bit through the insulation and made contact with the cable's central conductor, allowing a network connection to be made without cutting the cable. ThickNet may be dead, but vampire taps are still being used in cheap strings of Christmas lights!)

The legacy of those two concepts that I met almost at once in 1980—Ethernet and the Internet—lies everywhere in today's computer industry. Wi-Fi is in fact a flavor of Ethernet, and I'll explain that relationship in this chapter. Much of Wi-Fi is driven by a need to connect to the global Internet, and I'll explain that part of the machinery in Chapter 3. If you can get a conceptual grip on Ethernet and the Internet, you won't have any trouble grasping Wi-Fi, nor putting it together in your home or small office, and using and maintaining it over time.

Nonetheless, networking is an *extremely* complex subject, and I'm going to have to ask you to take a great deal of it "on faith." Someday I intend to write a detailed book-length introduction to Ethernet/Internet networking, but we're not there yet. For here and now, everything points to Wi-Fi, even if (on the surface) it doesn't appear to.

There is a lot to cover, so let's get going.

Networking from Square One

A network consists of two or more computers connected through some sort of medium, passing information among them over that medium. "Medium" here is jargon; it refers to anything capable of acting as a data pipe. Various types of wires have long been used, and wire will always be the commonest network medium. Wi-Fi uses microwaves as its network medium. Infrared light can also act as a network medium, and Windows XP contains support for an infrared-based "Personal Area Network" within a single room. Surprisingly, the type of medium used in a network doesn't matter much, and it can be changed very easily without much disruption. If you already have a wired network, you can "swap out" wires for Wi-Fi and very little else changes.

Today's networks are "packet-based." Data moves over the network medium divided up into packets. A *packet* is just a smallish chunk of data with a destination address and a sender address. Every computer on a network has its own unique address. To send data to another computer on the network, a computer measures out a packet's worth of data, places its own address and the destination computer's address on the packet, and shoves the packet out onto the medium. The packet may pass by many other computers on the network (or all of them!) but only the computer to which the packet is addressed will grab the packet from the medium and read the data inside the packet. There may be more data to be sent than will fit in one packet, so the originating computer may simply repeat the process, measuring out data into packets, addressing them, and sending out the packets over the network one by one until all the data has been sent.

The Ether Vibrates

That, in a nutshell, is how virtually all networking works, not just Ethernet. At the bottom of it, it's about slapping addresses on data packets and getting those packets to their destinations. What we call "Ethernet" is now mostly a standard way of dealing with packets and addresses. However, the word "Ethernet" provides a fascinating hint at the logistics of getting packets from point A to point B.

Let's return to the dawn of networking time (that is, the Disco era of the 1970s) and consider how the original Ethernet worked. The fat yellow cable that connected all computers on a primordial Ethernet was a *coaxial cable*. (I explain coaxial cable in some detail in Chapter 8.) Coaxial cables don't just carry electricity. They are designed to carry radio-frequency energy, confined within the cable so that it doesn't radiate freely into space and get into trouble. (Ethernet began to get in *that* kind of trouble with the advent of Wi-Fi...) Ethernet signals are technically streams of digital pulses, but they happen so rapidly that in terms of the laws of physics they *are* radio energy.

 It's a common metaphor to suggest that coaxial cable is a pipe or hose for radio waves, which is true to an extent. However, when we think of things moving through a pipe, we imagine them going in one end and coming out the other after some time spent in passing through the pipe.

Radio waves travel at the speed of light, which is 186,000 miles per *second*. Considering that a local area network is generally confined to one building, the farthest two computers are likely to be from one another is a couple hundred feet. Radio waves can move two hundred feet in so little time it almost doesn't matter. Inject a radio signal into two hundred feet of coaxial cable, and in practical terms the signal is just *there*, everywhere, filling the cable what might as well be instantaneously.

So it isn't really accurate to say that a computer stuffs a packet into the data pipe, where the packet starts trucking gamely along the pipe toward its destination. The packet is in fact a species of a radio signal, and when a computer injects that signal into the cable, the entire cable essentially vibrates with that signal all at once. The "ether" was a Victorian term for the (imaginary) medium in which radio waves propagate. Radio waves were vibrations in the ether. That's why Xerox's research scientists (who had a legendary whimsical streak) coined the term "Ethernet."

I don't mention this just for local color. Bear with me; it's important. See Figure 2.1, which depicts four computers on one of those original, coaxial-cable based Ethernets. Each computer has an address, from 001 to 004, and I'll refer to the computers by their addresses.

Computer 001 has a packet for computer 003. So, having placed 003's address on the packet, 001 places the packet on the cable. For a (very) short period of time, the entire cable vibrates with that packet. All computers on the network glance at the address tag, but only 003 copies the packet off the cable into its own storage.

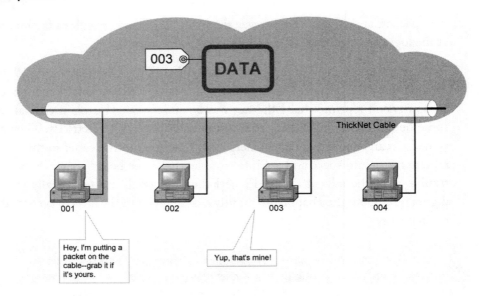

Figure 2.1
A Packet on the Ethernet.

What's important here? Not the nature of the cable so much as the fact that *all computers connected to the cable share that one cable*. All packets placed on the cable "touch" all computers on the cable, though that touch is brief and only extends to examining the address. All computers, furthermore, are absolute peers. Nobody is "boss" and no computer sits at the center of things directing traffic in any way. Traffic isn't directed at all. It's just "out there" on the cable, and whatever computer finds its address on a packet grabs that packet.

Better Wires: Category 5

The fat yellow cables that vibrated with early Ethernet packets was expensive, bulky, and hard to deal with. (I learned a few new words looking over the shoulders of the Xerox Ethernet installers back in 1980.) It had to be cut to a very precise length, it could only be so long, and those vampire taps could be positioned only in certain places. However, in 1980 it was the best we could do. Radio energy is fussy in ways I can't fully explain here, but over the years we've gotten much better at making it do what we want it to do. As the 1990's drew to a close, the early Ethernet coaxial cables were abandoned for a new type of cable: the *twisted pair*. Actually, inside this new king of networking cables were no fewer than *four* pairs of wires, with the two individual wires of each pair twisted around one another. A twisted pair of two wires has special properties with respect to radio-frequency energy, just as coaxial cable does. When two wires are twisted around one another, they shield one another, and radiate very little of the signal that travels within them.

In normal network service, only two of the four pairs are actually used to carry data. The two unused pairs are sometimes used to carry DC power to remote Ethernet devices like wireless access points or bridges mounted on poles to create a point-to-point connection between two buildings or other locations. This is called Power over Ethernet (PoE) and I describe it more fully in Chapter 6.

This type of cable has come to be called *category 5 twisted pair*. Most people call it CAT 5 for short. The end connector looks a lot like a modular telephone plug, only wider, to accommodate eight wires instead of a phone cable's four (see Figure 2.2). There are four lesser categories of twisted-pair cable, down to category 1, which is for humble analog telephone service only. Category 5 cables are extremely flexible, quite small, and very cheap compared to almost any kind of coaxial cable. They have basically driven coaxial cable networks into the sea.

The very common term "10Base-T" refers to Ethernet networks based on CAT 5 cabling. The "10" indicates that the network operates at a maximum of 10 million bits per second, abbreviated Mbps. The "Base" stands for *baseband*, which means that signals are injected onto the network at a single frequency. The alternative to baseband is *broadband*, which uses many different frequencies to pass different sorts of signals simultaneously over the same cable. Cable TV systems are broadband

Figure 2.2
A Category 5 End Connector.

systems, which is why you can receive both TV signals and Internet data over a single piece of wire. Finally, the "T" stands for "twisted pair."

100Base-T is similar, but operates at the higher speed of 100 Mbps rather than 10 Mbps. Very recently, computer equipment has become available for 1000Base-T networking, also called *Gigabit Ethernet*, which operates at one *billion* bits per second, abbreviated Gbps. 1000Base-T networks require a better class of cabling called category 5E or category 6. Gigabit Ethernet networks can be run over existing category 5 cables, but higher error rates will trigger more packet resends, slowing the system down well below its gigabit potential.

Most all of the networking cables and equipment you'll use in home office and small office networks these days will be 100Base-T.

A Change in Topology

For all the radical difference in shape, size, and cost, twisted pair cabling works pretty much the same way as coaxial cabling for Ethernet networks. A packet is placed on the CAT 5 cable and the whole cable vibrates with that packet. What has gone away is much of the physical radio-wave fussiness of the cable, in terms of how long it must be, where the taps must be, how the ends must be terminated, and so on. In addition to purely physical flexibility, CAT 5 cables are much more flexible in how they can be strung around and connected. Although a single run of CAT 5 cable has a maximum length of about 295 feet, individual runs of cable can be any length less than that. (There are no "magic lengths" for cable runs as there were with the original Xerox Thicknet networks.) Finally, CAT 5 cabling allows something that was impossible with coaxial cable: a *switched* network. I'll come back to switched networks later in this chapter.

Stringing computers out along a single run of coaxial cable, as was done in early Ethernet systems, is called a *bus topology*. ("Topology" here is jargon for "functional shape.") Bus topologies work, and they were the best we could do in low-cost networks prior to the 1990s. They work, but when they fail, they fail badly. Due to electrical peccadilloes in the technology, even a momentary break in the cable could bring the entire network to a screaming stop. This was not an issue in the first ThickNet systems, where the cable was a single, uninterrupted wire. However, a later variation on coaxial Ethernet gave us ThinNet, which used a modular type of coaxial cable that had bayonet-style push-and-twist connectors on each end. The modular cables were joined at the back of each networked computer by inexpensive

T-connectors that were far from robust. If a connector got dirty or loose, the slightest tug or twist would break the electrical connection within the larger run of cabling, and the whole network would freeze.

Finding such "weak links" in a long run of linked cables was infuriatingly difficult, rather like figuring out which bulb had gone dead in one of those miserable 1950's series strings of Christmas tree lights. It was such weaknesses that gave bus topologies a bad name, though in fairness it was cheap bayonet connectors and not the topology itself that made the technology failure-prone.

Nonetheless, bus topologies are now mostly extinct. The development of cheap category 5 cabling allowed a new shape for local area networks: the *star* topology. In a star-topology network, each computer is connected to a central point called a *hub*. I've drawn it out in Figure 2.3.

For the simplest sorts of hubs, called *passive* hubs, there's nothing at the center but all the various wires from the networked machines connected together. A more sophisticated class of devices called *active* hubs contain amplifiers that help overcome

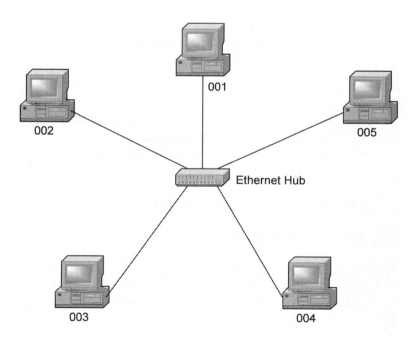

Figure 2.3
A Star Topology Ethernet Network.

signal loss and disruption due to resistance in the cables, as well as static induced from motors and other nearby electrical machinery. When a packet enters the network from one leg of the star, the active hub's amplifiers strengthen it and retransmit it down all the other legs of the star.

But fundamentally, a hub changes nothing: Each computer places a packet on its end of a connecting cable, and the whole star sees the packet at once. All computers on the network examine the address field on the packet, and the computer whose address is on the packet grabs it.

The primary value hubs bring to networking is reliability: If a cable connection breaks, only *one* device is cut loose from the network. Finding the bad connection is as simple as following the cable from the *incommunicado* computer back to the hub.

Hubs do not eliminate a problem that plagued other early Ethernet systems: *Packet collisions.* Whether it was a hub network or a star network, only one packet could be sent out on the network at a time. If two computers by chance decided to launch a packet at the same moment (which on a busy network is almost inevitable) the two packets would collide, and one or both packets would be lost. Ethernet engineers were forced to create a complicated set of protocols to minimize packet collisions. These protocols did the job, but they took time and bandwidth that could otherwise have been used to send more packets across the network. The more computers joined on a single network, the more likely collisions became, and the slower the whole business of networking grew.

For this and other reasons, hubs were eventually superceded by better technology, as I'm about to explain. However, the simple idea of a network hub is one you should keep in mind: When we finally get back to Wi-Fi networking, it will return, bringing all its triumphs and its sorrows.

Bogging Down on Bandwidth: Switching to Switched

Simple Ethernet networks built with hubs eventually fell victim to their own success. As networking hardware and software became more common, more and more computers were hooked up to networks. Still, every packet sent by *any* computer was received by *all* computers, even though in most cases that packet was addressed to only one computer. On a busy network, where most computers are sending packets most of the time, 90% of the network's computers spent most of their network time waiting for all the other computers' packets to "play through." The total capacity of the network to move data around, which we refer to as the network's *bandwidth*, was fixed, but was shared by all the network's computers. As the number of computers on the network grew, each got a smaller slice of the total bandwidth, and the network gradually slowed down until eventually it all but ground to a halt.

The solution proved to be perhaps the most significant technological advance in networking since the invention of networking itself: the *network switch*.

Simply put, a network switch creates a momentary, dedicated high-speed data connection between two computers. When one computer wishes to send a packet to another, the switch isolates both computers from the rest of the network just long enough for a packet to pass from one to another, and for an acknowledgement to be returned, indicating that the packet had gotten through. Because for that moment both computers are alone on a temporary, two-computer network, there is no fear of collisions, and thus no time or bandwidth must be spent on collision avoidance. Most significant of all, there is no bandwidth wasted carrying packets to computers that don't need to see them. The two computers engaging in that momentary conversation have the full bandwidth the network can offer all to themselves.

I've drawn a LAN switch schematically in Figure 2.4. The switch can very quickly create a data connection between any two computers on its network. Note that this diagram is schematic only: The actual switch mechanism is purely electronic and has no moving parts.

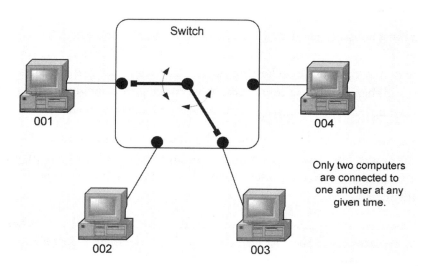

Only two computers
are connected to
one another at any
given time.

Figure 2.4
A Network Switch.

The connection created by the switch lasts only as long as it takes for that one packet to move between the two connected computers and acknowledgement passed back. If more than one packet needs to pass between the same two computers, that packet may have to wait its turn. The switch is careful to allow each of the connected computers to pass packets in turn so that no computer sees the network as slow or paused. Packets move so quickly through a modern Ethernet network that it almost seems like all machines can be in full connection with all other machines at once, all the time. Packets move through even slow Ethernet networks at a rate of ten million bits per second, so a typical 1,500-byte packet can move between two computers in a small fraction of a second. More modern 100-Base-T networks are ten times faster than even that.

Switches, Ports, and Addresses

A network switch is *much* more than a hub. It has some considerable intelligence built into it, most of which is devoted to determining what devices are on its network and what their addresses are. In a hub network, only the computers need to pay attention to the addresses attached to packets. In a switched network, this burden is moved to the center and placed on the switch.

A switch contains a number of switchable connection points called *ports*. (Most switches used in home office networks have four or perhaps eight ports. Switches for large corporate networks can have a great many more, sometimes hundreds.) One computer or other networked device (like network printers and other networkable gadgets) can be attached to each port.

Each port must be associated with a unique network address. The switch keeps a table inside itself, relating a network address to a switch port. When a packet arrives at the switch, the switch looks at the packet's destination address, looks up that address in its port table, and then creates the connection between the port belonging to the sender of the packet and the port belonging to the packet's intended recipient.

The switch has several tricks that it uses to build and maintain its internal table of network addresses, but most commonly, a computer will broadcast its network address over the network when it powers up or reboots. The switch sees this broadcast and records the address.

Network switches are common, small, and inexpensive. Most of the switches I've used in home networks in the past were from Linksys, like their 5-port EZXS55W model shown in Figure 2.5.

Figure 2.5
A 5-Port Switch for Home Networks. (Photo courtesy of Linksys.)

Don't run out and buy a network switch yet—simple switches lack critical machinery for dealing with the Internet, as I'll explain in Chapter 3. Only when your home network is completely disconnected from the Internet does a dedicated network switch make sense, and such networks are getting rarer all the time.

Media Access Control (MAC) Addresses

The nature of network addresses is worth some discussion, because they come up now and then in Wi-Fi work, and in certain cases you'll be called upon to determine the addresses of some of your network gear. The network addresses used in Ethernet networks are formally called *media access control* (MAC) addresses. The term comes from the network machinery that controls what devices get access to the network medium, which if you recall is the generic term for whatever carries packets from one device to another. It can be cable, glass fiber, or microwaves, but it's still a medium, and access to the medium has to be managed in an orderly fashion.

Any device or part of a device that represents an interface to an Ethernet medium has a MAC address. Your computer's network interface controller (NIC) has a MAC address. Your Wi-Fi client adapters each have a MAC address. Some devices have more than one MAC address, because they contain more than one Ethernet interface. The best example is the wireless gateway, which I'll describe in detail in Chapter 6. A wireless gateway acts as a communications center to which a wired network, a wireless network, and the Internet are all connected at once. There is a separate MAC address for the wireless interface, a MAC address for the Ethernet cable interface, and yet a third for the Internet interface.

Theoretically, *every MAC address ever issued by any equipment manufacturer is unique.* No other device ever made in the past (and if the rules are followed, ever made in the future) will carry that same exact address. If more than one device with the same MAC address were to show up on a single network, packets could go to the wrong destinations, and network switches could become very confused. Nothing's perfect, and there have been duplicate MAC addresses issued through error or carelessness, but it happens rarely enough as not to be a major problem.

A MAC address is a number, usually expressed in *hexadecimal,* which is base 16 rather than our familiar base 10. In hexadecimal, values from 10 through 15 must be represented as single digits, so the letters A through F are used to represent values from 10 to 15, respectively. This is why a MAC address may look like this:

0080C8ADAC0B

What looks like letters are actually used as numbers in hexadecimal notation. Each pair of hexadecimal digits represents one byte, and each byte contains eight bits. The full number thus contains 48 bits, and 48 binary bits are capable of expressing 281,474,976,710,656 different values. In other words, 281 *trillion* values and change—that's a lot of network interface controllers, so we're not going to run out of MAC addresses any time soon.

Each MAC address is divided into two groups of three bytes. The first three bytes are a manufacturer code. The last three bytes contain a serial number of devices built by that manufacturer. This manufacturer code can be misleading, because manufacturers often build subsystems and then sell them to other companies who build them into final products. You won't necessarily see the company name that "owns" your MAC address on the gear the MAC address belongs to.

For example, the 24-bit hexadecimal value 00022D is the manufacturer code for Lucent/Agere, the originator of the Orinoco line of Wi-Fi client adapters and access points. The value 004096 is the code for Aironet Wireless Communications, which is now owned by Cisco. A full MAC address for a single Orinoco Wi-Fi PC card might look like this:

00022D-6749A4

The hyphen is a frequent notational convention, and separates the 24-bit manufacturer code from the 24-bit device identifier. A lot of MAC address blocks are assigned to faceless Pacific Rim conglomerates whose names don't go on the box. 24

bits allows a manufacturer to make over 16 million different devices, each with a unique address. That's actually not an impossible number of circuit boards for one manufacturer to stamp out, but there's nothing to prevent a manufacturer having more than one block of addresses. Xerox Corporation, in fact, has thirteen blocks, including the first nine.

MAC address blocks are assigned by the Institute of Electrical and Electronic Engineers (IEEE) as part of their standards programs. A complete list of what manufacturers have what MAC manufacturer codes can be found at the following Web site. As you might imagine, it's *immense*: **http://standards.ieee.org/regauth/oui/oui.txt**

 If you look on the underside of your Wi-Fi gear you'll often find its MAC address printed right on it, sometimes on a sticker, often next to a bar code. The MAC address of a piece of Wi-Fi gear is almost always displayed somewhere on the configuration utility belonging to that piece of gear, and if it's not printed on the device somewhere that's the first place you should look. Figure 2.6 shows the back of a Cisco Aironet 342 PCMCIA card. Look at the bottom of the card and you'll see a line beginning "MAC ID:" The number that follows is the card's MAC address.

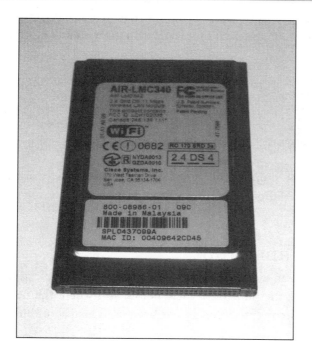

Figure 2.6
A MAC Address Label.

Privacy paranoids need to understand that *no* effort is made to associate an individual device's MAC address with the person who owns it, but be aware that barring some clerical screw up, no other device anywhere in the world carries the same address. Your Internet IP address may change each time you dial in to the Internet, but your Mac address changes only when you swap in new network hardware. And each time you connect to an Ethernet network, your Wi-Fi client adapter proudly announces your MAC address to the entire network—which is something to meditate on if you ever find yourself thinking about "liberating" bandwidth from an unprotected Wi-Fi network.

Switches vs. Routers

Note well that a *switch* is not the same thing as a *router*. (I'll be talking about routers in detail in Chapter 3.) A lot of people are confused about the differences between routers and switches because in virtually all home office and small office networks, the router and switch are combined into a single box, like the famous Linksys BEFSR41. This isn't absolutely necessary, and hasn't always been the case. You can buy routers without switches and switches without routers, but the two work so well together for small networks like those used in homes that they usually travel together. Separate switches and routers are far more common in larger and more complex corporate networks.

 Here's the way to keep switches and routers separate in your mind: Switches govern communication between different computers on a network. Routers govern communication between different networks. Routers are critical to establishing and using an Internet connection from your network, and that's a lot of what's in the next chapter.

In a sense, the switch has the more fundamental job. It creates a network from several separate computers. Without any networks to intermediate, a router has nothing to do.

Mixing Switches and Hubs

Using hubs and switches isn't an either-or proposition. They're often mixed in the same network simply because the hubs were there before and where the network has been extended, newer switching technology has been used instead of hubs.

Typically, a hub will connect to one of a network switch's ports as though it were a single computer, as a sort of starburst off the end of an Ethernet star. I've drawn this in Figure 2.7. The switch doesn't have the ability to create a separate single connection between a computer on one of its ports and each one of the computers attached to the hub, so it does the best it can do, which is wall off the hub and the other switched computer into the smallest possible subnetwork.

In Figure 2.7, the shaded lines indicate the path that the switch will create when it responds to computer 003's request to send a packet to computer 006. The packet will also be sent to computers 004 and 005, but once they examine the destination address they will ignore the rest of the packet, just as on a fully hubbed network. It's not as fast or efficient as a fully switched network, but it's much better than it would be with all networked devices sharing the same bandwidth equally.

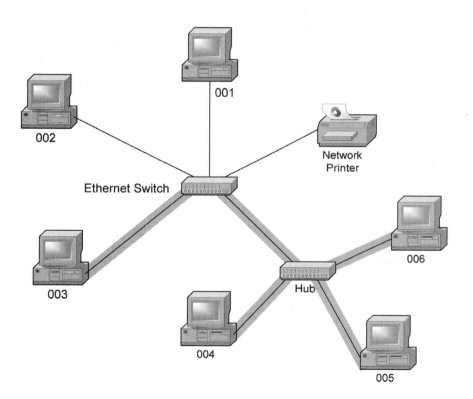

Figure 2.7
A Hub as Part of a Switched Network.

From Wires to Wireless

What I've given you so far is a pretty complete overview of what a *local area network* is. Machines within a single building are connected through hubs or (more recently) switches, so that any computer can send packetized data to any other computer or device on the network. Many higher-end printers these days come with built-in Ethernet ports, and these can be hooked up to a network the same way computers can.

A wireless network works just about the same way—only without the wires. I've drawn Figure 2.8 to give you an idea of how a wireless network fits into what I've told you so far. Just as in Figure 2.7, there's a network switch and a hub. But this time, there are no wires connecting computers 002, 003, and 004 to their hub. The hub is a *wireless* hub, which we more precisely refer to as a *wireless access point*.

Whatever we may choose to call it, a wireless access point *is* a hub. It's a meeting point for devices that have wireless ability in the form of a *wireless client adapter*. Just as devices on a wired network may be plugged into a hub with CAT 5 cables, wireless client adapters *associate* with a wireless access point over the air. It's done with

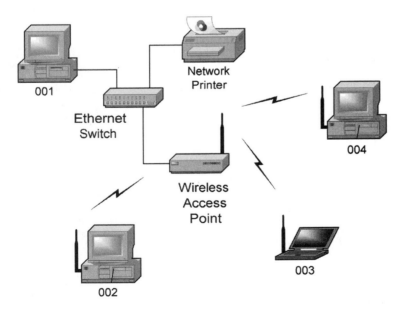

Figure 2.8
A Network with a Wireless Access Point.

microwaves, not cables, but connecting to an access point is very much the same, functionally, as connecting to a wired hub. It's a transition from one medium to another, but the packets travel across any legal Ethernet medium with equal agility.

An access point pretty much *has* to be a hub. An access point operates on a single frequency. It doesn't have the power to set up a "private" connection between any two devices, as a switch does. The data that it sends to one of its associated computers goes out to all of them, because radio waves just go everywhere.

Consider an example involving Figure 2.8. When computer 001 sends a packet to computer 003, the switch creates a connection between computer 001 and the access point. The access point receives the packet from 001 and transmits it out into space. Because all computers associated with the access point are listening to the same Wi-Fi channel that the access point is using, computers 002 and 004 see the packet as well. As they would on a hub, they inspect the destination address, see that it's not for them, and ignore the rest of the transmission.

This has a downside for access points, just as it does for hubs: All devices associated with a single access point share the maximum bandwidth of that access point. In using Wireless-B Wi-Fi gear, that maximum bandwidth is relatively limited: 11 Mbps. Bring more than five or six Wi-Fi equipped computers into a Wireless-B access point, and the network can slow down to a crawl. This may not be a serious problem in most home networks, but it definitely has to be taken into account when planning Wi-Fi networks for small offices. Wireless-A and Wireless-G access points both have more bandwidth than Wireless-B, and can support a greater number of simultaneous users before performance falls noticeably.

 The technical term for the type of wireless network depicted in Figure 2.8 is infrastructure mode. Here, a central access point is associated with one or more wireless client adapters. You'll see it now and again as you learn more about Wi-Fi. Both access points and client adapters can work in different ways under specialized circumstances, which I'll speak of later in this book. But nearly all of the time, you'll be setting up Wi-Fi gear in infrastructure mode.

Just Like Ol' Grand-Dad: Ad-Hoc Mode

Although it's not nearly as common as infrastructure mode, there is an entirely different way to connect computers via Wi-Fi technology. Recall the original, ancient-style Ethernet network I drew out in Figure 2.1: a group of computers are all connected via a single run of cable. There is no center point, no hub, nothing concentrating, switching, amplifying, or otherwise directing traffic. Now consider the network in Figure 2.9. Five computers are all wirelessly connected directly to one another, by way of their wireless client adapters. There is no access point, no hub, no switch, no cable. Every device talks to every other device. This is called an *ad-hoc network*, because all the client adapters are operating in *ad-hoc mode*.

Here, if computer 002 wants to send a packet to computer 003, computer 002 just transmits the packet out into the air as though it were an access point. The packet exists in a little field of radio energy that touches all the computers in the ad-hoc network, and as with the old-style Ethernet in Figure 2.1, the computer to whom the packet is addressed grabs it.

Without any wires or extra hardware to buy, configure, and use, ad-hoc networks sound terrific, and under certain circumstances they can be extremely useful. However, they have their downsides:

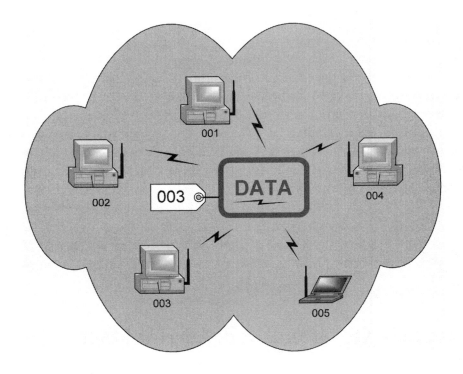

Figure 2.9
An Ad-Hoc Wi-Fi Network.

- As with any hubbed network, there is a fixed amount of bandwidth available to an ad-hoc network (for Wireless-B, only 11 Mbps) and all computers in the network share that bandwidth. If everybody's passing packets at once, it slows down in a hurry.

- Unless every computer belonging to the network can "hear" *all* the other computers in the network, strange things can happen. This is called the *hidden node problem*, and it's nasty for ad-hoc networks. It's best to use ad-hoc networks only when all computers in the network are very close together, ideally in the same room.

- Each computer in the network attempts to maintain contact with every other computer in the network. This leads to a sort of combinatorial explosion of "housekeeping" efforts as the number of computers goes beyond five or six.

- For reasons I have yet to completely figure out, Microsoft Windows doesn't always establish network connections correctly at the Windows level when a Wi-Fi ad-hoc network is established among Windows computers.

People use ad-hoc networks most commonly at meetings and events, when several people have a need to exchange files. I'll speak more of ad-hoc networks in Chapter 5, since they represent a sort of spontaneous network community.

The Missing Ingredient

The network setup in Figure 2.8 is very close to the simple wireless home network that a great many people are now using in their homes and small offices. It's a true Ethernet system from one end to the other. However, one very important thing is still missing from Figure 2.8: the Internet. The switch and the wireless access point alone can't deal with an Internet connection. We'll need to add a little additional machinery for that, which is what I'll be describing in Chapter 3. Keep reading!

Your Net and the Internet

The idea of local area networking and the Internet evolved separately but concurrently over the period of time from (roughly) 1965 to the current day. They're really two very different things, as I'll explain shortly. Both local area networking and the Internet are very big topics, and I can't treat either in detail in this book. What I'm really trying to spotlight are the places and ways that local area networks (LANs) and the Internet connect. It's a very rare LAN these days that doesn't have an Internet connection, and the #1 reason people put home or small office networks in place (be they wired or wireless) is to share a single, high-speed Internet connection among the several computers in the home or office.

It's true enough that when everything works correctly, you don't need to know much about how the Internet works under the hood. On the other hand, when things don't work—or when they stop working—the more you know about how your computers and networking equipment operate, the more likely it is that you can put things right without having to depend on other people to fix it for you.

In the Wi-Fi world, you sometimes need to know what a "subnet" is, and there may come the (dreaded) day when a bright young tech support rep asks you over the phone, "Can you ping any of your other machines?" What I'm going to focus on in this chapter are those aspects of Internet operation that you're likely to encounter in Wi-Fi work. I encourage you not to stop there, but to keep going, and read up on both local area networks and the Internet.

A Network of Networks

As I described in Chapter 2, a local area network is a group of computers connected together so that data can move among them. In the simplest terms possible, the Internet is a network of *networks* rather than a network of computers. It's a general approach to moving data among separate local area networks, some of which may be half a world apart.

Odd as it may seem, the Internet grew out of a desire to create a communications system that could survive nuclear attack. Not surprisingly, the Pentagon was the driving force in the early years, accompanied by the RAND Corporation and researchers at universities and large technology companies like Xerox Corporation. A military group called the Advanced Research Projects Agency (ARPA) worked with the civilian sector in the late 1960s to design and test ways of passing data among widely separated nodes. The data had to be sent in such a way that if one or more nodes were destroyed by military action, data could be routed around the damage and still be delivered to its destination.

What was originally called ARPANET first went live in 1969, and grew quickly and steadily throughout the 1970s, even though it was still limited to government, university, and corporate research organizations. In those years there were no personal computers, and "local area networks" were small groups of large and extremely expensive mainframe computers and minicomputers, which were "mini" only in comparison to the mainframes. (Minicomputers were "only" the size of refrigerators rather than the size of New York studio apartments.) Being on ARPANET was a fairly rare privilege back then, and remained so until ARPANET "went public" and became the Internet in 1989. Even then, the general public had a hard time finding a way onto the Internet until 1992 or 1993, when Internet access exploded into a growth business.

The notion of the Internet as a network of networks is subtle. From where you sit at your computer, it looks like the Internet is a gigantic local area network of countless separate computers. The Napster file-trading program was used by tens of millions of people, all connecting directly from one computer to another to trade MP3 music files. Nonetheless, the Internet is really a way to connect networks—and then it's up to the networks to connect to individual computers.

Backbones and Interstates

A simple metaphor for the Internet is the Interstate Highway System. All across the United States are cities and towns of many sizes. Each city is a cluster of homes and businesses, arranged on a network of streets and roads. Connecting many of these cities are the huge highways we call the Interstates. There are no homes nor businesses built right on the Interstate highways. The highways are strictly for moving between cities.

So it is with the Internet. There are a fair number of high-volume data conduits called *backbones* running around the United States and much of the rest of the world, connecting networks into the Internet. In very simplified form, the structure of the Internet is shown in Figure 3.1.

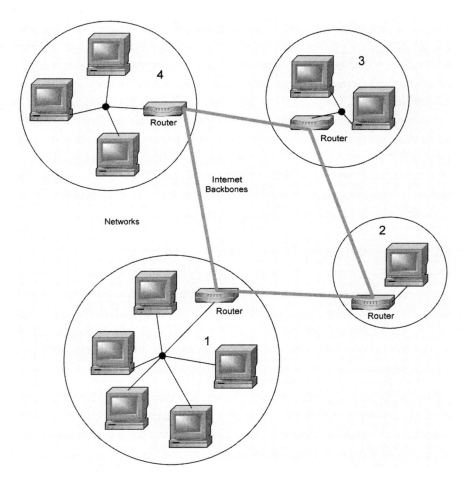

Figure 3.1
Interstate Highways for Data.

Each of the bubbles in Figure 3.1 represents a network, and the lines running between them represent the various Internet backbones. Each of the networks is a group of computers belonging to one organization or individual. They can be of various sizes, from immense (imagine how many computers Microsoft or IBM has!) down to a "network" of only one computer.

The networks are very much as I described them in Chapter 2, except that each has something new this time: a router. A *router* is a device that facilitates communication among networks. It accepts data from one of the computers on its own network, and routes that data to the network containing that data's destination computer. A router's job is to know where other networks are and how to get data to the next router on a trip that may involve numerous hops among several routers.

Not all networks are connected directly to all other networks. A path from one network to another may require intermediate stops at a fair number of other networks. In Figure 3.1, getting from Network 1 to Network 3 requires an intermediate stop at either Network 2 or Network 4. Although one of those two paths may be by convention the "normal" path, either path will do. And if someone drops a nuclear bomb on Network 4, Network 2 can take over and get the data where it needs to go. It's possible to blow holes in the Internet, and whereas the Internet might slow down as some of its capacity is destroyed, it would be very hard to bring it completely to a halt. The Internet is very "fault tolerant," and although it has weaknesses (like "denial of service" attacks—deliberately caused packet floods) dependence on a particular set of physical connections is not one of them. Any connection will do, and the Internet is an ace at finding connections.

Networks within Networks

Routers rule the Internet. The Internet is, in fact, a kind of "router's club," in that the routers are the ones that know how to get data from here to there, and cooperate tirelessly in making all necessary connections happen. In fact, routers are so good at managing traffic *between* networks that they are also used to manage traffic *within* networks, by cutting up large networks into smaller subnetworks, with a router governing communications at the gateway to each subnetwork.

The best example would be a mid-sized company that is divided into departments. The whole company might have 200 computers, but there are four departments, each with 50 computers. Most of the traffic that moves from computer to computer stays within department boundaries, simply because people who do similar work tend to work on similar data—and often the same data. Each department has a router on its network, and that router confines departmental network traffic within the department, unless it explicitly has to go outside the department. Instead of one huge network of 200 computers, there are now four smaller networks of 50 computers, each acting mostly independently.

The Internet began as a peer network, in which all networks stood as peers to one another. As the number of both networks and computers attached to networks grew stratospherically, the Internet became a hierarchical network, with immense networks containing large networks containing small networks. Big routers handle communications among big networks, and smaller routers handle communications between the smaller networks contained in the big networks. So it goes, with networks inside of networks, smaller networks containing still smaller networks, until at some point we find you.

Your Place on the Internet

If you use the Internet, somewhere along the way you signed up for an Internet account. Although you think of that account as allowing you to connect to the Internet, what it really allows you to do is connect to someone else's network for a fee. This network, in turn, is connected to the larger global Internet. An Internet Service Provider (ISP) is a company that sells access to the Internet. They do so by creating a network to which their customers can connect. These connections may happen through a dialup modem, a cable TV system, or high-speed DSL links through your phone line. Back when I lived in Arizona, my own connection was a two-way wireless system in which an antenna on my roof connected to an antenna on a mountaintop almost forty miles south of my house.

However the connection happens, you connect to your ISP's network. Once you're part of your ISP's network, you reach the rest of the Internet through your ISP's router or routers. Schematically, it looks something like Figure 3.2.

Even though you're not in the same building with all the rest of your ISP's customers, you're still very much a part of a "local" area network. The connection is by way of modem (dial-up, cable, or DSL) but at your ISP's central location your connection is networked with the connections of other customers through a hub or switch, as I described in Chapter 1. The ISP's router then acts as your gateway to the Internet.

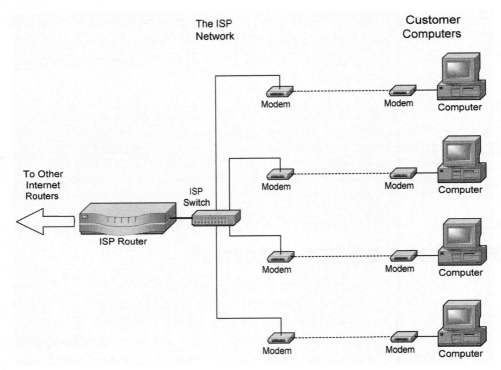

Figure 3.2
Your Computer on the ISP Network.

IP and TCP/IP

Understanding your own place on the Internet is essential for you to understand the way that routers and computers on the Internet find one another. Like Ethernet, the Internet deals in data divided up into small units (typically about 1,500 bytes each) called *packets*. The collection of rules and techniques that enable packet-based communication over the Internet is called the *Internet Protocol*, abbreviated IP. Within the Internet protocol is an addressing scheme based on a type of numeric address called the *IP address*.

The Internet Protocol is intimately connected with a slightly higher-level protocol called *Terminal Control Protocol*, abbreviated TCP. The Internet Protocol is focused on addressing and routing *packets*; the terminal Control Protocol is focused on establishing and maintaining *connections* between computers so that packets may be transferred. TCP is the Internet's delivery mechanism: It makes sure that packets actually get where they're going, and that the *order* of a stream of packets is preserved as it travels from computer to computer. IP and TCP work together and are rarely used separately. This is why most of the time you see them referred to as TCP/IP.

Although the details of how TCP operates are interesting, understanding TCP is much less useful than understanding IP addresses, where they come from, and how they're used.

IP Addresses

An IP address has two parts: One is the address of a network and the other is the address of a particular node (in Internet jargon, a *host*) on that network. A host is anything that can be gathered together into a network: computers, printers, or other networkable devices. (An Internet host doesn't have to "host" anything.) A router can be a host, which means that a network (which a router governs) may be a part of a larger network, as I explained earlier.

Expressed in the conventional way, an IP address looks like this:

```
264.136.8.101
```

Each group of numbers separated by periods is called an *octet*, because the value in an octet must be expressible in no more than eight bits. By the rules of binary numbers (which aren't necessary for you to understand) the value of an octet thus must always lie between 0 and 255. If you're sharp you'll see that the IP address shown above is invalid, because 264 is greater than 255. That's deliberate: I don't want to be using somebody's real IP address in my examples here in this book. Just assume that in the real world, an IP address would contain no octets greater than 255.

Where, then, is the division into two parts? (It looks more like the IP address is split into four parts.) I can't answer that question right now; tuck it in the back of your mind for a moment. In the meantime, look at Figure 3.3.

In the example shown in Figure 3.3, the first three octets represent the address of a network. The last octet contains a unique address for each host on the network. Because each octet can express numbers from 0 to 255, there can be no more than 256 different hosts on this network. (The real number is actually less than 256, for various technical reasons.)

In the real world, that's a fairly small network, but just as there are many more small companies than enormous companies, the larger network address has enough "space" to allow millions of different networks, each with as many as (but no more than) 256 hosts.

Because the world contains networks of many different sizes, the architects of the Internet created three different classes of IP addresses for normal network use. (Two additional classes of IP addresses exist for special purposes, but I won't be covering

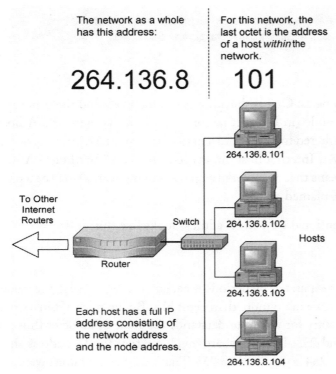

The network as a whole
has this address:

For this network, the
last octet is the address
of a host *within* the
network.

264.136.8 | 101

264.136.8.101

To Other
Internet
Routers

Switch

264.136.8.102

Hosts

Router

264.136.8.103

Each host has a full IP
address consisting of
the network address
and the node address.

264.136.8.104

Figure 3.3
The Two Parts of an IP Address.

those in this book.) I've summarized the ways the three classes of IP address are
structured in Figure 3.4.

Now we can return to the question of how IP addresses are split into two parts. It's done
by class: The shaded octets in Figure 3.4 are the network portion of the IP address, and
the white octets are the host portion of the IP address. In Class A addresses, only one
octet is used for the network address. This means there can only be 126 Class A networks, but each network can have almost seventeen *million* hosts. In Class B addresses
there are more possible networks, but not as many possible hosts. And in Class C networks there are millions of possible networks, but each network is limited to 254 hosts.
(Two host addresses are reserved for special uses in each address class.)

Routers and other equipment can determine the address class (and thus where to
split the address) by inspecting the first octet. Figure 3.4 shows the possible values
allowed for each octet by class. For example, if the first octet is 129, the address is a
Class B address, and the address is split down the middle, with two octets for network
and two for host.

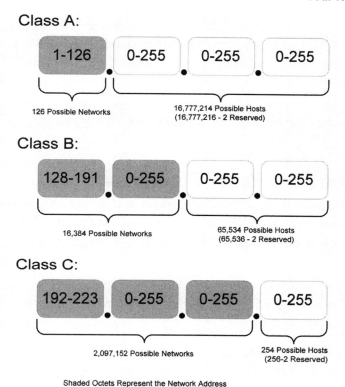

Figure 3.4
IP Address Classes.

All octets but the first octet may have any value from 0 to 255.

IP Addresses and TCP Ports

An IP address is applied to a host (that is, a computer or a router) to allow it to be located on a network. A host, however, may be running many different kinds of software. There are hundreds of different kinds of servers, for example, and dozens of different servers may be available on a single host. A Web server, an email server, and an FTP (File Transfer Protocol) server may reside on the same host computer. You can get to the computer with an IP address. How do you get to a specific server out of many on a single host?

The TCP protocol includes the definition of *ports*, which are numbers that are assigned to individual entities (usually software) residing on a host. Web servers are usually assigned port 80, and FTP servers are usually assigned port 21.

Think of an apartment building with a single street address, like "6817 N. Ozark Avenue." Inside the apartment building are several apartments, each with numbers:

#1, #2, #3, and so on. The address will get you to the building, but to find a person living in the building, you need the apartment number as well. To reach Ms. Kathleen Prendergast, who lives in the building, you need to use the full address: "6817 N. Ozark Avenue, #2."

 Even if you're not interested in servers, ports are still important as the key to making Network Address Translation (NAT) work—which is very important. More on that shortly.

How to Determine Your IP Address

Knowing how to find your own computer's IP address is important. Windows doesn't always make it as easy as it should be. For Windows NT, 2000, and XP, you have to open a command line window. At the command prompt you enter the command:

```
ipconfig
```

and press enter. The ipconfig utility will display a very simple summary of your IP address details. An example is shown here:

Ethernet adapter Local Area Connection:

```
Connection-specific DNS Suffix  . :
        IP Address. . . . . . . . . . . . : 192.168.1.102
        Subnet Mask . . . . . . . . . . : 255.255.255.0
        Default Gateway . . . . . . . . : 192.168.1.1
```

Your values, of course, may be different. (They may also be exactly the same! More about that, and also about subnet masks and default gateways, a little later.)

Under Windows 9x and ME, you bring up the Start|Run dialog, and type the following program name

```
winipcfg
```

and click OK. You'll then see the utility pop up in its own window, as shown in Figure 3.5.

Running out of IP Addresses

When the architects of the Internet defined the suite of Internet protocols that include the IP addressing system, they never imagined that the general public would ever be connecting to the Internet by the hundreds of millions. They also didn't envision that devices as mundane as coffee machines, TV sets, and refrigerators

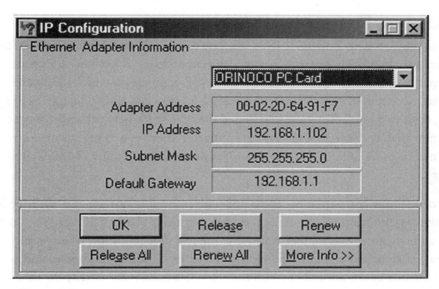

Figure 3.5
The Windows 9x winipcfg Display.

would someday want their own IP addresses for home automation purposes. This has led to a serious problem: There aren't enough different IP addresses to give one to every person (or refrigerator) on Earth who wants one. We're in good shape now, but the shortage could begin to pinch in another ten years or so.

Several things are being done to deal with this shortage of IP addresses. The high road is to create a whole new addressing scheme with larger addresses, which is being done in the IPv6 project. The IPv6 "address space" is almost beyond imagining, supporting up to 2^{128} different addresses. That number works out to 3.4 X 10^{38}, which probably exceeds the number of stars, planets, moons, and odd chunks of loose rock kicking around in the observable universe.

But that's still for the future. In the meantime, we have an Internet to run. There are two different approaches to conserving IP addresses that are of considerable interest to people creating home office and small office networks. (Another, called Classless Inter-Domain Routing, is of interest to networking gurus only.) Let's take a close look at both, as they're related.

Static vs. Dynamic IP Addresses

When they go into business, ISPs are given a block of IP addresses for their subscribers. In Olden Tymes (that is, prior to 1995 or so) when you created an Internet account with an ISP, the ISP gave you your very own IP address to plug into your computer. This IP address remained yours and didn't change as long as you had the account. Any time you dialed into the ISP's network and accessed the Internet, that IP address was how the Internet knew you. This system provided Internet account holders with a *static IP address*; it was "static" because it didn't change.

Millions of new Internet subscribers put a strain on this system, and after 1995 or so a new system came to prominence: ISPs put their block of IP addresses into a pool, and whenever a subscriber dialed into the ISP network, a special server program pulled a currently unused IP address from the larger pool of addresses and sent it down the line to the subscriber computer. This IP address was used by the subscriber only during the time the subscriber was connected to the ISP network. After the connection was ended, the IP address went back into the IP address pool, and became available for use by the next subscriber to dial in.

This way, IP addresses were assigned *only* while they were in use, which allowed much more efficient use of IP addresses. Many people would log in for only an hour or so a day; why tie up an address 24/7 for use maybe 5% of the time? This new system provided a *dynamic IP address*. At the current time, virtually all consumer IP addresses are dynamic. Static IP addresses can still be had, but ISP's charge a premium price for them.

This system works because static IP addresses are generally required only when someone intends to operate a server, like a Web or file transfer protocol (FTP) server. Few ISP subscribers want to run servers, and the ISPs discourage it for various reasons. For the things most people do on the Internet (access the Web, use email, get on chat servers) static IP addresses are not required at all.

DHCP and Dynamic IP Addresses

The way dynamic IP addresses are generated is important. Back at ISP headquarters, the central ISP server computer runs a type of server program called a Dynamic Host Configuration Protocol (DHCP) server. When your computer connects to the ISP network, one of the first things it does is request an IP address. The DHCP server pulls an address from the free IP address pool and sends it (along with a few other things) back down the line to your computer.

The DHCP server gives you a *lease* on the IP address it sounds down the line. A lease in this case has nothing to do with the money you pay the ISP for the account. It's really a time limit on the IP address. When the lease expires, the IP address goes back into the free address pool. If you happen to be connected to the ISP network when your IP address lease expires, your computer simply requests that it be renewed. This leasing process is used to keep abnormal disconnections and other networking glitches from "losing" IP addresses. If your computer for any reason fails to release its IP address when disconnecting from the ISP network, the lease on the IP address will eventually expire and the IP address will again become available for re-use.

DHCP servers actually do a little more than this: Additional network parameters like subnet masks and default gateways are also sent out with IP addresses. I'll return to those additional parameters a little later.

Local IP Addresses

Dynamic IP addressing via DHCP is one way to conserve our limited supply of IP addresses. The other way of interest to home network people involves reserving a number of IP addresses strictly for *local* use, entirely within local area networks. Such addresses are various called *local IP addresses*, *private IP addresses*, *unregistered IP addresses*, or *non-routable IP addresses*.

This last term is key to understanding the concept: A local IP address can't be processed by a router. The router knows that IP addresses within certain ranges are local, and it ignores such addresses. They are "non-routable" and are known *only* within a local-area network. Because routers govern all communication between one network and another, a non-routable IP addresses is stuck on one side of the router and can't be accessed from beyond the router, from other networks or from the Internet as a whole. The governing body IANA (Internet Assigned Numbers Authority) is responsible for setting aside blocks of IP addresses for local use. There are several blocks of local IP addresses. I've summarized them in Table 3.1.

Table 3.1   Local IP Address Blocks.

Class A	10 .0 .0.0 - 10 .255.255.255
Class B	169.254.0.1 - 169.254.255.254 (Reserved for Microsoft)
	172.16 .0.0 - 172.31 .255.255
Class C	192.168.0.0 - 192.168.255.255

Because local IP addresses can't be seen from beyond the local router, any local area network can use the exact same IP addresses. Millions of people can happily use an IP address like **192.168.1.102**, all at the same time, and no confusion results. This makes millions of additional IP addresses unnecessary.

Why is this useful? First of all, certain devices are inherently local in nature and don't need to be seen from outside the local area network. Networked printers are a good example: Why allow people from Singapore to access your printer over the Internet? And if you really need an IP address for your refrigerator, why not keep it local? (It's tough enough keeping the neighbor kids out of the fridge, much less the global cracker community.)

If you run a DHCP server somewhere inside your local area network, your DHCP server can hand out local IP addresses to all the computers, printers, and other networkable devices on your home network. These addresses are completely functional, and allow the TCP/IP protocol to operate within your local area network. Although designed originally for establishing communication among networks, TCP/IP works just as well on local area networks, and it currently is by far the most common way that local area networks pass data around within themselves.

You may be using two different DHCP servers: One owned by your ISP, which gives your home office router its IP address, and a second DHCP server inside your home office router, which gives local IP addresses to all the computers and other devices on your home network. Every network, big or small, may have its own DHCP server.

Network Address Translation (NAT) and Home Office Routers

The good news about local IP addresses is that they're invisible to the Internet as a whole. If network crackers can't see your IP address, breaking into your computer from the Internet is a *lot* harder. The bad news, of course, is that if your IP address is invisible to the Internet, it's kind of hard for a Web server to send you satellite weather images or anything else.

The solution is something called Network Address Translation (NAT). NAT is a software service that can run on a computer or (more commonly) inside a router. Quite simply, NAT translates a non-routable local IP address into a "normal," routable IP address. There are several different types of NAT software. I'm going to focus on the kind that runs inside a small router, because that's the place NAT runs in most simple home office networks.

If you create a home or small office network using a router or wireless gateway, (gateways contain routers, so when I say "routers" in this discussion I'm including gateways too) your router is the device that gets the IP address that you receive from your Internet Service Provider. Routers are the "entrance points" to networks, and your IP address is the address "over the door."

Anything you do using the TCP/IP protocol (which, over the Internet, is virtually everything you do) involves a connection between your computer and a computer somewhere else. A connection requires two ends, and both ends must have IP addresses. The hangup (as I mentioned earlier) is that a local IP address cannot be accessed beyond your router. To use the Internet from your computer, you must have a routable IP address.

NAT provides this. Take a look at Figure 3.6. This is a sketch of a very common home network setup: Four computers, a router, and a switch. (In many or even most cases these days, the router and the switch are combined into a

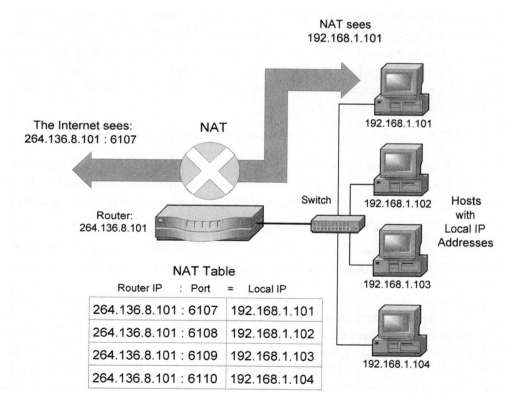

Figure 3.6
How NAT Works.

single unit. I break them out here for conceptual clarity.) Each of the network's four computers has a local, non-routable IP address. NAT is running inside the router. NAT keeps these local IP addresses in a table that it maintains within itself.

The router has a public, routable IP address that is the only address for the whole network that can be seen by the outside world. When a server or some other program needs to create a connection to one of the computers inside the network, the router takes its own public IP address, and adds a TCP port number to that address. It tucks this "extended" IP address in its internal table beside the local IP address of the computer in question. *Which* port number isn't important, as long as it isn't already being used by anything in that particular network. (There are over 65,000 different port numbers, so finding a free one in a small network is rarely a problem.) In this way, NAT creates the table as a sort of "internal phone book" for the devices on its network. This table is not accessible from the Internet. Only NAT can read it or change it.

When one of the computers inside the network wants to connect to a Web server, NAT takes the Web page request and places the extended IP address (the router's IP address plus a port number) into the request. When the Web server establishes a connection, it uses this extended IP address, and not the internal, local IP address of the computer to which it connects. The connection is thus established with the *router*, not the computer—and the router decides what material delivered from the Web server can reach the computer.

NAT thus provides two very important benefits to a small network:

- It makes good use of scarce unique public IP addresses. Only *one* is needed for the network as a whole. Computers on the network all have local IP addresses, which may also be used locally by other networks, even millions of other networks.

- It provides considerable security. No computer may connect to a computer inside the network without the router's consent and cooperation.

Virtually all home office routers include both DHCP servers (which provide local IP addresses to devices on the network) and NAT servers, which intermediate between local IP addresses and the global Internet. Rounding out the equipment lineup on home routers is usually a switch with several hardware ports (no relation to TCP ports!) for plugging in computers and other network devices, like Wi-Fi access points. One of the first big successes in this product category was the Linksys BEFSR41, shown in Figure 3.7.

Figure 3.7
The Linksys BEFSR41 Router and 4-Port Switch. (Photo courtesy of Linksys.)

If you add a wireless access point to a router/switch appliance like the BEFSR41, you'll have a wireless gateway. I'll cover this in more detail in Chapter 6.

Firewalls

Because of the protection it provides to a network, NAT is sometimes called a "NAT firewall." The generic term *firewall* refers to any system that controls what sorts of connections are made from one network (like the global Internet) to another network. NAT is certainly a firewall, and a good one, but it is not nearly as sophisticated as many firewall products.

One limitation of NAT is that it's almost entirely outward-looking. It controls what sorts of connections come into your network from outside, but it does little to monitor what connects to the outside world from *inside* your network. If you install a piece of software that includes the ability to access the Internet, NAT won't quibble with it and will just let it play through, assuming that everybody inside the network is legitimate.

This isn't always true, alas. Some software applications contain "spyware," which is software that covertly "phones home" with information gleaned from inside your network. Similarly, some virus and Trojan horse programs can hijack your computer for various purposes (more on this in Part 3, which focuses on security issues) and NAT can do little or nothing to prevent them.

So even if you have NAT running inside your router or gateway, having a separate firewall program is a very good idea. Firewalls on home networks have not been popular until recently, because configuring a firewall is a very tricky business—and if you misunderstand something and do it

badly, you can blow holes in your own defenses and allow various bad guys to get into your network. Until you get a very good handle on network operation, I don't recommend manually configuring a firewall. Excellent books have been written on general Internet security and firewalls, and I refer you there to learn more.

However, most recent firewalls are configured a different way. They "learn" what's permitted and what isn't—and you teach them, based on how you use your computer. The best example (and the one I recommend) is Zone Labs' Zone Alarm Pro. It works like this: When you install Zone Alarm, by default it permits *nothing* to connect to your computer, neither from the outside world of the Internet, nor from inside your network on your own computer. Each time you run a program that needs to access the Internet, Zone Alarm asks permission by popping up a dialog (see Figure 3.8). If you grant permission, Zone Alarm allows the program in question to "play through." If you don't grant permission, the access is blocked.

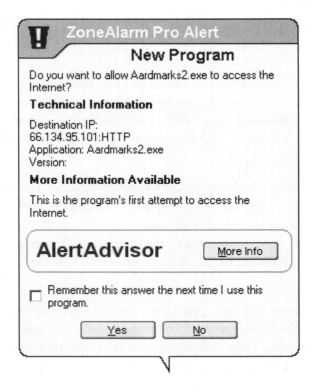

Figure 3.8
Zone Alarm's Pop-Up Permission Dialog.

The first day you use it, you'll see a lot of dialogs popping up to ask permission. But very quickly, all your customary programs will have received permission, and if anything weird ever asks to go out on the Net from your computer, Zone Alarm will report it, and you will be able to decide whether to permit it or not.

For more on Zone Alarm Pro, see the Zone Labs Web site:

www.zonelabs.com/store/content/home.jsp

Default Gateways

Routers keep routing information in a *routing table*, which is a special purpose database allowing the router to determine where to send a packet on its journey to another network somewhere else in the world. The way routers do this is fearsomely complex, and I can't go into it in detail here. What you need to understand is that routers come in many different sizes and degrees of power; the largest ones that shuttle packets around the various Internet backbones can be called supercomputers in their own right. Smaller routers have less built-in intelligence and can accomplish less. The very smallest routers (like the ones used in small office and home office networks) may not have a routing table at all.

Your router needs to know how to find other routers on the Internet. It can either do this directly (through information that it maintains in a routing table) or it can delegate the job to another, more powerful router. This router is typically owned by your Internet Service Provider. This larger router is the only way that packets from your network can access the Internet, because home office routers rarely maintain their own routing tables. Because it acts as a gateway to the rest of the Internet world, this larger router is called your *default gateway*.

Your own home network router needs to know the address of its default gateway. You may be given this address to enter manually, typically when you are given a static IP address. Much more commonly, your router receives the default gateway address when it requests a dynamic IP address from your ISP's DHCP server.

The default gateway address becomes a sort of minimal default routing table: Any packets that need to go out to the Internet are sent to the default gateway, and the default gateway (which is a router, generally at your ISP's site) knows how to take it from there.

Subnet Masks

One of the values that your computer must have to participate in a TCP/IP network is a *subnet mask*. The subnet mask comes from your Internet Service Provider. They either hand it to you in a list of values to be entered manually, or (more commonly) it comes from your ISP's DHCP server, along with your IP address and default gateway address.

Subnet masks exist to give network administrators fine control over the division of an IP address into a network address and host address. A subnet mask specifies what portion of an IP address is the network address, and what portion is the host address. The best way to get a handle on this is to look at the three default subnet masks, one for each of the three classes of IP addresses. Table 3.2 lists the three default subnet masks.

Table 3.2   The Three Default Subnet Masks.

Class	Mask
A	255.0 .0 .0
B	255.255.0 .0
C	255.255.255.0

Look back to Figure 3.4, and compare the structure of the subnet masks shown above to the structure of the three classes of IP address. Note that subnet mask octets containing 255 indicates the network address portion of the IP address, whereas octets containing 0 indicate the host address portion of the IP address.

Subnet masks are really binary-number bitmaps. 255 is the value represented by a byte in which all 8 bits are set to binary 1. If you've done any work in programming (or certain types of mathematics) you may have used sequences of binary bits like this to "mask off" parts of a number or another bitmap. By adding additional bits to one of the three default subnet masks, it's possible to cut a network into subnetworks. How this is done is fascinating but would take a chapter all to itself. What's important is how to recognize when two devices are on the same subnet.

When Routers and Access Points Fight

This comes up sometimes in Wi-Fi work, and a fairly common experience provides a good example. Wi-Fi access points contain miniature Web servers, and their setup pages are accessed through a Web browser. (I'll have more to say about this in later chapters.) In the access point's manual, you're usually given a particular local IP address for the setup page. The D-Link DWL-900AP+, for example, comes with its setup page at 192.168.0.50. If you build this IP address into a Web-formatted URL, you can bring up the setup page from any computer on your network. That is, you can bring it up *if* the IP address given is in the same subnet as your router—and therefore within the address range that your router recognizes as present in your network.

In my case, I had a Linksys BEFSR41 router on my network. It comes pre-set for a local IP address of 192.168.1.1, and the Class C subnet mask of 255.255.255.0. I plugged the D-Link access point into one of the router's switch ports and typed in its setup IP address.

Nothing.

It might have been cause for panic (or a tech support call) but one look at the two IP addresses told me that they were not on the same subnet. Table 3.3 lines them up so you can see what I saw.

Table 3.3 Conflicting Subnets.

Network Address	Host Address	
Network Subnet Mask	255.255.255.	0
Router Setup IP	192.168. 1.	1
Access Point Setup IP	192.168. 0.	50

The "255" octets of the subnet mask specify the network address portion of an IP address. I've highlighted them along with the corresponding octets of the two device IP addresses. The shaded portions of the two device addresses are not identical—and that means that they're not technically on the same network!

Here's how I fixed this problem:

1. I went into the router's setup page and changed its setup page IP address to 192.168.0.1.

2. Router and access point were then on the same network. (Can you tell why? Look back at Table 3.3 if you're not clear on this!) That allowed me to bring up the access point's setup page at 192.168.0.50.

3. I changed the access point's configuration so that instead of relying on a fixed local IP address, it requested a local address from the network's DHCP server when it powered up. This guarantees that router and access point will always be on the same network address, because the router's DHCP server only issues host IP addresses in the same network address as the router itself.

4. I logged back into the router's setup page and changed it back to 192.168.1.1.

5. I powered the access point down and up again. This forces it to request a new IP address from the DHCP server.

6. I logged back into the router's setup page and inspected its DHCP clients table to get the new local IP address for the access point.

7. I used this IP address to bring up the access point setup page, and configured the access point.

Now technically, stopping after Step 1 would have allowed everything to work... *if* nothing else depended on the address of the router. In my case, I had documented my network's setup to include a particular setup page address for the router, and I wanted to keep that setup as it had been. This isn't an arbitrary preference: I feel it's better practice to configure *all* network devices to pull their IP addresses from the network's DHCP server. The router should stay where it is, and everything else on the network should follow it.

The lesson taken from this incident is that when things don't work, take a *close* look at the various IP addresses you may have to use to set up a network. Communication among the various devices on your network requires that all devices have host addresses on the *same* root network address. The subnet mask tells you what part of your IP address is the network address.

You might well ask: What if one of the numbers in the subnet mask is something *other* than 255 or 0? This is less common in small networks, but it's perfectly legal. Unfortunately, it's also much more difficult to explain. You'll have to study the subnet masking process in detail, or call for expert help.

 *You may not get much help from manufacturers of routers and access points, some of whom will refuse to support their products when used in conjunction with products of other manufacturers. This is shameful, but it's a fact of life, and the main reason I suggest to non-technical people the following: Buy all your network gear from the **same** manufacturer!*

APIPA: IP without DHCP

The TCP/IP protocols have become so pervasive in local area networking that Microsoft wants each Windows machine to have an IP address at all times, even when there's no DHCP server to request one from. So in circumstances where a computer discovers no connection to the outside world, or no DHCP server anywhere it can reach, the computer can give itself an IP address.

The technology is called Automatic Private IP Addressing (APIPA) and it's present in Windows 2000, Windows XP, and Windows 2003 Server. If a computer looks for a DHCP server and can't find one, APIPA takes over, and generates a local IP address from a special block of non-routable IP addresses reserved by the Internet Assigned Numbers Authority (IANA) for use by Microsoft in Windows: 169.254.0.1 through 169.254.255.254. APIPA also provides a Class B subnet mask of 255.255.0.0.

Because each computer gives itself an IP address under APIPA, there's always the possibility that two computers on the same local area network might by chance pull the same number. A protocol called ARP (Address Resolution Protocol) prevents such conflicts, basically by having each computer's APIPA module ask permission over the network before using a particular IP address. If one of the other computers is already using that address, it responds negatively, and APIPA repeats the process, choosing another address and asking permission until no other device on the network objects.

 APIPA is strictly a hole-filler technology, and the Windows APIPA module checks for the presence of a DHCP server every five minutes. If a DHCP server comes back online somewhere on the network, APIPA will request configuration from DHCP, and the local IP address that comes back replaces the one generated by APIPA.

Typically, an IP address generated by a router appliance intended for home networks will be in the block 192.168.X.X. If you check the IP on your computer and you see an IP address starting with 169.254, you can be fairly confident that that address came from APIPA and not DHCP.

APIPA is important in Wi-Fi work under very particular circumstances: If you create a wireless ad-hoc network (more on which in Chapter 5) there is typically no DHCP server available, and all computers joining in the ad-hoc network will have IP addresses generated by APIPA. This is extremely useful, as the alternative is to configure each computer with a local IP address by hand, making sure that no two computers are using the same address. This is definitely something better left to computers to do.

Barely Scratching the Surface

TCP/IP networking (that is, Internet-style networking) is a complicated and subtle business. About the best I can do in this chapter is allow you to get your bearings. Most of the time you can treat network machinery as a black box and not pay a great deal of attention to how it works. Now and then, however, you may need to know something about it to troubleshoot problems, especially those involving mixing networking products from different manufacturers. (This is the primary reason that I recommend buying all your Wi-Fi devices from the same manufacturer if you're not at least moderately up on networking theory and practice.)

Knowledge is good, and the more you know about networking the easier it will be to make your network do precisely what you want it to do.

In the meantime, it's time to get down to some serious Wi-Fi network design, which is the subject of the next chapter.

Designing Your Wi-Fi Network

B y this point, I hope you're comfortable enough with the basic principles of Ethernet networking and Wi-Fi to sit down and start working out what your new wireless network is going to look like. The design process is really one of gathering facts and making decisions. For small networks deployed in a single-family home, the design process is trivial, although there are some speed bumps to think about, which I'll show you how to overcome. For something requiring multiple access points that serve a medium-sized company, the design process may be infuriatingly difficult. (The behavior of radio waves in the real world of bricks, mortar, and steel framing is notoriously hard to predict.) In fact, my experience has shown that the design process bleeds seamlessly into the deployment process. Certain things you just won't find out until you put a Wi-Fi access point up somewhere and start feeling out the "microwave presence" of the building you're in. Certainly remember this:

Canned solutions will fail. Manufacturer's specs are for rough guidance only—emphasis on *rough*.

My rule of thumb: The design won't be complete until the network works.

In this chapter I'll present the basic concepts involved in developing a Wi-Fi network. We'll start by exploring the requirements that you will likely have for your home or small office. After we walk through the critical design requirements and questions you should ask yourself, I'll present a basic design solution that will likely work for many readers. Of course, there is no such thing as a "one-size-fits-all" Wi-Fi solution, so I'll devote the second half of the chapter to design solutions for the unique problems and situations that you might encounter while setting up a Wi-Fi network for your home or office.

Getting Started

You have to begin somewhere, and you begin by thinking about your requirements and making certain decisions. What follows is a list of some of the facts you will need to gather and decisions you will need to make. This is not a linear list. Some of the decisions interact with others.

- Where will people be accessing the network?

- How many people will be accessing the network?

- What wireless networking technology should I use?

- What sort of area (both size and shape) do I need to cover?

- Can I get by with one access point, or will I need multiple access points?

- If I need more than one access point, how can I arrange multiple access points to provide full-speed coverage of my target area?

In the rest of this chapter I'll talk about these points in more detail. Before I do, however, I'd like to briefly discuss product vendors and prices.

I didn't include "decide how much you want to spend" in the design process decisions list for a number of reasons. For small offices and home offices, Wi-Fi gear has mostly become a commodity, in that Wi-Fi products deliver a standard service (vendor-independent wireless connectivity) that doesn't vary much among products and vendors. Spending more won't necessarily get you "better" Wi-Fi. Comparison shopping can save you money, and I encourage you to shop aggressively. What the goods go for is what you'll have to spend. For a home network consisting of a wireless gateway and three client adapters, you should plan on spending $250 to $350. If you can get the goods for less than that, it's gravy. Prices have fallen steadily since 2001 and may fall further. Vendor and retailer rebates add additional uncertainty to the pricing mix, as does the possibility of buying older but still completely functional gear on the used market.

On the other hand, if you spend any amount of time cruising online catalogs, you'll notice that there is often a huge spread in prices for what seems to be equivalent Wi-Fi hardware. This is especially true of access points. Admittedly, the spread has come down as the Wi-Fi idea has become more "mainstream" and thus more price-competitive, but some product lines are consistently more expensive than others. The Cisco Aironet 350 access point, for example, sells for between $400 and $500, whereas the Linksys WAP-11 runs for about $60 from online vendors and $75 in retail stores, sometimes less on sale. Both are Wi-Fi-compliant, Wireless-B access points. Why should one cost so much more than the other?

Cisco designs their products for a particular market: Large corporate shops that need to integrate Wi-Fi with very large, very fast, and highly protected networks. Cisco has thus "filled the holes" in the Wi-Fi standard with proprietary technology that plays to the high-end corporate market. Their access points have a lot more muscle in certain areas like virtual private networks, 802.1X authentication frameworks, and other things that home office and small office networks don't need and in most cases can't even use.

More really can be better—if you need the "more" that a high-end product offers. If you can't use 802.1X integration, it's wasted. As you design your Wi-Fi network, be realistic about your needs, and don't buy features that you can't put to work.

Sketching Network Usage Patterns

Your physical location is a given: You have a house or an office to equip with a Wi-Fi network. A good first step is to determine where people will be establishing wireless connections to the network. If you have a scale drawing of your home or office, it's a good idea to make a copy and mark where network access will be required.

There are two different kinds of client connections to an access point: Fixed and roaming. Fixed connections are easy to spot: People in your home or office have desks at which they work, and their desktop computers can be equipped with Wi-Fi client adapters to let them connect.

Roaming access is less well defined. At home, I use my laptop in three places: On the dining room table, on the coffee table in the living room, and out in the small bay of the garage where I have my woodworking and metalworking shop. Anywhere you may need a "work surface" is a likely candidate, as is your easy chair where you read.

In an office, your conference rooms will be the main roaming destinations, followed by the break rooms. Staffers sometimes bring their laptops into one another's offices, but if a desktop machine is already connected in an office, a laptop will usually be able to connect as well. If you have a warehouse or mailroom, you may need to think a little harder about whether those areas (which can be substantial) need Wi-Fi coverage.

In a home network, the number of people connecting will usually be small and isn't generally an issue. In an office "cube farm," however, you may have enough people in a small area to overload a single access point and drag access point throughput down to dialup levels. All clients connecting through an access point share that access point's throughput (its capacity to carry data) on an equal basis. If you get more than five people on a Wireless-B access point and if they all use the connection simultaneously, the connection will slow down a *lot*. Wireless-A and Wireless-G will support as many as 10 or 12 simultaneous connections. They are also much better for "cube farm" environments.

Once you know how much area your prospective network has to cover and how many people the network must serve, you can begin making decisions about what technology to choose.

To start designing your network, I suggest you follow these guidelines:

1. Get out a piece of paper and draw out your home or office configuration. In this drawing indicate where your computers are currently located and the areas where you may be working (assuming that you have one or more laptops).

2. Try to mark your fixed and roaming connections on your drawing; that is, indicate which locations have desktop machines that don't move around, and which (like the kitchen table) might be popular laptop hangouts.

3. Indicate where your access point might be. (Hint: Where's your broadband Internet connection?) You should also be mindful of the distance from your access point to your fixed and roaming connections. Marketing hype aside, a hundred feet is a long distance in the Wi-Fi world when you're inside a building packed with metallic structural members, stainless-steel kitchen appliances, and water-filled objects like tropical aquariums and human beings.

4. If you have an office that spans multiple floors, assume that you'll need multiple access points. This means creating an Extended Service Set (ESS), which requires more care and cabling. (I'll explain how to design an ESS later in this chapter.) A single access point can often fill a two-story home, but if you're planning to stretch from attic to basement—or if you're dealing with something like a four-story brownstone—do not assume a single AP will do the job.

The 85% Design for Very Simple Home Networks

Most of this chapter is unnecessary if you're establishing a wireless network in a small house for the purpose of sharing an Internet connection. What most people do (and at least 85% of the Wi-Fi networks I've seen and worked on fall into this category) is place a router and Wi-Fi access point near where your Internet broadband modem (cable, satellite, or DSL) is located.

Most people who create small home networks already have a broadband Internet connection, and there is usually a computer on a desk somewhere in the house where the connection is already in use. If the house isn't enormous, it doesn't matter much where in the house this is. You can park an access point or wireless gateway near the cable/DSL modem and install a Wi-Fi client adapter in all the other computers in the house, and you're done. There really aren't a great many more decisions to be made.

This "85% design" is shown in Figure 4.1. The "wired" portion of the network is all on or under the desk where Dad keeps his computer. The wireless gateway (like the Linksys WRT54G) connects to Dad's computer and to the cable/DSL modem with short runs of Category 5 networking cable. Each of the other three computers in the house is equipped with a Wi-Fi client adapter. And that's your whole network!

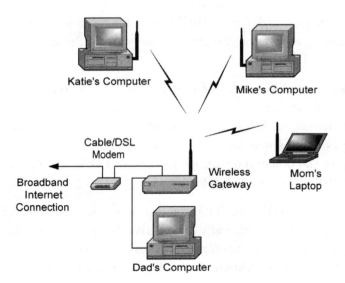

Figure 4.1
The "85% Design" for Very Simple Networks.

I recommend that you read the rest of this chapter, even if this simple design will work for you—but if you're impatient, you can skip ahead to the beginning of Chapter 5, or even Chapter 6 if you're in a fever to get on with your Wi-Fi implementation.

Choosing a Wireless Networking Technology

This book is nominally about Wi-Fi; that is, 802.11-family wireless networking. Wi-Fi is the overwhelming leader in the wireless networking world, but it's not the only technology available to you. Competing wireless networking technologies exist, such as HomeRF and Bluetooth, neither of which I will discuss in detail in this book. HomeRF never quite caught on and is gradually becoming extinct, and Bluetooth isn't really a competing technology, though some vendors claim it is. This issue may be worth a word or two.

Local Area Networks vs. Personal Area Networks

The problem I call "Bluetooth confusion" is really due to confusion between two very different (if related) concepts: the local area network (LAN) and the personal area network (PAN). LANs are networks of individual computers located within a building and connected somehow for continuous, rapid communication. This book is about wireless LANs and how to design and build them. LANs allow you to move files from one computer to another, and share a gateway to the Internet among several computers.

A PAN, by contrast, is a network consisting of a single computer and several related peripherals or devices that connect to it. It's very rare for the devices comprising a PAN to be in separate rooms, or farther than about thirty feet from one another. Most of the time, PAN devices may be resting on a single desk or table. We're talking about a computer and one or more printers, scanners, PDAs, or cell phones that need to be connected to that one computer.

Bluetooth allows for a "wireless PAN," in that it connects a computer to devices like printers, scanners, and PDAs. Bluetooth really doesn't have the speed nor the bandwidth to connect computers to other computers, except perhaps to synchronize email and address book data between a computer and a laptop or a PDA. In a sense, Bluetooth was created to get rid of the rat's tangle of cables drooping down the wall behind your computer desk. Whether it's been successful or not at this task is a topic for another book. What's important here is that you don't confuse the idea of a LAN with a PAN.

The 802.11 Family of Wireless Networking Standards

Within the 802.11 family, you currently have three standard choices: Wireless-A (802.11a), Wireless-B (802.11b), and Wireless-G (802.11g.) By 2006, a fourth standard will be added to the Wi-Fi family: Wireless-N, a specification for a much faster technology being developed right now by the IEEE's 802.11n task group.

I say "standard" here for a reason: There are non-standard wireless networking technologies that claim ancestry in the 802.11 world but are really non-standard proprietary technology from specific chip manufacturers. For a couple of years now, Texas Instruments has sold a chipset implementing a Wireless-B variant called 802.11b+ that boosts throughput by about 50% over what standard 802.11b Wi-Fi can offer. (D-Link uses 802.11b+ technology in its AirPlus line of wireless networking gear.) Much more recently, chipmaker Atheros has begun offering chipsets to support Super G, an extension of the Wireless-G standard that doubles the 54 Mbps Wireless-G bitrate to a whooshing 108 Mbps. The catch with all such proprietary technologies, of course, is that their special benefits are available *only* in networks where *all* networking equipment uses the proprietary technology. If all the wireless gear in your network uses TI's 802.11b+ chipset, you can get 50% more throughput. However, a connection between an 802.11b+ unit and a standard Wireless-B unit moves data no faster than standard Wireless-B. I'll cover more on 802.11b+ and Super G later in this chapter.

Most of the differences among the three standard contenders center on bit rate and throughput, which I discuss elsewhere in this chapter and, in some detail, in Chapter 1. Other important issues include compatibility and range. Price may be a factor but price is a notoriously changeable parameter. Although Wireless-A gear has always been more expensive than Wireless-B gear, you could get Wireless-A gear for almost the same price as Wireless-B if you luck into a promotion or sale. Wireless-G gear now provides most of the benefits of Wireless-A for a consistently lower price so there's little reason to go with Wireless-A anymore.

A good first step is to understand what the various technologies have to offer, and what parameters affect your decision. The chart in Figure 4.2. summarizes the various 802.11-family wireless networking technologies, and the following section discusses the decision parameters in detail.

IEEE Standard				Proprietary	
Wireless-A 802.11a	Wireless-B 802.11b	Wireless-G 802.11g	Wireless-N 802.11n	Texas Instruments 802.11b+	Atheros Super G
Year					
2000	1999	2003	2006?	2001	2003
Top Bit Rate					
54 Mbps	11 Mbps	54 Mbps	320 Mbps?	22 Mbps	108 Mbps
Compatible with					
None	802.11g 802.11b+ Super G	802.11b 802.11b+ Super G	?	802.11b 802.11g Super G	802.11b 802.11b+ 802.11g
Pros:					
Inference is rarely a problem as it works in the uncrowded 5 GHz band. Few network crackers have tools to sense and subvert it.	Cheap, esp. on used market. Shaken out and very reliable. As fast as any broadband Net connection. Long range at top bit rate.	As fast as Wireless-A across greater range. Most gear has WPA support. Not a lot more expensive than Wireless-B.	Details are still thin; we'll know more by 2005.	Highly compatible with Wireless-B at Wireless-B bit rates. Cheap.	Highly compatible with Wireless-G and Wireless-B at their lower bit rates. Very high bit rates and throughput.
Cons:					
Expensive. Antennas are not removable, by FCC rules. Highest bit rates are available only across a very short range. Won't connect to most public hotspots. May be abandoned now that Wirelss-G is common.	Slow for moving large files around. Most gear will never support WPA. 2.4 GHz band is crowded and interference is a growing problem.	Network bit rate drops when Wireless-B clients associate with a Wireles-G AP. 2.4 GHz band is crowded and interference is a growing problem.	Unknown. May be expensive	22 Mbps bit rate only available for connections with other 802.11b+ gear. Most gear will never support WPA. May be abandoned now that Wireless-G and Super G are common.	108 Mbps bit rate only available for connections with other Super G gear. Operates only on channels 5 & 6. Uses wide swath of 2.4 GHz Wi-Fi band and has potential to interfere with other nearby networks.

Figure 4.2
Wireless Networking Technology Selection Matrix.

Which Will It Be? A, B, or G?

I'll now help you get your head around the parameters that govern the A vs. B vs. G buying decision. I've cooked down most of the head work to five parameters, which I've posed in the form of questions that you should ask yourself, and take note of the choices following each question.

Parameter 1: *What is the primary use you intend to make of a wireless network?*

- If your primary need is simply sharing an Internet connection, go with Wireless-B, which is cheap, easy to deal with, more than fast enough, and highly standard.

- If your primary need is moving lots of files (or a few very large files) from machine to machine *within* your home or office, go with Wireless-A or Wireless-G.

Discussion: I have yet to see a broadband Internet connection that was much faster than a Wireless-B network. No matter how fast you can bring material down from the Net, Wireless-B can keep up with it. Nearly all broadband connections operate at 2 Mbps (megabits per second) or less. At its top bit rate of 11 Mbps Wireless-B can easily handle that, with throughput of 4-4.5 Mbps. Even at its second-highest bit rate of 5 Mbps, your wireless throughput will be at least 2 Mbps. (Don't forget that bit rate and throughput are *not* the same! If you're still fuzzy on the difference, look back to the discussion in Chapter 1.)

A slim handful of broadband connections will give you peak speeds of 5 Mbps, and with some care in the placement of your access point, 802.11b will support close to 5 Mbps. Remember that few Web sites, especially busy ones, will serve data as quickly as a broadband connection can deliver it to your network. In most cases, the Web servers themselves will be your throughput choke point, and even if your connection tests out at 5 Mbps, you won't be getting data anywhere near that quickly from Internet servers of any type.

In terms of moving large files around locally, however, Wireless-A or Wireless-G wins hands down. The two faster standards support the same top bit rate of 54 Mbps. In most home office and small office applications, A and G works at a bit rate of either 36 Mbps, 48 Mbps, or (sometimes) 54 Mbps. As a rule of thumb, your throughput will be about 40% of one of these rates. You can safely count on 20-23 Mbps for the 54 Mbps bit rate, or 13-15 Mbps for the 36 Mbps bit rate.

That's pretty fast as networks go, and faster, in fact, than the common 10-Base T wired networking system that many older and inexpensive PCs use. A and G are fast enough to stream video without disruption. This is sometimes said about Wireless-B, but I've tried it and it's not always true. For data speed, go with Wireless-A or Wireless-G. But before you pull out your credit card, consider Parameter 2.

Parameter 2: *How big an area must your wireless network serve?*

- If the network service area is longer than 100 feet in any dimension, go with Wireless-B or Wireless-G, otherwise any of the three standards will work well, and you can let other parameters drive your decision. For every interior drywall wall the network must penetrate, subtract 20 feet. For any exterior wall, subtract 40 feet.

- For smaller areas, or if you can afford and manage multiple access points, any of the three standards will work fine.

Discussion: The *big* disadvantage to Wireless-A is its limited range *at high data rates*. The buzz about "high rate" Wireless-A networking often doesn't come with the fine print: The bit rate drops like a stone as you move farther away from the access point. The Wireless-G and Wireless-B data rate drops with distance as well, but it doesn't drop *nearly* as fast. The Wireless-B bit rate does the best of all three standards over distance.

The maximum Wireless-A bit rate of 54 Mbps may, in many cases, be available *only within the confines of a single room*. If you move 25 or 30 feet, or go through an interior wall, your rate will drop to 48 or even 36 Mbps. The 36 Mbps data rate is what you're most likely to see with Wireless-A around a single floor of a typical single-family home, and possibly up to the second floor immediately above the access point. That's over three times the Wireless-B rate, so it's still a win for the home office. When you get into a small business that has five or six thousand square feet of space, however, people in offices on the edges of things are not going to be seeing a bit rate at anything over 18 or 24 Mbps, and possibly even less, with throughput down in the 7 Mbps to 10 Mbps range.

When Wireless-A was your sole high-throughput choice, this was simply the way it worked, and you had to deal with it—often by buying multiple Wireless-A access points and creating a zoned network. Since mid-2003, we've had Wireless-G, which provides the same high bit rates and throughput as Wireless-A, and provides them across a significantly longer range.

Wireless-B bit rates drop with distance and walls as well, but the 11 Mbps bit rate can be good out to 100 feet from the access point, where Wireless-A has already dropped to 18 Mbps.

 At this writing, Wireless-G is still very new and its bit rate vs. range curve appears to fall somewhere between that of Wireless-A and Wireless-B. For this reason, I really don't recommend Wireless-A anymore except in certain circumstances that I'll mention in this chapter and the next.

Parameter 3: *How many users will be connected via wireless?*

- If you have four or more users, all requiring simultaneous high bit rates, go with Wireless-A or Wireless-G.

- If you have four or fewer users and don't need high data rates all the time, any standard will work.

Discussion: A wireless access point is a network hub. (See Chapter 2 for a description of network hubs.) As with any network hub, all users of a single access point *share* that access point's bit rate. Every user of a Wireless-B access point doesn't get his or her own 11 Mbps connection. Two users will each get one half of that bit rate. Three users will each get one third, and so forth. Pretty soon you're down to a crawl.

The additional throughput available from a single Wireless-A or Wireless-G access point can solve the "cube farm" problem, in which you have a lot of users within range of a single access point. In an open-plan cube farm, you can easily have ten or twelve users within range of an access point, but ten or twelve users will completely swamp a Wireless-B access point. Wireless-A and Wireless-G will both support more users on a single access point. Twelve users is probably as many as you can cram onto an A or G access point and still get acceptable performance from the network, but that's still almost three times what a Wireless-B access point will support.

You can add additional access points to give more users greater bit rates, but this adds both cost and complexity to the overall network, as I'll explain later in this chapter, in connection with *extended service sets*.

Parameter 4: *How important is wireless security?*

- If security is a major issue, go with Wireless-G and WPA support.

- If security is not a major issue, any standard that supports WEP security will do.

Discussion: The original 802.11-family security technology, called *Wired Equivalent Privacy*, or WEP (see Chapter 13), has some serious defects, and it is possible for network crackers to reverse-engineer WEP passkeys, especially on heavily used networks. A newer technology called *Wi-Fi Protected Access* (WPA) is now available, and is being shipped with most Wireless-G gear. The occasional Wireless-B or Wireless-A product will support WPA, but few manufacturers have gone to the trouble of implementing WPA on gear following the older standards. Certainly you will not be able to upgrade Wireless-B gear purchased a year or two ago to WPA— the internal processors inside the devices do not have the computational muscle to handle it.

For lightly used home networks, WEP is still pretty strong protection, as I'll explain in the security section of this book. However, if you have a small business network that handles high volumes of sensitive information, *do not settle for WEP!* WPA is *very* strong security, and until we've had a year or two to determine whether it has "holes" like WEP, I recommend that small business users either choose or upgrade to WPA-capable gear as soon as possible. Right now, that means Wireless-G.

There are some "early adopter" issues involving WPA that you need to be aware of, primarily that many vendors are limiting WPA support to Windows XP. This may not always be the case, but you need to research WPA compatibility thoroughly before you buy. I'll explain this in detail in Chapter 14.

There are other options beyond WPA for larger corporate networks, but these options are complex, expensive, and take expert attention to administer and maintain. I do not have the space to discuss those in detail in this book, which focuses on home and small business networks.

Parameter 5: *How important is cost?*

- If money is a really big issue, go with Wireless-B.

- If money is not an issue, go with Wireless-G. Wireless-A is almost never cost-competitive.

Discussion: Wireless-A hardware has always been much more expensive than Wireless-B or Wireless-G hardware. You can sometimes find Wireless-A on sale, or catch a deal on the used market. Wireless-A, for the most part, is vanishing from the Wi-Fi scene now that Wireless-G has matched it on its major advantage of high bit rate.

The hinge issue here is used Wireless-B gear. In the wake of Wireless-G's appearance on the market in quantity, *huge* numbers of Wireless-B access points and client adapters are appearing on the used market as people upgrade. Unless they're mounted outdoors or mistreated somehow, wireless gear does not "wear out." Even a three-year-old device, if it works at all, probably works as well as it did when it was new. Consumer-class Wireless-B client adapters regularly sell on eBay for $20 or $25 (I've seen them go occasionally for as little as $12!) and as time passes, they will only get cheaper. There will come a day, I predict, when retailers will no longer choose to sell Wireless-B gear, and will dump their remaining inventory at astonishingly low prices. Keep your eyes open.

The Mixed-Network Throughput Problem

The higher throughput of Wireless-G networks sounds great, and it is. G's compatibility with Wireless-B sounds even better, since you can retain your earlier investment in Wireless-B gear. However, there's a *really* ugly catch: Once a Wireless-B client adapter associates with a Wireless-G access point, the bit rate of the access point drops to Wireless-B bit rates, which means you might as well be using a Wireless-B network.

Why is this? Remember, an access point is a wireless *hub*. It has only one transmitter and one receiver. Multiple clients associated with a single access point can operate through that access point simultaneously. Since a Wireless-B client cannot transmit at those higher Wireless-G bit rates, the entire access point has to drop back to a bit rate that Wireless-B clients can keep up with. This blows any advantage you might gain by using Wireless-G gear.

What can you do if you must have both B and G clients connecting to the same network? Get a Wireless-B access point and add it to the network. As long as you keep it about six feet or more away from the Wireless-G access point, the two APs should operate independently without interfering with one another. Note well that you *must* configure the two access points to operate on non-overlapping channels, of which there are only three on the Wi-Fi band: 1, 6, and 11. I'll have more to say about this later in this chapter. With a separate Wireless-B access point on your network, your Wireless-B clients can happily connect to the network at 11 Mbps, without interfering with the ability of your Wireless-G clients to connect at their full bit rate of 54 Mbps.

Is Wireless-A Passé?

Since the beginning of 2004, I have not recommended Wireless-A to my clients except in very special circumstances. Wireless-G now offers identical bit rates, and can sustain higher throughput than Wireless-A across greater distances, and through more interior obstructions like walls. Very few public wireless hotspots support Wireless-A, so it doesn't help you much when traveling. Given that Wireless-G is invariably less expensive than Wireless-A, there's now very little reason to go with A.

Wireless-A does have one thing going for it, though it's a hard one to quantify: Wireless-A networks are less prone to interference than either Wireless-B or Wireless-G networks. The frequencies on which the 802.11a standard operates are *much* less crowded, and the gear is often better behaved. If you've had trouble with interference from microwave ovens, cordless phones, or other rowdy denizens of the 2.4

GHz frequency band, Wireless-A may be a fix—but you won't know how bad interference is until you've already invested in B or G gear. Unfortunately, there's no reliable way to test for interference before you deploy at least a minimal network.

Looking forward, my intuition is that Wireless-A gear will become less and less common in coming years. There is a strong possibility that it may be abandoned entirely by the industry, in favor of Wireless-G and eventually Wireless-N.

What About 802.11b+?

Texas Instruments was a little late to the Wi-Fi party, so the chipset that they fielded in 2001 added something to the mix: A new modulation scheme called Packet Binary Convolutional Coding (PBCC) which raises the bit rate to 22 Mbps. The TI technology is backward compatible with standard 802.11b Wireless-B gear, but only at the top Wireless-B bit rate of 11 Mbps. The actual throughput is much less than 22 Mbps, and although it's higher than standard Wireless-B throughput, it's not *radically* higher. My own tests show throughput in the range of 6-7 Mbps on an all-802.11b+ network (using D-Link AirPlus equipment) as opposed to 4-4.5 Mbps on standard Wireless-B gear. This is good and useful, but not dazzling.

The best-known user of TI's 802.11b+ technology is D-Link, in their AirPlus product line. I've tested networks incorporating AirPlus gear, both in "mixed mode" (AirPlus along with "ordinary" Wi-Fi gear) and all-AirPlus. As long as you use AirPlus products exclusively, everything works well, and you get the throughput increase. Mixing things is, well, a mixed bag. As expected, the bit rate falls back to 11 Mbps, but I also experienced unexplained drop-outs and disconnects between the DWL-900AP+ access point and non-AirPlus clients.

As to whether you should use AirPlus gear or other wireless gear based on the 802.11b+ technology, well, that's a hard call. Here is a summary of the issues:

- Unless you use *all* AirPlus gear, there's little point in using it at all. You get no benefit from the 802.11b+ technology in a mixed network.

- I haven't tested D-Link's products with those of other vendors using TI's 802.11b+ technology, but there is no guarantee that 802.11b+ products from different vendors will be fully compatible. Any time you deviate from a strong standard, you must cross vendor boundaries with *great* care!

D-Link has regularly posted driver and firmware upgrades for their AirPlus product line, and if you own AirPlus gear, I encourage you to keep its drivers and firmware updated. Most vendors are reasonably good about addressing incompatibilities in drivers and firmware once these incompatibilities come to light.

What About Super-G?

Toward the end of 2003, products appeared based on a new and very aggressive technology from chipmaker Atheros: Super-G. Super-G provides a way to literally double the top bit rate of Wireless-G to a breathtaking 108 Mbps. As with TI's 802.11b+ technology, this is a proprietary extension to the Wireless-G standard, and the 108 Mbps bit rate is available only between wireless units incorporating the Super-G chipset, and operating in all Super-G modes. Typical throughput through an all-Super-G network is about 37-40 Mbps at about 30 feet, dropping steadily with distance. Within a single room, throughput can approach 50 Mbps!

Super-G clearly works, and companies like Netgear and D-link are shipping relatively inexpensive gear based on the Super-G technology. D-Link's Xtreme-G product line is based on Super-G and has gotten excellent reviews.

Super-G has an interesting catch that you should be aware of: A Super-G network is fixed on two "bonded" channels that act together to carry a much higher bandwidth signal than a single channel can carry by itself. Those two channels are 5 and 6, and this cannot be changed. Using two channels at once would not in itself be a bad thing, but many have reported that Super-G signals "spread out" in use and significantly overlap "band edge" channels 1 and 11 and everything in between. In a sense, a Super-G gateway will take the entire 2.4 GHz Wi-Fi band within its immediate vicinity.

This isn't a problem if you're the one who owns the Super-G network in question, but if you live in a townhouse or other close quarters with other Wi-Fi networks, the possibilities for interference with the other networks are high. I have not tested Super-G at this point, but accounts I have read indicate that there should be some distance (at least 150 feet) between a Super-G network and a conventional Wireless-B or Wireless-G network.

For an excellent, in-depth discussion of the problem, see Tim Higgins' Super-G Need To Know in his Small Net Builder:

www.smallnetbuilder.com/Sections-article59.php

One Access Point or Several?

Two major factors bear on the decision of how many access points you'll need to serve a given network:

- The size, shape, and construction of the building being served.

- The number of people connecting through each access point.

A single access point will "reach" only so far, and how far that is can be really tough to predict before you actually put it in place and test it. Metal absorbs microwave energy and casts microwave shadows. Dense exterior walls will absorb more energy than interior wallboard walls. Certain construction techniques like stucco over metal mesh and metal studwork can play hob with the size and shape of a microwave field. All of this is just to say that prediction will only get you so far—and not very far at that. You have to test performance "in situ" by temporarily installing an access point and then walking around "auditing the field" with a laptop, to see what your actual coverage is. More on this shortly.

 A more subtle issue is the bandwidth load to be placed on each access point. Remember from Chapter 2 that an access point is really a hub, not a switch. In a hub, all computers connected to the hub share the maximum bandwidth that the hub can provide. In a switch, each connection through the switch happens at maximum bandwidth.

A Wireless-B access point has a maximum bit rate of 11 Mbps and a maximum throughput of about 5 Mbps. All client adapters connected to an access point share this bandwidth on an equal basis. If five clients connect, the maximum throughput available to each client is 1 Mbps. Each time you add another client, you cut the throughput available to all clients by an additional fraction. At some point, you begin to overload the access point and your users will feel like they're dialing into the network through a phone modem.

The same issue applies to Wireless-A and Wireless-G access points; the only difference being the number of clients that may connect simultaneously without dropping each client's throughput unacceptably. What this means is that you may need additional access points even if a single access point can *physically* reach all clients in the network. If you have a fairly compact cube farm in your office with fifteen people in the cubicles, each with a computer, you can't expect a single access point to serve up sufficient bandwidth for all of them, even if the physical space is compact enough for all fifteen users to connect.

My rule of thumb is this: Five users per Wireless-B access point, or 12-15 users per Wireless-A or Wireless-G access point unless the network is to be very lightly used. If you go beyond the 5-or-15 rule, and if all users are constantly passing files and working on the Web, they may experience a radical reduction in response time.

A network with one access point is significantly different from a network with more than one. Let's talk about some of those differences.

Basic Service Set (BSS) vs. Extended Service Set (ESS)

The term *basic service set* (BSS) is IEEE standards jargon for a wireless network containing only a single wireless access point. Figure 4.3 shows a basic service set. The vast majority of small office and home office networks fall into the BSS category, since the range of a typical access point or wireless gateway is designed to "fill" a typical residence or small office.

In a larger office, or a large and oddly-shaped residence, a single access point may not provide coverage "out to the corners." The overall 802.11 standard provides for a network in which multiple access points are connected to the wired portion of the network, operating from the same router. Such a network is called an *extended service set* (ESS). The basic idea of an ESS is shown in Figure 4.4.

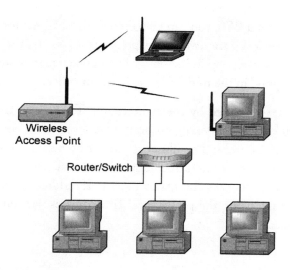

Figure 4.3
A Basic Service Set (BSS).

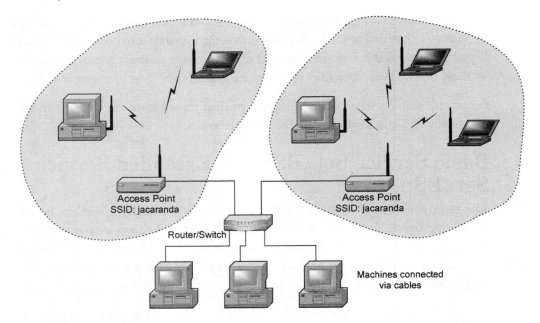

Figure 4.4
An Extended Service Set (ESS).

Here, there are two access points, but both have the same SSID. This is a crucial point; remember that the SSID is the identifier of the *network*, not the access point! (For ease in telling access points apart within a BSS, you can give them individual names, as I explain in Chapter 6.) The coverage of the two access points is shown by the gray clouds. For clarity, the clouds do not overlap in the figure, but in practice they should overlap slightly to avoid "dead spots" in the middle of the home or office.

Note that both access points are managed by the same router. That's key: Unless you're willing to do some really serious mucking around, *all access points in an ESS must be addressed within a single subnet*, and a subnet is almost by definition controlled by a single router. (For more on routers and subnets see Chapters 2 and 3.) This usually means reconfiguring all access points to request IP addresses from a central DHCP server, rather than using the preset local IP addresses written into access point firmware at the factory.

Central management of more than two or perhaps three access points is a serious challenge, especially in terms of Wired Equivalent Privacy (WEP) encryption keys. More on this in Part III, which focuses on wireless security.

Setting up an ESS may seem straightforward, but there are technical issues that just don't arise in setting up a basic service set. The first is service area overlap and channel interference. To avoid interference among the several access points, channels must be assigned to access points such that overlapping channels are not used by access points with overlapping service areas. There are only three channels in the American 2.4 GHz Wi-Fi channel set that may be used simultaneously without overlap: 1, 6, and 11. (To get a sense for the overlap in the 2.4 GHz Wi-Fi channels, go back to Chapter 1 and see Figure 1.3.) If your ESS can function with only three access points, do your best to make it so, and use those three channels. Once you go beyond three, you have to take the spatial relationships of the access points into account to avoid having one access point interfere with another.

 Here's a point to always remember: Access points or gateways that incorporate the Atheros Super G technology are fixed on channels 5 and 6—with some bleed almost to the band edge— and should not be used in ESS applications.

Figure 4.5 shows how to avoid channel conflicts when using multiple access points to fill a large rectangular office space. In the example, five access points are used, all of them on one of the three non-overlapping channels. Note that nowhere do two fields intersect on the same channel. Theoretically, you can fill a space of any arbitrary size with only these three channels, and not have any fields overlap on the same channel. In practice, differences in field strength due to building shape and construction will still give you dead spots and occasional areas where two fields of the same channel are strong enough to conflict.

In other words, setting up an ESS with more than three access points is more art than science.

ESS Networks and Roaming

The biggest hassle in creating an ESS, however, has to do with roaming. (I defined and discussed roaming conceptually in Chapter 1.) Ideally, you want to give your users the power to pick up their laptops and move from the conference room to their offices and back without logging into the networks again each time they enter the service area of a different access point. The overall 802.11 specification supports roaming to the extent that it specifies what needs to happen to support users who move from one access point's service area to another in an ESS. The spec, however, is "soft" about *how* that roaming support is to be implemented. Different manufacturers of access points have implementing roaming in different ways, ways that are not always compatible with those chosen by other manufacturers.

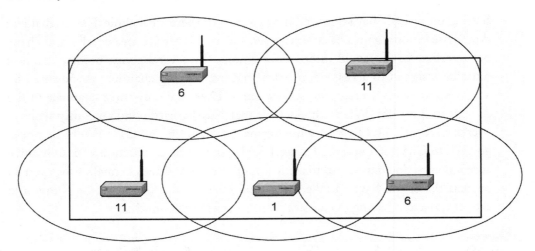

Figure 4.5
Avoiding Channel Conflicts in an ESS.

The IEEE 802.11f task group is working on a complete and formal specification for roaming support. When finished, the task group will have defined the Inter Access Point Protocol (IAPP), which defines how access points must communicate to follow users as they roam from service area to service area within an ESS.

With all that in mind, here's some advice about setting up an ESS to implement roaming:

- Before buying access points that must support roaming, check with the manufacturer to be sure that some sort of roaming support or IAPP is present and functional in the firmware. Many low-end access points (and most wireless gateways) include no roaming support at all.

- Until such time as we have a strong standard for IAPP, buy all access points of the same make and model. Cisco Aironet is good with roaming, but Cisco access points don't necessarily coordinate roaming with access points from other vendors.

- Even within the same model, watch out for differences in firmware level. Roaming is still a little bleeding edge, and manufacturers may issue enhancements in firmware that may cause incompatibilities *even within the same make and model* of access point. For supporting "advanced" features like roaming, you're going to have to master the art of flashing new firmware into your hardware, and checking firmware release levels to be sure all access points are running the same firmware release. Updating firmware is done differently for each vendor and even each device, so you have to obtain and closely follow instructions from the vendor of each device that you want to upgrade.

If this seems daunting, keep in mind that roaming is nice to have but you can manage without it. Doing without roaming simply means that staff will have to log in again in the conference room after walking there from their offices. Be careful not to spend large amounts of time and money implementing a feature that will be used rarely and by few.

Positioning Access Points

No matter how much design work you do on paper, you *cannot* know the range or service area shape of an access point before you install the access point and "audit the field." This is especially true if you expect an access point to work through floors and ceilings. There is some art in choosing your "first guess" of an access point's position, and that art can be sharpened with experience, but at some point you have to sit down with a set of blueprints and decide where to stick the device.

My experience has given me a rule of thumb of 75 to 100 feet as the *best-case* top-rate indoor range of an Wireless-B access point operating on a single floor. (You usually won't do that well. You will sometimes do *much* worse.) How much signal will get through the ceiling and floor to the level above (or below) is almost impossible to estimate, and depends heavily on how much metal is in the ceiling, and where and what shape that metal (HVAC ducts, cable plenums, power lines, water pipes, structural beams and whatnot) may be. Some will definitely get through, but *you will have large dead spots*. Don't count on anything but spotty coverage through a typical office building ceiling or floor. Houses are better because there is just less metal in residential construction. However, odd issues may surface: In an East Coast brownstone home with three or even four floors, reaching the top floor from the bottom (or vise versa) could be a challenge, even without metal framing. Put the access point on a middle floor if possible, if your home falls into that category. Also, a king-sized waterbed will cast a king-sized microwave shadow if it's on a floor between the access point and a client adapter. Water is about as transparent to microwaves as steel.

My experience has been that a single access point can "fill" a typical residence of about 2500 square feet and under, depending on its layout. Long, rambling ranch houses may be problematic if the access point is at one end of the house and users must be able to roam to the opposite end. My previous house in Arizona (a 3400 square foot ranch house) was just a little too big for complete end-to-end coverage with a single access point, and I had some really nasty dead spots. However, I had no way to run cables to bring in a second access point, so I stayed with a BSS and finessed the dead spots with better antennas. (See Chapter 16, which describes a "bandwidth expander" antenna made from a spaghetti sauce can.)

Auditing the Field

Prediction is mostly useless. The *only* way to be sure is to set up an access point temporarily in a prospective position, then walk around with a laptop running a field strength utility of some kind, drawing on the structure blueprints or sketch where the boundaries are between "green" and "yellow." Virtually all access points come with such utilities. (I like NetStumbler for field audits because it has a large and high-resolution field strength display—and it will also tell you if your staffers have installed any "rogue access points" on their own initiative. See Chapter 19.) Some people advise drawing circles with a compass on your blueprints with the access point at the center, indicating the range for various bit rates as defined by the manufacturer. That's naîve in the extreme—in a crowded, metal-strewn office environment, your field patterns will look like squashed bugs (with holes in them), not tidy circles!

If you have a convenient place to mount the access point but the service area has odd boundaries or doesn't reach very far, try a different antenna before moving the access point. There are a lot of different wall and ceiling mounted antennas available for office installations (variously called "patch antennas," "panel antennas," and "blister antennas") and while some of them are too ugly to put up with in your living room, they can definitely get the signal out better than the little 4" whips that come stock with most access points. See my description of commercial antennas in Chapter 8.

Needless to say, take into account the places where you'll want people to be able to connect at top speed. Conference rooms are key; break rooms less so, unless they function as your overflow conference rooms. (Ours at Coriolis Group Books certainly did!) Individual offices and cubicles are important, obviously, but there you have the option of fitting an external antenna or two where the field doesn't quite reach a laptop's built-in (and marginal) antenna. If you can solve a dead spot problem by Velcroing a cheap blade antenna or a tiny USB client adapter to a staffer's cube wall, that's better than spending another two days trying to tweak the position of the access point to reach everywhere. (Trust me, it never will!)

Finally, keep in mind that for offices and cubicles on the edges of your building area, a simple mesh reflector (see Chapter 18) propped behind an omnidirectional antenna can make the difference between connecting and not connecting. This is a good reason (low cost being another) why USB client adapters are very nice for desktop computer office installations: You can move them around, raise them above cube-wall level, and park reflectors behind them to reach beyond a dead zone. Some (like those from Linksys) even come with stick-on Velcro patches to make it easy to tack them to cubicle walls!

Residences and Cablephobia

Residences are a different challenge for ESS installation. If your multiple access points are widely separated, running cables may become a serious problem, especially where there is no easy access to attics or basements. Fortunately, in new high-end construction at least, many builders are running Category 5 Ethernet cabling as freely through houses as telephone wire. If you can afford a house big enough to require multiple access points, your cable may already be in the walls.

In a house, you may not be able to tack an access point to a wall or ceiling for the sake of appearances, so your options for mounting access points are much more limited. Here's a chance to be creative: You can sometimes hide an AP inside a decorative pot or basket or other nonmetallic ornament. If you have built-in book or media shelves with "media wiring" (power and cable/network outlets) in their rear walls, you can easily park an AP behind a row of books. Don't park it behind a (metallic) satellite receiver! Metal objects cast microwave shadows, especially when they're close to the access point.

For the most part, however, extended service sets will be in the domain of mid-sized offices. If you're rich enough to live in a house big enough to require multiple access points, you can probably afford professional help getting your network set up. The difficult part, of course, is that Wi-Fi is such a new field that "professional help" may be difficult to find. All the more reason to crack a few books on networking and do it yourself!

As Design Bleeds into Implementation

Purists insist that design and implementation are two separate tasks, and that design must always be completed before implementation begins. On the other hand, purists rarely *do* the actual work; mostly they just talk about it. This is true of software engineering, where I used to run into degreed "design experts" constantly who had never written a line of code in their lives (it showed!) and it goes double for wireless networking.

In Wi-Fi work, *the environment dominates the design.* You're not pulling cables through a tidy plenum, and so your design is utterly dependent on what your space is built of, what's been piled up in it, and how it's all arranged. Your design will therefore be a starting point *at best.* Do not assume that you can draw a diagram, install three access points, and get everybody in the office connected, all on one arbitrary Wednesday before lunch.

It's better to work this way: Do your sketch, and then place *one* access point, running a cable back to your router/switch cabinet by just laying it on the floor. Then take a laptop and see what the shape of your field is for that single access point. You may find that you're getting better coverage than you guessed, or worse. Take your laptop into all the cubes and offices that your network must serve, and make sure you can connect everywhere. Mark down where you connect poorly, or can't connect at all— that's the space that may need to be covered by an additional access point, or where client adapters may need external antennas. (The antennas on laptop client adapters are notoriously bad—but this means that if you can connect in a location with a laptop, a client adapter with a real antenna will connect as well or probably better.) If you record enough readings to get a sense for the boundaries of the field, it may suggest where to place the subsequent access points.

Modify your design based on your actual wireless network field audits. Then deploy a second access point in the same way, and see how coverage has expanded. (This is a good weekend project, when staffers aren't around to trip over cables and waste your time asking questions.)

The process will be difficult, especially the first time you have to do it. After you get a little experience, your designs will come closer to the mark at the outset.

The point I'm making is that wireless network design is necessarily messy, heuristic, and incremental, and the design won't be finished until the network actually works.

I'll explain more about network field audits in Chapter 9, which is really about network implementation. Between here and there, I'll be spending some time talking in detail about the hardware that makes up a Wi-Fi installation: Access points and wireless gateways, client adapters, and antennas.

Wi-Fi Communities

In early 1993, a year or so before the Internet was a household word, I was playing around with the idea of "electronic community." I was the editor of *PC Techniques Magazine* (a programmers' magazine that later became *Visual Developer* and is now defunct, alas) and wrote an editorial in the August/September 1993 issue that caused a bit of a stir. It was called "The Cableton Project" and it was an open question to my readership: If you lived in a small town with ubiquitous high-bandwidth connectivity, how would it change your life? What would you do with it? How would you work?

Opinion was almost evenly split between those who loved the idea of Cableton and would move there in a minute, and those who felt that small towns (networked or not) were hateful places where Blacks, gays, and Koreans were lynched on sight.

Whew. Stepped right into *that* one, didn't I?

My mailbox boiled with the debate for most of a year, and in all the yelling over "family values" and other city vs. country social dynamics (echoes of the "blue vs. red" phenomenon that emerged with the 2000 national elections) we got distracted from the technical issues standing in the way of implementing a heavily networked town.

Then, almost as a sidenote, one letter writer pointed out that the big barrier to creating Cableton was…the cable. Digging ditches and laying fiber costs a lot of money. How about putting short-range data radios up on poles, like TV antennas, and creating a *wireless* network?

It took ten years, but it's happening, and I'm glad to say I saw it coming. Cableton is being created—not where I originally expected it to be, and not with cables. It's a little too soon to offer you a blueprint (the technology is still in furious flux) but we've begun to see groups of people create wireless electronic communities using cheap Wi-Fi gear and obsolete "doorstop" PCs. In this chapter I'll explain what some of the issues and challenges are, and who's in the forefront of the effort. There's still a lot of room for experimentation, and if you're good with both networking and community dynamics, you could almost literally change the world.

I find it intriguing that the World-Wide Web went live just about the time I was writing the original Cableton editorial. Before the Web, the Internet wasn't about content. It was about other people. The Web distracted us hugely from what could be accomplished by person-to-person communications. In the past few years, pure "content" on the Web (documents, audio, video) has begun facing strong competition from forums and chat rooms using the Web simply as a foundation technology.

Again, it's about other people. It's *always* been about other people. Hollywood is just a distraction.

There are a number of different levels at which Wi-Fi communities can happen: on your dining-room table, at local community hotspots, and across entire towns. We'll start small, with ad-hoc wireless connections in small groups, and go from there to the promise of the heavily networked city.

Spontaneous Community: Ad-Hoc Networks

Virtually everyone who uses Wi-Fi does so by creating an "infrastructure network" with a wireless access point acting as a hub for one or more wireless client adapters. I've concentrated my discussion on infrastructure mode and infrastructure networks in this book, but there is in fact another way to connect computers via Wi-Fi. I find it interesting that so little has been written about *ad hoc mode*, which is sometimes called *peer-to-peer mode*. In ad-hoc mode, wireless client adapters connect to one another directly, without the intermediation of an access point. It's a way to create a spontaneous and usually temporary network community, often when people gather around a table with their laptops for some kind of meeting.

Ad-hoc Wi-Fi networks remind me very much of the early Ethernet days, when all computers were daisy-chained together on a single run of coaxial cable. With ad-hoc networks, all network traffic between any two machines "passes by" all of them.

There's no lightning-quick switched connection created between two computers wishing to communicate, as modern Ethernet switches provide. Multiple file transfers can be going on at once, but the bandwidth of the ad-hoc radio connection is shared by all concurrent file transfers, and eventually too many simultaneous file transfers can bog everything down to a crawl.

That's why even though up to 256 simultaneously connected computers can exist in an ad-hoc network, you're unlikely to get any useful work done with anything close to that many machines sharing a single Wireless-B 11 Mbps connection. I'd suggest keeping it to eight or ten at the very most, especially if an intense activity (such as interactive network gaming or heavy file swapping) is happening across the connection. With the ad-hoc mode, the more bandwidth the better so try to get everyone to pop for a Wireless-G notebook card for their laptops. It will make a world of difference. This is especially true because ad-hoc networks are generally assembled within the same room—often around a single table—and under those circumstances, the links are very likely to happen at the top Wireless-G bitrate of 54 Mbps.

An Ad-Hoc Scenario: A Family Genealogy Meeting

Say "file sharing" to most people, and "mp3s" follows along with the next breath. You can certainly swap music files using an ad-hoc network, but there are other uses, as you'll realize if you think about it for awhile. Here's a scenario I hope to put together myself someday:

Five cousins are researching their common ancestry, and have "split up" family lines to research. Each is gathering information and photos of ancestors, ancestral homes, and headstones for a common archive, eventually to be placed on CD-ROM. After six months of hard work, everybody gathers around the dining room table at the home of one of the cousins to share their data.

All five have Windows laptops with Wi-Fi client cards. Everybody puts their client adapters in ad-hoc mode, and all five laptops connect in a five-way connection. On all five laptops, the C:\Genealogy folder has been shared. Once it's all set up, the five cousins can sit down at the table and use Windows drag-and-drop to copy photo files and text files from one another's laptops. If they're really sharp, they can use a file-sharing utility like LANster, which provides the old Napster user interface model for file sharing across local area networks rather than the Internet (see Figure 5.1).

Lanster is free and may be downloaded from the author's home page:

www.warpengine.com/

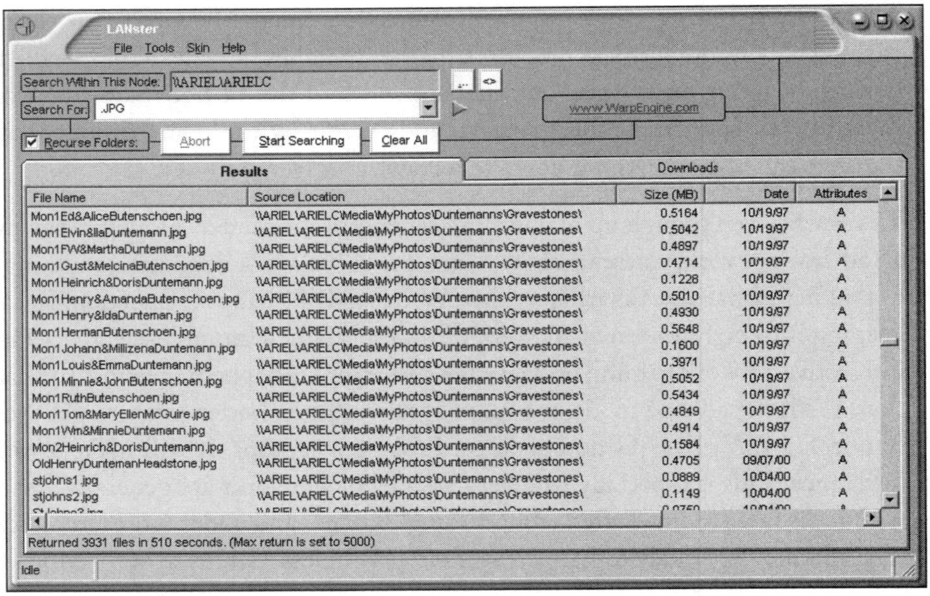

Figure 5.1
The LANster User Interface.

How to Create an Ad-Hoc Network

To set up an ad-hoc network, you'll need to make sure that all of the client adapters used are configured properly as presented here:

- All client adapters need to be using the *same* Wi-Fi standard. That is, all clients need to be running Wireless-B, or else all need to be Wireless-G or all Wireless-A. You cannot mix B, G, and A in the same ad-hoc network.

- All client adapters wishing to connect in ad-hoc mode must be set to the same SSID. Remember, the SSID is the name of the *network*, not the name of an individual client adapter or access point.

- All client adapters need to be set to the same channel. If there is an access point or wireless gateway in the vicinity, don't use the same channel as the access point or gateway.

- All client adapters need to be set to operate in ad-hoc mode.

- In most circumstances, you should leave WEP disabled for all client adapters. If you're paranoid you can use WEP, but key distribution is a hassle; if the network is temporary, it's unlikely that anyone will try to "break in" while everybody's gathered around a table for an hour munching popcorn and swapping files.

- Needless to say, if files are to be freely exchanged, all PCs must share appropriate directories for the purpose. This is not a Wi-Fi issue, but I've answered queries from people who can't understand why they can't swap files over ad-hoc Wi-Fi, when they had simply forgotten to share any directories under Windows.

- Personal firewalls such as Zone Alarm and Black Ice Defender can also be an impediment to sharing. You may have to adjust firewall parameters to get network directory sharing to work without problems. Many people just turn them off for the duration of the ad-hoc session.

The best way to make all these things happen is to create a profile for ad-hoc mode. A profile (as I explain in Chapter 7) is a collection of Wi-Fi parameters gathered under a descriptive name. When you select and apply a profile, those parameters are imposed on your client adapter. Every client adapter I've ever used allows named profiles to be created, though it's done in a different way (as you might imagine) for every manufacturer's product line. What you should do is create a profile called "Ad-Hoc," and in the profile provide an SSID (I suggest "LANParty"), a channel (I suggest 1), and the correct values for operating mode (ad-hoc) and WEP enable/disable.

 If everyone wishing to join the ad-hoc network is within client adapter radio range, booting up and then changing to the "Ad-hoc" profile should bring everyone into the network so that all machine names and their shares appear in "Network Neighborhood" or "Computers Near Me," depending on your Windows version.

The Curse of the Ad-Hoc People

Ad-hoc mode is part of the fundamental 802.11-family standard, and theoretically, all Wi-Fi certified client adapters, regardless of A, B, or G status, should support it. The problem is that the Wi-Fi Alliance didn't originally include testing for ad-hoc mode in their Wi-Fi logo certification program. This may explain the number of people in my acquaintance who haven't been able to make it work consistently. I regularly see inquiries on various Web forums asking, "How do I set up an ad-hoc network?" If they have to ask, there's something wrong. If everything's working correctly, ad-hoc networks happen *automatically*, once you apply your ad-hoc profile that puts your client adapter in ad hoc mode with the proper parameters.

 As often as not I've had trouble even getting my own machines to gang up in an ad-hoc network. There's never any obvious reason why, but sometimes I have to reboot one of the machines once or twice to get it to cooperate.

Even though at the Wi-Fi level you have a wide-open N-way connection, Windows doesn't always get the I's dotted and the T's crossed. Often you'll see all the machine names in Windows Explorer's "Computers Near Me" folder, but when you select some of them to see their shares, you'll get an error box that reads "The network path was not found." If this happens, reboot the machine you can't reach and try again.

If you encounter difficulty forming an ad-hoc network, make sure that all machines are getting a local IP address from somewhere, and that they're all in the same address block and subnet. Windows XP, once again, is best for wireless networking, with Windows 2000 close behind, and Win98 a distant third. (Don't even try it under Windows 95.) All of these versions support APIPA (Automatic Private IP Addressing) which can be considered a solo computer's fallback equivalent to network DHCP. (I described both in some detail in Chapter 3.)

If no DHCP server is detected at boot time, APIPA takes over and generates a local IP address in the reserved block 169.254.XXX.XXX. Make sure that all machines are using an IP address in the same block and subnet, which ideally should be the default APIPA block of 169.254.XXX.XXX and subnet 255.255.0.0. Typically, in an ad-hoc network no router or DHCP server is available, so all addresses will be assigned individually by APIPA and will be in the same block and subnet. If any are not, you may have to go deeper into the Windows networking machinery to troubleshoot further, and that falls outside the charter of this book.

The Dream of Community Hotspots

Meditate a little bit on the explosive success of Wi-Fi in America and you'll come to the same thought: What if *everybody* had a hotspot—and was willing to share that hotspot with others? Then no matter where you went, you'd be connected. The Internet would literally be everywhere, in the very air.

This is the dream of the community networks movement. Groups all over the country are discussing and experimenting and trying to figure out how to make this dream happen. The movement has arisen primarily in large urban areas, but there have been remarkable efforts in small rural towns to establish "bandwidth co-ops" to spread the considerable cost of broadband Internet connection where phone or cable companies don't want to do it themselves.

The "Last Mile" Problem

At the heart of the difficulty with getting broadband Internet into more hands is the simple fact that cable and telephone companies are monopolies, and as monopolies they have no reason to deploy anything broadly unless forced to do so. Telephone service exists in rural areas only because governments forced telephone companies to extend service beyond the cities. No such mandate has been placed on cable TV or Internet service providers, which is why cable doesn't go everywhere (even affluent but sparsely built areas like north Scottsdale, where I lived until 2003) and broadband remains the near-exclusive province of big cities and their suburbs.

As increasingly *unregulated* monopolies, cable and phone companies are hiking prices, being much happier to collect $80 per month from a few people than $20 per month from everybody. *They have no incentive at all to either lower prices or increase their service area.* Until governments force them to extend coverage, coverage will not be extended. As long as they are protected from competition, prices will remain high.

Community networks functioning as bandwidth co-ops solve what industry people call the "last mile problem": getting bandwidth from high-speed Internet backbones into a multitude of homes. (Some of us wish it were no more than a last *mile* problem rather than a last *twenty* mile problem…) In a wireless bandwidth co-op, someone installs a high-bandwidth data line (usually a species of leased line called a "T-1") and shares that bandwidth and its cost with others nearby. This often involves putting one or more wireless access points up on poles at the T-1 site, and then having co-op members point directional gain antennas at the access points. Wi-Fi gear has short range inside buildings with tiny "rubber duck" omnidirectional antennas, but with highly directional gain antennas pointed correctly across clear air to an access point, that range can increase to as much as a mile, sometimes (with an aggressive gain antenna like a parabolic dish) considerably more.

 I cover gain antennas and the associated math in Chapter 8, and in Chapter 17 I cover putting access points in weatherproof enclosures for outdoor mounting.

The wireless bandwidth co-op idea is still in its infancy, and it will be a few years yet before we can be sure the wireless solution to the last mile problem will work reliably. There is the further problem that in many very small towns far from any high-bandwidth backbones, even T-1 service is impossible. Some of the best-documented struggles in this area come to us from the tony wilds of Sonoma County, California, where Robert Cringely and Rob Flickenger have used every Wi-Fi trick in the book to bring high-bandwidth connectivity to their houses in the hills. See the NoCatNet Web site:

http://nocat.net/

There are, of course, a lot of places where the last mile problem has long been solved, and broadband connections are available via cable modem or DSL service. In such areas, the challenge to community networks moves up to the next level: Creating a "cloud" of wireless hotspots as a means of making the Internet generally available (ideally without cost) from public places.

On the surface this would seem to be easy: Just put an access point outside your bedroom window for the world to use. A lot of people are doing precisely this, but there are two major challenges: Internet service provider usage agreements and the gnarly issue called "the tragedy of the commons."

ISPs and Connection Sharing

Ever since Linksys and other companies began offering cheap router/switch combinations, people with broadband Internet connections have been using Internet connection sharing within their homes. A simple and cheap wired router/switch appliance like the venerable Linksys BEFSR41 allows you to run cables to your spouse's computer and your kids' computers so that the whole family can share the broadband Net connection coming into the house through cable or DSL. Internet Service Providers (ISPs) have often objected to this, since they would prefer to charge "by the machine" for Net access. However, the router technology (specifically Network Address Translation, or NAT, which I described in Chapter 3) insulates the computers from outside inspection, making it virtually impossible for ISPs to tell, remotely, how many computers are connected to the broadband link.

 With Wi-Fi, you can share a Net connection without the wires. You can share a connection right through the walls of your home. If you do that, your ISP can send somebody up and down the street to sniff wireless signals (see Chapter 19 to get a sense for how easy this is). If they trace those signals to your house, they can demand to "upgrade your service" (read here, charge you more) or shut your connection down.

Predictably, the larger Internet services are, with great bravado and wringing of hands, calling this "bandwidth theft." The problem I have with calling this theft is that people are paying for the bandwidth whether they use it or not. In other words, many of us pay our ISPs for "goods" (bandwidth) that they never deliver. If I order something from a catalog company, pay for it, and it's never delivered, that's theft. Works both ways, guys.

This is especially true since broadband companies have installed bandwidth caps (more on this shortly) on their broadband modems. A bandwidth cap limits your bandwidth to some maximum value. My sense is that if there's a cap on your bandwidth, *you're paying for that much bandwidth*, and what you do with it is not the ISP's business.

The ISPs, of course, make subscribers sign contracts, which, having been drafted by company lawyers, predictably cook down to a statement that "You owe us money and we are not obligated to provide you with anything at all." (Don't believe me? Go read your contract!)

Given the dominance of corporatism today, and the degree to which large companies buy legislators and legislation, this standoff isn't likely to be solved anytime soon. Monopolies fight deregulation as though their corporate lives depended on it, which they do. On the other hand, we live in the sort of interesting times where "interesting" means "anything can happen." In fact it did happen at one point in the early 90's when Congress acted to deal with some issues of cable pricing and practices because consumers had gotten angry enough to make it politically expedient to do something. Keep your eyes open—and if you get angry, let your legislators know it!

Bandwidth Caps

Virtually all broadband ISPs operate on a sort of "health club model" for selling bandwidth: All subscribers share a limited resource. Instead of a handful of treadmills, this is a certain maximum number of bits that can move across the data channel at one time. As with health clubs, broadband ISPs assume that most people are not online most of the time, and many use the connection rarely and lightly. Only a handful of fanatics make heavy use of the system, and it averages out.

This system assumes; nay, *requires* that most people are not doing intensive data transfers most of the time. For a long time this was inherent in the way people used the Internet. Querying a POP3 mailbox for email takes a few seconds for most people—perhaps a minute or two after coming home from a week's vacation, spam being what it is today. Surfing the Web can require lots of bandwidth, but only in fits and starts: Bringing a "rich media" page down may take a minute of constant data transfer, but once the page has been rendered, it sits there for awhile so that the user can read it. Download and pause, download and pause; this process averages out over many users to a manageable use of bandwidth.

Things got a little ugly in the heyday of Napster and its peer-to-peer descendents. Avid users of peer-to-peer MP3 trading kept their connections completely busy (in terms of bits moving both up-link and down-link) most of the time. In neighborhoods with an abundance of teenagers, the bandwidth well got sucked dry after supper on weekday evenings. This prompted broadband providers to replace their existing cable modems with newer models having *bandwidth caps*, which enforced strict limits on the number of bits moving through the modem on a per-second basis. Performance might still bog down in the evenings, but the effects of Napster-style constant data transfers were limited by the bandwidth caps.

I personally experienced this at my satellite office outside Chicago, in a peaceful post-WW II suburban neighborhood where most of the residents were retirees, and "cable" was thought of in terms of TV and not bandwidth. When the provider first installed broadband Internet access for me there, the data rate I was able to achieve was astronomical—over *eight megabits* per second. Of course, I was one of the few users of the system, and the system gave me whatever slice of the available bandwidth that nobody else was using. In early 2002, a mandatory cable modem upgrade was done, and after that, my downloads were remarkably consistent at about one megabit per second or less, even in the middle of the night. The new modem had a bandwidth cap.

It took some of the cleverer Internet hackers about ten minutes to figure out how to open up the new modems and disable the bandwidth caps, which in many cases were nothing tougher to change than a setting on a DIP switch. (Smarter hackers, who could foresee the inevitable reaction from the providers, didn't disable the bandwidth caps entirely but simply increased them to the next higher level.) The providers responded with fury and even involved the FBI in the search. Eventually, criminal bandwidth theft charges were brought against the malefactors. (Many think—and I concur—that in an era of aggressive terrorism this is a silly damfool waste of FBI resources.)

Community networks are coming to be seen as a new assault on shared bandwidth systems, and broadband providers are beginning to take action against people who share a single broadband connection with their neighbors through a wireless access point. Some providers are even taking action against people who share a connection among machines within a single home. This is virtually impossible for them to discover if you use a completely wired connection and a good router containing a NAT firewall; however, to learn if you have a wireless access point on your system, they simply have to sit out in front of your house in their trucks and run Netstumbler.

My point? Read your contract with your broadband provider and see if sharing a connection among multiple machines is one of those things outlawed by the contract. If so, keep in mind *that wireless access points cannot be hidden*, and if your broadband provider does a "sweep" in your neighborhood, you could be caught in their net.

The Tragedy of the Commons

Born of idealism, the whole idea of establishing community networks to put "Internet everywhere" depends on everybody pulling their weight. If everybody in an area had broadband and everybody shared bandwidth, there would be plenty to go around and there really wouldn't be a problem. The problem of freeloaders does arise, however, especially when broadband coverage is expensive and thus far from universal. People who use a community resource while sharing nothing create "the tragedy of the commons."

It's a difficult problem but not an unsolvable problem. The key to finessing the tragedy of the commons is a technology called the *captive portal*. (More on captive portals later in this chapter.) Briefly, a captive portal is a special entryway to a network that imposes certain restrictions on those who connect to the network. These restrictions are predicated on sharing. Those who share get more privileges than those who do not. People who belong to the network get priority over people who are just passing through, and the bandwidth of non-members is restricted.

Captive portals exist in the wired world, but in Wi-Fi circles they are actually "muscular" wireless access points. Unlike most access points (which are simple wireless hubs) captive portals contain firewalls that separate the owner's network from outside access. A captive portal "escorts" outsiders right to the Internet and does not allow them any access to or even knowledge of the owner's internal LAN.

So captive portals mostly solve the problem of network crackers getting into a Wi-Fi user's LAN. What they do not prevent is IP impersonation (see Chapter 12) though one captive portal system (Sputnik, a commercial hotspot turnkey system) has something called "spam radar" that watches for large volumes of email traffic. All problems with community networks have not been solved, but the movement is *extremely* new, and I think technology will appear in coming years to make most of the problems manageable, if not entirely solvable.

Table 5.1 lists some of the more active community network projects of which I am aware, and the more people who join them, the faster the movement's goals will be realized. If you want to experiment with community network technology and there is no project underway in your area, I recommend NoCatAuth because it's free and open source—and already running in many places. I also recommend starting your own local group. Sharing knowledge is every bit as important to the community networks movement as sharing bandwidth!

Table 5.1 Community Network Organizations.

Organization	Location	Web Site
Atlanta Freenet	Atlanta, Georgia	http://www.atlantafreenet.org/
Austin Wireless	Austin, Texas	http://www.austinwireless.net/
BAWUG	SF Bay area	http://www.bawug.org/
Brisbane Mesh	Brisbane, Australia	http://www.itee.uq.edu.au/~mesh/
Houston Wireless	Houston, Texas	http://www.houstonwireless.org/
NoCatNet	Sonoma County, California	http://nocat.net/
CAWNET	Northern Virginia/DC	http://www.cawnet.org/
NYCWireless	New York City	http://www.nycwireless.net/
Personal Telco	Portland, Oregon	http://www.personaltelco.net/
Sbay Wireless	San Jose, California	http://www.sbay.org/wireless-net.html
Seattle Wireless	Seattle, Oregon	http://seattlewireless.net/
Wireless Revolution	Boulder, Colorado	http://wireless-revolution.net/

Captive Portals

Most of the discussions on Wi-Fi security are focused on keeping the general public *out* of wireless networks. This kind of "brick-wall" security sees a sharp division between private and public use of Wi-Fi connections, especially those leading out onto the Internet.

The issue is not always so cut-and-dried. Some individuals and groups feel that making Internet access ubiquitous by sharing Net connections wirelessly is the way to go, especially in places where cable and telco organizations are keeping prices high on broadband services. Sharing Net connections makes the issue not one of *stopping* access to Wi-Fi networks by the general public, but one of *managing* it. Technological means have been suggested for doing this, and a few have begun to appear. By far the most important of these technologies is the captive portal.

The notion of a captive portal is older than Wi-Fi, and has been used for years to manage Internet access through "rented wires" in places like airports, hotels, and Internet cafes. (I've used Wayport's wired captive portal system in hotel rooms around the world. See Chapter 10 for more on Wayport.) In a Wi-Fi context, a captive portal is a feature-rich wireless access point, specifically designed to manage (and optionally charge for) connections to a wireless network by people not (entirely) trusted by the owner of the network. A captive portal's major tasks are as follows:

- It establishes a strong firewall between the wireless access mechanism and the wired LAN to which the portal is attached. Most access points are simply hubs and do not contain firewalls at all, and are usually connected *inside* the network firewall. This is usually trouble, especially in corporate applications.

- In those cases where the portal is part of a larger network of access points (often forming a community network or a fee-based network like Boingo) it identifies and authenticates members of the network community.

- It manages network traffic priority according to some sort of plan. Generally, the node owner has the highest priority for all bandwidth. Network members have lower priority, and non-members have the lowest priority of all.

- It sets limits on the bit rate that certain classes of users are allowed. As with traffic priority, the node owner generally gets the highest bit rate the node supports. Network members may be limited to a lower bit rate, and nonmembers to an even lower bit rate.

Some captive portals support additional features, but these are the major tasks that define a captive portal *vis-a-vis* a simple wireless access point.

Keep in mind that an "access point" isn't always a dedicated little box you buy in a shrink-wrapped package at Best Buy. A computer with an Ethernet network interface controller (NIC) and a wireless client adapter can operate as an access point under the control of appropriate software. The software "overrides" the software store inside the client adapter (the client adapter's *firmware*) and makes the client adapter operate differently. If all the correct software functions are available, the computer will look like an access point to client adapters in the vicinity, and will coordinate associations with those client adapters just as an access point would. Most (but not all) captive portal implementations use a computer with a client adapter card installed in it. We've begun to see the emergence of turnkey captive portals that consist of an access point with additional software running as its firmware and a separate management package running on a PC. The Sputnik system works like this, though it's expensive—about $900 for one AP and the management package.

What a User Sees

The captive portal implementations that I have used are all based on the Web protocol (http) and Web browsers. If you've ever used a fee-based wireless Net access system at a coffee shop or hotel (Boingo is typical), you have probably encountered a captive portal. Here's how it works:

1. You crank up your wireless laptop. The portal's hotspot is usually "wide open" and will associate with any wireless client adapter. However, the network connection isn't "live" yet, even once you associate. You must first launch a Web browser.

2. Your Web browser's requests for URLs are redirected to a particular Web address, which is the only address you can see at first. So no matter what URL you might try to request, you'll get the designated portal entry page. You are still a "captive" of that portal entry page, hence the term "captive portal." The portal isn't the captive...you are the captive of the portal!

3. This Web site may request a user name and password, or (for "open" community networks) simply display a "terms and conditions" page for legal reasons. If you don't have an account with that portal, the server may offer you the opportunity to create one. In one way or another, the portal authenticates you according to its established rules.

4. After authentication, the portal closes the authentication page, opens your connection to the Internet, and allows your Web browser's URL requests to go to their true destinations. You're "in."

That's the road warrior's view of captive portals, which I feel will become the standard way to access the Internet wirelessly through both free and fee-based hotspots.

There are some variations on this theme. Boingo, for example, depends on a Boingo-specific client application that you install on your laptop when you establish a Boingo account. When your laptop associates with a Boingo member hotspot, the client application handles the conversation with the captive portal. Boingo is one of the slickest Net access systems I've ever used, and I think its client-application authentication model will eventually be adopted by others. See Chapter 10 for more on Boingo and other wireless hotspot networks catering to business travelers.

Creating Your Own Captive Portal

People at the heart of the community networks movement have led the way in creating open-source (that is, free and "no-secrets" software) implementations of captive portals. The original free portal package is NoCatAuth, created by the people at NoCatNet in Sebastopol, California. WICAP is another, which runs under OpenBSD rather than Linux.

You can use a captive portal to share your broadband connection either as a lone wolf hotspot, or as part of a larger community or fee-based network. If you want to join a fee-based network like Boingo, the software will generally be handed to you as a turnkey solution—at a price. For use in a community network, the software is usually free, but you'll have to do a fair amount of pretty technical work yourself.

That's a serious issue and something to keep in mind: If you aren't fairly adept with the Unix command line and Unix networking, you're going to have trouble. All of the free portals I know of are based on some flavor of Unix, either Linux or BSD. Windows 9x is completely hopeless from a server-side networking standpoint, and Windows 2000 Server is neither cheap nor as reliable or easy to use as Microsoft insists. Linux, on the other hand, will run for months without requiring a reboot. (I once had my Linux box going for 96 days straight, between power outages here, and it never burped. Try *that* with Windows!) Needless to say, you had also better be *keenly* familiar with TCP/IP, firewalls, routing, DHCP, and all that other server-side machinery. Knowing Perl helps. (NoCatAuth is a Perl app.)

The free portal software runs on a dedicated PC—you can't run the portal on a computer and then use the computer for other things as well. The PC can be pretty minimal; NoCatAuth will run tolerably well on a 486 with as little as 32 MB RAM. Typically, a portal requires:

- A working Intel motherboard, 486-33 or better, 32 MB RAM or better

- A modest-sized hard drive

- An Ethernet NIC

- A wireless client card, ideally one incorporating the Prism chipset

Junker PCs in this class lurk almost everywhere in suburbia, hiding in basements and closets because people have this hangup about putting something out on the curb when it once cost them $2,000, even if its current value asymptotically approaches zero. Ask around; you'll get one, and maybe a spare—or if you're not careful, a garage full.

In addition to free open-source software like NoCatAuth and WICAP, commercial captive portal software packages are now available that turn junker PCs into full-fledged captive portals. One of the best-known is ControlAP, a $150 product that allows you to set up a free or a fee-based captive portal. Unlike NoCatAuth, ControlAP runs on Windows, Mac OS X, and PocketPC as well as Linux. It is much easier to install and configure, and also handles billing for commercial hotspots. A free demo version is available from the ControlAP Web site:

http://controlap.com/

The very best way to learn about community network implementation is to join or form a group in your area, and work with other people who may have more experience than you do, or experience in different areas. These groups are appearing all over the country; ask around or search on the Web. Good, detailed books on the topic will appear over time, but in these early stages there's nothing to beat face-to-face cooperation with other interested people.

As useful as they are in building community networks, there is a physical problem with captive portal systems running on old PCs: It's very difficult to put them close to an outside antenna, particularly one set high and in the clear to increase the size of your hotspot. Losses through runs of coaxial cable longer than ten or twelve feet can be crippling unless you use Andrew Heliax or Times Microwave LMR 600 or LMR 900, all of which are fairly stiff and extremely expensive. (Heliax N connectors alone cost $30 to $40 each!) You can sometimes scrounge odd lengths of Heliax at amateur radio hamfests (basically flea markets for technology junk; that's where I've gotten mine) but it's hard to be sure you'll find just what you want precisely when you want it.

There's *lots* of room for experimentation here. If you're good with PC hardware you can probably buy a small-footprint Intel motherboard and build a weatherproof PC to mount right up on the roof, and control it remotely. (The reigning champ in the tiny motherboard wars is the Mini-ITX—see **www.mini-itx.com**.) Surplus military steel ammunition cans are cheap and abundant and worth exploring for uses like that. People are building the Mini-ITX into toasters; surely you could build it into an ammo can!

Another thing to do is follow the progress of the OpenAP project, which actually replaces an ordinary access point's firmware with an implementation of Linux. When last I looked they didn't have captive portal software for OpenAP, but it's an obvious thing to do with a Linux-programmable access point, and I suspect it will happen eventually. See **http://opensource.instant802.com/home.php**.

To help you learn more abut the available captive portal programs and projects (like OpenAP) that may lead to them, I've included a set of reference links in Table 5.2.

 The subject of captive portal installation, configuration, and use is an extremely technical topic, and tightly tied to the larger issue of community networks. I can't do that topic justice in less than an entire book. A lot is happening on this front, so stay tuned.

Table 5.2   Captive Portal Products and Related Links.

Program Name	Link	Comments
NoCatAuth	http://nocat.net/download/NoCatAuth/	In perl, for Linux
ControlAP	http://controlap.com/index.html	Commercial; $150
OpenAP	http://opensource.instant802.com/	Linux running on an AP!
Sputnik	www.sputnik.com/	An AP with custom CP firmware
WICAP	www.geekspeed.net/wicap/	Runs on OpenBSD

SSIDChalking

UK Wi-Fi enthusiast Matt Jones became instantly famous in April 2002 for his suggestion of *warchalking*, the marking of sidewalks near Wi-Fi hotspots to indicate to passing wibos (a UK-ism for Wi-Fi enthusiasts that is a compaction of "wireless hobos") that an access point was nearby, and what sort of access point it was. (I discuss warchalking and the rest of the war-memes in detail in Chapter 19.)

The idea of warchalking quickly became a meme (an idea that resonates deeply with people and takes on a life of its own) even though, on examination, it doesn't make a great deal of sense. Chalk marks tend to vanish after a hard rain (it never rains in London, right?) and chalk is one of those things, like dead fish and loose iodine crystals, that do annoying things if you carry them in your pockets. I don't know how it is in England, but over in the States there are places where you can get tossed in jail for drawing things on private and public property.

But at the core, Matt was on to something: It would be useful to be able to tell, at a glance, when there's a public access hotspot in the vicinity. So I have a counter suggestion: Build ASCII representations of the Jones warchalking symbols into the first part of an access point's SSID. Any wibo without a stumbling program isn't serious, and stumbling programs detect and display SSIDs as part of their primary mission.

So consider these two hypothetical SSIDs:

```
<< O >> nutmeg
<< )( >> coriander
```

The first is a private node, not to be messed with or connected to. The second is a public-access node. The enclosing << >> symbols are to give some future generation of stumbling utilities an unambiguous way of separating the symbols from the SSID text proper, and would allow additional symbols if that would be useful, as in nodes that are available to the public but fee-based, as in T-Mobile or Boingo:

`<< )( $ >> coriander`

I suggested this to Matt Jones in an email and he seemed receptive. Others have since posted independent suggestions on **warchalking.org**, but I believe I thought of it first.

Why is this important? As Wi-Fi hardware becomes ever more widespread, mistakes are going to be made, and there will eventually be legal consequences for connecting to an unprotected access point, even by mistake, if that access point is not intended by its owner to be public. SSIDchalking will allow a stumbling program (or something like Boingo's connection utility) to protect its users by discriminating between truly open public community hotspots and private hotspots owned by the clueless who can't figure out how to turn on security.

The Dream of Wireless Mesh Communities

The term "wireless community networks" embraces a lot of territory, from free community hotspots and "clouds" (overlapping hotspots that cover a wider area than only one can) to the creation of "rooftop LANs" of wireless connections that could theoretically span and connect an entire city. To conclude this chapter, I'll need to take a half-step beyond what has been definitively accomplished and talk about the dream of a wirelessly networked town or city. To avoid the confusion inherent in using the broader term "community network" I prefer to call such a creature a *wireless mesh community*. The term comes from a group called the Brisbane Mesh in Brisbane, Australia, which in my research most clearly exemplifies the idea. A wireless mesh community is in fact a wireless version of what I predicted in 1993, with my "Cableton" editorial: A Cableton without cables, using Wi-Fi appliances.

Mesh communities are *not* about the creation of public hotspots, though public hotspots may be part of the mix. A wireless mesh community has the following general characteristics:

- Individuals create wireless nodes that connect to other wireless nodes with roof-mounted antennas.

- Traffic among nodes is routed, via some kind of router appliance, usually a PC running some flavor of free Unix like Linux.

- Even if there is no connection between the mesh community and the global Internet, local community servers support Internet protocols like email, chat, newsgroups, and Voice over IP (Internet telephone.)

A mesh community, being a routed network based on Internet protocols, is actually a parallel Internet, which wireless guru Rob Flickenger calls a *paranet*.

The Brisbane Mesh

Although mesh community projects appear to be popping up almost everywhere, one of the earliest and best-documented is the Brisbane Mesh project in Brisbane, Australia. The project's Web site is here:

www.itee.uq.edu.au/~mesh/

A very nice forum (you must register to participate) on Brisbane Mesh is here:

www.itee.uq.edu.au/~mesh/forum/

A very active email list server devoted to the Brisbane Mesh may be found here:

www.itee.uq.edu.au/~mesh/list/

The three kinds of nodes used in the Brisbane Mesh architecture are trunk nodes, access nodes, and leaf nodes. Trunk nodes communicate with one another and with access nodes. They form the mesh community backbones, and use high-gain antennas and high-bandwidth access point technologies (like Wireless-A and G) to transport packets in volume across significant distances. Access nodes provide connections to individual leaf nodes that are within easy Wi-Fi distances. Access nodes communicate with one another, and also with trunk nodes. Leaf nodes are for ordinary users without the desire or means to relay packets from other users. This all shows better than it tells, so take a close look at Figure 5.2.

The Brisbane Mesh project has a brilliant node directory system that allows prospective participants to determine whether there are any access nodes within line of sight, and provides contact information for node operators. The directory is public and may be found here:

www.itee.uq.edu.au/~mesh/db2/index.php

The Hinternet: Amateur Radio's HSMM Initiative

In mid-2003, a movement arose within amateur ("ham") radio to create a parallel Internet for amateur traffic, using standard Wireless-B or Wireless-G hardware. One little known Wi-Fi factoid is that the federally-licensed Amateur Radio Service has a band that overlaps half of the American Wi-Fi band at 2.4 GHz.

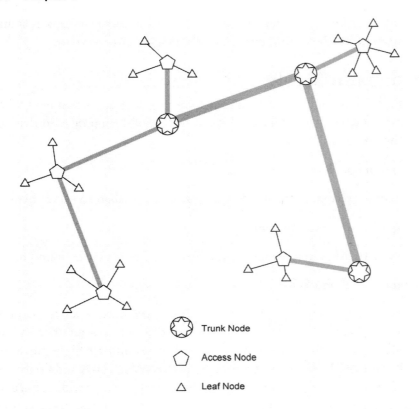

Figure 5.2
The Brisbane Mesh Topology.

People who get ham radio licenses are often imagined by the general public as gray-haired retirees pounding Morse code into 100-foot antenna towers, but the truth is considerably more complex. Amateur radio no longer requires a Morse code test for licensing, and the body of technical knowledge required is considerably less than required for, say, MCSE certification. With the Amateur Radio license comes the right to use much higher power and huge swaths of electromagnetic spectrum, from just above the AM broadcast band up through millimeter microwaves.

Let's just say that it's worth the trouble to get the license. I've been in ham radio for 32 years now, and currently hold callsign K7JPD.

The High-Speed Multimedia (HSMM) Radio initiative coalesced in 2002, and is currently in the design stages. Sometime in the next couple of years, hams will be mounting Wi-Fi repeaters on towers and moving data through high-powered Wi-Fi links between high-gain parabolic dish antennas. Two amateurs near Colorado

Springs used a pair of scrapped 6-foot satellite dishes in 2002 to establish a Wi-Fi link across a 23-mile path, at the full Wireless-B bit rate. On each end of the link was a humble Linksys WUSB11 client adapter, bolted at the focus of the dish. No amplifiers of any kind were used. Over in Utah at the end of 2003, a pair of amateurs did considerably better, and bridged a record-breaking *82-mile* path with a pair of unmodified 100 mw Cisco Aironet 350 Wireless-B cards.

The HSMM Radio initiative is being spearheaded by the American Radio Relay League (ARRL), the national association of radio amateurs. If you're already a licensed radio amateur (or would like to become one) and HSMM radio interests you, here are some pertinent links:

ARRL home page for HSMM radio   **www.arrl.org/hsmm/**

An article from ham radio journal QST   **www2.arrl.org/tis/info/pdf/0304028.pdf**

Challenges Facing Mesh Communities

It's still much too soon to say what sort of mechanism works best for a mesh community. We'll need the next several years to see what works and what doesn't, and how well. There are some issues to keep in mind if you're considering launching such a project:

- Even if the connections among mesh participants is free, connection to the global Internet usually is not. Some way of sharing the cost of a connection to the Internet may need to be worked out. Many people will not participate if they can't "surf the Net" through the connection.

- Most modern suburban subdivisions have a peculiar and deadly hatred of antennas, even small ones. There are deed restrictions that go so far as to prohibit *ownership* of "transmitters," though how enforceable such provisions are has not been tested. The same hateful people who once used deed restrictions to forbid ownership of suburban homes by minorities are behind such things, and they make a hobby of meddling in other people's business. The energy and money they can bring to bear on those who disagree with them can be awesome. If such restrictions exist in your area, your only out may be to use a surplus satellite dish, as such devices have been granted a certain amount of immunity to deed restrictions by the FCC. Investigate carefully, and keep a low profile.

- The technical burden of coordinating IP addresses and configuring routers is not to be underestimated. Once you exhaust your pool of enthusiastic and network-savvy volunteers, sharing the work required to keep the whole thing coordinated and running may become a serious problem.

- Security remains a gnarly problem, because even with WEP (and much more recently, WPA) to exclude outsiders, there is nothing to prevent packet-sniffing by less-than-ethical mesh members. A mesh community has much in common with the old "party line" rural telephone line sharing systems. Privacy needs to be an added layer on top of the network, using some sort of point-to-point tunneling protocol. More research must be done here, but the problem, while difficult, is not unsolvable.

In short, a mesh community is a *very* big project, and a great deal of work. Furthermore, you can expect political opposition from several quarters, including the antenna hater crowd and local telecommunications companies who feel that they're being edged out of a market. If that doesn't scare you off, I encourage you to give it a try. The good news is that you can start small, and experiment with the technology with two or three other people in your general vicinity. Once you get a three-house rooftop LAN together and the bugs wrung out, you can begin adding additional nodes within line-of-sight.

For more on community networks you'll need to scour the Web. Rob Flickenger's short book *Wireless Community Networks* is helpful, but is mostly an overview of the technical issues involved. We don't yet know enough about how community hotspots and mesh communities will work over the long haul for a definitive reference to be written.

Such a book will happen, but it'll be a little while yet. Stay tuned.

In the foreseeable future we can expect to see more and better software systems to make developing and administering wireless community networks easier. As that happens, and perhaps as special hardware bundles and other items drop in price we could start to see quite a bit of growth in this area. There is clearly some economic incentive to enable these projects not to mention the challenge and fun of developing community through technology too.

Access Points and Gateways

I f you read Chapter 4 carefully, you should understand the shape of a typical Wi-Fi setup. An "infrastructure" network provides a central point to which your various computers connect via microwave links. To take part in the network, each computer must be equipped with a *client adapter* (which I'll cover in depth in Chapter 7). A client adopter is usually a plug-in board containing a computer-controlled data radio.

Two or more Wi-Fi client adapters can create a sort of egalitarian electronic mob by going into *ad-hoc mode* and talking to one another, but in 98% of all cases, what people need in their wireless networks is an infrastructure network. The linchpin gadget in Wi-Fi infrastructure is that central connecting hub called an *access point*, or its all-in-one big brother, the *wireless gateway*, which combines an access point with an Internet port, a router, and a network switch.

I've described access points conceptually in earlier chapters. In this chapter, we'll look more closely at what access points do, how they work, and how you control and maintain them. At the end of this chapter, I'll provide some advice on how to choose an access point or wireless gateway for your own network.

Access Points: Broad Power, Limited Agenda

Access points have never been especially large, in physical terms, and it surprises many to learn that an access point is first of all a *computer*, and a relatively powerful one. What keeps access points small is that their computing power is extremely focused. They do only one thing, and do it well, and do it without a lot of extra equipment. Figure 6.1 shows a very common access point, the Linksys WAP-11. It's about the size of a fat paperback book, and smaller than many dialup modems from Ye Olden Tymes.

Access points don't store a great deal of data, so they don't need hard drives, floppy drives, or CD-ROM drives. They don't communicate directly with their users very often, so they don't need keyboards, monitors, or mice. (They communicate with their users when necessary through other computers' peripherals.) They need a network interface port (or two, in the case of wireless gateways) and a Wi-Fi radio system. That's it.

Not having to deal with fast disk drives and (especially) video graphics allows an access point's computer to get a lot more done without having to run at 2 GHz with 512 MB of RAM in the box. Slower computers need less power and generate less heat, and can fit in smaller enclosures without fans. If you get rid of drives, video, fans, and power supplies capable of sourcing a spot welder, you can get a lot of networking done in a very small package.

That access points are general-purpose computers is borne out by the fact that the OpenAP group has written a version of the Linux operating system that runs on certain brands of access point. The OpenAP software replaces the access point's

Figure 6.1
The Linksys WAP11 Access Point. (Photo courtesy of Linksys.)

own software (called *firmware*, more on which shortly) and allows a lot more control over what the access point can be made to do. To learn more about this, visit the following Web site:

http://opensource.instant802.com/

OpenAP is definitely a project for serious Linux network experts, but it shows how much computing power is actually available inside a $79 access point.

Firmware

Access points are not alone in being computers beneath the covers. A covert revolution in consumer electronics has occurred in the last ten years or so (with roots going back to the 1970s) that has placed complete and fairly powerful computers inside virtually all sophisticated consumer devices. New high-definition TVs and stereo tuners are all computers at their core, as are disk-based video recorders like TiVo. What makes this a revolution is the simple fact that most of what all these gadgets do is now driven by software, and not hardware. Increasingly, the hardware is simple and cheap. The value-added in consumer electronics is mostly in the software.

In smaller devices like Wi-Fi gear, this software resides not on a hard drive but on special *non-volatile* memory chips, so called because they retain their contents even when power to the device is turned off. These memory chips are unlike the RAM found in your Dell or Compaq desktop or laptop computer. You'll often hear non-volatile memory called "flash RAM" or "flash memory."

Software residing in non-volatile memory isn't quite as "soft" as software residing in ordinary RAM. This is why engineers coined the term *firmware* to describe software written into non-volatile memory such as flash RAM or older ROM (read-only memory) chips, and used to control the operation of "embedded processors" hidden inside devices that are not used as general-purpose computers.

The really great thing about firmware residing in flash memory is that it can be updated. In a technology advancing as quickly as wireless networking, this is a tremendous bonus. In the old days, computer gear was obsolete almost as soon as you took it out of the box, and there was no way to add new features or fix design defects. Today, you can download a new firmware file for an access point or client adapter, and "flash" the update into its place inside the device. Some of my Wi-Fi gear is almost as old as the 802.11b standard itself, but because I've kept its firmware up-to-date, it now holds its own against brand-new gear. The Orinoco Gold PCMCIA card in my laptop now offers features that didn't even exist when it was manufactured, including crucial things like weak IV filtering (see Chapter 13). By performing firmware updates with files provided by the manufacturer without charge on their Web site, I've gotten almost three years of use out of my Wi-Fi gear, with no necessary "end of life" in sight. That said, there may be older gear that cannot be upgraded to the WPA security standard because an older device may not have the internal resources—computing, memory—to support WPA. This is something you have to research, starting with the vendor Web site.

I'll explain how to perform firmware updates on your own gear a little later in this chapter.

Computer-Controlled Data Radios

An access point can be thought of as a computer-controlled data radio. I've sketched out a block diagram of a typical access point in Figure 6.2. How the functional blocks translate to chips inside actual products depends on the manufacturer, but it's been cooking down to fewer and fewer chips as competition drives manufacturers to seek lower unit manufacturing costs. Dedicated Wi-Fi chipsets now dominate the industry, in which large, complex chips combine several necessary functions onto a single silicon die. The Atmel AT76C510 processor chip, used in popular products like the Linksys WAP11 access point, actually contains two independent RISC CPU units, one to handle overall device control, and another to perform continuous translation of 802.11b frames to Ethernet packets. The two work in parallel, accomplishing much more than either could do alone.

An access point has two *medium access controllers*. If you recall from Chapter 2, Ethernet networking can transfer data over several different "mediums": wire, fiber optics cable, infrared light, or microwave radio signals. A medium access controller is a type of translator that sits between a network port and the physical medium over which data is transferred, governing the passage of data between the medium and the network. It controls access to the medium, hence its name.

 The really interesting (and difficult) part of an access point is the radio subsystem. The rest of the subsystems (the computer and medium access controller logic) are "old stuff" and well-understood. The real brilliance in Wi-Fi hardware lies in the silicon that controls the reception and generation of microwave radio energy.

Right now, a relative handful of chip manufacturers are slugging it out for dominance in the Wi-Fi radio chipset realm. Intersil leads with its PRISM product line, with Agere and Texas Instruments having most of the rest of the market. This is significant, since much of the "character" of a given access point proceeds from the quirks and feature set of its radio chipset. You'll hear people say things like, "Oh,

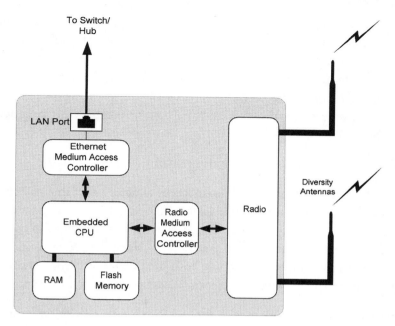

Figure 6.2
Access Point Functional Blocks.

that AP uses PRISM 2," which speaks volumes to Wi-Fi industry geeks. Power output, power consumption, noise figures, and many other radio-related things mark the difference between a so-so access point and a killer access point.

Newcomers to the Wi-Fi chip field often try to compete in areas outside the true mass market, which was original Wireless-B and is now Wireless-G. Chip maker Atheros first chose to compete primarily in the 5 GHz 802.11a chipset market, but now that Wireless-A has begun its long sunset, Atheros has taken a deep position in Wireless-G, with bit rate enhancements called "Super G." (I described Super G in some detail in Chapter 4.) Other companies emerge from the noise on a regular basis. Breakthroughs and surprises can't be predicted but can be expected. We live in very interesting times.

Command and Control

Even though access points don't have their own dedicated keyboards, displays, or mice, you still have to communicate with them. Access points come out of their boxes with reasonable default values for all their configurable options, and the good news is that in most cases you can simply plug them in, connect the cables, and be up and running.

That's also the bad news: It's so easy to make Wi-Fi gear function that many people never bother to learn how to configure their access points. 60% to 65% of access points queried by wardrivers (see Chapter 19) do not have any security enabled at all, and about 40% are put "on the air" with their default SSID values intact and unchanged, veritably *screaming* "Clueless network owner here!" It's important to learn how to configure your Wi-Fi gear, starting with your access point or gateway.

Communication with access points is done in one of the following ways:

- A serial port or USB port in the AP connects to a mating port in a physically adjacent computer. The administrator of the AP opens a "terminal window" or dedicated serial port utility of some kind on the adjacent computer to configure the AP. This method has a security advantage, since the person doing the configuring must have physical access to both the AP and the computer to which it is connected. However, few recent access points have this feature.

- An administrator communicates with the AP through its network port, and uses a protocol called SNMP (Simple Network Management Protocol) to query and set configuration options. The label says "simple," but SNMP has a serious learning curve and is really intended for use by large organizations with a multitude of networked devices to manage in some sort of coordinated fashion. Unless you already know SNMP from your work experience, there's little point in learning it to manage one or perhaps two APs.

- An administrator communicates with the AP through its network port, and connects to an internal Web server using an ordinary Web browser. This is how virtually all modern APs and gateways are configured, and the only method I'll discuss in detail here.

It surprises some people to learn than most access points contain their own Web servers. That's not difficult—a Web server is not a complex thing, and is really just a sub-program in the AP firmware.

The key issue is that any Web server must have an IP address. (See Chapter 3 for more on IP addresses.) An access point can obtain an IP address in one of two ways:

- An IP address may be preset into the access point by its manufacturer. The popular Linksys BEFW11S4 and WRT54G wireless gateways come with a default address of **http://192.168.1.1**. Once your AP is connected to your router (or once your gateway is connected to your primary computer and

Internet connection) you can type that address into a Web browser and the unit's configuration screen will pop up in your browser, ready to work.

- The AP may request an IP address from the local network router or some other device that is running a Dynamic Host Configuration Protocol (DHCP) server. The Cisco Aironet 340 access point works this way: When it powers up, it requests an IP from the local DHCP server. (Again, see Chapter 3 for more on DHCP.) You have to inspect the local DHCP client table to find out what the IP address is, before you can enter it into a browser to begin configuration.

Many APs support both methods, but virtually all come "out of the box" with a preset IP address. In both methods, the IP address will be a "local" or *non-routable* IP address. This kind of address is local to the network, and cannot be accessed from outside of your local network. There's no reason for your AP's configuration screen to be reachable from the Internet at large (and plenty of reasons why it shouldn't!) so its address is pulled from a block of IP addresses reserved for local network use. (I describe this in more detail in Chapter 3.) Most non-routable addresses you'll see used by access points and gateways are in the block 192.168.X.X.

Talking to Your Access Point

Once your network has been physically assembled, your access point or wireless gateway will be connected via Ethernet cable to at least one computer. This is required, because configuring an access point affects its ability to operate "over the air" and a solid connection is required to change its configuration parameters. Theoretically, you can configure an access point through its wireless link, but if you change a parameter that affects the wireless connection, you can be cut off from the access point before the job is complete.

Typically, the wired connection is through a router/switch appliance, or to the switch built into a wireless gateway. More on this later.

To communicate with your access point's configuration screens, follow these steps:

1. Bring up a Web browser on the computer with a *wired* connection to the access point.

2. In the browser's URL entry field, type "http://" followed by the access point's IP address, and press Enter. The complete URL will look something like this: http://192.168.1.1. The precise URL will depend on the particular IP address.

The one you should use should be present in the device's documentation. If you don't have the documentation, try using 192.168.1.1 or 192.168.0.1. Those are the two commonest. Some access points may request their IP addresses from your network's DHCP server, and you'll have to go to the DHCP server's clients table to find out the IP address of the access point. More on this shortly.

3. Assuming you used the correct IP address, a user name/password dialog will appear. If it's the first time you've brought up the configuration screen, the dialog will respond to a default user name and password. These should be given in the product documentation. Enter the user name and password and click Enter.

4. The configuration screen will appear in the Web browser. Most such screens have tabbed interfaces with several separate subscreens containing configuration information and data fields in which configuration parameters may be entered. A typical screen is shown in Figure 6.3.

Alas, the documentation I've seen for low-end Wi-Fi gear is pretty sparse, and usually written so poorly it's a wonder it can still be considered English. A little later in

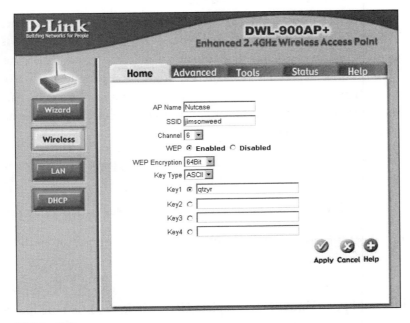

Figure 6.3
The D-Link DWL-900AP+ Configuration Screen.

this chapter I'll describe many of the common configuration parameters you'll have to deal with in setting up simple Wi-Fi networks. Some of the precise details may be specific to a particular make or model of access point, and for this you'll have to read carefully and perhaps experiment a little to fully understand what a parameter means.

The majority of configuration parameters can be left with their default values in place and don't need to be changed. For those that must be changed, I'll provide ample guidance in Chapter 9 and later chapters.

Access Points and DHCP Servers

Most of the low-end access points and wireless gateways come with a pre-set IP address, as I explained above. Sometimes an access point will not have a pre-configured IP address, but instead will automatically request an IP address from the network's DHCP server when it powers up. (I explained DHCP servers in Chapter 3.) My ancient Cisco Aironet 340 access point works this way, and as best I know the newer Cisco 350 series does as well.

To configure such an access point, you must look up the access point's IP address in the DHCP server's *clients table*. In most home networks, the DHCP server and its clients table are part of the router/switch appliance, or wireless gateway. Somewhere in the menu structure of your router/switch appliance or wireless gateway you'll find a tab or screen for DHCP server status. Here you'll find either a listing of the clients table or a button you can click to bring up the clients table in a separate window.

The location of the DHCP clients table listing is different in every network device I've ever used, so you'll have to explore the menus or (horrors!) look it up in the documentation. Once you go to the DHCP clients table, you should see your access point listed (along with all the various computers connected to the network) with an associated IP address like 192.168.1.104. That's the address you should type into your Web browser to bring up the access point's configuration screen.

Wireless Gateways

Even though sharing a broadband Internet connection is the top use driving Wi-Fi networks in the home, there is nothing inherent in a wireless access point to support the Internet. As I explained in Chapter 2, an access point is just a wireless Ethernet hub, and can be used to create a network without any Internet connection at all.

Internet connection sharing requires a router and a Network Address Translation (NAT) server. A Dynamic Host Configuration Protocol (DHCP) server is also very useful in a network based on the Internet protocol suite. Taken together, these items comprise a *gateway*, that is, an interface between two networks: your network and the global Internet.

It's easy enough to bundle a router, a NAT server, and a DHCP server into a single package with a wireless access point. To make local area networks easier to create, most vendors also add an Ethernet switch (see Chapter 2) to the mix as well. Router, NAT, DHCP, switch, and access point together become an "all-in-one" wireless network appliance focused on providing an Internet gateway to a local area network. I call such an appliance a *wireless gateway*.

Not everyone uses the term "wireless gateway," but there is a crying need for a new descriptive word or phrase to replace awkward concretions like "Wireless access point + cable/DSL router and switch." (That awful mess is what Linksys calls their very excellent BEFW11S4 and WRT54G products.)

Wireless gateways are quite common and very effective for small office/home office (SOHO) local area networks, and both save money and reduce cable clutter considerably. Perhaps the best-known example of a wireless gateway is the LinkSys WRT54G, shown in Figure 6.4. This unit is consistently shown as the best-selling Wi-Fi appliance in any stack rank of sales I see on the Web, including the bestseller list on Linksys'

Figure 6.4
The Linksys WRT54G Wireless Gateway. (Photo courtesy of Linksys.)

own Web site. In small networks needing only a single access point, a wireless gateway like this (there are many on the market) is the only piece of networking gear you'll need, apart from network client cards (either wired or wireless) installed in all computers or other devices connected to the network. Wireless client adapters connect to the built-in wireless access point. Wired Ethernet client adapters connect to one of the several Ethernet switch ports on the back of the unit.

How these connections are made is fairly simple, as shown in Figure 6.5. A Category 5 patch cable connects your cable or DSL modem to the wide-area network (WAN) port on the wireless gateway, and any computers requiring wired access are similarly connected to one of the four switched ports on the gateway. Machines with Wi-Fi client cards installed communicate with the gateway via its wireless access point.

Many wireless gateways have an expansion port, which allows the connection of a "slave" switch to provide additional wired ports. The Linksys BEFW11S4 (and its newer Wireless-G descendant, the WRT54G) has such a port, which it calls the

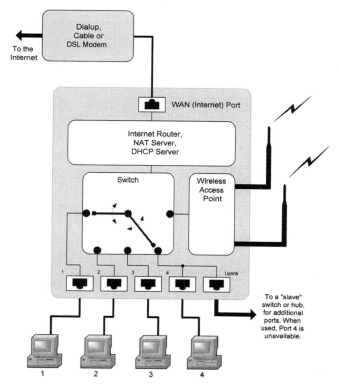

Figure 6.5
A Wireless Gateway.

"uplink" port. The uplink port is attached to port 4, and when the uplink port is connected to a slave switch, port 4 is unavailable.

The router inside the gateway manages access to the "wide area" network world beyond your LAN (usually the Internet), and uses its NAT server to share the WAN connection among the several computers on your LAN. (I explained NAT operation in Chapter 3.) The switch directs those packets to the correct machines, and the access point provides wireless connection to machines not connected to the gateway by CAT 5 cables.

The wireless access point is switched just as the hardwired computers are. All computers connected wirelessly to the access point share one switched connection, and thus share the data throughput of that one switched connection. (Never forget that a wireless access point is an Ethernet hub, not a switch!)

One caution about using wireless gateways: They're *not* suitable for networks that must support roaming. In other words, if your house or office is so large as to require multiple wireless access points to cover it all, don't attempt to use multiple wireless gateways, or a wireless gateway with an access point cabled to its switch. Roaming (being able to walk around with a Wi-Fi-equipped laptop or PDA and connect seamlessly through multiple APs) is a very sticky issue in Wi-Fi right now. The original 802.11 standard calls out roaming as a requirement but does not specify in detail how roaming is to be handled, so different manufacturers handle it in different (and often incompatible) ways. If you need to implement roaming, always inquire of your Wi-Fi vendor to make sure a given access point supports it, and then use the same manufacturer and model for *all* APs in the network. Once the 802.11f roaming standard is widely implemented, roaming will be easier to implement. In the meantime, you're better off with higher-end access points (like those from Cisco) if you need reliable roaming among several APs.

Another thing to keep in mind if you're thinking about experimenting with bridge mode or with access points in client mode: None of the wireless gateways I've tried support either bridge mode or client mode. They're not designed for versatility, and they're really one-trick ponies. Still, for 85% of the people who implement a Wi-Fi network, that one trick is all they need the device to do.

"Dual-Mode" Access Points and Gateways

In the fall of 2002, several manufacturers began shipping "dual-mode" Wi-Fi gear. In their first release, these products provided Wireless-A and Wireless-B in the same package. This means that in a single access point or wireless gateway, there were entirely independent 2.4 GHz Wireless-B and 5 GHz Wireless-A data radios, capable of connecting to clients using either Wireless-A or B technology.

The release of the Wireless-G standard in mid-2003 made it possible for dual-mode products to support all three Wi-Fi standards, and very quickly "dual-mode" meant three standards rather than two. The reason is that both Wireless-B and Wireless-G operate on the 2.4 GHz band, and thus can share much of their radio machinery in common. Once we got into 2004, the change was complete, and now it's rare to see a multi-mode Wi-Fi product that doesn't support all three standards.

Dual-mode access points and gateways are one way to keep your investment in older Wireless-B gear while using Wireless-A gear for speedier, in-network file transfers. However, because Wireless-G gives you all the speed of Wireless-A and even greater range, there's little reason to adopt Wireless-A anymore, except for compatibility with existing gear and networks.

Keep in mind that the additional cost of dual-mode gear is huge—often more than twice the cost of an equivalent Wireless-G (which also supports Wireless-B) device. A recent check of online prices shows that the D-Link AirExpert A-B-G DI-774 wireless gateway goes for a street price of $230, whereas the comparable DI-624 Wireless-G (and B) gateway goes for $88. That's a $142 premium for Wireless-A compatibility. Given that Wireless-A is sliding from niche status toward abandonment, I'm sure that's not a particularly good tradeoff. Unless you have a truly compelling reason to use Wireless-A, I recommend saving your money: That $142 could buy you two additional client adapters!

Diversity Reception and Dual Antennas

Most (though by no means all) access points and wireless gateways have two antennas. Two antennas allow *diversity reception*, a feature that improves the reliability of your Wi-Fi connection through the access point or gateway.

Microwaves bouncing around a room sometimes reflect back to their source and interfere with themselves, creating "ghost signals" that weaken the link and reduce its quality. It's analogous to "ghost images" on a broadcast TV signal, which happen when the signal arrives at the TV's rabbit-ears antenna twice: once on a direct path, and another on a path that bounces off a hill or tall building or even a jetliner flying overhead.

For technical reasons that I can't explain in detail here, a pair of antennas located at least one wavelength apart will rarely both experience this sort of interference at the same time. When one antenna is beset by reflective ghosting, the other will typically not be. Diversity reception allows the access point to choose which antenna to take its signal from. The access point's radio subsystem continually samples the signal strength from both antennas, and it takes the stronger of the two signals.

One wavelength at Wireless-B and G frequencies (2.4 GHz) is a little under five inches, and if you measure the distance between the two antennas on an access point, that's how far apart they'll be, or a little more.

Note well that diversity reception is about *reception*, not transmission. The signal transmitted from an access point or gateway always goes out through the same antenna. Many access points allow you to select which antenna is the receive antenna, but in operation, the transmit antenna never changes, even if the receive antenna does. (Wi-Fi gear is "half-duplex," meaning that a device will either transmit or receive at a given time, but will never transmit and receive simultaneously.) The only exception I know of is the high-end Cisco Aironet 350 product line, which offers a diversity option on the transmit side. The documentation says little about it and it's unclear what diversity on transmit accomplishes.

All else being equal, an access point or gateway with two antennas will have a greater range than similar devices with only one antenna. This is not because both antennas transmit at once, but because the signals received by the access point are less subject to ghosting interference.

Some client adapters also have dual antennas, but that's much less common. The Cisco Aironet 350 and the Asantè AL-1511 "X-Wing" PCMCIA cards are the only ones I'm sure of, and because there isn't room on a PCMCIA card to put 5" between antennas, the effectiveness of their diversity reception isn't optimal.

Common Access Point Configuration Parameters

Not all access points are alike, obviously, and it would be impossible to give detailed instructions on setting all the various configuration options you'll encounter on your AP's configuration screens. I'll summarize the most important ones here, so you'll at least have some idea of what they are and what different values might imply.

Be aware that different manufacturers sometimes call the same parameter by different names. SSID and ESSID, for example, mean precisely the same thing. "Header type" and "preamble type" are the same as well.

- *SSID*: This is the Service Set Identifier, and it is the name of the network to which the access point belongs. It is *not* the name of the access point itself! (When there is only one access point in a network, that's an easy enough mistake to make.) All access points come with a default value like "default" or "linksys." Definitely choose something and change it. Leaving the default in place makes you look like low-hanging fruit to those drive-by bad boys. The SSID is limited to 32 characters, but may contain spaces and punctuation.

- *ESSID*: Extended Service Set Identifier, a slightly different name for SSID used by some manufacturers. The two terms mean the same thing, and the "extended" is intended to emphasize that the SSID is the name of the *network*, and not an individual wireless device.

- *Access Point Name*: Many (but not all) access points allow you to enter a descriptive name for the access point itself. It's actually the host name for your access point, and is usually blank by default. The access point name appears in DHCP client lists, and if you have multiple access points it is *very* handy to give each a different descriptive name so you can tell them apart when looking at the DHCP client list. Don't make this name the same as your SSID!

- *Channel*: In the U.S., there are 11 frequency channels on which Wi-Fi gear may operate, and you're free to pick one. Which channel you use generally isn't important unless you install multiple access points (each of which must be on a channel that doesn't overlap that of adjacent access points) or have other networks nearby—like your neighbors' in the adjoining condo or townhouse. Only three channels are completely without frequency overlap: 1, 6, and 11. Nonetheless, if you must create a "cloud" of wireless coverage with many access points, you can create a "tessellation" of access points using channels 1, 6, and 11 such that no two wireless fields abut one another with overlapping channels. See Figure 4.5 in Chapter 4 for an illustration of how such tessellations are created. Note also that Super-G devices (see my discussion of Super-G in Chapter 4) operate on channels 5 and 6 at once, and cannot be moved to any other channel.

- *Wireless Network Mode*: In access points or gateways that support both Wireless-B and Wireless-G, the device can often be placed into one of three modes: B-only, G-only, and "mixed" mode, which allows both B and G clients to connect. Your greatest throughput will come from G-only mode, but in G-only mode, Wireless-B clients will not be able to connect. The default is mixed mode, and if your network is to support only Wireless-G clients, you can change this to G-only. Note that this is *not* the same as "access point mode" (see below) which determines whether the device will function as an access point, bridge, or repeater.

- *LAN IP Address*: This is the IP address to which the device responds, typically through a Web browser. If you embed this address in a URL and type the URL into a Web browser, the internal Web server in the device will display its configuration screen.

- *LAN Subnet Mask*: A subnet mask indicates what part of an IP address specifies the network, and what part specifies the host (that is, a particular computer on the network.) I explained subnet masks in Chapter 3. If two devices (say, an access point and a router) have different subnet masks, they may not be able to coexist on the same local area network. This happens sometimes, and can be a problem when you mix hardware from different manufacturers on the same network. Still, unless you understand IP addressing thoroughly, do not change the LAN subnet mask. The best way to solve this kind of problem is to configure your access point to request its IP address and subnet mask from the network's DHCP server.

- *LAN Default Gateway*: Your default gateway address is the IP address of the device that "guards the gate" to the outer network world, typically the Internet. If you have a router (as you must if you are to have a home network) this is the IP address of your router. If your router is part of a wireless gateway, this is the IP address of the gateway.

- *LAN IP Address Static/Dynamic*: This option (generally a radio button) determines whether the LAN IP address is static (entered into a field) or dynamic (pulled from a DHCP server). Virtually all low-cost access points default to a *static* IP address, which is listed in the user documentation so that you can type it in and bring up the configuration screens. Once you have your network assembled, it's better to change this to *dynamic* IP address, as I'll explain in Chapter 9.

- *WEP Enable/Disable*: This option (generally a radio button) specifies whether the Wi-Fi encryption system is on or off. WEP (Wired Equivalent Privacy) keeps other people from reading or connecting to your network. Leaving it off for long periods of time is trouble. See Chapters 13 and 14 for detailed information on WEP and how to set it up.

- *WEP Key Length*: Most access points and gateways support two and sometimes three levels of WEP encryption. These are usually 64-bit, 128-bit, and (more rarely) 256-bit. Only the 64-bit level is standard. Using longer key lengths in networks containing Wi-Fi gear from multiple manufacturers can be trouble. I discuss this in more detail in Chapters 13 and 14.

- *WEP Keys*: Once you enable WEP you must enter encryption keys into your access point or gateway, as well as all the computers that will be part of your wireless network. This field (four fields, usually) is where those keys must be entered. In many low-cost devices, only Key 1 is used. I explain this process in detail in Chapters 13 and 14.

- *Authentication Type*: This parameter specifies how clients are authenticated (that is, their identity verified) before the access point or gateway allows them to connect. Your options (generally radio buttons) are typically "shared key," "open system," and "auto" or "both." Alas, there is a lot of confusion on what these actually mean. Although the greater 802.11 standard defines both terms, manufacturers seem to implement them in different ways. The default is invariably "auto" or "both" and I recommend leaving it there.

- *Access Point Mode*: Many access points (but very few gateways) can operate in several modes. The default mode is access point, but other modes may include bridge mode, point-to-multipoint bridge mode, repeater mode, and client mode. I discuss bridge mode in Chapter 17. Unless you're doing something exotic (and know what you're doing) this option should be left alone.

- *DHCP Enable/Disable*: This option (generally a radio button) selects whether the DHCP server inside the device is active or inactive. Virtually all wireless gateways contain a DHCP server. Many (but not all) access points do as well. The general rule is that there should be *one* DHCP server per local area network segment—and most home office networks have only one segment. It's good practice to use the DHCP server associated with your router or wireless gateway. Unless you have no other DHCP server, leave any DHCP servers inside access points disabled.

- *DHCP Server Starting Address*: When enabled, your DHCP server hands out IP addresses to devices on the local area network that require one. These addresses are issued sequentially from a starting value, which is the value in this parameter. Unless you know precisely what you're doing (and have an unusual need) there's no need to change the default value for this parameter.

- *DHCP Lease Time*: Some devices that incorporate a DHCP server allow you to specify the "lease time" used by the server. This is simply a time interval after which a DHCP-issued IP address expires and must be renewed. (I explained DHCP in Chapter 3.) The default is typically 1 hour, but for home networks there's not much point in changing this value, so whatever the default is, leave it unchanged.

- *DHCP Client List*: This isn't something you have to set or change. It's a list of all the IP addresses that your DHCP server has handed out, along with their host names. Once you set your access point to request an IP address from a DHCP server, you look up its name in the DHCP clients list to find its IP address. You can then use this local IP address to bring up the AP's configuration screen.

- *Preamble Type*: (Sometimes called "header type.") Many access points and gateways allow you to choose between long preambles and short preambles. What a preamble is and why you actually have a choice is technical and difficult to explain, but if you configure all your wireless gear to use short preambles, you will achieve a small increase in throughput. Don't bother unless you're an enthusiast. The increase is at best minor.

- *SSID Broadcast Enable/Disable*: Your access point or gateway broadcasts a notification of its presence every 100 milliseconds or so. This allows computers that don't know it's there to find it and associate with it. It also makes it easy for you to configure a newly installed Wi-Fi client adapter, by displaying a "site survey" of available networks and selecting your network from the list. (I'll demonstrate this in Chapter 9.) Disabling the SSID broadcast means your network won't appear in a site survey list, and setting up new clients becomes all the more difficult. You can disable the SSID broadcast if you like, but it doesn't help you much, contrary to what the non-technical press may say. *Network crackers do not need your SSID broadcast to find you.* My recommendation is to leave this option alone.

- *Antenna Selection*: On access points and gateways with dual antennas, you'll have an option to select diversity reception (using both antennas) or an option to select and use one or the other of the antennas exclusively. Diversity is the default, and should be left there *unless* you attach an external gain antenna to the device. Then (obviously), you have to select which antenna jack is used for the gain antenna, or your signal will be going to an empty jack!

- *MAC Address Filters*: Most access points and gateways allow you to enter a list of Media Access Control (MAC) addresses of computers permitted to connect to your network. This is supposedly a "security" feature, but it is absurdly easy to "sniff" a permitted MAC address and "spoof" your way into the system using another computer's address. MAC address filtering is worthless for security. As I'll explain in Chapter 9, the real use of MAC address filtering is for "load balancing" in networks having more than one AP to serve the same physical space. This is a fairly arcane application, so unless you need to do load balancing, don't mess with MAC address filtering.

- *Radio Output Power*: A few of the higher-end access points and wireless gateways allow you to select a power output level from a drop-down list of several. Most access points operate at about 30 to 35 milliwatts of power. Some will offer output as high as 100 milliwatts, but the really interesting options are those offering lower power levels. If your network is in a small house, townhouse, or apartment, you may be able to drop power without losing a top-rate connection among your networked devices. Reducing power makes it harder for people outside your walls to connect, and if those people are fairly close (as in adjacent townhouses) it becomes a worthwhile security precaution.

- *PPPoE Username and Password*: Certain broadband Internet systems (typically those using ADSL) incorporate a technology called Point-to-Point Protocol over Ethernet, abbreviated PPPoE. Your Internet service provider (ISP) will tell you if you need to provide values for these parameters, which are used in authenticating your network before it is allowed to connect to the Internet through your ISP's network.

I will discuss the use of some of these parameters in Chapter 9, when we go through network implementation.

Firmware Updates

Updating your access point or client adapter's firmware can fix bugs and add whole new features, and sometimes crucially important ones. An early 2002 update to the firmware for the Orinoco Gold PCMCIA card added weak IV filtering, which I considered *the* most significant new feature to appear for Wi-Fi until the release of Wireless-G in mid-2003. Often a manufacturer will issue a firmware update to bring a Wi-Fi device into line with newly approved IEEE task group specifications. This field is moving quickly, and firmware updates allow you to keep your investment in hardware even when advances in technology might otherwise render it obsolete.

Firmware updates are generally packaged as executable archives with a .EXE extension. This makes it easy to do the update: You download the executable, run it, and follow instructions. The only decision you really have to make is whether your Wi-Fi device is already up-to-date or not, and that depends on its firmware release level.

The details vary wildly by manufacturer, but in general terms firmware updates are done this way: You go to the manufacturer's Web site and check their list of firmware updates (often under the "Downloads" item on their main page, products page, or support page) to see if any are available for your unit. If any updates are dated after you bought your unit, it's a sure thing: Download the update and install it. If updates are dated before you bought your unit, you'll have to check the firmware release level on your unit to see if it's older than the release level of the firmware update.

The easiest way to do this may well be to download the firmware update and attempt to install it. For most firmware updater utilities, the utility queries the Wi-Fi device to be updated and discovers its firmware release level. It displays this along with the release level of the update in an initial window (see Figure 6.6).

In Figure 6.6, note the description of the current state of the client adapter in the "Card identification" block. The existing firmware is version 7.28, and the update is to version 8.10. The device needs updating. Had the numbers been the other way around (or the same) updating would not be necessary. Some updater utilities allow you to "go back" to an earlier firmware release level and some do not. I've never known this to be necessary, and you certainly don't want to do it by accident. Check those numbers!

Some updater utilities may not make it as easy as others. You may need to go into a client utility or other configuration screen (like the Web-based screens used by most recent access points) to find the current version of your firmware. It may take a little digging, but I've always managed to locate the firmware level without much trouble. Most modern access points, for example, update their firmware through their Web-based configuration screens.

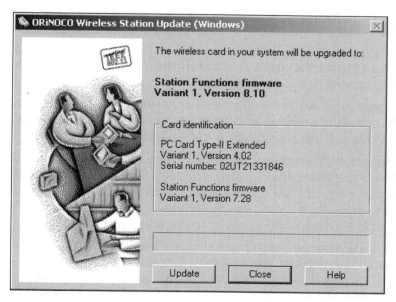

Figure 6.6
The Orinoco Firmware Update Utility.

Once the update begins, it may take a few seconds. Let the software run, and don't do anything else with the computer until it indicates that the update process has been completed.

Updating your firmware may be crucial if you bought "draft-G" gear in that period (which was most of the year 2003) before the final IEEE 802.11g standard document was finalized and implemented in new Wireless-G gear. Before the 802.11g standard was finalized, equipment vendors were guessing about certain details within the standard, and these guesses can degrade compatibility with other Wireless-G gear. After the standard was published in its final form, many vendors wrote new firmware to bring the device up to full (or almost full) 802.11g standard compliance. To get that full standards compliance, you must download and install the updated firmware. Even if the product you bought is not marked "draft-G," check for firmware updates anyway. Some vendors fudged a little on full disclosure early in the Wireless-G era. You may think you have full 802.11g compliance when you do not. If the 2.4 GHz/54 Mbps box is not checked in the Wi-Fi compliance logo on the box, you have *no* guarantee that the product inside is full 802.11g-compliant!

Updating firmware is especially important when you buy used gear and don't know how old it might be. Firmware updates have been issued with surprising frequency in the last two years, and a year-old Wi-Fi client adapter or access point is already considered "ancient."

EXAMPLE: Updating Firmware for the D-Link DWL -900 AP+ Access Point

The D-Link firmware update process is not quite as automated as is that of the Orinoco Gold client adapter, and I've found that it's pretty typical of consumer-class Wi-Fi gear. The steps below will guide you through it. Important note:

Do not initiate a firmware update over a wireless link! Make sure the Web browser you use to configure your DWL-900AP+ is running on a computer connected to the DWL-900AP+ via cables. (This is typically your "main" machine where your router/switch and broadband Internet connection are.)

1. *Determine your current firmware level.* Bring up a Web browser and enter the device's configuration address. Unless it's been changed since I wrote this, the address is http://192.168.0.50/ Log in and navigate to the Tools tab. Click the Firmware button in the left margin to reach the Firmware Upgrade screen. At the center of the screen will be the line reading "Current Firmware Version:" followed by a number. That's your current version. Write it down.

2. *Determine if a newer firmware release exists.* Bring up a Web browser and go to the D-Link support Web site: http://support.dlink.com. Click the Products button in the button bar under the main D-Link logo. This will bring up a full-screen list of D-Link products. Find the "D-Link Air Plus" line and click on DWL-900AP+. Scroll down to a subwindow entitled "Firmware" and see what the level of the most recent firmware release is. If that level is greater than the current level of your DWL-900AP+, you can go ahead to Step 3 and download the firmware. If your unit is up to date from a firmware standpoint, there's nothing more to be done.

3. *Download the firmware archive file to an empty directory.* Click the "Download Now" button for the latest firmware release listed. Your browser will begin a typical download process, allowing you to choose where to store the downloaded file. The file is a self-extracting ZIP archive, with a .EXE extension. Store it in an otherwise empty subdirectory.

4. *Extract the firmware from the self-extracting archive.* The firmware file itself is compressed inside the .EXE file you download. Using Windows Explorer, navigate to the directory where the archive is stored, and double-click on it to run it. The archive is set to extract to a default directory. You will probably have to navigate back to the directory where you stored the archive. Click Unzip and the archive will self-extract the .bin file to the directory that you specified.

5. *Perform the firmware update.* Return to the Firmware Upgrade screen in the DWL-900AP+ Web configuration screen. Click on the Browse button at the center of the screen and navigate to the directory where you stored the firmware .bin file. Highlight the file name and click Open. The path to the file will appear in the field to the left of the Browse button. Click the Apply button to kick off the actual firmware update. Don't do anything with the machine while the firmware update is working, which will take several seconds. When the update is finished, a new screen will appear with a Continue button on it. Click it…and you're done!

Power Over Ethernet (PoE)

Here's a problem that you might encounter in setting up your Wi-Fi system: You have an access point that you want to install in the clear and up in the air. Perhaps you want the access point to act as a wireless bridge to another similar access point some distance away, on top of the next building—or in the next town. Getting power up to the access point can be a real problem and a significant expense. Fortunately, a new technical standard for power transmission over Ethernet cables will help. The IEEE standard for *Power Over Ethernet* (PoE) will reduce the number of wires needed to get the job done. The IEEE task group is 802.3af, and that's the number to look for on product packaging. This new standard (finalized in June, 2003) will let you string a single Ethernet cable to an access point and provide it with both data and power through the same cable.

In a nutshell, PoE allows the same Ethernet category 5 (CAT 5) cable to carry both data and electrical power to an access point or other Ethernet device. There's nothing magical about it. CAT5 cables have more conductors than they need to carry Ethernet data, so PoE uses two of the otherwise idle conductors to carry DC power through the cable.

The trick, of course, lies in knowing *which* two idle conductors. There are four possibilities, and the primary benefit of the standard will be industry-wide agreement on the conductors that carry power. Some vendors already offer PoE adapters, but those designed before the 802.3af standard was published have their own schemes. If you decide to go with PoE pre-standard, keep in mind that you may be stuck with non-standard adapters once the IEEE 802.3af standard is adopted. If you must use non-802.3af PoE devices, use *only* adapters from that same vendor. Adapters from other vendors may use other pairs of wires and simply not work together—or worse, may damage your equipment!

 For a good write-up on some of the implementation details of 802.3af, see this link:

www.us.design-reuse.com/articles/article6889.html

Why PoE?

Why is PoE important in the Wi-Fi world? Simple: A need to keep the access points as close to their antennas as possible. If you want an antenna way high up, you have to mount the AP way high up as well, or you'll simply dissipate the AP's signals (both transmitted and received) in the coaxial cable between the AP and the antenna.

This is important when creating a point-to-point bridge (see Chapter 17) because such bridges are often "rooftop to rooftop" with the endpoints as high as possible to avoid intervening obstructions. People implementing community hotspots may want an AP in a weatherproof housing up on a 30-foot pole with an omnidirectional antenna attached directly to the AP.

The key is keeping the cable length between the AP and its antenna to an absolute minimum. In my experience, coaxial antenna cables longer than three or four feet are *poison*, absent a very expensive, low-loss variety of cable. (See Chapter 8 for a detailed discussion of this problem.) It's easier and cheaper to send Ethernet data over long runs of cables than microwave signals. PoE allows you to send power to the AP right through the same CAT 5 cable that carries Ethernet data to the AP.

How PoE Works

Power is applied to a run of CAT 5 cable through a small device called an *injector*. At the other end of the CAT 5 cable, power is taken from the cable using another small device called a *tap*. (Sometimes a tap is called a *splitter*, but I consider that term confusing for various reasons and won't use it here.) The injector is typically in the server closet, or wherever Ethernet data must be sent to a device like a wireless access point. The tap is near the device being powered. The tap has a power jack on it, and the AP (or other device) plugs its power cable into the tap (see Figure 6.7). Some higher-end APs have a tap built right into them, and I think more will be designed this way in the future, now that the 802.3af standard has been finalized. Check with the AP vendor to be sure.

Note that the injector and the tap both pass the Ethernet conductors through without any kind of interruption.

Passive and Active Devices

Injectors and taps come in two varieties: passive and active.

Passive injectors and taps simply provide a connection for power to a chosen pair of the "spare" conductors inside the CAT 5 cable. Passive injectors and taps can be made from small networking junction boxes, if you have some skill and experience handling wire and simple hand tools.

Active injectors and taps provide additional electrical services:

- An active injector typically provides short-circuit protection, which is something like a circuit breaker: It stops current flow if a short-circuit occurs in the

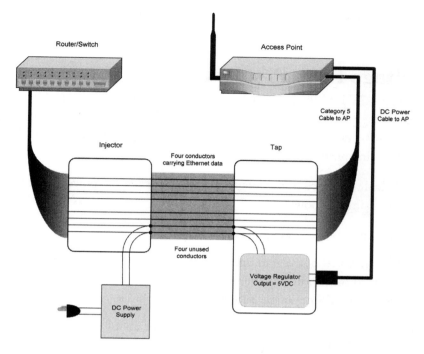

Figure 6.7
How Power Over Ethernet (PoE) Works.

power circuitry somewhere. This prevents the cable from overheating and possibly causing fires and damage to the remote device or devices being powered.

- An active injector may also provide overcurrent protection. This limits current from the power supply in case the device at the other end of the CAT 5 cable attempts to draw excessive current for some reason. (This often happens when multiple devices are powered through the same CAT5 cable. Too many devices may demand more current than the power supply can provide without damage.)

- An active tap usually includes a voltage regulator, which takes DC power from the CAT 5 cable and converts it to the specific voltage required by the device being powered. This way, voltage changes in the cable will not affect the device being powered.

Commercial active injectors typically put either 24V or 48V DC into the CAT 5 cable. For each device powered through the cable, an active tap is chosen with an appropriate voltage regulator inside. A Linksys access point, for example, may require

5V DC. An active tap with a 5V regulator would be used to convert the 24V in the cable down to 5V.

The Voltage Drop Problem

Why not just put 5V into the cable and avoid the cost of active devices? There is an unavoidable voltage drop across significant lengths of cable (more than twenty feet or so) that must be taken into account. This voltage drop depends on two things, according to a principle of physics called Ohm's Law:

1. The electrical resistance in the length of cable between the power source and the devices using the power

2. The total current being drawn through the cable

If either factor (or, worse, both) goes up, the voltage available at the other end of the cable goes down. At some point, the voltage will drop so far that the devices drawing power from the cable will no longer function.

Each conductor in a CAT 5 cable has a resistance of about three ohms per one hundred feet of cable. If you use a long enough cable (and power enough devices through it) the voltage available to the devices under power will drop so low that the devices will no longer work. One device, in fact, may be enough. The governing equation is this:

Voltage drop across the cable = Current in amperes X resistance in ohms

EXAMPLE: Dealing with Voltage Drops

Say you're powering a wireless access point (AP) through one hundred twenty feet of CAT5 cable. At 3 ohms per hundred feet of cable, the resistance in that length of cable would be 1.2 x 3 ohms, or 3.6 ohms. If the AP draws 1.4 amperes of power through the cable, you have:

Voltage drop = 1.4 amperes x 3.6 ohms = 5.04 volts

How bad is this? Well, that depends on what voltage your AP requires. The Linksys line of access points use a 5 Volt power source, so if you drop 5.04 volts through the cable while putting only 5 volts into the opposite end, you have... *no voltage at all.*

Not good. Fortunately, there are two ways out:

- Use active injectors and taps that provide a high enough voltage level through the cable that modest voltage drops may be absorbed without problems. Even if your cable drops 5V, if you begin with 24V, you'll still have 19V at the other end of the cable, which an active tap can regulate down to 12V or 5V as needed.

- Use passive injectors and taps and calculate (or measure) the voltage drop through the cable, and choose a power supply that provides *precisely* enough voltage to compensate for the measured loss in the cable. In the example shown above, you would need to use a 10V power supply, so that losing 5V in the cable would still leave 5V to power the access point.

Using passive injectors and taps is less expensive, but tricky, and unless you have some skill with electrical calculation and test equipment, you should stick with commercial active PoE products. Recent PoE product introductions from companies like D-Link have taken the cost of injectors and active taps down to $39 for a set containing one of both, so there's less and less reason to make your own as time goes on.

 If you decide you're willing and able to construct PoE injectors and taps on your own, perform a search on the Web to see some of the sites posted by others who have done this. The process involves some Ohm's Law math and some bench electrical work, plus some test equipment. A variable voltage power supply is extremely helpful—and egad, a soldering iron!

The Power Connector Problem

Another unexpected problem in using PoE with some Wi-Fi gear is that certain units take power through non-standard power connectors on their back panels. The Cisco Aironet 340 access point runs on 5V—but it uses a connector you won't find on a rack at Radio Shack or anywhere else, except perhaps direct from Cisco. Many Linksys products, on the other hand, use a standard "coaxial" or "barrel" DC power connector which you can buy at almost any electronic parts retailer. If you're designing a system that will require PoE, take a look at the power connectors on the devices that will have to draw power through the Ethernet cable. Make sure you can buy or cobble together a jumper cable to run from the tap to the Ethernet device.

Commercial PoE Products

You can buy readymade PoE injectors and taps from a number of companies, including industry leaders Linksys and D-Link. Until very recently they were outrageously expensive for what they are, which is what has prompted many people to construct their own. My own experience leads me to recommend the D-Link PoE product, the DWL-P100, which lists for about $40, or a little less if you shop aggressively (see Figure 6.8).

The DWL-P100 is a kit containing an injector, a tap, and a fairly gutsy power supply, plus all the associated cables you'd need to power one of the D-Link access points remotely through its Category 5 cable. In Figure 6.8, the injector is at the bottom, and the tap is at the top. The modules are 3" long, $1\,^3/_4$" wide, and $^1/_2$" thick.

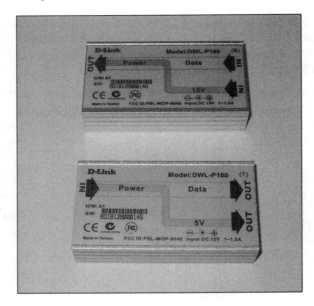

Figure 6.8
The D-Link DWL-P100 Power over Ethernet (PoE) System.

One caution: The D-Link PoE system works beautifully—*with D-Link products*. I still haven't seen many 802.3af compliant PoE products on the market, and D-Link's remains a proprietary system. To use the D-Link PoE devices with other vendors' access points requires that you know enough about electricity to know whether the voltage and available current at the tap are correct for the device you want to power. Tread carefully here—burning out an AP by feeding it excessive voltage will void the warranty and make you feel like a total idiot.

Choosing an Access Point or Gateway

Having read this chapter so far, you should know enough to be able to make an intelligent decision as to what access point or gateway products to buy for your home or small office network. To conclude this chapter, let me offer some points to keep in mind as you make your buying decisions.

1. *If at all possible, purchase all your Wi-Fi gear from the same manufacturer.* There are gaps and fuzzy areas in the Wi-Fi standard, and some of them (like WEP security) are crucial. Your chances of having everything talk to everything else on your network are greatest if both access points and client adapters are from the same manufacturer. If you make exceptions, make them for PC cards for your laptop. (See Chapter 7 for more on the various types of client adapters.)

If you intend to use an "enhanced" Wi-Fi technology like 802.11b+ or Super-G, you *must* use gear from the same manufacturer, or you will lose the benefits of the enhanced technology. I covered this in detail in Chapter 4.

2. *If your network only requires one access point, buy a wireless gateway.* This applies to the "85% solution" I described in Chapter 4. Small houses, townhouses, apartments, and condos are unlikely to require more than a single "center point" for your network. You can make things *much* easier to set up and configure by using a wireless gateway rather than a separate router and access point. On the other hand, consider the next issue…

3. *If you might need multiple access points, use a separate router appliance and add access points to the network as required.* Large homes, oddly-shaped homes (including very tall and very slender row houses and brownstones), and mid-sized offices may require you to place access points somewhere other than where your broadband Internet connection enters the premises. My experience in adding additional access points to networks based on wireless gateways has *not* been good. Once you step away from the 85% solution, go with a wired router and separate access points, not wireless gateways.

4. *Choose access points or gateways with dual antennas, ideally removable antennas.* Some access points and gateways have their antennas built right into the plastic case, which in my view is a bad idea. You can sometimes finesse a weak spot or a dead spot by re-orienting an access point's external antennas—remember TV rabbit ears?—and products with external antennas are not automatically more expensive. Removable antennas allow you to mount external omni gain antennas if you need to. See Chapter 8 for more on this issue. Note well that antennas on devices that support Wireless-A are *not* removable. That's an FCC rule, and it applies to "dual" mode and A/B/G gear.

5. *Unless you have a very particular need for Wireless-A, stick with B or (ideally) G.* Wireless-G is every bit as fast as Wireless-A, and that speed extends out to a greater range. Wireless-A doesn't have a lot to recommend it anymore, except in those circumstances where Wireless-B or G equipment experiences unacceptable interference from other equipment or other services using the 2.4 GHz band. There are a fair number of these, and virtually all of them have a better claim to the band than Wi-Fi does. See Appendix B for a full explanation of this issue.

6. *Finally, if you possibly can, buy gear that supports the WPA security standard.* Wi-Fi Protected Access (which I'll cover in detail in Chapter 14) plugs the most egregious of the security "holes" that have been discovered in the original Wired Equivalent Privacy (WEP) security system. For the moment, the vast majority of products that supports WPA are brand-new Wireless-G units. New Wireless-B gear may eventually support WPA, but for now, WPA is mostly seen in Wireless-G equipment. There is a check box on the latest Wi-Fi compliance logo (see Chapter 1 for more on the logo and how to read it) indicating WPA-compliance. Look for that box when you shop!

What About Used Gear?

People regularly ask me if I think buying used gear is a good idea. Sure—as long as you can be sure you're not being taken. I have been astonished to see used Wi-Fi gear sold on eBay for more than the street price for the same gear new through reliable channels, which is a weirdness I doubt I will ever understand unless this has to do with Wi-Fi's demand in countries that already have a hard time importing gear. Here are some pointers to consider when shopping for used gear:

• Know the *current* new price. Do some Web research. Prices are volatile and can drop radically without warning. Some people can't bear to sell used gear for much less than they paid for it, especially if they haven't had it long, so don't assume that a used price is lower than the new price!

• Pay attention to details like version numbers, firmware release levels, and precise model numbers. D-Link has a DWL-900AP and a DWL-900AP+, and they are *not* the same device! Linksys has a USB client adapter (the WUSB11) with three radically different configurations under the same name. Version 2.5 has a removable antenna, but version 2.6 does not. The cases are not the same size and shape.

• If you're buying gear from people you know, ask to try it out.

• Make sure you get all the parts: software CD, printed manual, power supply, connecting cables, detachable antennas. It helps to check a manufacturer's Web site to learn what's in the new package before you buy something used.

My Recommendations

I have used both Linksys and D-Link wireless gear on the consumer side with great success, and recommend both for fairly simple networks. Both companies offer very complete product lines, and their prices are quite competitive. Once you get into enterprise territory, Cisco Aironet becomes pretty compelling, especially if you intend to integrate wireless with a centralized authentication server and virtual private network endpoints. Aironet products are exquisitely configurable, and come with PDF-formatted manuals that are hundreds of pages long. Getting the most from Aironet gear requires serious study, and some previous experience in Ethernet networking.

One issue as I write this is that a great deal of equipment that hit the Wireless-G market early is not yet certified as Wireless-G compliant by the Wi-Fi Alliance. Some smaller firms that entered the Wireless-G market after the final standard was published have already received Wireless-G certification, and among these I recommend Buffalo Airstation. Buffalo has the further distinction of building antenna jacks into their PC card client adapters, which can be very useful for things like wardriving (see Chapter 19). I have had less experience with Buffalo gear than the majors, but all of it has been very good.

I recommend D-Link's very inexpensive AirPlus DWL-900AP+ access point for bridging (to another identical unit—see Chapter 17) but I am less enthusiastic about it for use in infrastructure mode, as it only has a single antenna and thus cannot support diversity reception. The DWL-900AP+ uses 802.11b+ technology, and so is about 40% faster than standard Wireless-B. If you need more throughput in your bridge and are willing to pay a little more for the endpoints, D-Link's DWL-2000AP provides all the same modes, and both standard Wireless-G throughput and a Super-G mode offering you a bitrate of 108 Mbps. Prices on this unit have come down radically in recent months, and soon it may cost no more than the DWL-900AP+.

The Linksys BEFW11S4 Wireless-B gateway is a personal favorite of mine for very simple 85% solution networks. It's gotten quite cheap and my unit held up well in continuous service for the 18 months that I used it. However, among Linksys products, the one I now recommend for new networks is the WRT54G, which is the Wireless-G equivalent of the BEFW11S4. D-Link has a similar product in its DI-624 wireless gateway. (They call it a "wireless router," but that's just another word for "wireless gateway.")

Often it makes sense to decide what sorts of client adapters you need for your network before you buy your access point or gateway, to be sure that you can get everything from the same manufacturer. Not all vendors offer a Wireless-G USB client adapter, for example, and if you want a single-vendor G-only network, you may need to look at what sorts of client devices are available before choosing a vendor. On general principles I recommend reading Chapter 7 and thinking hard about what sorts of clients you need before committing to either a vendor or an access point or gateway model.

Wi-Fi Client Adapters

I f your access point is the sun of your network, your client adapters are its planets, moving as they must but never out of the influence of their sun's gravitational field. Each and every computer that intends to connect to your Wi-Fi network must be equipped with its own client adapter. There are six major types of client adapter: PC (PCMCIA) cards, Compact Flash (CF) cards, Secure Digital I/O (SDIO) cards, PCI cards, USB client adapters, and Ethernet client adapters. As you'll learn in this chapter, the differences between the several different types are mostly differences in how they interface to your computers: via a card slot in your laptop or PDA, PCI expansion slot in a desktop PC, or through a USB or Ethernet port.

In this chapter I'll describe the different types of client adapters and offer some tips on which to choose and how to make good use of them.

What's Inside Client Adapters?

Client adapters are generally smaller (sometimes *much* smaller) than wireless access points or gateways, so you'd imagine there's simply less to them internally. Not so: Most client adapters have nearly everything inside them that access points have. (Wireless gateways have more, of course, to do the extra work that they do.) In fact, a surprising number of access points contain PC Card client adapter cards as their basic machinery, with additional hardware (generally an Ethernet interface subsystem—see Chapter 2) to talk to the wired network. The firmware controlling the device is different, however, even if the PCMCIA module looks identical. So you can't necessarily open up the access point's case, pry out the card, and use it in your laptop as a client adapter.

Recent advances in semiconductor technology allow the workings of a client adapter to be placed on a mere handful of silicon chips. There are two major subsystems in a Wi-Fi client adapter, each of which is usually (but not always) a separate chipset:

- A microwave *software-controlled radio* system. This handles the physical microwave reception and transmission, including modulation and frequency control.

- A *media access control* (MAC) system that enables Ethernet networking over the radio system. The medium here is microwave radio. Ethernet client adapters are distinctive in that they have two MAC systems: One for the radio medium, and another for the wired Ethernet medium. (Because Ethernet client adapters essentially establish a bridge between the two media, they are sometimes called *wireless bridges*.)

In addition, there is some sort of standard system interface that connects the adapter to a computer. Both major subsystems are microprocessor-controlled, sometimes with a separate microprocessor for each subsystem, sometimes with a single microprocessor controlling both.

Chipset Differences

There are dozens of manufacturers of Wi-Fi client adapters, and within a single manufacturer's product line there may be a dozen different models. There are, however, only a handful of semiconductor firms selling silicon chipsets that provide Wi-Fi functionality. Most of the time, you need to be aware of chipset differences only if you intend to run certain wireless-specific utilities that may be chipset-specific as well. NetStumbler (see Chapter 19) is a good example: It goes *way* down deep into the guts of wireless client adapters, so its author has had to write chipset-specific code to do the job. This means that not all client adapters are supported by Netstumbler. Even though its author adds support for new Wi-Fi clients on a regular basis, supporting multiple chipsets is a lot of work.

Chipset differences can, however, come into play for ordinary users when manufacturers offer proprietary extensions to the 802.11b standard. The best example is Texas Instruments, which sells the ACX100 chipset. ACX100 provides functionality for enhanced Wi-Fi gear falling under the "802.11b+" category. The most popular user of the ACX100 chipset is D-Link, which has a full product line called AirPlus.

802.11b+ gear uses a proprietary modulation scheme called *packet binary convolutional coding* (PBCC) to achieve higher throughput than "stock" 802.11b. It's not outrageously higher (typically 6 Mbps versus 4 Mbps) but high enough to be worthwhile in certain circumstances.

What you need to understand is that you achieve the full benefits of the ACX100 chipset only when the access point and all client adapters are based on 802.11b+ technology. 802.11b+ is backward compatible with 802.11b, and if you add an 802.11b adapter to the network, it will communicate at the lower 802.11b rates.

Dual Antennas and Diversity Reception

A very thin handful of client adapters have two antenna connectors, allowing the client adapter logic to support diversity reception. Simply put, in diversity reception, there are two antennas spaced some distance apart, and the control logic for the radio subsystem in the adapter continuously senses which antenna is bringing in the stronger signal, and uses that antenna. Both antennas are thus used for diversity reception, but the transmitted signal does not benefit from the use of both antennas, and only one antenna actually transmits. The majority of Wi-Fi access points and wireless gateways support two antennas for diversity reception, as I explained in Chapter 6.

Few client adapters support diversity reception because there simply isn't room for two antennas on most of them. To be most effective, the twin antennas need to be a very specific distance apart: one wavelength at the frequency of interest. For the Wi-Fi frequency band on 2.4 GHz, this is just under five inches. If you have an access point or gateway with two antennas, measure the distance between them and it will be very close to that.

Diversity reception is important because microwave signals in enclosed areas bounce off walls and floors and other intervening objects, creating reflected "ghost" signals that interfere with the primary received signal and cause signal fading. For technical reasons, if one antenna is subject to fading, an identical antenna one wavelength away is unlikely to experience fading at the same time, hence the distance between the two antennas.

Some PC card client adapters support diversity reception with miniaturized antennas in their "bulge" extensions (look ahead to Figure 7.1 a few pages on) but these antennas are quite close together and their effectiveness is pretty low in my experience.

"High-Power" Client Adapters

Most Wi-Fi client adapters are rated for output power at 15 dBm (see Chapter 8 for more on power measurements) or about 32 milliwatts (mw). Some PC card client adapters are billed as "high performance" and have higher transmitter power. I have seen adapters with power output as high as 200 mw (23 dBm) with numerous models offering 180 mw or 100 mw.

High power levels are generally available only in PCMCIA client adapters. The reason is pretty simple: The "bulge" antennas present on PCMCIA clients are terrible, both because the antennas are physically small and also because they are horizontal while most access points' antennas are vertical. This "cross polarization" effect reduces the range and the bit rate of PC clients, and the higher power adapters transmit additional power to make up for the deficiencies of their bulge antennas.

I'm a little leery of any Wi-Fi adapters that put out more than 100 mw (20 dBm). Microwaves cause tissue heating, and their long-term effects on human tissue (particularly the eyes) is still subject to debate. High-power gear is acceptable in point-to-point bridging applications (see Chapter 17) because the bridging access points and gain antennas are usually mounted up in the air, away from living things. Having a client adapter spraying 200 mw of microwave energy in all directions from my laptop strikes me as a bad idea. If you have trouble "getting in" from your laptop, consider a USB or Ethernet client adapter, both of which avoid the cross-polarization problem and have greater range than almost any PC card client at similar power levels.

Client Profiles

An awful lot of people—myself included—have a laptop that they carry back and forth between home and work. Back when I worked for Coriolis Group Books, I had a Wi-Fi network at home, and another at the office. Since both were Wi-Fi networks, a single Orinoco Gold card could connect me at home and also at the office. However, no two Wi-Fi networks are (or should be) entirely alike. The SSID at home was not the same as the SSID at the office. More to the point, my WEP keys at home were not the same as the WEP keys at the office. (See Part III for more on WEP and WEP keys.)

Virtually all Wi-Fi client adapters allow you to store several different networking setups under descriptive names and choose between them as circumstances demand. These setups are basically lists of parameters like the SSID and WEP settings. A stored networking setup is called a *profile*. When you boot your laptop at the office, you select your work profile, which sets up your client adapter for use with the Wi-Fi network at work. When you go home again and boot your laptop at home, you choose your home profile to connect to your Wi-Fi network at home.

Those are the most common uses of profiles, but there are others. I have a third profile for wardriving (see Chapter 19) in which the SSID field is left blank, and yet a fourth profile for setting up my laptop to communicate directly with other machines in ad-hoc mode.

Every client adapter manufacturer has a different system for creating and editing profiles. Check your product documentation; it's usually one screen or sometimes (as in the case of the Orinoco Gold) a multi-screen wizard. There is usually a "default" profile, which you modify and save out under different names, like "Home," "Work," "Stumbling," or (for ad-hoc work) "Lan Party."

The Different Kinds of Client Adapters

There are six major varieties of Wi-Fi client adapters. In addition to those six there are a few outliers. Some Wi-Fi access points (like D-Link's DWL-900AP+) claim to be able to operate as client adapters, but I've had indifferent success with such devices and don't recommend them in service as client adapters. A few very recent computer models like some Tablet PCs and few notebooks are being shipped with built-in Wi-Fi client adapters. Sometimes the built-in clients can be disabled and an external client adapter installed; sometimes what you get is... what you get, forever and ever, amen. Down the road you might want to (or need to) move to a Wireless-G network, perhaps to connect to a G-only wireless network at your office, so if your computer comes with a built-in, non-removable and non-disable-able client adapter, you could be completely out of luck.

In my view it's still a little too soon to be building Wi-Fi client adapters inextricably into computers, because the field is simply evolving too quickly, and the useful lifetime of a client adapter is probably less than the useful lifetime of a computer. Therefore, if you're shopping for any device with built-in Wi-Fi hardware, check carefully to see if it can be disabled and other Wi-Fi devices installed instead.

There are also some special-purpose client adapters, which are in most cases consumer electronics devices with wireless networking features added to them. Wireless network cameras (like D-Link's DCS-100W) are one, and wireless media receivers (like the Linksys WMA11B) are another.

Here are the six major general-purpose client adapter categories:

- PC (PCMCIA) cards

- Compact Flash (CF) cards

- Secure Digital I/O (SDIO) cards

- PCI cards

- USB client adapters

- Ethernet client adapters

Each different type of adapter has its strengths, weaknesses, and miscellaneous peccadilloes. I'll run through the list of categories to give you a sense of what each type of client is like. At the end of this chapter I'll provide a list of pros and cons for each category to help you decide which type to use in what circumstances.

PC (PCMCIA) Cards

Most people these days refer to PCMCIA cards as "PC cards," a term that differs so little from the term "PCI cards" (which I'll discuss next) as to cause occasional confusion. Nonetheless, that's how current usage in the industry has evolved, and I'll go with it. The original PCMCIA acronym stands for Personal Computer Memory Card International Association, the industry group that defined the PCMCIA card spec in the late 1980s. While originally intended to allow people to easily add memory to laptops, the spec has become general enough to support virtually anything that can be attached to a computer expansion bus.

The three types of PC cards include:

- Type I cards are for simple things like memory. They are 3.3 mm thick.

- Type II cards are for more complex devices, including modems, network interface cards, and wireless networking client adapters. They are 5.5 mm thick, but can have protruding extensions for connectors or antennas. (I call such extensions "bulges.")

- Type III cards are used for plug-in disk drives, and are 10.5 mm thick.

All Wi-Fi PC cards that I have seen are Type II.

Just as there are three types of cards, there are three types of slots: Types I, II, and III, each capable of holding one card of the corresponding type. Larger slots can also hold multiple cards in certain combinations; for example, a Type II slot can hold one

Type II card or two Type I cards. Most modern notebook computers have one or two Type II slots. Type I and Type III slots are far less common.

A typical PCMCIA client adapter is the D-Link DWL-650, shown in Figure 7.1. Most other cards look very much like it, except for the shape and size of the antenna bulge.

The Cardbus Compatibility Problem

As if that weren't confusing enough, PC cards come in two "generations." The original PCMCIA specification was 16-bit in nature. In 1999, a new, 32-bit descendent of the original spec appeared in products. These 32-bit PC cards go by the name "Cardbus." Cardbus cards can handle more data more quickly, and also contain new technology to reduce power consumption, which is a critical issue in battery-operated laptops.

The downside to Cardbus cards is that they require 32-bit Cardbus slots, and will *not* plug into an older, 16-bit slot. (16-bit cards, however, will plug into Cardbus slots and work properly.) If you have an older laptop or other computer equipped with PC card slots, be careful what Wi-Fi client adapters you buy. Computers made before 1999 probably won't be Cardbus compatible. Not all Wi-Fi PC card client adapters are Cardbus cards, but the ones offering higher bit rates than Wireless-B generally are. This includes 802.11b+ products (like D-Link's AirPlus line) and both Wireless-A and Wireless-G.

Figure 7.1.
The D-Link DWL-650 PC Card Client Adapter. (Photo courtesy of D-Link.)

Unfortunately, I have seen a fair number of Cardbus Wi-Fi client adapters that do not say "Cardbus" anywhere on the box. The Linksys WPC54G is one of these. Like all high-bitrate PC card clients, it really has no choice but to be in the 32-bit Cardbus architecture, but it will not insert into pre-1999 computers. I feel that it's irresponsible not to indicate on the package that the WPC54G is a Cardbus device. If you're shopping for a PC card client for your laptop, look carefully. *High-bitrate PC cards always require Cardbus slots.* If you have an older laptop, you may be stuck with Wireless-B.

If you're not familiar with installing PC cards in a slot, it may even be difficult to tell when a Cardbus card isn't fully installed. A Cardbus card will go all the way to the end of a pre-Cardbus Type II slot, but it will refuse to go the final 1/8" of an inch or so that establishes electrical connection. That last 1/8" has a different "feel" to it than simply a card sliding into a slot: It feels like something is "taking hold" of the card.

 If a Cardbus card won't seat all the way in a slot, the card itself won't work. If you attempt to install a PC card client adapter and it won't work, check to be sure that you're not trying to install a 32-bit Cardbus card in a 16-bit slot.

The Battle of the Bulge Antennas

The problem with PC card client adapters is simple: The antenna bulge isn't large enough to contain a reasonable antenna, and the antennas that will fit in the bulge (apart from being small, inefficient, and generally weak) exhibit something called *horizontal polarization.* Without going into the physics here, think of it as an alignment problem: Your access point antennas are typically vertical (pointing up) and your laptop antenna is horizontal. A radio transmitter and receiver can pass a stronger signal between them if their antennas are either both horizontal or both vertical.

This problem haunted me for a couple of months back when I lived in Arizona, during which time I could not get my laptop to connect effectively to my access point from the living room, which is at the opposite end of the house from my office, where the access point lives. I was forced to build an external gain antenna, which I plugged into my Orinoco Gold PC card while working in the living room. Details of this antenna and how to build one yourself (if you're so inclined) are in Chapter 16.

One recent and interesting innovation around the polarization problem is Asanté's FriendlyNet AeroLAN AL1511 PCMCIA adapter, shown in Figure 7.2. It has a pair of hinged antennas that fold horizontally for storage, and then unfold vertically for use. Asanté claims that using the antennas vertically can improve signal strength by 17%, and I can well believe it. (I have not tested this unit myself.)

External Antenna Jacks

One crucial difference among PCMCIA client adapters, especially for Wi-Fi performance fanatics and adherents of the wardriving hobby (see Chapters 19 and 20) is whether there is a jack on the antenna bulge for attaching an external antenna. The Orinoco Silver and Gold Classic cards have a very small jack for an RMC connector on the edge of the antenna bulge. (See Chapter 8 for descriptions of the types of connectors you'll encounter in Wi-Fi work.) The jack comes with an inconspicuous flat plastic plug that isn't easy to see and may take a knife point to pry out—look closely!

Note well that some of the newer PC cards labeled "Orinoco" may not have an antenna jack at all. The addition of the word "Classic" to the product name is usually the clue, as there is a generation of newer Orinoco cards that lack antenna jacks. You have to shop carefully, as the model nomenclature is ambiguous and sometimes misleading. When in doubt, ask the retailer—and be prepared to take the device back if the jack isn't present.

This as an aspect of a general problem in the electronics world: A particular make and model has a feature early in its history, and this feature changes—or vanishes—

Figure 7.2.
The Asanté AeroLAN 1500 Client Adapter (Photo courtesy of Asanté.)

later on, without any change in the device name and model number. I have heard, for example, that later Compaq WL110 client adapters lack the antenna jack that earlier WL110's have. I can't verify that from personal experience but I do know that Linksys changed the design of the WUSB11 USB client adapter a couple of times, and in one update the device lost its removable antenna. So be very careful what you buy.

The Cisco Aironet line is high-end and expensive compared to products from Linksys and D-Link, but the line includes several models with antenna jacks. The current Aironet 350 is an intriguing design: The entire antenna bulge pops off, exposing two MMCX connector antenna jacks. (The card may also be purchased without the bulge antenna, thus requiring you to attach antennas to one or both of the antenna jacks.) There are two jacks because the bulge contains two separate antennas, and the card itself uses the two antennas to support diversity reception, for better throughput. An external antenna can be connected to either, or to both.

The Cisco Aironet 342 PC card is an older model, now out of production, but interesting in that it acted as the "guts" of Cisco's PCI product for the PCI expansion bus. The PCI card consisted of a Type II PCMCIA slot with some associated logic, and a short run of coaxial cable from one of two MMCX antenna jacks to a connector on the metal card spine. You can actually remove a small retainer bracket and pop the card out and use it in your laptop, assuming you have an external antenna with an MMCX plug.

With the jack-equipped Orinoco client adapters becoming harder to find, it's nice to see that a relative newcomer to the field, Buffalo Technologies, has released a Wireless-G client adapter with an antenna jack: The Airstation WLI-CB-G54A. Buffalo seems to have adopted external antenna jacks as a general product line feature. All of their client adapters have such jacks, and their PC cards are cheaper than the Orinoco Gold Classic.

I powerfully recommend using PCMCIA cards with antenna jacks, so that if you find yourself in a dead spot with your laptop, you have the option of using an external antenna. Without that jack, you're out of luck—and do not misunderstand me as to how completely miserable the typical PCMCIA card "bulge" antenna really is!

Table 7.1 lists all the PC card client adapters I'm aware of with antenna jacks. See Appendix A for Web site references and suppliers.

Table 7.1   PC card client adapters with external antenna jacks.

Card Name/Connector	Type	Std.	Notes
Aironet 342	MMCX (dual)	B	Lacks antenna bulge. No longer sold new.
Aironet 350	MMCX (dual)	B	Can be had with/without antenna bulge
Avaya Silver World Card	MC	B	Identical to Orinoco Silver Classic
Avaya Gold World Card	MC	B	Identical to Orinoco Gold Classic
Buffalo WLI-PCM-L11	MC	B	
Buffalo WLI-CB-G54A	MC	G	Cardbus card
BreezeNet PC-DS.11b	RP-SMA	B	By Alvarion, formerly BreezeCom
Compaq WL110	MC	B	Rebranded Orinoco Gold Classic
Compex WP11A+	MC	B	Rebranded Orinoco Gold Classic
Demarc Tech Reliawave	MMCX (dual)	B	High power output: 180 mw
Dell TrueMobile 1150	MC	B	Rebranded Orinoco Gold Classic
Orinoco Silver Classic	MC	B	Only supports 64-bit WEP
Orinoco Gold Classic	MC	B	Like Silver except has 128-bit WEP
Orinoco Gold B/G 8470WD	MC	G	Branded "Proxim"
Signull	MMCX	B	A modified D-Link DWL-650
Teletronics	MMCX	B	With or without integrated antenna
ZComax XI-300	MMCX (dual)	B	Prism 2. 35 mw
ZComax XI-325	MMCX (dual)	B	Prism 2.5. Also in 100mw & 200mw

PCI Cards

If you want to add Wi-Fi capability to a typical desktop PC (as opposed to a laptop) the conventional way is to open the PC's case and add a Wi-Fi PCI (Peripheral Component Interconnect) plug-in card to the PC's card bus. The card bus on most desktop PCs will accept four or five PCI cards, and these days, with more and more PC functionality on the PC motherboard, most of those slots go unused.

Wi-Fi PCI cards run about $60 to $90 street price. The popular Linksys WMP11 product is shown in Figure 7.3, and is fairly typical of its class. PCI client adapters are often more expensive than PC card client adapters, because many actually contain PC card client adapter cards in a framework allowing them to plug into a computer's PCI expansion bus. The Cisco Aironet PCI adapters are simply PCI bus hosts for Aironet PCMCIA modules without integrated antennas.

Most Wi-Fi PCI card products have a short flexible antenna on the card spine, which protrudes behind the PC when the card is installed. This is a much better antenna than is present on Wi-Fi PCMCIA (PC) cards, which are the type of client

Figure 7.3
The Linksys WMP-11 PCI Client Adapter. (Photo courtesy of Linksys.)

adapter used in laptops. Sometimes adjusting the angle of the antenna can improve your signal strength slightly, which is worth trying when you're on the outskirts of your access point's range. The better antennas can both pivot from side to side and tilt forward back.

The antenna can be removed, and an external antenna (like a commercial blade antenna or a tin can antenna you make yourself) can be attached if the standard antenna can't quite "reach" the associated access point. This requires a short coaxial cable jumper called a *pigtail* (see Chapter 8) to run from the antenna connector on the card spine to the gain antenna. For a Linksys WMP11 or D-Link DWL-520, you'll need a pigtail with a RP-SMA (Reverse Polarity SMA) connector on one end and an N male connector on the other. Other brands (like Cisco, which uses an RP-TNC connector) use other connector types, but pigtails are generally available for all major card models. These may be obtained from Fleeman, Anderson, & Bird and other vendors (see Appendix A).

If the back of your tower PC is a huge mess of wires, you may find that your PCI client adapter antenna gets lost in the tangle. The wires can distort the field coming from the antenna, and partially shield it from incoming signals. An external antenna on a short length of coaxial cable can often make a big difference. Long lengths of coaxial cable are bad news in Wi-Fi work, as I'll explain in detail in Chapter 8. If you use an external antenna on a PCI client adapter, keep that cable short!

A second form of Wi-Fi PCI card is actually a plug-in adapter for a PCMCIA (PC) card, like those used in laptops. The Linksys WDT11 is a PCI card that plugs into your PC's card bus (see Figure 7.4). In turn, it has a slot in its metal spine into which you can plug a PCMCIA card like the Orinoco Silver or Gold, the Linksys WPC11, or the Cisco PCM340. The WDT-11 costs about $35, but it allows you to share a Wi-Fi PCMCIA card between your laptop and your desktop PC. This might once have been an advantage, but Wi-Fi cards have gotten so cheap it hardly seems worth spending $35 to save $50!

 Installing PCI cards means some simple screwdriver work, and a computer that opens up without a serious struggle. (Not all do.) If you don't want to take the step of opening up your PC, consider a USB adapter, which is a Wi-Fi client adapter that stays outside your PC's case and connects to your PC via a USB port. I'll talk about those next.

USB Adapters

By now, most people are familiar with the Universal Serial Bus (USB) technology that has been present in nearly all Intel-based PCs since 1997 or so, and fully supported by Windows 98, ME, 2000, and XP. (Windows 95 and NT do not support USB at all, and the patches distributed to add USB support to them are *extremely* dicey. Attempting to use USB under Windows 95 or NT is an invitation to fury.) The original USB 1.1 specification allows data to move at up to 12 Mbps (megabits per second) over a USB connection, though in practice that top speed is usually not quite achieved. Over the past year, USB 2.0 ports have become increasingly popular,

Figure 7.4
The Linksys WDT-11 PCI PC Card Adapter. (Photo courtesy of Linksys.)

with a breathtaking maximum bit rate of 480 Mbps. USB 2.0 ports look no different from USB 1.1 ports, and you can't tell which version a given port is simply by looking at it. You have to check your system documentation to be sure. This is especially important because some PCs have two of each kind.

Most Wi-Fi manufacturers now offer client adapters that connect to your computer via a USB port. These are hands-down the easiest Wi-Fi client adapters to install and configure: You don't have to open the case of your computer (as with PCI Card adapters) and you have a great deal more flexibility in positioning your client adapter antenna without losing signal strength by connecting an external antenna through a pigtail made of coaxial cable. (With a PC card and a laptop, an antenna/pigtail is your only option to improve the generally execrable performance of the card's built-in antenna.)

A USB adapter has the advantage that it resides completely *outside* your computer's case. This gives it an unappreciated edge over PCI and PC card adapters: You can move it around, up to a distance of 15 feet (the longest recommended USB cable run) to improve the quality of your link. What most people don't understand is that a typical home with a wireless access point or gateway in it (usually upstairs or in the den) is full of microwave "shadows" and "dead spots" where the access point's signal is weak or nonexistent. If your desktop or laptop finds itself in one of those Wi-Fi twilight zones, your only options are to move the computer or attach a movable antenna. Moving the computer is usually problematic (desks are where they are, as a rule) and external antennas must be used with great care, lest you lose all your signal in the coaxial cable running from the computer to the antenna. In a USB adapter, the microwave signal does *not* move through the connecting cable, so nothing is lost, even across the maximum cable length of 15 feet.

And although I'm not entirely sure why this should be so, USB adapters are currently the cheapest type of client adapter. Their street price is down to about $50 at major online retailers like Amazon.

Finally, little things do matter, and USB client adapters have the small advantage that they are powered through the USB port and do not require yet another wall wart to take up a space (or maybe two) on your computer power bar.

The USB adapter I've had most experience with is Linksys' WUSB11. It comes with software on a CD that you must install first. Once the software is installed, you plug in the device itself, and it just works. The WUSB11 is *tiny* (see Figure 7.5, where a WUSB11 sits next to my business card) and weighs less than two ounces. It can be easily packed along in a briefcase for connection to a laptop.

Figure 7.5
The Linksys WUSB11 USB Client Adapter.

The "Popsicle stick" antenna folds down into a slot until you need it. The WUSB11 comes with six feet of USB cable, which allows you to position it where it picks up the best signal without having to move your laptop around.

The WUSB11 does have a downside for road warriors: Boingo does not currently support it. Ditto for Wardrivers: Netstumbler does not work with it.

 My experiments in parking a rectangular-parabolic mesh reflector (see Chapter 18) behind a WUSB11 show that a little $^1/_4$" mesh hardware cloth can almost double the reach of one of these little blue gems.

Bit Rates and USB Versions

The first generation of USB client adapters were all Wireless-B. There were no USB Wireless-A adapters for a very simple reason: USB 1.1 ports only move bits at a rate of 12 Mbps—barely fast enough to accommodate the 11 Mbps Wireless-B standard. Toward the end of 2003, Wireless-G USB clients began to appear, but with a catch: They had to be plugged into USB 2.0 ports to operate at anything close to Wireless-G speeds.

The only Wireless-G USB adapter I have tested (the Linksys WUSB54G) will work in both USB 1.1 and USB 2.0 ports. However, when plugged into a USB 1.1 port, it will only move data at Wireless-B speeds, even when associated with a Wireless-G access point in G-only mode. If you buy a Wireless-G USB adapter and can't seem to get its throughput beyond Wireless-B levels, check the version of its USB port.

Although they might exist, I have not yet seen a Wireless-A USB adapter. If any exist, they will also require connection to a USB 2.0 port to achieve Wireless-A bitrates.

USB Dongle Adapters

The Linksys WUSB11 and WUSB54G client adapters are "conventional" USB adapters: Small boxes connected to your PC's USB port by a six foot length of cable. In 2003, a new type of USB adapter became popular. This device doesn't have a cable. The adapter is *tiny*—the size of a man's thumb—and one end of the device is a USB connector. You plug the entire adapter into the USB port as though it were the end of a cable. The antenna is built into the device body. Power comes from the USB port. This type of adapter is called a "dongle" because it resembles a family of copy-protection keys that plug into a USB or printer port as physical proof that a PC has the right to run a given (usually high-end) application.

Like most USB devices, dongle adapters are hot-swappable, meaning that you can pull them out of the USB port or insert them while a PC is running. Several firms offer USB dongle adapters for Wireless-B, although I have not yet seen one for Wireless-G. The Linksys WUSB12 adapter, as shown in Figure 7.6, is typical. Dlink's DWL-122 is roughly the same shape and size, and has comparable specifications, as does the Buffalo WLI-USB-KB11. One end of the device is simply a protective cap, which pulls off to expose the USB male connector. (They always remind me of "stubby" highlighter pens in that respect—but then again, I'm a book editor in my day job.)

Dongle adapters are most often used with laptops, as replacements for PC card client adapters. Often a compact notebook PC has only one PC card slot, and it may be needed for some other device. A USB dongle adapter is small enough to drop in a briefcase with a notebook PC, and can be plugged in any time a Wi-Fi connection needs to be made, without having to reboot the PC.

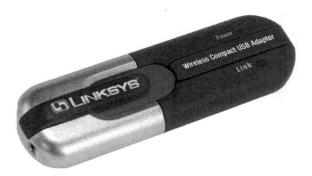

Figure 7.6.
The Linksys WUSB12 USB Dongle Client Adapter. (Photo courtesy of Linksys.)

Ethernet Client Adapters, AKA Ethernet Bridges

Ethernet client adapters represent a small and slightly odd category of Wi-Fi clients. These are not plug-in cards, but desktop devices that interface via a category 5 patch cable to your computer's Ethernet network adapter.

Physically, Ethernet client adapters resemble USB client adapters, in that they are separate devices connected to your computer by a cable, and the length of the cable is usually not a serious limitation. At the very least you can put eight or ten feet between your computer and the adapter, meaning you can park it atop your cube wall or on a bookcase to get it up and above metal objects that weaken your reception of your access point's field. They are unlike USB adapters in that they require a separate power supply. (Someday, if the new Power over Ethernet standard 802.3af becomes universal, an Ethernet client adapter may get its power through the category 5 cable as well.)

The first widely available Ethernet client adapter was the Linksys WET11, a Wireless-B device shown in Figure 7.7. Linksys calls it a *wireless Ethernet bridge*, which may be confusing to people who assume bridges are strictly for linking two networks together. (That's what "bridge" means in the insider jargon of networking enthusiasts.) Although two WET11s can certainly be used to bridge two networks, most people use them as client adapters for connecting Ethernet-capable computers or other devices to a Wi-Fi access point. D-Link offers a very similar Wireless-B Ethernet client adapter, called the DWL-810. Ethernet client adapters cost from $60 to $80. Wireless-G Ethernet client adapters began to appear early in 2004. The Linksys WET54G is typical, but still quite expensive—about $140. D-link's DWL-G810 is similar, and slightly less expensive.

Figure 7.7
The Linksys WET11 Ethernet Bridge. (Photo courtesy of Linksys.)

Ethernet client adapters may be truthfully called Ethernet bridges because, unlike every other category of client adapter, they "bridge" two Ethernet media: microwaves and cable. You can use a pair of Ethernet bridges to "break" a length of Ethernet category 5 cable. When two such devices are used together, it's proper to call them bridges—but when used to connect an Ethernet device like a game adapter or printer to an access point, it's better to refer to them as Ethernet client adapters. Note well that certain access points can also function as bridges, as I explain in Chapter 17. (D-Link's are especially good in that regard.) If you intend to create an Ethernet point-to-point bridge, you can sometimes save money by hunting for two bridge-compatible access points rather than using two Ethernet client adapters, which are still expensive compared to most Wireless-B access points.

The primary use for Ethernet client adapters so far has been to wirelessly connect game consoles like the Playstation 2 and Microsoft's XBox to a Wi-Fi network, as a means of connecting to Internet online multiplayer game systems like Xbox Live. Game consoles, while computers internally, lack the customary I/O of a desktop or laptop machine. An Ethernet network adapter is the only way to connect them to a network, so a Wi-Fi Ethernet client adapter is the only way to network game consoles wirelessly. The other common use is to connect Ethernet-equipped printers to a network through an access point.

The WET-11 has an interesting configuration system: You plug it into a network router/switch port, or simply into a computer's Ethernet port, and then run a configuration utility from CD-ROM without installing any software anywhere. The CD-ROM based utility allows you to enter parameters like SSID, channel, and WEP keys. Once the unit is configured, it stores the configuration internally in flash memory, and you can then unplug it from the computer or network and attach it to a game console (or some other computer or device) with a short category 5 patch cable. Without any further configuration, it "just works."

You don't need a CAT 5 crossover cable with the WET-11, because there is a crossover/straight through switch on the side of the device. The straight-through switch setting is for connecting the WET-11 to a network switch or hub; the other (the crossover setting) is for direct connection to a computer or game console's Ethernet network port.

The WET-11 works very well, and I predict that the Ethernet client category will become quite popular in the future, especially if increased competition drives the price down. In the meantime, if your main use for an Ethernet client adapter is networking a game console, I now recommend the Linksys WGA54G, which is faster and has additional features, like a mode that lets you connect two such adapters for console-console play within wireless range.

Compact Flash (CF) Client Adapters

Adding Wi-Fi features to a PDA or cell phone has always been a gnarly problem. Even though PC cards are relatively small, few PDAs—and no cell phones—have PC card slots. A new type of client adapter began to appear late in 2002. The Compact Flash (CF) client adapter is built into a very small case designed to plug into a Compact Flash memory/peripheral slot. Most of the major vendors offer them now, including Linksys, D-Link, Buffalo, Netgear, and Belkin. Typical of the category is the Linksys WCF12, shown in Figure 7.8.

The Compact Flash standard emulates the PCMCIA-ATA standard, which is the same standard implemented in PC cards. In fact, $10 adapters are available that will accept a CF device and allow it to plug into a Type II PC card slot (see **www.delkin.com**). The CF card is smaller and the connector is different from the PC card, but most operating systems and devices that will support PCMCIA-ATA will support Compact Flash.

All that said, you need to shop carefully if you're considering a CF client adapter. There are two types of CF device: Type I and Type II, with two corresponding types

Figure 7.8
The Linksys WCF12 Compact Flash Adapter. (Photo courtesy of Linksys.)

of CF slot. A Type 1 CF device is 3.3 mm thick, and a Type II device is 5 mm thick. Both types are identical in width and height: 43 × 33 mm, roughly 1 $\frac{3}{4}$" × 1 $\frac{1}{2}$". A few Type II Wi-Fi client adapters are available but most are Type I. (Linksys offers one of each!) A Type I card will fit in a Type II slot, but a Type II card is too thick to fit in a Type I slot, and requires a Type II slot.

The CF architecture was originally designed for memory, and most CF devices today are memory cards, which are very popular in digital cameras, camcorders, and MP3 players. The CF architecture dates back to 1994, but was enhanced in recent years as CF I/O to embrace devices like modems, wired network adapters, and Wi-Fi client adapters. Before installing a CF Wi-Fi card in a device, make sure that its CF slot is in fact a CF I/O slot. Most expansion slots in current PDAs—or anything with an accessible operating system—are CF I/O. Most expansion slots in cameras and other consumer electronics devices are not.

If you're shopping for a CD adapter to use in a PDA, read the device's technical specifications carefully. Although they're physically small, CF adapters are not necessarily low-power. Early CF client adapters drew almost as much current from the system power source as a PC card, and could greatly shorten the life of a charge in a PDA. Newer CF adapters incorporate intelligent power management schemes that power-down the radio when no packets are being passed between client and access point.

Finally, not all PDAs support all CF client adapters. For example, the PocketPC operating system (which is a small-footprint version of Microsoft Windows) is much more Wi-Fi friendly than PalmOS. Before you put your money down, do the research necessary to make sure a particular client adapter will work in your PDA.

Secure Digital I/O (SDIO) Client Adapters

Hands down, the newest category of Wi-Fi client adapters is also physically the smallest: Secure Digital I/O (SDIO) cards. They are similar to CF cards in that they are an extension of a memory add-in architecture. Secure Digital (SD) memory cards have become quite popular in recent months in digital cameras and other devices requiring digital data storage. They are phenomenally small; both SD and SDIO cards are only 2.1 mm thick—.0825". SDIO cards require an SDIO-enabled slot. SD slots intended only for memory devices will *not* support SDIO devices like Wi-Fi clients.

The first SDIO Wi-Fi cards appeared in the second half of 2003, and are currently available from SanDisk and Socket. Both are Wireless-B. (I have not yet seen a Wireless-G SDIO client, but they will be available eventually.) They are still fairly expensive—over $100 at this writing—but for unobtrusive wireless networking, they have no equal. Figure 7.9 shows the Socket SDIO Wi-Fi client adapter, with a quarter coin beside it for scale. The appearance of SDIO Wi-Fi client adapters marks the first time I will actually admit that PDA-based Wi-Fi networking is actually practical and convenient. You don't have to embed your PDA in a fist-sized expansion sleeve. Another advantage is that power management is better than that of any other client adapter category, although adding an SDIO client card will reduce your battery life somewhat (how much depends on how heavily you use the network connection).

At this writing, both the SanDisk and Socket SDIO clients are supported under the PocketPC platform only. PalmOS 5.x drivers are under development, but have been repeatedly delayed and are not yet on the market. This could change at any time, but as with Compact Flash client adapters, you need to read all the fine print—and check the vendor Web site—to be sure that your PDA supports the device you've chosen. *An SDIO slot does not guarantee compatibility!*

In terms of power management and drain on your PDA's battery, SDIO clients, being recent developments, do better than any other device type. They are, however, very thin and therefore a little fragile. Once inserted in your PDA, there is still about half an inch of .0825" plastic tab protruding from the slot, and if you catch it on something and bend it even slightly, you could break the internal PC board and be out $100. Be careful.

Figure 7.9
The Socket SDIO Wi-Fi Client Adapter. (Photo courtesy of Socket Communications, Inc.)

Which Client Adapter to Choose?

With all of that in mind, let me summarize some of the issues involved in choosing what client adapter to buy. Price is sometimes an issue, but price differences are being squeezed by increased competition and are less and less significant all the time, at least on gear targeted at consumers. Cisco and certain other vendors are still getting premium prices from corporate buyers, but the premium covers features that you're unlikely to need or even be able to use in a home office or small office environment.

It often makes sense to decide what sort of client adapters you want for your network first, and then choose an access point from the same company. You're better off with access points and client adapters from the same manufacturer, all else being equal. (The Wi-Fi Alliance reports that over 25% of products submitted for Wi-Fi logo certification testing fail the test. Companies do, however, ensure that all of their own products work together.) Getting all your gear from the same company gives you your best chance at having everything work the first time, and it gives the vendor's technical support people no excuse for shrugging their shoulders and blaming "outsiders" for network problems. Stronger WEP encryption (128 bits and up) is non-standard, and works best when all gear is from one company.

If you want to take advantage of a non-standard extension to the Wi-Fi standard (like Texas Instruments' 802.11b+ and Atheros' Super G) you must buy all your gear from the same company, ideally all of the same product line, like D-Link's AirPlus.

Here are some other thoughts to bring to bear on your decision, sorted by adapter type:

PC Card and Cardbus Client Adapters

• PRO: They're tucked away inside your laptop or notebook and don't require any additional wires or power supplies.

• PRO: They install fairly easily. Generally you install some software from a CD-ROM and then plug the card into an empty slot. Windows Plug and Play takes it from there.

• CON: Their antennas are uniformly horrible, having the worst "reach" by far of any antenna in the Wi-Fi world. In laptops they almost always install horizontally, and thus are "cross-polarized" with respect to vertical access point antennas, which reduces range. Few adapters, furthermore, provide a jack for an external antenna.

• CON: Many laptops allow you to "stack" two Type II PCMCIA cards in a dual slot. The problem here is that Wi-Fi PC cards are notorious for physically obstructing adjacent MCMCIA slots, usually with their antenna bulges. PCMCIA Wi-Fi clients often insist on being in the "top slot." If another of your PCMCIA card adapters makes the same demand, you may be out of luck. If you already depend on one PC card in a two-card slot, be very careful which WI-Fi PC card you buy for the other slot. With their thin antenna bulge, Cisco Aironet is very good in this regard. Most others are not so good.

• CON: Many newer PC card adapters (including all Wireless-G and 802.11b+) are 32-bit Cardbus cards, and may not plug into older, pre-1999 laptops.

• CON: High-power adapters like Cisco's 100 mw Aironet 350 attempt to compensate for the lousy bulge antenna, but place a much greater burden on your battery, and will radically reduce the time between charges. Be aware of the power drain of whatever adapters you buy!

PCI Client Adapters

- PRO: PCI adapters are "out of the way" inside your computer and add nothing to the "cable clutter" on your work surface. There are no wall wart power supplies to fool with, and nothing to take up additional space on your desk.

- PRO: PCI adapters use antennas that are adjustable and work relatively well. Also, their antennas are usually removable, so if you need to use a gain antenna at some point you have that option.

- PRO: PCI card products are available that allow you to insert and remove a PCMCIA card client adapter through the card spine, allowing you to share an adapter between a desktop and a laptop computer. (Note that this type of product is usually sold "empty"—without a client adapter, which you have to buy separately.)

- PRO: PCI adapters are inside the case of the PCI and not easily removed. In office environments, small, easily removable adapters like USB and PC cards can be easily popped out of computers and pocketed.

- CON: PCI adapters require opening up the computer, sometimes pulling out a subchassis, and often fighting your way past fragile ribbon cable runs that get in the way of easy access to the PCI slot into which you hope to plug the card. If you're not completely comfortable opening up your PC (and have no one close by to do it for you) don't even *think* of going there!

- CON: If your PC is a "tower" case and mounted vertically, and if you have a lot of cables attached to the back panel, your PCI card's antenna can be partially shielded by all the draping cables, reducing the strength of your signal. This is one case where the (small) loss in a short length of coaxial cable is justifiable, to get the adapter's antenna away from all the cable clutter.

- CON: PCI adapters are inexplicably expensive, perhaps because many of them consist of a PCMCIA card attached to a PCI plug-in circuit board.

USB Client Adapters

- PRO: They're cheap. Many are now under $50.

- PRO: For ease of installation, little beats a USB adapter. Typically, you install a client driver from a CD-ROM, and then plug the device in.

- PRO: They're very easy to remove from one computer and plug into another if you ever need to do that.

- PRO: Unlike most "external" devices, they take power from the USB port and don't have a separate power supply.

- PRO: They're on the end of a wire, so if you're working on the fringe of your access point's range you can move them around a little to find the best signal. Sometimes getting the adapter up to the top of your cubicle wall is all it takes.

- PRO: They're usually pretty small, and don't take up much room on your desk. Some models (like the Linksys WUSB11 V2.0 and later; avoid V1) even provide a Velcro patch so you can literally stick them to a cubicle wall.

- CON: USB 1.1 ports are not fast enough to support higher bit rates than Wireless-B. USB client adapters for Wireless-G, but these require higher bitrate USB 2.0 ports. If your PC does not have a USB 2.0 port, your Wireless-G USB adapter will operate at Wireless-B bitrates only.

- CON: Few USB adapters have dual antennas or even removable antennas, which you might expect in an external device like this.

- CON: They're on the end of a wire, and if you don't need the flexibility of positioning (or a better antenna than a PCMCIA card) the wire may be a nuisance.

- CON: As with any physically small external adapter, in an unsecured office environment, USB adapters are easily unplugged and stolen.

Ethernet Client Adapters

- PRO: For connecting game consoles or printers with Ethernet ports to your Wi-Fi network, Ethernet clients are often your only option.

- PRO: Most Ethernet client adapters can act as wireless bridges with others of their own kind.

- PRO: All Ethernet client adapters that I've seen have external antenna jacks, which are important in point-to-point bridging applications.

- PRO: Many models can simply be plugged in and used, without any drivers or other software to install. (There's still some configuration to be done, but it's reasonably easy, and once done, the adapter can then be placed on different computers without reconfiguration.)

• PRO: As with USB client adapters, Ethernet clients are on the end of a cable and can be moved around without any signal loss. This ability can be useful if your desk sits in a weak spot or a dead spot. (Mine did!) You can move the client to the top of your cube wall or bookcase to get a better shot at your AP.

• CON: They're new and fairly uncommon, and thus are more expensive than most other kinds of client adapter.

• CON: They require external power, and add yet another wall wart to your collection.

Compact Flash (CF) Client Adapters

• PRO: They're quite small, and many PDAs have CF I/O slots to accept them without having to resort to expansion sleeves.

• PRO: More recent models have good power management features, and don't drain your PDA battery as quickly as PC cards.

• CON: Some older models lack good power management and will drain your PDA battery quickly. Read the fine print and shop carefully.

• CON: Not all PDA operating systems support all CF client adapters, even if the PDA in question has a CF I/O slot. Read the fine print, ask around, and shop carefully.

• CON: I have yet to see a CF client adapter with an antenna jack.

Secure Digital I/O (SDIO) Client Adapters

• PRO: They're miniscule, and don't add any bulk to your PDA or smart phone.

• PRO: They're very recent technology, with excellent power management, probably better than any other category of Wi-Fi client adapter.

• CON: So far, all products I've seen are Wireless-B.

• CON: I haven't yet seen an adapter that can be installed in a desktop PC.

- CON: They are very thin (only .0825" thick) and can be broken with careless handling.

- CON: They are still significantly more expensive than similar devices in other categories as to be expected for new and bleeding-edge technology.

My Recommendations

I have had excellent luck with Linksys and D-Link equipment, and recommend both manufacturers because they both offer complete product lines. You can find every type of Wi-Fi access point, gateway, and client adapter in both lines and thus can create a very versatile network and still be completely sure that all devices are compatible with all other devices. The only exception I will grant on this point is for the Orinoco Gold PCMCIA adapter for laptops; see my note on this below. In my own testing, it works very well with Linksys, D-Link, and Cisco gear. I've also had very good luck with some smaller vendors like Buffalo Technology, but you may not find as full a selection of gear as with larger vendors.

Cisco Aironet gear, while excellent, is often overkill for small offices and home offices. You're paying extra for "corporate" server-dependent features like RADIUS authentication that you probably can't use even if you wanted to.

All else being equal, I recommend USB adapters for desktop computers. They're cheap, easy, versatile, and don't require that you open up the computer.

For your laptop, Orinoco PCMCIA cards are compelling for two reasons:

1. They have an external antenna jack. Lacking that, if you find yourself in a dead spot, your laptop network connection is just… dead.

2. Orinoco Wi-Fi gear filters out "weak IV" values (see Chapter 13) that compromise WEP security. More and more client adapters are being released (or upgraded to) this ability, but it's often hard to tell if a particular adapter filters weak IVs or not.

Unfortunately, the rest of the Orinoco product line is fairly expensive. It's excellent, but you'll pay 30% to 40% more for it. Also, they do not (as far as I know) offer a USB adapter.

To network an Ethernet-equipped game console, I recommend the Linksys WET-11 for Wireless-B, or the Linksys WGA54B for Wireless-G.

Ready to Network

At this point you're about ready to buy the hardware and start assembling your network. The next chapter is optional; it's about external antennas, how they work, and how they affect the strength and quality of your Wi-Fi signal. For most installations, and especially if you're a newcomer to networking, Chapter 8 is optional. Feel free to skip ahead to Chapter 9, where we begin putting things together.

In the meantime, go shopping. Have fun!

Antennas, Cables, and Connectors

Wi-Fi is a radio technology, and radio implies antennas. Every wireless access point, wireless gateway, and client adapter has an antenna. (Many access points and gateways have two.) Sometimes these antennas are embedded in the device's case or are otherwise hidden, but they're there. And for most Wi-Fi work, what you get is good enough. Once you get everything hooked up and working you can squint a little and pretend it's magic rather than radio.

On the other hand, if your circumstances aren't ideal and things don't quite connect, understanding antennas becomes crucial. Some of Wi-Fi's inherent limitations can be circumvented with a little antenna smarts, and many of the more advanced things that Wi-Fi technology can do (like bridging two separate networks in two different buildings; see Chapter 17) actually focus on special-purpose antenna systems.

In this chapter I'm going to explain briefly how antennas work, how you connect them to your Wi-Fi hardware, and how you can make sense of radio power math, which includes antenna gains and cable losses and absolute power levels delivered by Wi-Fi access points and client adapters.

Let me say up front: *This is a technical chapter.* If you're simply going to equip a small home or office with a minimal Wi-Fi network, virtually nothing in this chapter has to be learned, so you can skip immediately to Chapter 9, in which I explain how to assemble and test a Wi-Fi network using "stock" equipment. Later on, if you want to fool with external antennas, you can always come back for a second look.

How Antennas Work

One way I like to put things to my students is that coaxial cable (more on which later) is a hose for radio waves, and antennas are nozzles. The hose transports the radio energy from a transmitter to a different location (like someplace outside and up high) and an antenna sprays that radio energy out into the air. And just as you can have many kinds of nozzles that spray water in lots of different patterns, from a straight, strong stream in one direction to a uniform spray in all directions, so it is with antennas: They can "spray" radio energy in different patterns, either in every direction at once or in a very narrowly focused beam.

The water metaphor pretty much ends there, but it's a good start. Different types of antennas emit radio waves in fields of different shapes, and that makes all the difference in the world. For the moment let's set aside discussion of the physical form and materials of which antennas are made. (I'll get back to that.) The crucial issue is the shape of the radio field.

The Mythical Isotropic Antenna

With Wi-Fi work we'll be most interested in the shape of the radio field produced by particular antennas, so let's start by positing an antenna that emits radio waves equally in all directions. If we could somehow magically see the radio field around the antenna, it would be in the shape of a sphere, with the antenna at the center. Such an antenna doesn't actually exist in the real world, but it has a name nonetheless: an *isotropic antenna*. It radiates equally in all directions. It's a mathematical abstraction, created specifically to give us a sort of "base point" against which to measure the performance of real-world antennas. The closest we come in real Wi-Fi work is in the *omnidirectional* antenna, which creates a somewhat lumpy field spread out mostly evenly *in the horizontal plane*. "Omni" here doesn't necessarily include "up" and "down." (More on this a little later.)

The idealized isotropic antenna is important in Wi-Fi work because antennas that you buy for your Wi-Fi equipment are rated in units called "dBi," which I will explain in more detail a little later in this chapter. Quite simply, the dBi unit is a measurement of antenna "reach" relative to the mythical isotropic antenna, which has the shortest "reach" possible of any antenna, given the same amount of input radio energy. The more dBi, the greater the gain of the antenna, and the farther it can reach.

 To understand this notion of "reach" (which is my coinage and not a technical term!), recall that the mission of an antenna is to get a readable radio signal from point A (the antenna's location) to point B. The longest distance from A to B is the antenna's reach, and a good measure of its effectiveness as an antenna.

An isotropic antenna radiates radio energy in a perfect sphere. Point A is at the ball's center, and Point B is somewhere on the sphere's surface. If you imagine the field of an antenna to be something like a balloon filled with water, a sphere is the most compact form a volume of water in a flexible container can take. The distance from the center of the balloon to its surface is as short as with any shape the balloon can take. On the other hand, a balloon can be pulled or squeezed into other shapes without changing the volume of water it contains. No matter what shape you squeeze the balloon into, if you change its shape into something *other* than a sphere, the distance from its center to its farthest extent will be *greater* than what it was when it was a sphere.

The Shape of the Field

If you're careful how you squeeze the balloon, you can change its shape to something long and thin, so that Point A at the center is way farther out than Point B on its edge. That's how antennas work: They change the shape of the radio field they emit from a sphere (as an isotropic antenna would emit) to something else, something that moves the edge of the field farther away from the center, or something that has a shape that more nearly "fills" a building or other area.

Figure 8.1 is a view from above, looking down on three different antennas and their fields. Antenna A is our mythical isotropic antenna, which has a spherical field, seen here as a circle. Antenna B is a "picture frame" antenna, which changes the shape of the field to something nearly all to one side of the antenna, with a corresponding increase in the distance from A to B. And Antenna C is a parabolic dish antenna, which squeezes almost all of the field into one long arm, pushing A and B much farther apart.

The picture frame antenna's mission isn't to get a signal across long distances, but to concentrate the field almost entirely to one side of the antenna. Hanging on a wall (hence the name) a picture frame antenna will "fill the room" with a Wi-Fi radio field. The parabolic dish antenna, however, is designed to create as narrow a beam as possible, sometimes a beam that can reach across several miles of open space.

If you'll need to evaluate commercial antennas, your best single source of information will be the radiation pattern charts most manufacturers publish. An excellent example is shown in Figure 8.2, which is the horizontal plot of Pacific Wireless' PAWIN24-10 directional panel, or picture frame antenna. In this plot, you're looking at the radio field of the antenna from the side rather than from above. Most manufacturers will publish two such charts, one viewed from the side (horizontal) and the other from above (vertical).

Isotropic Antenna

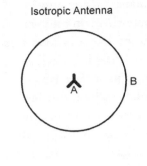

"Picture Frame" Antenna

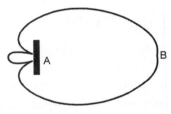

Parabolic Dish Antenna

Figure 8.1
The Shape of Antenna Fields.

 The field boundaries are not smooth curves, but have bumps and lumps and odd little tucks. These might seem to be problems, but remember that the field boundaries are not walls, but simply plots of equal field strength, like contour lines on a topographic map. A bulge is an area of slightly greater field strength whereas a tuck is an area of less field strength.

I emphasize understanding the shape of an antenna's radio field, because an antenna's gain figure in dBi isn't the whole story. A gain antenna has gain in very specific *directions*. If you don't understand the directions in which an antenna's gain is distributed, you can buy the wrong antenna for the job. If your Wi-Fi setup doesn't then work as it should, you can't blame the antenna. (See my later discussion on picture frame antennas for a detailed example.)

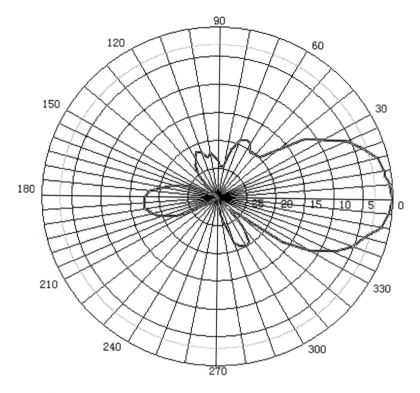

Figure 8.2
A Commercial Radiation Pattern Chart. (Chart courtesy of Pacific Wireless, Inc.)

The Threat from the Third Dimension

People who scrutinize the radiation pattern of an antenna as viewed from above (as they're almost always plotted and viewed) often forget that an antenna's radiation pattern has a third dimension as well. Even "omnidirectional" antennas are omnidirectional *only* in the horizontal plane. They don't necessarily radiate up (or down) with the same intensity that they radiate outward.

The cheap and very simple rubberized omnidirectional antennas shipped with most access points radiate pretty randomly in most directions, including up and down. The better and more expensive omnidirectional gain antennas get their gain by "squeezing" the vertical dimension of radiation down into the horizontal plane.

Think again of a completely spherical balloon. Push down on it from above, and it spreads out horizontally. Push it hard enough and it will take on the form of a round sofa cushion or even a doughnut. That's precisely what happens with the radiation pattern of an omnidirectional gain antenna. The energy that would have been radiated up or down is redirected more horizontally.

This becomes an issue in several facets of Wi-Fi work. "Picture frame" Wi-Fi antennas intended to be hung on office walls often have considerable gain. In part this gain is directional: The bulk of the antenna's energy is radiated in a "sector" in the shape of a fan that may be 140 degrees or so in angular extent. However, my tests have shown that picture frame antennas are *very* horizontal in their radiation. They work very well at filling office cube farms on a single floor. Go one floor upstairs or down, and the signal drops like a stone. This may be good—if your competitors rent the floors above or below you. But don't try to use a picture frame antenna to service more than a single floor. Between the inherent shielding of the floor's construction (especially in steel-framed office buildings with jungles of wires and HVAC ducts between floors) and the vertical directionality of the antenna, you won't get the kind of full-bitrate coverage you want.

In my tests I found that picture frame antennas don't work well even in wood-frame residential construction, when you intend to service even two floors of an ordinary ranch house. For a side-view look at the radiation pattern of a picture frame antenna, see Figure 8.2.

In a completely different realm, wardrivers (see Chapters 19 and 20) have found that omnidirectional gain antennas miss access points on the higher floors of office buildings. Think of driving down LaSalle Street in Chicago, with 50- and 70-floor office towers on every side. On the higher floors, the access points are almost directly above a cruising vehicle, and with a horizontally directional antenna, anything much above the fifth or sixth floor won't be detected.

A Quick Word on Frequency and Wavelength

Space prevents me from going much more deeply into general antenna theory, but I need to put frequency and wavelength into a Wi-Fi context. Radio signals are electromagnetic waves, and have complementary aspects called frequency and wavelength. The *frequency* is how many complete waves occur each second. The *wavelength* is how much distance one of those waves cover at the speed of light.

Radio waves travel at the speed of light, 186,000 miles or 300,000 kilometers per second. A radio wave with a frequency of one cycle per second will thus cover 300,000 meters during one of those cycles. It would then be said to have a wavelength of 300,000 meters. (That's much too long to be a radio wave, and I use it here simply as a conceptual example.)

Lower frequencies have longer wavelengths. Higher frequencies have shorter wavelengths. The frequency of the center of the AM radio band is 1 megahertz (million cycles per second, abbreviated MHz) and its wavelength is about 300 meters, roughly 1,000 feet. The frequency of the center of the FM broadcast band is 100 MHz, and its wavelength is about 3 meters, roughly 10 feet. The frequency of the Wi-Fi band is 2.4 gigahertz (billion cycles per second, abbreviated GHz) and its wavelength is just under 5 *inches*. We're in extremely short wavelength territory here, compared to more familiar radio and TV broadcasting. This is why Wi-Fi signals are said to be *microwaves*. (They're actually on the big side for microwaves, which go down in wavelength to very small fractions of an inch.) The major advantage of being in microwave territory is that good antennas are quite small and inexpensive, and easy to build if you're handy with tools.

The Different Families of Antennas

Let me now take you on a quick tour of the Wi-Fi antenna kingdom. Most varieties of Wi-Fi antenna are of limited use for homes and small offices, but I'll mention the "big guns" just the same, so you'll know what's out there and recognize the terms when you read them in the Wi-Fi literature.

One caution: In smaller homes and very small offices you may not need anything more than the small rubber omnidirectional antennas shipped with the access point or wireless gateway. Test access point coverage *before* you spend your money on an external antenna! Don't provide gain where none is needed, especially where the home or office in question is very near others. Too much Wi-Fi coverage is as serious a problem as too little, albeit a very different kind of problem. If your Wi-Fi field reaches into adjacent floors or buildings, people on those floors or in those buildings can use packet-sniffing tools to identify and possibly break into your network—and you may have no way to know what they're doing. The higher gain your antennas have, the farther away a drive-by network cracker can be and still test your defenses. Why make things easier for them?

Omnidirectional Vertical Antennas

The simplest and commonest Wi-Fi antennas are *omnidirectional* antennas. The 4" long rubberized rod antennas that come with Wi-Fi access points are the best examples. They're called "omnidirectional" because they radiate roughly equally in all directions. The operative word is "roughly"—their radiation patterns are by no means spherical. They will, however, fill modest-sized houses (under 2,500 square feet) with a top-bitrate field, and if you find slow spots or dead spots in your house you can adjust simple access point antennas to some extent by rotating them and tilting them in various directions—just like the old "rabbit ears" TV antennas!

 Some access points have two such antennas, while many have only one. Why two? Two antennas allow something called diversity reception, which reduces the effects of certain kinds of reflection interference. I explained this in detail in Chapter 6.

Omnidirectional Vertical Gain Antennas

These are special-purpose outdoor antennas, used for either point-multipoint bridging or (less commonly) for servicing Wi-Fi clients in an open area like a university quad. In point-multipoint bridging, a centrally located omnidirectional vertical gain antenna provides a network link to networks in nearby buildings, each of which has a directional gain antenna pointed at the omnidirectional vertical. They are generally weatherized fiberglass tubes from 12" to 40" long and under an inch in diameter. They cost from $100 to $400.

Omnidirectional vertical gain antennas can have as much as 12 dbi gain. One problem with omnidirectional antennas with this much gain is that their vertical beam width is quite narrow (as little as *7 degrees* for a unit like Pacific Wireless' 12 dbi omni) and if the antenna is mounted too high, the bulk of its radiation never reaches the ground! This may, of course, be a *good* thing, if you want to minimize access to rooftop point-to-point data links by people on the ground who shouldn't be able to tap into that link.

 I use a 5 dBi magnetic-mount omnidirectional vertical gain antenna for wardriving. For more on this antenna and why wardriving requires that sort of antenna, see Chapter 19.

PC Card Integrated "Bulge" Antennas

By all measure the *worst* Wi-Fi antennas are the ones baked into the PCMCIA PC card client adapters that you plug into your laptop. These "integrated" antennas are inside the plastic bulge that extends beyond the end of the card. They are miraculously small, but they are also oriented horizontally, and most Wi-Fi antennas are vertical. Radio signals have an orientation aspect called *polarization*, and when a vertical antenna emits a radio field, it is picked up most effectively by another vertical antenna. It is picked up *least* effectively by a horizontal antenna, and this accounts for most of the shortcomings of integrated PC card antennas.

Although integrated antennas work acceptably in most cases, on the fringe of your Wi-Fi field they may come up short. This is why I always recommend buying a Wi-Fi PCMCIA client adapter with an external antenna jack, like the Orinoco Classic Gold card and the several PC card Wi-Fi clients from Buffalo Technology. You can buy simple external antennas (like blade antennas, which I'll describe next) to extend the reach of PC card integrated antennas. In Chapter 16 I describe homemade antennas that can be used for the same purpose.

Blade Antennas

A *blade antenna* is a very simple, small omnidirectional antenna built into a thin, flat (hence the name) piece of plastic. Blade antennas are often literally glued or velcroed to walls (sometimes cubicle walls) to finesse a Wi-Fi dead spot, where the signal from an access point won't otherwise reach at full speed or perhaps at all. Figure 8.3 shows a typical blade antenna from Maxrad. This model costs about $50, and has a

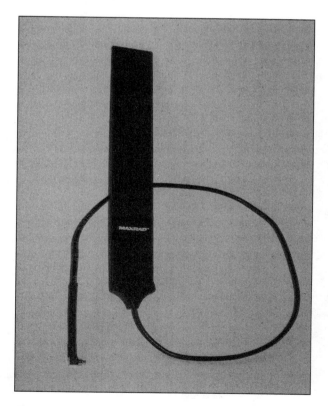

Figure 8.3
A Maxrad Blade Antenna.

short length of low-loss coaxial cable terminated in an MC connector, for use with an Orinoco PCMCIA card. They can be obtained with most of the commonly used coaxial connectors.

A blade antenna rarely delivers any significant gain (except in comparison to a PC card's miserable "bulge" antenna) and is used mostly to "catch" signal by allowing the antenna to be a short distance from the computer. Sometimes mounting a blade antenna just two feet above a cubicle desktop will allow a computer to connect to the network where it otherwise wouldn't.

Breezecom makes a $70 blade antenna mounted on a little desk stand so you can park it on a flat surface rather than Velcro it to the wall. The Breezecom unit is bulky and less versatile than an unmounted blade. If you want the Maxrad to stand up on your desk, make a stand from a candle holder and some modeling clay, or glue a clothespin to some sort of nonmetallic base. I've used the (admittedly ugly) lashup shown in Figure 8.4 with good results finessing a couple of weak spots at work. It's

Figure 8.4
A Blade Antenna on a Home-Made Desk Stand.

nothing more than a clothespin stuck into the center hole of an octal tube socket mounted on a little masonite slab.

I've also used a blade antenna to wardrive from the back seat of a taxi, by hanging it from a suction cup stuck to the cab's window. It's handy to have one in the drawer for such special applications.

Ceiling Blister Omnidirectional Antennas

Antennas are almost universally considered ugly (unless you're a real tech freak like me) and there are products designed specifically to make them less obtrusive for indoor environments. Ceiling blister antennas are designed for use in the ceilings of large office spaces (above cube farms, for example) to provide omnidirectional coverage without looking too much like antennas. Gain is not the point here, and ceiling blister antennas usually offer only about 3 dbi of gain.

Blister antennas for Wi-Fi use are about the size and shape of a large smoke detector: flattish and round, between 5" and 8" in diameter and 3" to 4" thick. Most are shipped with about a foot of pigtail, terminated by an N female connector. The idea is to mount them into a wallboard or dropped ceiling and place access points immediately above them, with Category 5 cable connecting the access point into the network. In my experience, ceiling blister antennas are overkill for residences, unless you're outfitting something in the 10,000 square foot range. See Figure 8.5 for a typical blister antenna from Pacific Wireless.

If Wi-Fi connectivity really catches on in corporate environments (it's still a little exotic), we're likely to see low-cost ceiling blister antenna assemblies that actually contain access points, making it even simpler to deploy an ESS (Extended Service Set) wireless network in the ceilings above cube farms.

Waveguide Antennas

At very short wavelengths (like those of Wi-Fi signals) it becomes possible to pass signals literally through a metal pipe. The laws of physics tell us that, introduced into a round or rectangular pipe of the proper dimensions, radio waves will line up like soldiers and march in formation through the pipe with minimal loss, even if the pipe bends or turns right-angle corners. Such a pipe, of a size calculated according to the correct formula, is called a *waveguide*. Waveguides are used extensively in radar installations to conduct high-power radar signals safely between transmitters and antennas.

Figure 8.5
A Ceiling Blister Antenna. (Photo courtesy of Pacific Wireless, Inc.)

A short, straight section of waveguide can be used as an antenna, if one end is closed and the other left open. Such *waveguide antennas* are fairly light and compact, and can be made very cheaply. Short waveguide antennas have moderate gain (about 10 to 12 dBi) and are quite efficient if made correctly. Figure 8.6 shows the Super Cantenna, a commercial waveguide antenna that sells for about $20 (see **www.cantenna.com**).

 If you're not fussy about appearances and have some skill with hand tools, you can make your own waveguide antennas from coffee cans, food cans, tennis ball cans, or even "Tetra Brik" foil-cardboard soup and milk boxes. I lay out the math and provide detailed step-by-step instructions on how to build your own in Chapter 16.

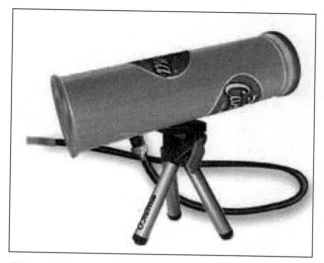

Figure 8.6
The Super Cantenna Waveguide Antenna. (Photo courtesy of Cantenna.)

Parabolic Grid Antennas

For point-to-point network bridging work across distances I favor parabolic grid antennas over their chief competition, Yagi "fishbone" antennas. Both are extremely focused gain antennas, but Yagis are long and skinny with lots of easily bent parts and are simply more difficult to mount and adjust. I've had excellent results with the parabolic grids from Pacific Wireless. Their top-of-the-line 24 dbi model is shown in Figure 8.7. It sells for about $75 new. Smaller models down to 15 dBi gain can be had for as little as $50.

Parabolic grid antennas are light and compact and the wind blows right through them, which isn't the case for some of the used and surplus satellite TV parabolic dish antennas that some people have pressed into Wi-Fi service for very high gain. For more photos of parabolic grid antennas used to bridge two networks, see Chapter 17.

Picture Frame Antennas

"Picture frame" is my coinage here; these antennas have a lot of names, including panel antennas and directional patch antennas. They are generally square or rectangular and may be hung on or bolted to a wall. They are directional in that they are designed to radiate forward and to their sides, but not behind them. The idea is to "fill the room" with signal as much as possible, but not send signal backwards through the walls they're mounted on. Audio people will understand when I say that the antenna has a "cardioid" radiation pattern, as shown in Figure 8.8. The little

Figure 8.7
A 24 dBi Parabolic Grid Antenna. (Photo courtesy of Pacific Wireless, Inc.)

"tail" sticking out straight behind the antenna is not very strong and will be attenuated by the wall.

The radiation pattern shown in Figure 8.8 is the "free space" pattern, and I've super-imposed it on the rough outline of a typical home or small office, as you would do to evaluate an antenna of this type. The actual shape of the pattern will depend heavily on the building and what it's made of, but you can assume that the top bitrate field boundaries will not extend quite so far outside of the structure. Note that the radiation pattern as shown isn't an all-or-nothing proposition. What I show is roughly the boundaries of where the maximum bit rate can be achieved; outside that boundary the bitrate will drop to an intermediate level. There may be "slow spots" or dead spots within the boundaries, depending on metal obstructions and how the structure is built. You won't know until you walk around with a laptop and test the field!

The antenna I've used in installing wireless networks for some of my clients is the 10 dBi gain Pacific Wireless PAWIN24-10. It's quite compact: 8.5" x 7.5" x $1^3/_4$" thick, and costs about $50 (see Figure 8.9). It's excellent for small and medium-sized offices or larger single-level homes, where the access point is at one end of the

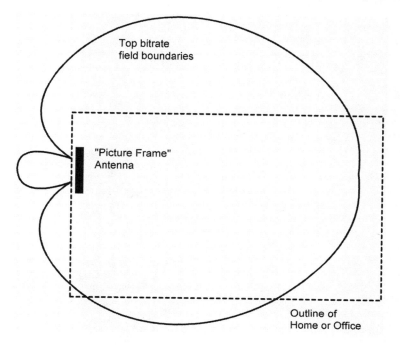

Top bitrate
field boundaries

"Picture Frame"
Antenna

Outline of
Home or Office

Figure 8.8
A Picture Frame Antenna's Radiation Pattern.

structure to be covered, rather than at the center. It's not suitable for multi-story homes or offices, because it has a fairly narrow radiation pattern in the vertical dimension. (Look back at Figure 8.2, which is a side view of its radiation pattern.) In my own two-story house back when I lived in Arizona, my wife was unable to connect from her office almost precisely below and a little behind the antenna, and the signal was marginal in our first-floor living room, irrespective of the 10 dbi gain directed square at (but above) the living room.

Sector Antennas

Sector antennas are large, heavy outdoor gain antennas, designed to confine their radiation to a specific fan-shaped pattern of a specified angular width. This pattern is a sector of a 360-degree omnidirectional radiation pattern, hence the name. 900 Mhz sector antennas are used in virtually all cell phone towers, and you've probably seen them without knowing what they were. They are long, narrow rectangular devices mounted vertically, and when mounted in high places are sometimes tipped slightly off vertical for optimum delivery of radio energy to devices at ground level.

Figure 8.9
The Pacific Wireless PAWIN24-10 Antenna.

Sector antennas are sometimes used by business or university campus Wi-Fi systems to cover wide areas. They're quite expensive (generally over a thousand dollars) and are not of much interest to residential and small office wireless users.

Backfire Antennas

A backfire antenna is a compact gain antenna for outdoor use. A typical backfire antenna for Wi-Fi frequencies is a little under 11" in diameter and looks like a pie plate with a can in the middle of it. Pacific Wireless makes a $50 backfire with 14

Figure 8.10
A Pacific Wireless PAWES24-14 Backfire Antenna. (Photo courtesy of Pacific Wireless, Inc.)

dbi gain. For outdoor gain antennas I prefer parabolic grid antennas because they present a lower profile to the wind. Figure 8.10 shows a Pacific Wireless backfire antenna, the PAWES24-14.

Yagi Antennas

The canonical rooftop TV antenna is a species of Yagi antenna. The Yagi antenna's characteristic "fishbone" structure is key: A long spine (called the *boom*) to which perpendicular elements are attached in a row at precisely calculated intervals.

The longer the Yagi antenna, the more focused its radiation is in a single line. Yagi antennas can be made quite long (especially at microwave frequencies, where the fishbone elements are only a few inches long) and have tremendous gain, generally from 12-20 dbi. Their extremely narrow radiation patterns make them suitable only for point-to-point work, bridging networks in different buildings, and more rarely allowing an outlier Wi-Fi client to connect to a distant access point.

Because Yagi antenna elements at Wi-Fi microwave frequencies are so short, the fishbone elements can be disks instead of rods, and many Wi-Fi Yagi antennas look like fender washers spaced out along a length of metal rod. (That's often precisely what they are.) The structure of commercial Yagi antennas is often hidden inside a length of white PVC pipe, so that you don't necessarily see the disks or rods that the antenna is made of.

You'll see a lot of articles on the Web by people who have built their own Yagi antennas for Wi-Fi use, often by stringing fender washers on a length of threaded rod, with carefully cut lengths of metal tubing acting as spacers. This can be done, but my own experiments show that it's not nearly as simple as certain experimenters make it sound, and I won't provide instructions in this book. It's *way* easier to make a waveguide antenna from a spaghetti sauce can or a Tetra Brik soup box. I explain how in detail in Chapter 16. If you're not a machinist and really need the gain of an extra-long Yagi, I recommend commercial parabolic grid antennas from vendors like Pacific Wireless.

A Special Case: The Pringle's Can Antenna

As best I can tell, the well-known (nay, legendary) Pringle's can Wi-Fi antenna was first published on the Web by Andrew Clapp, and later made famous by the much more visible Rob Flickenger of O'Reilly Books. Rob calls the antenna a "shotgun Yagi," and technically that's what it is, and more or less looks like: A long tubular thing made from PVC pipe and a Pringle's can, with a very narrow directional pattern and 12 dbi gain.

Rob's article on the antenna is very good, and I suggest you read it carefully: **www.oreillynet.com/cs/weblog/view/wlg/448**.

I've always been suspicious about making waveguide antennas from Pringle's cans because a waveguide antenna needs to be a conductive cylinder with one end closed with conductive material. Early Pringle's cans had an interior surface of silver-painted cardboard. In my own tests I could not find good conductivity in the silver layer, which was either paint or some kind of silver-colored ink. Sometime in 2003, Pringle's began to line the interior of the cans with actual aluminum foil. This foil lining is in fact conductive, but it's very thin and difficult to make electrical conduct with. Electrical contact between the lining and the body of the coaxial connector that connects the can to a Wi-Fi device must be good, and after butchering a number of cans I could not get sufficient electrical contact to make for a decent antenna.

Rob's antenna works—if you do it Rob's way. He adds a short Yagi director array using washers, and that's where I believe the bulk of the antenna's gain comes from. However, a lot of people speak of using the Pringle's can as though it were a contiguous metallic cylinder, and thus a waveguide. It's true that if you build a quarter-wave probe into it (look ahead to Chapter 16 if you don't understand this) you will get some measurable gain. However, if the body of the probe doesn't make good contact with the foil lining—and if the metal bottom of the can does not also have good contact with the foil lining—you don't have a waveguide antenna. What gain happens under those circumstances is probably due to the metal bottom of the can acting as a very simple reflector.

Finally, the can is on the small end of the envelope for a good waveguide antenna at 2.4 GHz. You can do the calculations yourself, using the formulas I cite in Chapter 16, which is about making your own waveguide antennas.

On the balance, if you really want a gain antenna, you can do much better with other designs. One purely practical objection I have to a high-gain (and thus highly directional) antenna made of cardboard is that directional antennas are most useful mounted permanently for point-to-point work, such as linking wired networks in two close but unconnected buildings. This means mounted *outside*—in the rain and the snow, which would make quick mush of any cardboard tube.

The Pringle's can antenna is more valuable in the Wi-Fi community as an emblem of the marvelous gonzo innovative style that wireless experimenters have brought to the Wi-Fi field. You can make an even better antenna out of spaghetti sauce, juice, or coffee cans—see Chapter 16—that will stand up to the weather, but that's just not as, well, nuts.

dB, dBi, dBm: The Decibel Family

If you intend to simply buy off-the-shelf Wi-Fi gear, plug it in, set it up, and go, you don't need to deal with decibels and their children. On the other hand, as soon as you begin to fool with external antennas, coaxial cable, bridge mode, and things like that, power levels, signal levels, and losses begin to loom large. The decibel family of units are ways to get a grip on those things.

Simply put, a decibel (abbreviated *dB*) is a measure of *relative* power or signal strength. "Relative" means it's not a question of absolute units (like watts for power, or volts for signal) but a *comparison* of two values.

The easiest way to understand the idea of relative power is to think of an amplifier. An amplifier takes a signal of some sort at its input, and reproduces the signal at its output—at greater power. The power of the output signal may be compared to the power of the input signal in terms of decibels. This value in decibels is the *gain* of the amplifier, and doesn't depend on whether the amp is a small signal amp or a power amp. You can have a 6 dB gain amplifier the size of a matchhead, or the size of a trash barrel. One amplifies signals measured in microvolts; the other amplifies power measured in kilowatts. What matters is the *relationship* of output to input, expressed in decibels.

Losses in a length of coaxial cable can be expressed in decibels as well. (Especially at microwave frequencies, a length of coaxial cable is like an amplifier in reverse.) The relationship of power levels leaving a cable to the power entering into the cable indicates the loss occurring inside the cable. The decibels figure in that case is negative, but it's still the relationship between input and output.

It's not a simple ratio, say, output over input. Decibels express a base-10 logarithmic scale. The relationship between two power levels expressed in decibels is calculated this way:

$$10\log\left(\frac{Output}{Input}\right)$$

An amplifier that outputs 32 watts for 2 watts input would have a gain of 10 x log (32 / 2), or 12.04 dB.

For losses, it works the same way. Say you put 5 watts into a run of coaxial cable, and measure 1.8 watts at the other end of the cable. Your cable loss would be 10 x log (1.8 / 5) or −4.43 dB.

Note the x 10 factor in the equation. There is a unit called a *Bel* (after telephone inventor Alexander Graham Bell) which was developed by telephone engineers seeking to capture the logarithmic nature of human hearing. A Bel is simply the logarithm of a ratio of two signal levels, but the magnitude of the results of the logarithmic equation is smaller than is convenient for most real-world work. So a new unit with one tenth the magnitude of a Bel was defined and named the decibel. Using decibels rather than Bels is simply a mathematical convenience that gives us an appropriate unit of measure; it's very much like choosing to measure the distance from Denver to Chicago in miles rather than inches.

Eyeballing Gains and Losses

All the math may obscure the real value of decibels: They make it possible to easily calculate (often in your head) combinations of gains and losses as represented by radio amplifiers, antennas, and runs of coaxial cable. The total gain (or loss) of a system may be calculated by simply adding the gains and losses of its various parts, all expressed in decibels. For example, say you have a 6 dBi gain antenna (I'll explain "dBi" in a moment) fed by a run of coaxial cable that loses 2.7 dB. Adding 6 to –2.7 gives you 3.3 dB, which is the total gain of the system represented by the antenna and the cable.

 A convenient rule of thumb is that 3 dB represents a doubling of power, and –3 dB represents a halving of power. 6 dB is thus a doubling of a doubling, or quadrupling (4x) of power, and –6 dB divides your power by 4.

One critical role of gain antennas is to compensate for inevitable losses in coaxial cable. At microwave frequencies, losses in runs of coax longer than a few feet can be crippling, especially if you try to use coax not designed for microwaves. Coaxial cable is rated at loss in dB per 100 feet. (You can calculate shorter runs as simple proportions.) If you intend to use coax in your Wi-Fi installations, you need to be able to calculate the loss that happens inside the cable and make sure that your cables aren't simply eating your power and leaving none for the radios and antennas!

Antennas and dBi

If you shop for commercial Wi-Fi antennas, you'll see most antennas rated for gain in units called *dBi*. A dBi is not a different unit than a decibel. It's an abbreviation of "dB gain over an isotropic antenna." As I explained a little earlier, gain antennas aren't exactly like amplifiers. They don't add power to your signal. They *focus* your signal, like a lens focuses light. Instead of spraying radio waves equally in all directions, they concentrate radio energy in a particular direction, while reducing energy in other directions.

An *isotropic antenna* is in fact an antenna that *does* spray radio waves equally in all directions, including up and down. Such antennas don't really exist in their ideal form, but the uniform theoretical radio field of an isotropic antenna provides an input value for comparison against a gain antenna's output value in the direction of greatest gain. A dBi is a decibel of gain realized by a gain antenna, compared to what that theoretical isotropic antenna would do with the same radio power input. As a unit it actually has more to do with degree of focus of radio energy than gain in the sense that an amplifier provides.

The dBi gain of an antenna tells you, in a sense, how much additional power you would need to get the same performance from an isotropic antenna. The dBi allows you to perform gain/loss calculations that incorporate antennas as well as amplifiers and cables.

Watts and dBm

Unlike dBi, the unit *dBm* is quite different from the decibel. The dBm unit indicates *absolute* power levels, not relative power levels. In that it's very much like the watt, and in fact you can convert any dBm value to an equivalent value in watts. So why not use watts?

Just as the dBi unit allows you to easily calculate antenna gain into the total gains and losses in an RF system, the dBm unit allows you to easily calculate absolute power levels into an RF system that includes radio transmitters (which generate RF power) amplifiers, coaxial cables, and antennas.

The term dBm is an abbreviation for "power relative to one milliwatt." (A milliwatt is one one-thousandth of a watt, or .001 watts.) The unit dBm assumes one milliwatt of absolute power as a 0-based value, and expresses absolute power values both above and below one milliwatt on a logarithmic scale. (0 dBm is equal to one milliwatt.) The equation for calculating dBm from watts is similar to the first equation I presented for decibels:

$$dBm = 10Log\left(\frac{Power}{.001}\right)$$

This allows you to calculate the equivalent of a power value in watts in dBm units. For example, say the radio output stage of a Wi-Fi client adapter puts out 85 milliwatts of RF power. Plug that value into the *Power* variable, expressed in watts. That makes the calculation cook down to 10 x log (.085 / .001), or 19.29 dBm. Make sure you express the *Power* term in *watts*, not milliwatts!

Think back to the rule of thumb for decibels. The same scale applies here. One milliwatt is 0 dBm. Two milliwatts is 3dBm. Half a milliwatt is −3 dBm.

Learning to think of power in dBm terms allows you to do easy gain and loss calculations that tell you how much absolute power actually comes out of an antenna. This is important, since by the FCC's Part 15 rules, Wi-Fi power is limited to either one watt of actual transmitter output power, or four watts effective radiated power, which depends on the gain of your antenna and the losses in whatever cables links your Wi-Fi device to your antenna.

Calculating that effective radiated power value is much easier when your Wi-Fi client adapter or access point output is expressed in dBm. Here's an example: Say you have a client adapter that puts out 85 milliwatts. As shown above, that's 19.29 dBm. You connect the adapter to an antenna with 14 dBi gain, through a 30' run of cable rated for loss at 8 dB per 100 feet. What is the effective radiated power coming off the antenna?

First figure the total loss in your coaxial cable, in dB. If 100 feet of cable has 8 dB loss, 30 feet has 30/100 x 8 dB, or 2.4 dB. Next, add your radio output power to your antenna gain, and then subtract your cable loss: 19.29 dBm + 14 dBi − 2.4 dB = 30.89 dBm of effective radiated power. How much is that in watts? Converting backward from dBm to milliwatts is done this way:

$$mw = 10^{\,dBm/10}$$

Divide your 30.89 dBm figure by ten, giving you 3.089, and then raise ten to that power. 10 raised to the power 3.089 equals 1227.4 milliwatts, or 1.23 watts. Your system is thus still on the right side of Part 15!

Coaxial Cable

Making radio waves go where you want them to go is more art than science, and a lot of that art lies in the design and use of *coaxial cable*. Coax (as insiders call it) can be thought of conceptually as pipe for radio waves. Radio energy travels inside it without being radiated into the air. It's used to carry radio energy between an antenna and a radio; in this case, a Wi-Fi client adapter, access point, or wireless gateway.

Coax comes in a lot of different thicknesses and is made from many different materials, but the essential design is the same: an inner conductor (generally copper wire) surrounded by a layer of insulation, surrounded by an outer conductor (generally cylindrical copper-strand braid) encased in a protective plastic sheath. You can get coax as thin as .1" in diameter, or as thick as your arm. Some is as flexible as simple copper wire, while some is as stiff as water pipe. For most ordinary Wi-Fi work, you don't need to fuss with coax. But to do certain things and fix certain problems, you're going to have to use coax, and not all coax is created equal, especially at the lofty frequencies at which microwaves operate.

What Coax Is For

When you do require coax, you're most likely going to use it to bring signal to and from external antennas. When Wi-Fi enthusiasts speak of *pigtails*, they mean short lengths of coax with specific coaxial connectors soldered to each end. These are used to connect client adapters and access points to external antennas. You may be used to thinking of "external" antennas being used outdoors, or in exotic applications like linking separate networks in bridge mode, but the commonest use of external antennas is to extend the reach of a Wi-Fi client adapter that's just a little too far away from its access point to sustain a good connection. For example, I built myself a tin can antenna to allow my laptop to share my broadband Internet connection at full speed from my living room. (For more on this, including how to build your own, see Chapter 16.) The antenna connects to my laptop through a pigtail consisting of 19" of thin coax.

External antennas are sometimes used to get signal into a "dead spot" where a Wi-Fi signal doesn't quite reach because of intervening obstruction from walls and metal objects. Sometimes getting the antenna just a few feet away from the computer is all you need, and again, a pigtail and an external antenna are just the thing. In modern corporate cube farms with metal cube walls and integrated overhead file cabinets, it sometimes takes a blade antenna tacked unobtrusively to the top of the cube wall to pull in the company Wi-Fi signal, which may be blocked by the metal in the cube structure and fittings.

Frequency, Power, and Loss

The key phrase here is "just a few feet away." There's a problem with coaxial cable: It eats radio signal energy unavoidably, in a predictable way at a predictable rate. The amount of signal you lose depends on both the length (and type) of the cable, and the frequency of radio energy you're using. The 2.4 GHz frequency at which Wi-Fi operates is up in the microwaves, and at microwave frequencies, coax is positively voracious in the way it eats signal.

The degree of loss present in a specific type of coax depends on its dimensions and the materials it's made of. In very broad terms, thick coax is less lossy than thin coax. It's also less physically flexible, to the extent that a lot of microwave coax should be considered "bendable" rather than flexible.

Table 8.1 summarizes the loss exhibited by the most common types of coax used at microwave frequencies. The loss is given in dB per 100 feet. For the common LMR 240 coax, the loss is 12.7 dB per 100 feet. (I explained decibel calculations earlier in this chapter.) For the moment, consider this rule of thumb: A 3 dB increase means your power doubles; a 3dB loss means your power is cut *by half*.

Table 8.1 Coaxial Cable Loss at 2.4 GHz. (All loss figures are per 100 feet of cable.)

Manufacturer	Cable Type	Loss / 100 ft
Andrew Heliax	1 5/8" LDF	1.4 dB
Andrew Heliax	1 1/4" LDF	1.7 dB
Andrew Heliax	7/8" LDF	2.3 dB
Andrew Heliax	1/2" LDF	3.9 dB
Andrew Heliax	1/2" Superflex	6.17 dB
Andrew Heliax	LDF 4-50A	3.3 dB
Andrew Heliax	Superflex	6.84 dB
Belden	9913	7.7dB
Times Microwave	LMR 1700	1.7 dB
Times Microwave	LMR 1200	1.99 dB
Times Microwave	LMR 900	2.63 dB
Times Microwave	LMR 600	4.4 dB
Times Microwave	LMR 500	5.48 dB
Times Microwave	LMR 400	6.6 dB
Times Microwave	LMR 300	10.4 dB
Times Microwave	LMR 240	12.7 dB
Times Microwave	LMR 195	18.6 dB
Times Microwave	LMR 100A	38.9 dB
(Many)	RG 213	13.2dB
(Many)	RG 214	13.2dB
(Many)	RG 58	35 dB

It adds up, with every 3 dB of loss meaning your power halves again. A 6 dB loss means your power will be only one fourth of its original level. A 9 dB loss means you have one eighth left; a 12 dB loss means you have one sixteenth left, and so on. At some point you needn't bother: Pass a Wi-Fi signal through 100 feet of RG 58 (much used by CBers and amateur radio operators for far lower frequencies) and only four ten thousandths of your original signal will come out the other end, and that's almost too small to measure.

Calculating Coaxial Cable Losses

In terms of the length of the cable, the loss increases (or decreases) linearly. In other words, if 100 feet of cable loses 6 dB, 50 feet will lose 3 dB, and 25 feet will lose 1.5 dB. To calculate the loss for a shorter length of coax, multiply the stated loss in Table 8.1 by the length in feet divided by 100. For example, calculate the loss present in nine feet of LMR 195, which has a loss of 18.6 dB per 100 feet:

$$\frac{9}{100} \times 18.6 = 1.67 dB$$

To calculate the power ratio associated with a dB value, divide the dB value by 10 and raise 10 to that power. If the dB value was negative (in other words, if you're calculating a loss) take the inverse of that value:

$$\frac{1}{10^{0.167}} = 0.68$$

If your run of coax gives you a 1.67 dB loss, that means you'll have only 68% of your input power at the output of the cable. And that's only nine feet of cable!

Clearly, you want to keep your coax runs (if you use them at all) down to the absolute minimum. You can counteract cable loss, to some extent, with antenna gain, as I explained a little earlier in this chapter.

Other Loss Effects

Damaged cable and cable that has been exposed to water for a long time will exhibit higher loss than when new and undamaged. Bad solder joints or clumsy crimp jobs in coaxial connectors increase the loss present in a coaxial cable run. Don't kink coax or damage the braid through abrasion or pinching, and unless you're experienced with attaching connectors to cable, buy pre-made pigtails or cable sections with the connectors professionally attached. Some coax is designed to be exposed to the elements; most is not.

Even perfectly attached coaxial connectors introduce a measure of additional loss by creating an impedence bump (basically, a short section of radio turbulence) in the transmission path. To avoid this, don't use more connectors than you must.

Pigtails

A relative handful of Wi-Fi PC card clients for laptops are equipped with a tiny coaxial jack on the outer edge of the antenna bulge. The jack allows the connection of an external antenna with much higher gain, directivity (a narrow beam) or both. A short length of coaxial cable used to connect a wireless card to an antenna is called (colloquially) a *pigtail*.

The cable is short because at microwave frequencies like 2.4 GHz, radio energy losses in coaxial cable are quite high. Typical pigtail length is from 19" to 42", with an N connector on the antenna end and one of several types of small coaxial connectors on the wireless card end. Such pigtails may be obtained from several Web-based vendors for prices between $20 and $40.

That sounds like a lot of cash for two feet of wire and two connectors. This has led some folks to make their own pigtails, but there are gotchas. A badly-made pigtail will eat a lot of your signal.

Any connector in an RF transmission path will create an impedance bump (a short region of turbulence for radio waves) that increases the loss of signal in the path. The severity of this impedance bump depends heavily on how carefully the connector is soldered or crimped to the cable. Connectors like the RMC and MMCX are *tiny*, and soldering coaxial cable to it is an art, not a science. Do it badly, and the loss in your pigtail will skyrocket.

I've purchased most of my pigtails from Fleeman, Anderson, & Bird. See the vendor list in Appendix A for contact information.

Coaxial Connectors

The small metallic screw-on ends that terminate pigtails and other runs of coaxial cable are called *coaxial connectors*. There are probably close to a hundred different kinds of coaxial connectors used in radio work today and in times past, but only a handful are in regular use in the Wi-Fi industry.

Complicating the picture is the fact that most Wi-Fi connectors are used *only* in the Wi-Fi industry for Wi-Fi products, and are unknown in other sectors of radio technology. (The main exception is the ubiquitous N connector.) In this section I'll briefly describe the connectors you may encounter in Wi-Fi work.

Reverse-Polarity Connectors

One reason that Wi-Fi connectors are specific to the Wi-Fi industry is that the FCC would prefer that it be difficult for basement tinkerers (like thee and me) to connect Wi-Fi things in ways not explicitly tested and approved by the FCC. So in traditional government fashion, it decreed that Wi-Fi connectors used in consumer products like access points and client adapters be nonstandard. This hasn't made them especially difficult to obtain, but it has made them more expensive.

So that connector manufacturers wouldn't have to completely retool their equipment to make utterly new types of connectors, these nonstandard connectors were devised by flipping the sense of the plugs and the sockets on existing standard connectors. Traditionally, a male connector has a little pin protruding from its center, within a larger free-turning threaded metal sleeve. A female connector has a little spring-loaded cylinder into which the male pin slides to make electrical contact, set into a narrower threaded sleeve that does not turn. In reverse-polarity connectors, the FCC has mandated a sort of sex change, in which the female connectors now have a pin, and the male connectors now have the cylinder.

This is easier to show than describe (see Figure 8.11). I've drawn both normal and reverse polarity coaxial connectors in cross-section to show the reversal of the pin and the cylinder. Note that the figure doesn't depict any particular type of coaxial connector, but most of the microwave connectors you'll encounter in Wi-Fi work

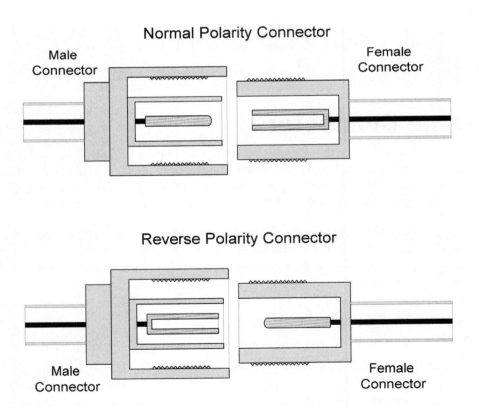

Figure 8.11
Normal and Reverse Polarity Connectors.

are constructed roughly the same way, and differ mostly in size. Male connectors are customarily used on the ends of coaxial cable runs, and female connectors are customarily used on the equipment itself.

N Connectors

I've been told that the "N" here stands for" "Navy," but the truth is that the "N" is for Bell Labs scientist Paul Neill, who designed the connector for use by military (primarily Navy) radar equipment during World War II. N connectors are the largest of the Wi-Fi family of coaxial connectors, being about $^3/_4$" in diameter. Most of the larger external antennas without integrated pigtails connect through female N connectors. The better N connectors are silver plated for lower losses (see Figure 8.12).

MMCX Connectors

Several models of Wi-Fi PC card clients, including the Cisco 350 series, allow for connection of an external antenna through a very tiny gold-plated connector called the Micro-Miniature Co-aX (MMCX) connector. The MMCX is the microminiature adaptation of the older Miniature Co-aX (MCX) connector, which is not used in Wi-Fi hardware to my knowledge (see Figure 8.13).

The older Cisco 340 PC cards lack this connector—except those cards built into the 340-series PCI cards, which carry the 342 model number. The connector in Figure 8.13 is shown with the Cisco Aironet PCI 342 client adapter of which it is a part, with a dime for scale. The v2.5 build of the Linksys WUSB11—USB client adapter also has an MMCX connector. (The v2.6 build of the WUSB11 and later removed

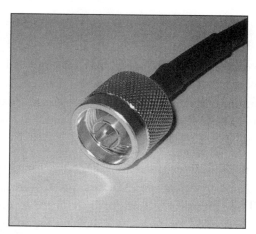

Figure 8.12
A Male N Connector on a Coaxial Pigtail.

Figure 8.13
An MMCX Connector.

the connector for reasons unexplained, and the "Popsicle stick" antenna used in those later versions is non-removable.)

The MMCX is about the same size as the MC connector used in Orinoco Classic Silver and Classic Gold cards, and the Buffalo Technology PC cards, but unlike the MC, MMCX is fairly common and easy to obtain "loose" (that is, not bound into a pigtail). Still, its extremely small size makes it very difficult to work with, and if you need an MMCX connection, buy a commercial pigtail. (See Appendix A for a list of suppliers.)

MC Connectors

The extremely popular Orinoco Silver and Orinoco Gold PCMCIA wireless LAN cards have a feature that many such cards lack: A jack for an external antenna. The jack, on the edge of the external "antenna bulge," is extremely small and easy to miss, since it is only about 1/8" in diameter and protected beneath a small button of black plastic that blends well with the rest of the bulge.

The tiny coaxial plug that connects to the jack is called an MC connector. (I don't know what the acronym "MC" expands to—perhaps "Microscopic Connector.") Technically, it's the RMC-6010-B. This connector was originally haunted by distribution limitations imposed by Orinoco vendor Agere and was difficult for hobbyists to obtain, but since Agere was purchased by Proxim I've begun to see the connector offered without restriction by vendors like RF Parts (see Appendix A). I think Agere had been asked to restrict distribution by the FCC, which doesn't favor individuals fooling with Wi-Fi antennas.

Although there are now dealers who will sell single MC connectors to hobbyists, it makes more sense to buy the connectors as parts of factory-configured pigtails, usually with an MC connector on one end and an N female connector on the other. Soldering coaxial cable to the nearly microscopic MC and MMCX connectors (microscopic to middle-aged eyes, at least) is agonizing, and most people don't have the skill or equipment to do it correctly. Bad coaxial connections introduce intermittent connections, shorts, and impedance bumps into the coax line, which increase the already appalling RF losses inherent in thin coaxial cable. To keep as much of your signal as possible, let the pros do the cable-hacking.

RP-SMA (Reverse Polarity SMA) Connectors

The RP-SMA connector is the reverse-polarity form of the existing standard Sub-Miniature A (SMA) connector. Many popular PCI Wi-Fi client adapters (including those from Linksys and D-Link) use a detachable antenna mounted to the PCI card spine, and this antenna attaches through an RP-SMA connector (see Figure 8.14).

You can buy pigtails incorporating RP-SMA connectors from Fleeman, Anderson, & Bird, among other vendors. Most such pigtails cost from $22 to $30. See Appendix A.

The RP-SMA connector, while not quite as microscopic as the MC and MMCX connectors, is still very small and difficult to work with, and I do not recommend making up your own pigtails at home. If you insist, loose connectors are available from vendors like RF Parts. See Appendix A.

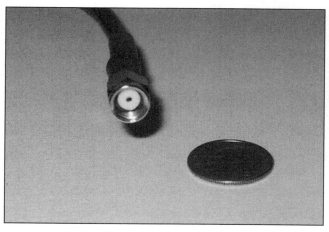

Figure 8.14
An RP-SMA Connector.

RP-TNC (Reverse Polarity TNC) Connectors

In the 1950's, Bell Lab scientists Paul Neill and Carl Concelman created a smaller version of Neill's WWII-era N connector, which became known as the Threaded Neill-Concelman (TNC) connector. The bayonet version of the Neill-Concelman connector is the well-known BNC (Bayonet Neill-Concelman) connector that was once ubiquitous in the old 10 Base-2 "Thin-net" Ethernet networks. The RP-TNC connector is the much more common TNC coaxial connector with a sex-change operation: As with the RP-SMA, where you'd expect to find the prong you find the hole, and vise versa. Most wireless access points with removable antennas are fitted with RP-TNC (reverse polarity TNC) connectors on their back panels.

RP-TNC connectors are reasonably sized (see Figure 8.15) and it's possible to make up your own coaxial jumpers from raw cable and RP-TNC connectors. Typically, what you need is a jumper with an RP-TNC connector on one end and a male N connector on the other. Again, if you're not an ace at making up coax assemblies, resist doing it yourself. Bad solder joints will cost you more power and signal at 2.4 GHz than at lower frequencies, so if you possibly can, buy readymade assemblies. See the vendor list in Appendix A.

Coaxial Connector Losses

Because every coaxial connector in a signal path creates a slight disturbance in the path (that impedance bump I've mentioned here and there) each connector contributes some loss to the path. How much of a loss depends on the frequency and on the

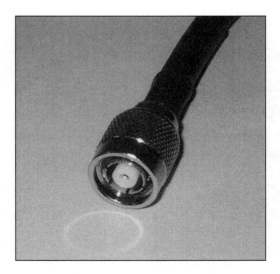

Figure 8.15
An RP-TNC Connector on a Pigtail.

connector, but it amounts to about .2 to .5 dB per connector. Note that for this calculation, joined connectors (in other words, a male and female connected together) are considered a single connector.

This isn't well understood in the Wi-Fi world, and there's nothing you can do about it anyway, but coaxial connectors work best at microwave frequencies when the coaxial cable they're attached to is of an appropriate size. N connectors, for example, create a pronounced impedance bump when used with very small or very large coax. Thin coaxial cable like LMR 100A works best with small coaxial connectors like the MMCX and MC.

The whole idea in a coaxial connector is to create a radio energy path through the connector that duplicates as closely as possible the path through the coaxial cable to which the connectors have been attached. If the diameter of the path through the connector is of a different size than the diameter of the cable, an impedance mismatch occurs through the connector, which increases losses through the connector slightly. Again, you can't always dictate what connectors you use in any given application, but it's useful to know why connectors exhibit losses and what makes those losses worse in particular circumstances.

In truth, connectors don't contribute a lot of loss to your signal path unless you use a lot of them, but try to keep them to a minimum when setting up any Wi-Fi system.

Path Loss

As if there weren't enough factors eating your Wi-Fi radio signal, well, empty space eats it as well. Your signal gets weaker the longer it travels through open air. How much? The basic formulas are pretty simple. Path loss in dB may be calculated this way:

$L_p = 32.4 + 20\log f + 20\log d$ (d given in kilometers)

$L_p = 36.6 + 20\log f + 20\log d$ (d given in miles)

In both equations, f is given in MHz.

For Wi-Fi work at 2450 MHz, across a path one mile in length, we'd calculate:

$36.6 + (20 \times 3.38) + (20 \times 0) = 104.2$ dB

You lose 104 dB just by being a mile away! That sounds grim, but that's physics—and the loss is ameliorated by the gain in your antennas and the gain in the amplifiers in your Wi-Fi gear.

What is a little discouraging is that many more factors enter into path loss that aren't as easily calculated. Primary among these are reflections off level ground and various objects like buildings and hills, and incursions by obstructions into what is called the *Fresnel zone*, which is an ellipsoidal region surrounding the line of sight between your two Wi-Fi antennas. If you're comfortable with the math and would like to learn more, there is an excellent technical discussion on the Web at:

www.tapr.org/tapr/html/ve3jf.dcc97/ve3jf.dcc97.html

The paper is available in PDF format as well for easy printing.

Calculating Link Budgets

If you're going to pull all this knowledge together to attempt to span a significant distance using Wi-Fi gear in bridge mode, you should see if the challenge is realistic by calculating a *link budget*. The idea is to gather all the various gains and losses represented by elements of a Wi-Fi signal path, add them up, and see if the final signal strength falls above or below a Wi-Fi receiver's signal threshold. If it's above that threshold, you're "in the black" and can establish the link; if it's below, you're "in the red" with the equipment stated and the link may not work. By using lower-loss cable or higher-gain antennas you might be able to push the quality of the link back up into workable territory.

Here are the variables you need to consider. Calculate or look up their values using the gear you have:

- Transmitter Output Power (dBm)

- Transmitter Antenna Gain (dBi)

- Transmit-side Coaxial Cable Loss (dB)

- Transmit-side Connector Loss (dB)

- Path Loss (dB)

- Receiver Antenna Gain (dBi)

- Receive-Side Coaxial Cable Loss (dB)

- Receive-Side Connector Loss (dB)

Once you have all of these figures gathered together, you simply add them. Gains are positive numbers, losses are negatives. The resulting figure is the signal strength at the receiver.

You may have trouble determining the receiver sensitivity (and hence the signal threshold) of your particular Wi-Fi access point or wireless gateway. Neither Linksys nor D-Link publish receiver sensitivity in their data sheets, online or off. Cisco does, and I'll use the Cisco 340 access point (with which I have some experience) in this example. You can ask a manufacturer's tech support people, but it's hard to tell if tech support even knows. If you can't find out your receiver's sensitivity, assume something on the order of −80 dBm. Most receiver specifications I've seen are a little better than that (in other words, they can pick up a signal with a lower strength of −83 or even −90 dBm) so it's a "safe" assumption.

A Link Budget Example

It usually helps to work through an example with real hardware and real numbers. For this example I'll use the following hardware components:

- Cisco 340 access point

- Pacific Wireless PMANT15 parabolic grid antenna, across a distance of one mile

- On each side I'll assume two connectors and two lengths of coax: One a 19" pigtail of LMR100 coax, the other a 48" pigtail of LMR400 coax. This is a typical setup for an access point mounted outdoors inside a weatherproof box; the short pigtail connects the access point inside the box to the bulkhead connector that passes through the box, and the long pigtail connects from the bulkhead connector outside the box to the antenna. (I describe such a setup in Chapter 17, which discusses creating Wi-Fi bridges.)

Given the hardware listed above, here are the variables themselves:

- Transmitter Output Power: 30mw, or 15 dBm

- Transmitter Antenna Gain: 15 dBi

- Transmit-Side Coaxial Cable Loss, total -.92 dB:

    1.58' (19") of LMR100 @ -38.9 dB/100' = -.66 dB

    4' (48") of LMR400 @ -6.6 dB/100' = -.26 dB

- Transmit-Side Connector Loss: 2 X .5 dB = -1 dB

- Path Loss @ 1 mile: -104 dB (calculated in previous section)

- Receiver-Side Antenna Gain: 15 dBi

- Receiver-Side Coaxial Cable Loss: total -.92 dB (same as transmitter side)

- Receiver-Side Connector Loss: -1 dB (same as transmitter side)

First we add together all the gain factors into a single gain factor: 2 x +15 dBi for the antennas, or +30 dBi.

Next we add all the loss factors together into a single loss factor:

Total cable losses: 2 x -.92 dB = -1.84 dB

Total connector losses: 2 x –1 dB = -2 dB

Total link loss = Path Loss -104 dB + cable loss -1.84 dB + connector loss -2 dB = -107.84 dB

Signal strength at the receiver will be the transmitter power plus antenna gain minus all the various loss factors:

Signal Strength = 15 dBm + 30 dBi antenna gain – 107.84 dB losses = -62.84 dBm

Most Wi-Fi access points have receivers that can pick up a signal at –80 dBm. Since -62.84 dBm is a stronger signal than –80 dBm (these are negative numbers, so "less" is "more") there is sufficient signal for the link to work.

Many network designers recommend a margin of 20 dB to cover difficult-to-calculate losses like reflections and other things that can interfere with the link's operation. If your signal comes in at more than 20 dB over receiver sensitivity, you're safely in business. In our example, we have 80 - 62.84 = 17.16 dBm margin. That's on the edge, but it will probably work. For the Cisco Aironet 340, the 11 Mbps sensitivity is –83 dBm, bringing us up to the comfortable 20 dBm margin.

What if you come up–"under budget?" Just as in monetary budgeting, where you can either increase revenues or cut expenses, in link budgets you can either reduce losses or increase gain. Gain antennas with more than 15 dBi gain are fairly common. Replacing the 15 dBi antennas in the example with a pair of 19 dBi antennas will give you an extra 8 dB of margin. Extra gain margin is good because there will always be factors in a link that you can't quantify, and those factors are rarely in your favor.

Because of the logarithmic nature of path loss, the loss across 2 miles is only 6 dB more than the loss across one mile—so with 8 extra dB of gain you can bridge another mile, with change!

Putting It Together and Testing It Out

As Bill Cosby once said (after talking for a good long while), I told you *that* story so that I could tell you *this* one. Everything in earlier chapters points to the task before you: Assembling, configuring, and testing your wireless local area network. Everything *after* this chapter is refinement, practice, and handy reference.

Basically, it's time to stop theorizing and actually put a network together.

My approach will be the following: First, I'll explain the general issues involved in assembling a network. After that, I'll show you three different networks, with explanations of the specifics for each, with diagrams. Finally, I'll explain how to test networks for throughput.

There's really not a great deal more to it than that. The one exception is security, which is a complex business all by itself. I've devoted Part 3 of this book (Chapters 11 through 15) entirely to Wi-Fi security, both theory and practice. Once you finish implementing your network as explained in this chapter, you should read Part 3 thoroughly, and then enable and configure either Wired Equivalent Privacy (WEP) or (if your hardware supports it) Wi-Fi Protected Access (WPA) as explained in Chapters 13 through 15.

My assumptions going into this chapter are the following:

1. You've read the book this far and have a good working understanding of simple networking and Wi-Fi hardware.

2. At least one of your computers has a standard 10/100Base-T Ethernet wired network adapter. Virtually all current Intel-based Windows

computers come with such an adapter built-in. The computer installed near your router appliance or wireless residential gateway is the one that should have this adapter.

3. You've spent some time thinking about the issues raised in Chapter 4 and you have decided what sort of network you need.

4. You've purchased (or are ready to purchase) your wireless hardware.

Making the instructions in this chapter literal, step-by-step, and "idiot-proof" is impossible. There are too many different Wi-Fi devices, each with its own quirks, to give you instructions that allow you to turn your brain off.

This is why I wrote a book instead of a pamphlet: To give you the background information you'll need to think your way through the network installation process. Success in creating a network rests on a three-legged stool:

1. Your knowledge, coming from places like this book, Web sites, and friends or co-workers who have been through it before.

2. The instructions that come with the network devices you're installing.

3. What your computer tells you about what's going on as you do it.

   In other words, do the research, read the instructions, and pay attention to what's on the screen. If you can integrate those three sources of information, your network is in the bag.

Notes on Platforms

This book is about Windows, because that's where my expertise lies. Both the Macintosh and Linux platforms deserve their own complete books on wireless networking, and I don't believe in trying to cover platforms as radically different as Windows, Mac, and Linux in a single volume.

There are several client-side versions of Windows, and providing detailed instructions on all of them would be difficult. I'm going to emphasize just three: Windows XP, Windows 2000, and Windows 98. Windows XP is the best version of Windows for wireless networking, with Windows 2000 close behind. XP and 2000 are built on the same operating system "chassis," but XP is two years newer, and has additional code to deal with Wi-Fi hardware. Windows 98 is at best so-so in terms of networking support, but a lot of people still use it, so I'll do my best. You're more likely to have problems with Windows 98 than with the others, and if it's possible to upgrade your computer to Windows XP or 2000, that would increase your chances of having a trouble-free network installation.

Windows 95 was created before networking was a commonplace for home offices, and for that reason is mostly hopeless for networking. Windows ME is close enough to Windows 98 so that you should be able to follow my instructions. Keep in mind, however, that Windows ME has terrible reliability problems and I do not recommend using it at all, network or no network. A computer that will run Windows ME will probably run Windows 2000 or XP, and I recommend upgrading to Windows 2000 or XP if you possibly can.

Installing a Small Wi-Fi Network: Overview

The following points provide an overview of the process I've found that works best for small networks. But before you study those points, here is an important meta-point that you shold consider:

Read this whole chapter to the end before you do anything!

Really!

Here's your general *modus operandi*:

1. Begin by installing your router appliance or wireless gateway, which should be installed near where your broadband Internet connection is. If any of your computers have Wi-Fi client adapters already installed, *turn those computers off* while you install the router appliance, gateway, and/or access points.

2. At least one computer must be connected, at least temporarily, to your router or gateway via category 5 Ethernet cable. Configuring a wireless link over the wireless link is just nuts. (This doesn't keep people from trying it.) This computer should not have a wireless client adapter installed yet.

3. Before changing *anything* on your router or computers, write down the existing settings that you're changing. Here's one place where paper trumps silicon every time: Keep your "changes log" on a paper notepad, in pencil.

4. If you already have a router-based network, make sure it's working correctly before attempting to add wireless functionality. DHCP must be enabled and operating.

5. Do your cabling with the power off to *everything*. Plugging and unplugging Ethernet cables with the power on may not physically damage anything, but the devices may get bollixed and post confusing messages on your screen.

6. If you're installing a network with two access points (or more), install one first and then audit the microwave field before installing the others. (I'll explain how to do this later.) It's impossible to tell ahead of time how well an access point will "fill" a structure, what its range is, or where your dead spots will be. *Your advance design is only an educated guess.* Where you mount the second or subsequent access points may depend on how well the first ones cover the required area. And, of course, there's always the chance that a single access point will do the job throughout the coverage area and you won't have to install the others. Still, you may wish to do so for "load balancing" if you have more than five or six client computers connecting wirelessly within the coverage area.

7. Once the access point or gateway has been cabled and powered up, use the computer connected to it via CAT5 cable to configure the access point or gateway. Record what you enter, and the defaults (if any) that you change by doing so. After configuration, test the network to be sure that Internet access works. If more than one computer or device is connected via CAT5 cables to the router appliance, gateway, or other switch or hub, test the wired portion of the network to be sure it's fully operable before installing any Wi-Fi client adapters.

8. Once you have the wired portion of the network installed, configured, and tested, install the first client adapter in one of your other computers. Perform the installation following the instructions provided by the manufacturer for that client adapter, but in general, you should install the drivers and utilities *before* plugging in the adapter itself. If you plug the adapter in first, Windows Plug and Play may install an older set of drivers automatically. If a laptop is among the several computers intended to connect wirelessly to the network, install the laptop client adapter first. This will allow you to audit the field by walking around with the laptop, to be sure the field is sufficiently strong in those locations where other Wi-Fi-connected computers will be based.

9. If your audit of the field looks good, install the other client adapters in your other computers one at a time, bringing each one up and testing it before going on to the next. If you're using Wireless-B, make sure each client computer connects at the top bit rate of 11 Mbps (22 MBps for 802.11b+). If

you're using Wireless-A or Wireless-G, you probably won't connect at the top rate of 54 Mbps everywhere, but you should be able to connect at 18 Mbps or more. If one of your client computers ends up in a weak spot or a dead spot, you may have to add an external antenna (see Chapters 8 and 16) or use a movable client adapter, like a USB or Ethernet adapter.

10. When all client adapters have been installed and their links tested, read Part 3 of this book (Chapters 11 through 15) and then enable either Wired Equivalent Privacy (WEP) or Wi-Fi Protected Access (WPA) for your network.

    Do not skip this step!

11. (Optional) If you're ambitious and reasonably tech-savvy, install the free throughput tester utility QCheck and test your data throughput across all your wireless links. (I explain how to do this later.) Record the results.

At this point, if nothing goes wrong, you're done, and you have a network. Be sure to keep your written notes and change logs in a binder of some kind, along with the rest of your computer configuration notes. Such notes are invaluable later on when things act up (not if), when you upgrade your network gear, or (most of all) when you buy an entirely new computer and want to add it to your network, in addition to or as a replacement for one of your existing computers.

What You'll Need from Your Internet Service Provider

If you're installing a wireless network, you probably already have a broadband Internet connection. When you obtained your broadband connection, your Internet service provider (ISP) gave you several configuration values. These may be listed in a booklet or on a sheet of paper. If not, they are probably accessible from the Windows Control Panel.

The key question is whether your ISP gave you static address information, or requires you to use their remote DHCP server to bring down dynamic address and mask information. The DHCP option makes things much easier. Getting a static IP address is pretty rare these days, and if your Internet connection is fairly new it's extremely unlikely.

However, if you do have static address information, the items you'll need are these. All are "dotted" sequences of four numeric octets, as explained in Chapter 3:

- A primary IP address (something like 264.148.8.221)

- A subnet mask (something like 255.255.255.0 or 255.255.0.0)

- A default gateway address, which is an IP address like but not identical to the primary address

- At least one but more likely two DNS server addresses, which are IP addresses like but not identical to the primary address

If you have a DSL broadband connection, you may have a login username and password as well. This depends entirely on your ISP.

 If you can't find the configuration information that you were given by your ISP, you can find it by looking in the right places in the computer directly connected to your cable/DSL modem. I'll explain how to do this in Appendix C.

I want to re-emphasize that virtually all consumer ISP accounts these days use remote a DHCP server to automatically hand your PC all the important values that it requires, which makes configuration a great deal easier.

Small Things Count!

There are a number of very small hints and disciplines that make computer systems and networks easier to maintain over time. These are general issues, not confined to wireless networks. Let me run through them before we move on and begin construction.

1. Keep a log on paper, not simply of your network installation but of any major configuration change you make to any of your computers and major peripherals. It may sound atavistic, but I keep a paper-based log of my computer and network configuration, changes, release levels, installed software, and so on. I keep it on paper so that even if all of my machines are down and unworkable, I can bring in a new one and start again from scratch.

2. Buy a selection of short CAT5 patch cables in different colors. Get as many colors as you can (I have five) in 3' or 5' lengths. I order them from CDW (**www.cdw.com**) but they are available in many places. The ideal is not to use more than one patch cable of a given color in the cable rats' nest around your router and access point. Record the uses of color in your log: The red cable goes from the router to your access point. The green cable goes from your main computer to your router, and so on. Cables tend to vanish into a shape-

less mess of wiring behind your desk, and it helps to find the "other end" if they're not all gray!

3. If you're using network appliances that "stack" (the Linksys line is the best example—see Figure 9.1) put the wireless unit (gateway or access point) on top. Putting something on top of the wireless box will interfere with the wireless unit's antennas and distort the shape of your microwave field. This may reduce the range of your unit or cause weak or dead spots.

4. Label your wall warts. As you acquire, experiment with, and replace computer gadgetry, sooner or later you will forget which wall-outlet power supply module (which most of us insiders call "wall warts") goes with which computer gadget. The name of the device is almost never on the wall wart, and in recent years even the manufacturer's name is absent. It's just a generic power supply manufacturer's name, plus the (nearly) ubiquitous legend, "Made in China."

Keeping the wart associated with its gadget is critical because the voltage and polarity of wall warts is by no means always the same. Computer devices and their wall warts are a little like Philip Pullman's fantasy characters and their daemons: They go together, and separating them means big trouble. Plug a wall wart into the wrong gadget and it can fry the gadget, so there's plenty of motivation to keep them sorted out.

Figure 9.1
Stacked Network Appliances.

I recommend labeling wall warts with the name of the devices that they came with. I use one of those electronic labelers made by Brother and other firms (see Figure 9.2).

My Three Networks

Wi-Fi-equipped networks for homes and small offices tend to fall into three general models:

1. *The 85% network.* This consists of a wireless gateway at the center, plus some number of computers connected via client adapters. The router is part of the gateway appliance, as is the wireless access point. This type of network is very easy to install, and works well for about 85% of people wishing to install an all-new wireless-capable network for a home office or small office.

2. *The simple add-on Wi-Fi network.* If you already have a wired network with a router appliance in place, you can add a single access point and wireless client adapters without junking your router appliance.

3. *The multi-zone Wi-Fi network.* Whether you already have a wired network in place or not, if you feel that you'll need more than one access point, it's best to use separate access points to handle your wireless connections, and a wired

Figure 9.2
A Labeled Wall Wart.

router/switch appliance to handle routing and wired connections. If you expect to support roaming (see Chapter 6) make sure your access points are of the same manufacturer, model, and firmware release level, with *known* roaming support. Check before you buy!

These are the networks that I will describe in this chapter. They have a lot in common, and even if you intend to install Network #2 or #3, read the section describing the 85% Network first. I won't repeat everything for all three networks.

There are a lot of refinements that you can add if you want, and sometimes you may find that wireless links just aren't possible from certain places. Basements are notoriously difficult, as are garages, and there are peculiar circumstances that you may encounter, like a king-sized waterbed casting a microwave shadow to floors either above or below it. Kitchens cast shadows (mine certainly does!) due to the presence of big refrigerators and cabinets full of pots, pans, and canned goods. You just won't know until you try. Nonetheless, these three "shapes" are the commonest ones, and I'll cover each one separately.

Building the 85% Network

Back in Chapter 4, I described what I call the 85% Network, because it meets the needs of probably 85% of those wanting a home office or very small office network. The core of the system is an all-in-one wireless gateway, which combines a router, a multiport switch (usually with four ports) a wireless access point, and essential firmware services like DHCP and NAT. Such units include the Wireless-B Linksys BEFW11S4, the D-Link DI-614+ (which uses 802.11b+ technology), the D-Link DI-764, the Wireless-G Linksys WRT54G, and numerous others from many manufacturers.

Figure 9.3. shows the cabling required for setting up the 85% network. Typically, there is a computer already installed where your broadband Internet connection's cable or DSL modem is. Absent a network, this computer is connected directly to your broadband modem with a category 5 Ethernet patch cable. The term "RJ-45" applies to the standard Ethernet network socket, into which category 5 Ethernet cables plug. It looks like a wider modular phone jack with more wires. (Ordinary telephone cable is in fact "category 1" in geek speak.)

The wireless gateway appliance becomes the new center point of your network. The broadband modem's "Network" jack is connected via patch cable to the wireless gateway's "WAN" or "Internet" jack. The adjacent computer is connected to one of the ports of the Ethernet switch on the back of the gateway. There are usually four

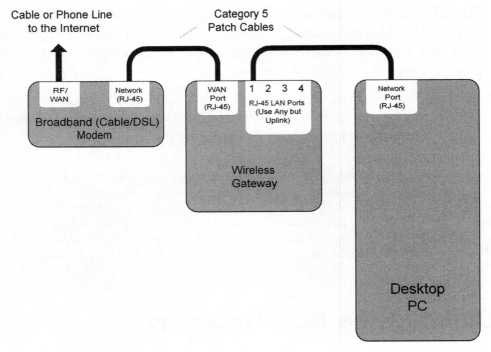

Figure 9.3
Cabling for the 85% Network.

ports (sometimes three, more rarely other numbers) and you can use any port but the one marked "uplink." The uplink port exists to allow you to attach other wired hubs or switches to the gateway, and that should not be necessary for a small home or office network.

The steps involved in setting up this network include:

1. Turn off power to the broadband modem and the computer.

2. Connect the CAT5 patch cables as shown in Figure 9.3.

3. Plug in the wireless gateway's power supply and cable.

4. Power up the broadband modem, and then the computer.

Configuring the Wireless Gateway

Every manufacturer provides instructions for configuring their gateway products, and it's done a little differently for each product. Follow the instructions shipped with the product you're using. I'll run through what's necessary for my favorite Wireless-B gateway product, the Linksys BEFW11S4. Note well that the details of the screens may be different for your own BEFW11S4, if your firmware release level isn't the same as mine. And needless to say, the configuration screens of other Linksys models and other manufacturers' products will be wildly different. The process, however, is broadly the same no matter what gateway you use. Think about what each of the steps below is actually accomplishing, and figure out how to do the same thing for your particular gateway product.

Nearly all current wireless gateway products are configured through an internal Web page. The manufacturer will list a URL containing a non-routable local IP address somewhere in the documentation. For Linksys BEFW11S4 and WRT54G gateways the URL is:

http://192.168.1.1

Bring up a browser on the computer, and enter the configuration URL into the URL entry field. Once you press Enter or click Go, a password dialog will appear (see Figure 9.4).

I show the dialog because I want to impress on you the need to change default values. The default username for Linksys network gear is blank and the default password is "admin." These values are useful to allow you to get into the gateway the first time to configure it, but in the process of configuring it you *must* change those default values to something different. I'll show you how in a moment.

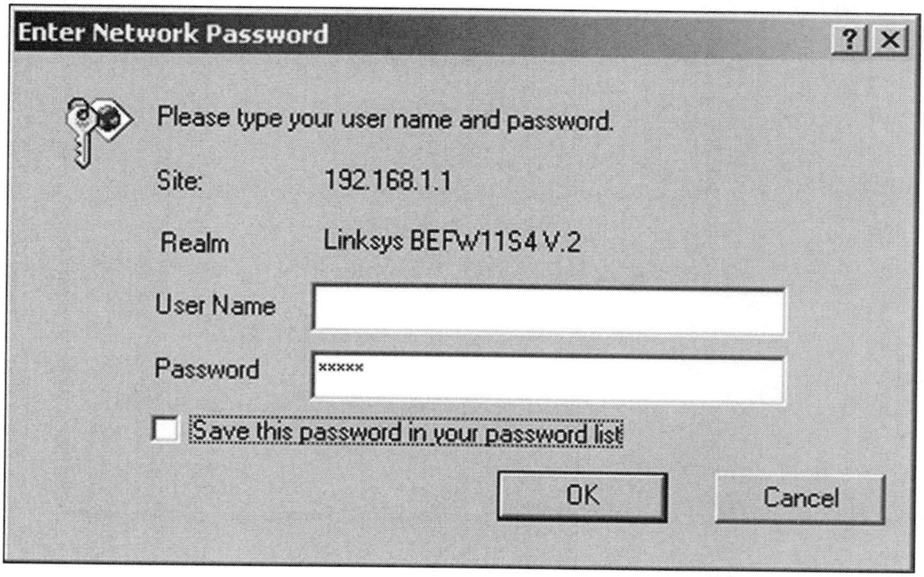

Figure 9.4
The BEFW11S4 Password Dialog.

Once you click OK, the internal Web server on the BEFW11S4 will hand you the screen shown in Figure 9.5. The figure as shown has some example changes in it already.

Once you see the setup screen, start down the list from the top, adding your own information as necessary:

1. If your ISP gave you a hostname or domain name (many do not) enter those.

2. The LAN subnet mask field (under Device IP Address) is *not* the subnet mask used to access the Internet! The default value (255.255.255.0) should not be changed unless you know exactly why and how, and what the consequences will be. If you don't, leave it alone.

3. Change the SSID from the default value ("linksys") to something of your own choosing. Don't give away too much about yourself in your SSID; something generic but memorable is best. I use the names of plants, like "nutmeg" or "coriander."

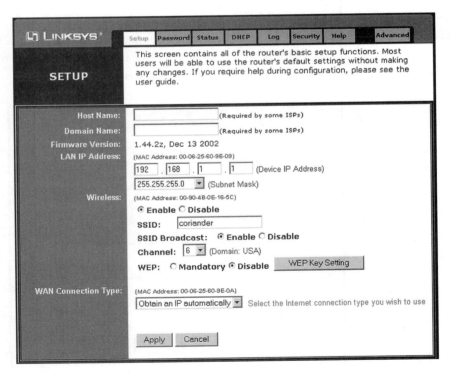

Figure 9.5
The Main Setup Screen for the BEFW11S4.

4. The SSID broadcast is a repeating radio beacon that your gateway sends out every tenth of a second, saying in effect, "I'm here and ready for connections!" This allows "site survey" windows to work, and makes it easy to associate a client adapter to a wireless network by choosing a network from a list. Changing the SSID Broadcast item from Enable to Disable gives you a *very* small security advantage, in that it allows you to hide from really stupid hackers. However, the really stupid hackers aren't the ones you need to worry about, and the smart hackers will find your gateway either way. Outweighing this minuscule security advantage is the fact that turning off the beacon at the beginning of configuration makes it harder to set up your client adapters through site surveys. If you really must turn off the SSID beacon, turn it off *after* your network is fully installed, configured, and running correctly. The rest of this chapter assumes that the SSID beacon is on.

5. Unless you know of other Wi-Fi networks in the vicinity on the same channel, you can safely leave the channel on the default one, which is Channel 6. It can be easily changed in the future if the need arises. However, even if you don't know of any nearby networks, if you live in a condo or townhome, or anywhere you may have close-in neighbors with networks, I recommend changing the default channel to something else. Choose from channels 1, 6, and 11. In other words, if your default channel is 6, change it to 1 or 11. If the default channel is 11, change it to 1 or 6, and so on. 1, 6, and 11 are the only three 2.4 GHz Wi-Fi channels that do not overlap at any point.

6. *Don't enable security yet!* You need to leave it off until all your clients are installed and configured and connecting successfully to the network. Enabling WEP or WPA merits their very own chapters in this book. Once you get to Chapter 15 you'll be able to turn on security with very little difficulty. It must, however, be the very last step you take in configuring your network.

7. Under WAN Connection Type you have several choices, most of which are "special cases" that don't turn up very often. (One is only used in Singapore!) The default is "Obtain an IP automatically" and that's almost certainly what you'll need. If your ISP gave you static address information, you need to pull down the list and select "Static IP." When you do that, the screen will expand, and you will see new empty fields for your IP address, subnet mask, default gateway, and DNS servers. Enter the data into the fields *precisely* as your ISP gave it to you. (A miss—or a bit—is as good as a mile!)

8. Once you get everything entered, click Apply. A "stand by" screen will appear for about 8 seconds, while the gateway is processing the changes. After that, you'll be back at the main setup screen.

The Linksys configuration screen is a tabbed screen, and the Setup tab is only the first of several. Once you're done with the setup screen, click the Password tab. This brings you to the screen where you define the password used to log into the configuration screen. It defaults to "admin." Change it to something you can remember easily but that is hard for other people to guess. I favor "vanity plate" codes for passwords, which use numbers to stand in for letters when the sounds come out right. For example, gr8pl8, pronounced "great plate." A Native American wrote once that he had used imnndn on his license plate. Get it? Think!

Be creative. Don't use your dog's name!

Linksys gathers virtually all the common configuration options on those first two tabs. For virtually all new networks, the rest can be left on their default settings. I should mention that the Status tab is a good place to go to see what the actual parameters are for several values, like your IP address, subnet mask, and other things returned by your ISP's DHCP server. The DHCP Clients Table button at the bottom of the status screen will bring up a window showing what computers have obtained their data, in turn, from the gateway's built-in DHCP server.

At this point, your gateway is configured, with the single (important) exception of security. (You can't set that until all your client adapters are installed, configured, and successfully connected to the network.) Make sure to record all the changes you made on paper for your configuration notebook.

Installing Your Client Adapters

Virtually all access points and wireless gateways are configured through a Web browser, and few require that any additional software be installed. Not so for client adapters: Typically, drivers must be installed for them. (The only exceptions are the fairly uncommon Ethernet client adapters like the Linksys WET11 and the D-Link DWL-810.) Each client adapter comes with installation instructions, and you should follow those instructions as closely as possible.

Windows supports hardware Plug and Play (PnP) in which the computer detects new hardware and installs drivers for it automatically. Windows itself comes with a great many drivers submitted by hardware manufacturers, so for many devices, you can simply run with what Windows has.

Not so for Wi-Fi. The technology is too new, and the software evolves too quickly to let PnP install whatever drivers Windows already has—if anything at all—for a Wi-Fi client. Assuming your client adapter comes with a driver CD, *install its drivers first*, before you install the adapter! At the same time, install any associated software, typically a "client utility" that shows you that the card is working and how strong your wireless signal is.

For best results, I recommend doing it this way:

1. Install the drivers and any associated software from the client's software CD.

2. Shut down the computer completely. (Mandatory before you install PCI cards!)

3. Install the client adapter hardware.

4. Power up and boot the computer. Windows will detect the new client adapter and kick off the PnP wizard. Answer the wizard's questions and Windows will use the drivers you just installed, regardless of whether it had any older drivers present in its database.

If for some reason Windows doesn't auto-detect the new client adapter when you power up, launch the Add/Remove Hardware wizard from Control Panel. I've had some intermittent problems with PnP for Windows 9x versions, for which many people call "Plug and Pray." The Add/Remove Hardware Wizard (called the Add New Hardware wizard in Windows 98) will make another attempt to detect the new device. If the device can't be found, the Wizard will show you lists of hardware already installed to see if the new device, for some reason, was determined to be an "old" device previously installed.

 If you can't get Windows to detect the device, it's possible that the device is electrically dead or defective. Make sure it's getting power and "lights up." For USB and PCMCIA card adapters, make sure they're fully inserted or plugged in. Note that 32-bit Cardbus PC card adapters will not completely insert into 16-bit pre-Cardbus slots. They will go in almost all the way, but will stop about 1/8" short of what should be their final position, and will make no electrical contact with the computer, and thus will appear to be dead. Old PC cards will work in new computers; new PC cards will often not work in old computers!

Configuring Your Client Adapters

Once the client adapter and its drivers have been installed, you need to configure the client adapter itself. Nearly all client adapters come with a client utility, which you use to configure the adapter. The client utility installs with the drivers. A heads-up here: Windows XP has such complete built-in support for wireless networking that many client adapters do not install their own client utility under XP. The D-Link DWL-650+ is a good example: It installs a client utility under Windows 2000 and 98 (and other older versions as well), but not under XP. For this example, I'll show you how the DWL-650+ client adapter is configured on both Windows XP (using Windows built-in support) and Windows 2000 and 98, using the D-Link client utility.

Configuring Windows XP

XP makes it easy. When you power up the PC after installing the client adapter and its drivers, and worked your way through the PnP wizard, Windows will display a small "talk balloon" pointing toward a network icon in the taskbar tray. The talk balloon instructs you to click on the icon to connect to a wireless network. Click the icon, and you'll see the window shown in Figure 9.6.

This is the Windows XP *site survey* window. It will display the SSID of any wireless network that is within range, assuming its SSID broadcast beacon is enabled. (This is why you shouldn't disable the SSID broadcast beacon until *after* all your clients are connected!) In most cases you'll only see your own gateway's SSID in the survey.

Figure 9.6
The Windows XP Site Survey and Connect Window.

If you have close neighbors with Wi-Fi networks, they may be listed as well. If you didn't change your gateway SSID when you installed it, it's possible that you may see two or more networks with the same (default) SSID, and it may not be the least bit obvious which one is yours!

Windows (rightfully) warns you that your gateway does not have security enabled, and that the connection is not secure from outside monitoring. We know that; all in good time. If you check the "allow me to connect" check box, the Connect button will become active, and you can click the button to connect. After you click Connect, Windows will establish a connection to your gateway, and another talk balloon will appear over the taskbar tray network icon, indicating that you're now connected.

XP's site survey window does most of your client adapter configuration for you, in that it sets the SSID from the network you chose from the list presented in the site survey. To finish configuration, you need to bring up the Network Connections applet from the Control Panel. Note well that until you go in to configure WEP or WPA security later on, there aren't any crucial configuration items remaining. The Network Connections applet is necessary if you wish to:

- Set your client adapter to ad hoc mode

- Change the "desired SSID" that your adapter is to look for and connect to when it powers up

- Change to short preambles

Other technical options are available but these are the most important, and the others are almost never changed in ordinary use.

Once the Network Connections applet is running, find your Wi-Fi client adapter on the list of network adapters, right-click on it, and select Properties from the context menu. Your wireless adapter will be named in a box at the top of the Properties window, above a button labeled Configure. If you click Configure, you'll see a multi-tab properties window for your client adapter. Click on the Advanced tab. You'll see the window shown in Figure 9.7.

This window presents a list of named properties on the left. Select a property, and its current value is shown on the right. To change the selected property, simply type a new value into the edit field on the right, and click OK. Note that you can only change one property value at a time. Click OK after changing each one or only the last one you change will "stick."

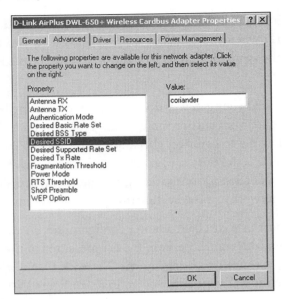

Figure 9.7
The Advanced Wireless Hardware Configuration Window.

Windows Versions Other than XP

Only Windows XP has a level of wireless networking support good enough to make client utilities unnecessary. For all other Windows versions, you *must* install and use the client utility. Client utilities are typically installed when you install the drivers for a client adapter. Each manufacturer has its own client utility, and for this example I'll use the D-Link client utility, as installed for the DWL-650+ Cardbus PC card client adapter.

D-Link's client utility posts a signal strength icon in the taskbar tray, and you must launch the client utility window by double clicking on the taskbar tray icon. When the window appears, click the Site Survey link in the left margin. You'll see the display shown in Figure 9.8.

Click the Refresh button to make sure the displayed information is current. Your network SSID should appear in the site survey list. If it doesn't, you're either out of range of the access point or gateway, or you turned off the SSID beacon broadcast. You may also see close-in Wi-Fi networks belonging to your neighbors. Highlight your own network and click Connect.

The client utility will bring up the screen shown in Figure 9.9. All the common configuration options will be listed. Note that some are "read-only" and cannot be changed. Settings like the SSID, mode and channel are controlled by the access point or gateway.

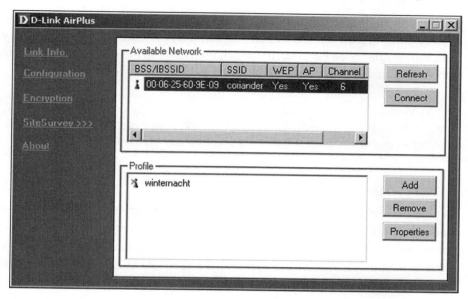

Figure 9.8
The D-Link DWL-650+ Site Survey Window.

At the top will be a profile name; it defaults to the SSID of your network, but you can change it (for example, to "Home" or "Office" or "Chicago Site") as appropriate. When you click OK, the utility will store the settings displayed in that window to a

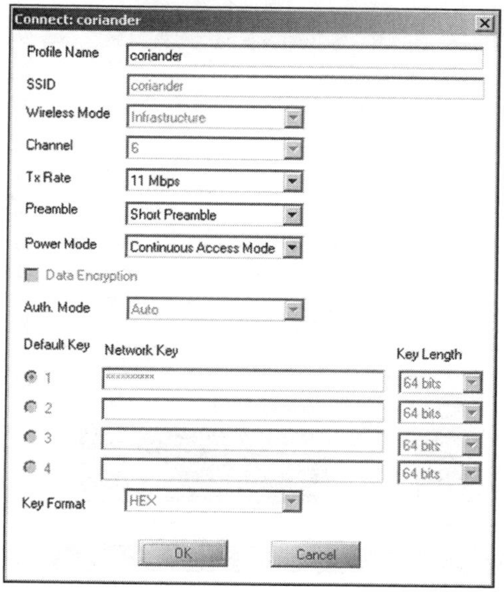

Figure 9.9
The D-Link Client Configuration Window.

profile with the name you left in the top field, and connect to the network you selected from the site survey. When you connect, the client utility will display the Link Info window (see Figure 9.10) which includes a signal strength and link quality display, and time-scrolling graphs showing packet activity over the network.

As good as Windows XP's built-in support for wireless networking may be, XP lacks the nice touches that the better client utilities provide, like D-Link's data rate graphics. This is why I prefer to use the manufacturer's provided client utility even under XP, when that's possible.

Auditing the Field

It's possible—even likely, in modest sized homes and very small office suites—that once you install and configure your client adapters, everything will connect to your gateway without a struggle, and your network will be almost done. (*Almost*—don't forget to read Part 3 about wireless security, and enable WEP or WPA encryption!) However, sometimes you'll find that one of your client computers lies in a weak or dead spot, and you won't be connecting at the top bit rate, or possibly not connecting at all. This is where the notion of "auditing the field" becomes important.

To "audit the field" is a geeky way of saying, "walk around with a laptop, checking the microwave field strength from your access point or gateway." As I've described in many other places in this book, your physical environment *powerfully* affects the

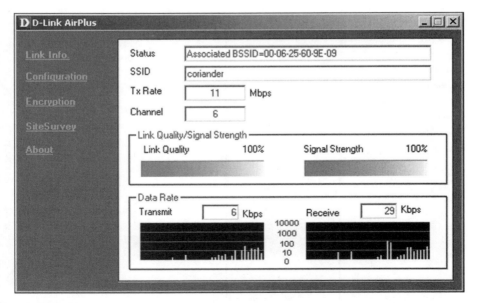

Figure 9.10
The D-Link Link Info Window.

quality of your connections. Many new-construction office buildings use steel framing members rather than 2 x 4s, and filing cabinets and modular cubicle walls often contain a lot of metal. Your coverage in a metal-rich environment will be hard to predict, at very least—and some places may be very difficult to reach with a low-power Wi-Fi signal.

You simply won't know until you "go look." You can perform a field audit with the field-strength graphs your client utility provides (see Figure 9.10 for an example from D-Link) but by far and away the best field auditing tool I've ever used is NetStumbler. I explain how to install and use NetStumbler in great detail in Chapters 19 and 20. It's free and very powerful, but its main drawback is that it doesn't work with all client adapters. If you do have a supported client adapter, nothing even comes close.

Audits can be as formal or as casual as you prefer. Some people print out a plan of their home or office and take readings at carefully indicated points (intersection of halls, center of the conference room, by the front door, and so on) and mark a dBm reading on the plan at those points. Take enough readings and you can create a rough drawing of the shape of the field by drawing lines connecting similar readings, like the elevation isoclines on a topographic map.

Most of the time, you're mainly interested in the useful outer boundaries of the field (in other words, how far away from the gateway or access point your microwave field extends) and where the dead spots are.

Here are some tips for auditing your field:

- Don't take a reading while you're moving. Stand still and give the laptop and its client adapter a few seconds to work. Take note of the reading before moving away again.

- The field can change significantly across just a foot or two of distance. If you have a dead spot, check the field two or three feet in any direction to see if the field comes up. Sometimes (generally near large metal objects) a distance of as little as a foot can make a radical difference.

- If you're checking a work location (desk or cubicle) check the field with the laptop in the typical computer position and yourself in the chair where a person would sit and work. People are mostly water, and water-filled objects can affect the strength of the field, especially on the fringes. (Staffers who are largely filled with hot air will affect the field much less!)

- If you're trying to map the general field dropoff with distance, or the outer boundaries of the field, don't take a reading right next to large metal objects or large containers full of water. Stay at least two feet away from refrigerators, large file cabinets, safes, aquariums, large machinery, or vehicles. Especially on the fringes of a field, large quantities of intervening metal or water distort the field and make the readings difficult to interpret. (Ponds or pools of water at ground level are not an issue unless you're trying to read a signal through them.)

- Keep in mind that the antennas in PC card client adapters used in laptops are close to worst-case. Almost any other kind of Wi-Fi antenna is better. If you read a weak or dead spot with a laptop PC card, a client adapter with a vertical antenna (like a USB or PCI adapter) will almost certainly do better. Field boundaries mapped with a PC card in a laptop will be *minimum* boundaries. If you need to map the *useful* boundaries of a field (say, for security purposes or implementation of a network with multiple access points) use an external antenna or an external adapter with an external (ideally vertical) antenna. I've used a Linksys WUSB11 USB client adapter literally taped to my belt to audit fields, and the readings obtained are much more "real life."

Once all of your clients are connecting to the gateway at top or near-top (for Wireless-A and Wireless-G networks) bit rates, your network is done. One last task: Read Part 3 of this book and enable security!

Building an Add-On Wi-Fi Network

Network #2 is really a simple add-on network to a wired network that you already have in place and working. The primary difference is that you add a wireless access point to your existing wired network rather than create the network around a single wireless gateway appliance.

I won't repeat everything I said about implementing the 85% network, even though most of it applies. Before building the add-on Wi-Fi network, read the part of this chapter describing implementation of the 85% network.

Most home office and small office wired networks that have an Internet connection are built around a combination router/switch appliance. The Linksys BEFSR41 is typical and extremely popular, and I have used them very successfully in small network installations for several years now. Many other similar products exist. The feature set common to all is this:

- An IP router, with a WAN port for connection to an outside IP-based network like the Internet.

- An Ethernet switch, usually with four ports. Products with 3, 5, and 8 ports are also common.

- A Network Address Translation (NAT) server, for sharing an Internet connection and isolating individual networked devices from direct connection over the Internet.

- A DHCP server, for providing networked devices with IP address, mask, and gateway information.

Cabling an Add-On Network

Creating the Wi-Fi portion of the network consists of adding a wireless access point and one or more Wi-Fi client adapters to computers in the vicinity. The bare minimum cabling of a typical wired + Wi-Fi network is shown in Figure 9.11.

Basically, you connect the access point to one of the switch ports on the router/ switch appliance, using a category 5 (CAT5) patch cable. Figure 9.11 shows only one computer on the wired network, but additional wired computers or printers may be connected using open ports on the router.

Adding Additional Wired Ports through the Uplink Port

On the other hand, if you already have a wired network, all of your switched ports may be in use. If you need more wired ports than the router/switch appliance has, most such devices have an *uplink port* for daisy-chaining additional switches or hubs to add additional wired ports. You connect a CAT5 patch cable from the uplink port on your router/switch appliance to any free port on the additional hub or switch.

One caution: In virtually all devices having an uplink port, the port physically adjacent to the uplink port is tied to it internally, and the two are really one port. You cannot use both the uplink port and its adjacent associated port at the same time. On the Linksys BEFSR41, for example, switch port #4 is tied to the uplink port. If you use the uplink port to attach an additional switch or hub, you must leave port 4 on the BEFSR41 empty. Figure 9.12 shows the details of using the router appliance's uplink port to attach an additional switch or hub to the network. Most of the unnecessary details in the figure have been removed for clarity's sake.

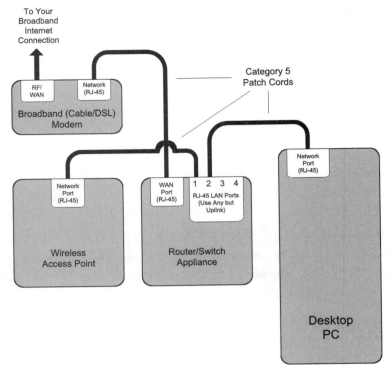

Figure 9.11
An Add-On Wi-Fi Network.

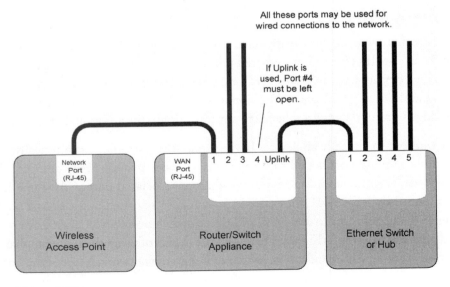

Figure 9.12
Using the Router Uplink Port to Add a Switch.

You can connect either a hub or a switch to the uplink port, but I powerfully recommend buying an Ethernet switch rather than a hub. (The switch I recommend is the Linksys EZXS55W 5-port model. A similar 8-port model is the EZXS88W. Except for the number of ports, they are identical.) All devices connected through a hub share the total bandwidth of the hub, whereas a switch creates temporary full-bandwidth connections between switched devices.

You may use as much as 300 feet of CAT5 cable between switch ports, but hubs should be on a much shorter leash. The rule of thumb is to keep hubs on no more than 50 feet of cable, or 15 feet if you daisy chain a hub onto an existing hub.

Configuration Screen Subnet Conflicts

Most low-cost gateways, router appliances, and access points come out of the box with their configuration screens "hard-coded" to a particular local IP address. (In other words, you type **http://192.168.1.1** into a Web browser to bring up the configuration screens.) This is a mixed blessing. It makes tech support much easier on the manufacturer, but if one device has a configuration address in a different subnet from another on the same network, there can be trouble.

The way things *should* be done is for the access point to request IP address data from the router appliance's DHCP server when it powers up. This is how the Cisco Aironet 340 access points work. To configure the 340, you must inspect the router's DHCP clients table to see what the access point's IP address is, and then build that address into a URL. That's a lot to ask of a non-technical newcomer to networking, so manufacturers of consumer-class networking equipment prefer to go with a fixed local IP address.

The most notorious problem of this type is the configuration address incompatibility between the Linksys series of routers and gateways and D-Link access points. Most Linksys routers and gateways respond to the local IP address 192.168.1.1. The D-Link DWL-900AP+ access point responds to the address 192.168.0.50. The two addresses are not in the same subnet, given the nearly universal subnet mask of 255.255.255.0. If you plug the D-Link AP into a Linksys router, the router will not be able to route packets to the AP, and thus you won't be able to bring up the D-Link configuration screen in a browser window. (Changing the subnet mask has other consequences, and I don't recommend it.)

If you run across a situation like this, try the following:

1. Boot a computer having a standard Ethernet port, without connecting to any network, wired or wireless. (Laptops work well for this.) If a Wi-Fi PC card or USB client adapter is present in the computer, pull it before you boot. If there's an internal Wi-Fi adapter, disable it. You do *not* want to connect to your network!

2. Connect the access point to the computer's Ethernet port through a *crossover* CAT5 cable. These can be had at any Best Buy or CompUSA store, and you should have one in your networking toolkit. They look like standard CAT5 cables externally, but the orientation of the transmit/receive wire pairs is reversed internally. A crossover cable allows you to connect an AP to your computer (or any Ethernet port to any other Ethernet port) without connecting through a hub or switch.

3. Browse the network adapters in the computer, and bring up the TCP/IP Properties window for the TCP/IP protocol bound to the computer's Ethernet port. If you're not familiar with this window, it is shown in the two figures in Appendix C at the end of this book, with instructions on how to navigate to the window from the Windows 2000, XP, and 98 desktops.

4. On the General tab of the TCP/IP Properties window, click Use the Following IP Address, and in the field below enter an IP address for the computer that is in the same range with the address of the AP you're trying to configure. Try a number one less than the AP's preset IP address. For example, for an address of 192.168.0.50, use 192.168.0.49.

5. Enter a compatible subnet mask, usually 255.255.255.0. You don't need to enter any DNS server addresses. Click OK on that and the previous windows until you're back to the desktop. Give the system 30 seconds or so to sort things out and get itself configured with the new address.

6. Bring up a Web browser, and enter the AP's configuration address. If you gave the computer an IP address in the same range, the AP's configuration screen should appear. Log in, and configure the AP to request IP address information from the local DHCP server. Make sure you click on OK (or whatever the AP offers you) to store the changes you made. The changes should now be stored in the AP's flash memory, and will remain even after you power down the AP.

7. Disconnect the AP from the crossover cable, and connect it via standard CAT5 patch cable to an open switch port in your router or gateway. Power the AP up. Give it a minute to request an IP address from the router or gateway's

DHCP server, then inspect the DHCP clients table to see what the AP's new IP address is. Use that address going forward to make additional configuration changes to the AP.

It's a real nuisance dealing with conflicts like this, and this is yet another reason—an extremely potent one—to use as much gear as possible from the same manufacturer. At the very least, get your router appliance and all access points from the same vendor. In an all-Linksys or all-D-link network, problems like this do not arise, because within a company's product line, the devices all respond to IP addresses in the same range and subnet.

Finishing off the Add-On Network

Once you get everything cabled up, and are able to reach the configuration screen of your new AP, configure the rest of the network as explained in the earlier section on the 85% network: Configure the access point and then configure your several client adapters.

The nice thing about an add-on network like this having a wired router appliance and a separate wireless access point is that you can add additional *identical* access points to the network in the future to expand coverage or do manual load balancing. I think it's very important that all access points in a network be of the same manufacturer, model, and firmware release level, especially if the access points need to cooperate somehow, as in roaming.

To learn how to build such a *multi-zone* network, read on.

Building the Multi-Zone Wi-Fi Network

There are two general reasons for having more than one wireless access point in a network:

1. Covering a wider physical area; that is, more space.

2. Providing additional bandwidth so that more computers can connect to the network at useful throughput levels, even if they're close enough to reach a single access point.

Roaming

If you simply need to cover a larger home or office, any access points will do. This is especially true if you don't need to support *roaming*, that is, the ability to walk around with a laptop or Wi-Fi equipped PDA and not lose your connection when you move from the field of one access point to another. Without roaming, you must move to a location and log into the network from that location. Move out of the field of the access point to which you're connected, and your connection vanishes, and you must re-connect from a new location in the field of a different access point.

Roaming has not been implemented consistently on low-end access points. Higher-end products (like those from Cisco and Proxim) implement proprietary solutions for roaming that work, but *only* work when *all* access points are "in the family" and support the proprietary technology. In August 2003, the IEEE 802.11f task group completed defining the Inter Access Point Protocol (IAPP) that will standardize 802.11 roaming, but 802.11f is still very new and has not yet been implemented broadly. Furthermore, roaming as a feature is not much needed in home or small office networks, and thus lower-end wireless gateways and access points may never actually be upgraded to support it.

All of this is just to say: If you want *reliable* roaming, you will have to spend big. Cisco Aironet 350 access points cost $600, not $100, because they support more features—and because they're targeted at corporations more willing to spend money than ordinary people.

The other reason for implementing a multi-zone network may take some explaining. Say you have a cube farm in your office with fifteen workers, each with a computer that needs to be networked through a wireless access point. If all fifteen workers connect to one access point, all fifteen would share that access point's throughput, which—for a Wireless-B access point—might be only 4 Mbps. (I cover measurement of throughput later in this chapter.) You might as well put them all on a dialup, especially if their work involves lots of heavy communication among their computers.

Load Balancing

Load balancing in this context means arranging a network so that multiple access points are installed in the same general area, and connections from wireless clients are distributed evenly among them. With three access points, you could have five clients connected to each access point, and your fifteen workers would all have a reasonably brisk network connection.

Load balancing is not a part of the 802.11 specification, and in my experiments has proven remarkably difficult to pull off with low-end hardware. The problem is that in a network with multiple access points, Wi-Fi client adapters want to connect to the access point with the strongest signal. Most client adapters provide no way to force them to associate with a particular access point when several are present on the same network. As with roaming, the higher-end access points from companies like Cisco and Proxim support load balancing through proprietary technology, either from a centrally administered utility or by manually assigning individual client adapters to access points by MAC address. On consumer-class access points, MAC address filtering is the only practical way to implement load balancing. You basically decide which computers are to connect to which access points, and give each access point a list of allowable MAC addresses, which you must harvest from the computers in question. This is done by running the ipconfig.exe utility with the –all parameter on each PC. I discuss load balancing in more detail later in this chapter.

 Be aware that there are only three channels on the 2.4 GHz Wi-Fi band that do not overlap in frequency and thus do not interfere with one another: 1, 6, and 11. Doing load balancing with more than three access points in the same area gets very dicey. My suggestion: Move to a technology such as Wireless-A or Wireless-G, which provide much higher throughput, and allow more client computers to connect to a single access point.

Cabling a Multi-Zone Network

In general terms, you create a multi-zone network by connecting multiple access points to your router/switch appliance or uplinked switches. A single run of Ethernet cable can go 300 feet before you start having problems, but a switch acts as a repeater and regenerates the signals passing through it. I like to keep single runs of CAT 5 cable to 150 feet where possible. If you need a longer run (and that's a *big* house!), uplink to a switch and continue the run from the switch. A simple cabling example is shown in Figure 9.13.

Running cables in office suites is usually pretty easy: Most modern construction has dropped or suspended ceilings over which cable can be run very easily. I did a lot of this years back, when we were still running RG-58 ThinNet coaxial cables, and while it can be dusty work it's no more difficult than pushing up the next ceiling panel a few inches and yanking the cable another two or three feet toward its destination.

Running a CAT5 cable to a second access point elsewhere in the house can be a challenge, especially if you don't have a convenient attic or basement for horizontal runs and access to the spaces inside walls for vertical runs. This is why for home installations I recommend installing your first access point near your broadband Internet modem, and then auditing the field in the rest of the house to be sure you really need additional access points. If you have an office or a bedroom on the fringe of your access point's useful field, weigh the cost and difficulty of cutting holes in the walls and pulling cables against the (minor) inconvenience of adding external antennas to the computers out on the fringe.

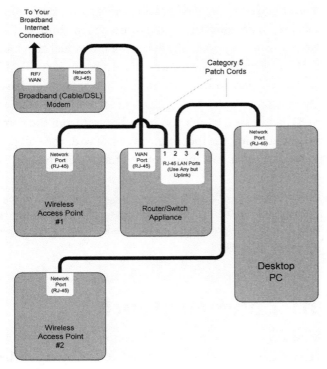

Figure 9.13
A Simple Multi-Zone Wi-Fi Network.

Here's a caution for amateur electricians. Do not attempt to pull CAT5 cable through a conduit already containing (or due to contain) AC power wiring! This is against all conceivable building codes, and a minor nick in the power cables' insulation could put 120V on your network conductors, destroying equipment and causing a potentially lethal safety hazard.

HomePlug Powerline Networking

Ironically, there are recent technologies that safely mix AC power and network data, by transmitting data over an RF signal conducted on power mains. Powerline networking is somewhat outside the charter of this book, but if you can't pull cable it might be an option to get data to the far corners of your mansion. The Homeplug Powerline Alliance acts like the Wi-Fi alliance to certify powerline networking products as compliant with the HomePlug standard. Linksys and Netgear are major players here, with full products lines that you can read about on their Web sites. HomePlug devices operate at a bit rate of up to 14 Mbps (somewhat faster than Wireless-B) and can bridge to a wired network. You can use a pair of HomePlug

Ethernet bridges to bring Ethernet data from your router to a wireless access point elsewhere in the house. Figure 9.14 shows schematically how this might be done.

The power lines carry Ethernet data from one bridge to another, just as a wireless bridge (like the Linksys WET11) would do, but without dead spots and interference from nearby electronic equipment. Alas, the technology is still fairly expensive: The Linksys PLEBR10 PowerLine EtherFast bridge costs about $80, and two are required for a connection through your home power lines.

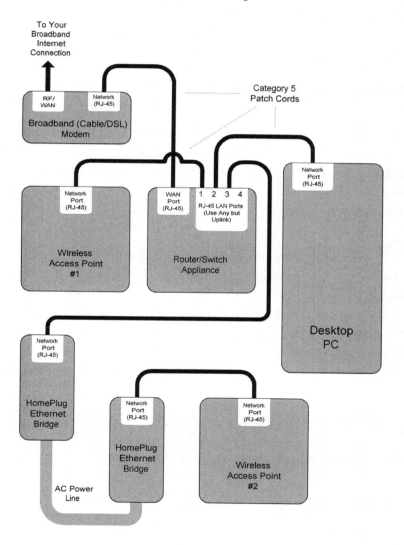

Figure 9.14
Using a HomePlug Powerline Link.

See these Web URLs for more information:

Homeplug Powerline Alliance **www.homeplug.org/index_basic.html**

Powerline Networking Test Drive **www.extremetech.comarticle 20,3973,9262,00.asp**

Powerline Technology eLibrary **www.homeplugandplay.com/index.shtml**

Access Point Configuration

There's nothing particularly difficult about configuring a network for multiple access points. Here are the major issues:

- All access points must have the same SSID value, because they all belong to the same network, and the SSID is the network—not the access point—ID.

- If the fields of the access points adjoin at any point, adjoining access points must be set to operate on non-overlapping channels. There are only three such channels (1,6, and 11) so if your network is to include more than three access points, you must begin paying attention to the geometry of the network, and where fields intersect. Turn back to Chapter 4 and Figure 4.5 to see how this is done.

- If your access points support the feature, give them descriptive names. This name is specific to the access point and should not be the same as the SSID. The name will be displayed in the DHCP clients list, and will allow you to tell which client is which without having to check a naked MAC address against a list relating devices to MAC addresses. Irrespective of how it's labeled by some access points, this name is not technically a hostname, and you can't ping the name over the network. (You can still ping an access point by using its local IP address, however.)

As long as you don't need to do anything exotic (like roaming) or something outside the Wi-Fi standard, that's about all you need to do. A client adapter can connect to your network from anywhere that lies within range of one of the network's access points.

Configuring Client Adapters

A Wi-Fi client adapter needs an SSID and nothing else to connect to an access point. (It also needs the security system encryption keys, assuming WEP or WPA is enabled for the access point. More on this in Part III.) If you're not concerned about which access point a given client connects to, there's not much else to do.

Left to their own devices, client adapters will choose which access point to connect to, typically in terms of signal strength: A client will choose the strongest signal it can hear from its location. Forcing a client to connect to a specific access point is more difficult than it should be. With some higher-end client adapters, there is a specific configuration parameter into which you enter the MAC address of the access point that you want the client to connect to. The Cisco 340 client adapters provide this parameter as part of the client profile. Figure 9.15 shows one of the client profile edit screens. Note the list of four fields labeled "Specified Access Point." You can set the order in which you want the client to choose an access point from the list of four. If it can hear and connect to #1, it will go with #1. If it can't hear or for some other reason connect to #1, it will try connecting to #2, and so on down the list. If it can't connect to any access point on the list, it will consider itself free to connect to any access point in the network that it can hear. (It will not, of course, try to go outside the network to something with an SSID different from the one specified in the profile.)

Cisco's system is the high road and it works very well. For access points without this feature, you must use MAC address filtering. MAC address filters are worthless for security purposes; that is, to keep out motivated hackers. (Dumb hackers maybe, but those you don't really need to worry about.) However, you can set an access point's filter to refuse connection from any client adapter not on its list.

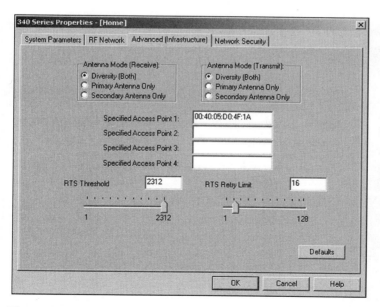

Figure 9.15
Specifying an Access Point for Client Connection.

This works. The downside is that there is no provision for fallback, as there is with Cisco's system of specified access points. If all access points but one refuse a client adapter, and that client adapter's own access point fails or otherwise becomes inaccessible, that client cannot connect to the network and is left out in the cold.

Every access point handles MAC address filtering in a slightly different way. Typically, you must manually enter the Mac addresses of the client adapters you want to allow to connect to the access point. Some access points, however, will show you a list of client adapters connected to them, and allow you to pick clients from the list to add to a MAC address filter. The D-Link DWL-900AP+ is particularly good at this (see Figure 9.16).

The MAC addresses of all clients connected to the access point are contained in the drop-down list labeled "Connected PCs." By clicking the Clone button, the displayed MAC address is added to one of the two MAC address filters (allow and deny) as desired.

Once you have all your clients up and running and connecting to your access points, your network is ready to secure. Read Part III on Wi-Fi security, and enable either Wired Equivalent Privacy (WEP) or Wi-Fi Protected Access (WPA) for your network. (Older gear will not give you the option of WPA, and you'll be stuck with WEP.)

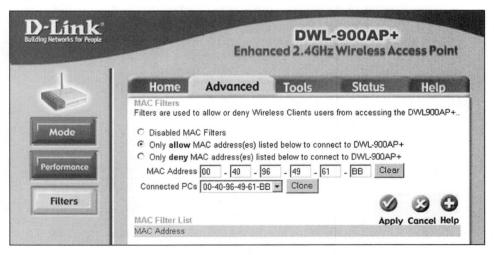

Figure 9.16
Choosing Clients for a MAC Address Filter.

If Things Don't Work...

The first time you install and configure a client adapter, it may not automatically connect to your access point or gateway. The easy way to connect is to bring up XP's site survey (or the client utility's site survey under other Windows versions) and choose a wireless network to connect to. This works most of the time. If it doesn't, here are some things to try:

- If you don't see your network SSID in a site survey window, check to be sure you haven't turned off the SSID beacon broadcast at the access point or gateway. If the beacon is on but you don't see the network, you're either in a dead spot or outside the useful boundaries of your access point or gateway's microwave field. Audit the field (as explained earlier) to see if you can mount an external antenna a little to one side or another and possibly finesse the dead spot.

- If a client adapter won't connect, make sure that you're not trying to connect a Wireless-B client to a G-only network. If you must mix Wireless-B and Wireless-G in the same network, the gateway or access point must be set to "mixed" B and G mode. Needless to say, a Wireless-B or Wireless-G client cannot ever connect to a Wireless-A access point. (Note: There are access points that provide both A and G radios, but what I mean here is that a Wireless-B client cannot connect to a Wireless-A radio, which for most Wireless-A access points is all you get on the radio side.)

- Windows XP has an option called "Repair This Connection," which you'll find in the Network Tasks pane of the Network Connections window when you select a particular network connection. When you click Repair Connection, XP probes the connection, refreshes some settings, and does whatever it can to make the connection work. I found this makes connections work most of the time, and if you're using XP it should be your first troubleshooting step.

- If you're running Windows 98, try running the Internet Connection Wizard. Windows may have some settings in place from a dialup connection or an earlier lack of any networking connection. Make sure you answer that you're connecting through a LAN when the wizard asks, and tell it to discover the proxy server automatically. (Most of the rest of the wizard is an attempt by Microsoft to sell Internet accounts.) This should definitely be your first troubleshooting step under Windows 98.

- Power down and reboot the balky computer and try again. This is a good way to request new IP address information from your local router's DHCP server, which can solve certain disconnects between a client machine and your router. (These can happen if you're configuring your router or gateway.)

- Make sure you do not have two DHCP servers operating at once. Many Wi-Fi access points contain DHCP servers, and although they almost always default to being disabled, if they become enabled somehow (typically by mistake—you meant to click something else!) computers on your network can get very confused.

- Make sure everything is completely plugged in (especially USB and PC card adapters), is getting power, has its antennas securely attached, and so on. Give every CAT 5 connector in the network a little shove to make sure it's fully seated.

- As a last resort, consider reinstalling the operating system on the computer that won't connect. I was forced to do this for Windows 2000 once, after it simply would not propagate the machine hostname across the network. Something in Windows had become corrupt, and reinstalling Windows put it right.

One thing you need to keep in mind as you assemble, configure, and troubleshoot networks: *It takes time for certain things to happen.* An access point doesn't necessarily receive an IP address from the local DHCP server the absolute bleeding instant you plug it into your network. Give it a minute before you panic and assume something is wrong. Setting a static IP address may require as much as 30 seconds on slower machines to "take." Don't despair and reboot too soon.

The MAC Address Authentication Problem

If you already have a broadband Internet connection (especially a cable modem connection) and are creating your very first network, you may run into a particular problem that has nothing to do with your network per se. The symptoms are simple to describe: You set up your network, and even though all computers connected through your home network can see and contact all the other computers, no computer can connect to the Internet.

This problem comes up on certain cable TV networks offering Internet service. I have personally encountered this problem on both Cox Cable in Arizona and Adelphia Cable in Colorado. What happens is this: The cable company uses the MAC address on your PC's network adapter to identify your PC to the network. This makes it more difficult for people to tap into the cable and freeload on the cable company's Internet service. The problem arises when you insert a router appliance or wireless gateway between the cable modem and your PC. The router appliance or gateway has its own unique MAC address, and this is not the MAC address that the cable system expects to see when a computer connects to the Internet from your home. Suspecting a freeloader, the cable's authentication machinery denies access to the Internet.

I've drawn this out in a diagram in Figure 9.17. The top half of the figure shows the original broadband Internet connection as installed by the Cable Guy. The cable system asks for a MAC address, and your PC responds with its network adapter's MAC address. Everything's fine. The lower half of the figure shows the situation after you install a wireless gateway. The cable system asks for a MAC address, and the wireless gateway replies with its own, but the gateway's MAC address is not the one the cable system is looking for. What to do, what to do?

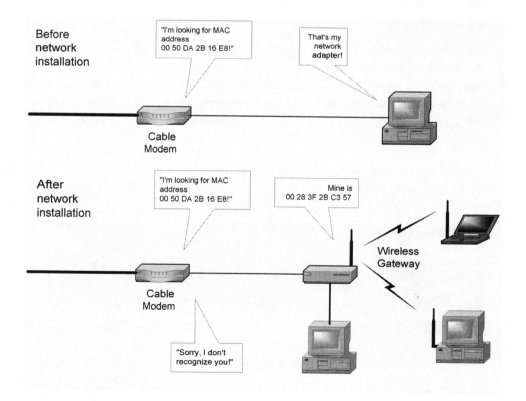

Figure 9.17
How a Wireless Network Breaks Cable System Authentication.

The solution to this problem lies in something called *MAC address cloning*. Almost every router appliance and wireless gateway that you can buy provides the ability to change the MAC address that the router or gateway presents when queried. What you do is determine the MAC address of your PC's network adapter, and then "clone" that MAC address in the router or gateway.

Determining your PC network adapter MAC address is easy. For Windows NT, 2000, and XP, you bring up a command prompt window and enter the command:

```
ipconfig -all
```

Look for the label "Physical address" in the display. The hyphenated number after the label is the network adapter MAC address.

For Windows 9x, you must run the little utility program winipcfg. From the window that appears, select "Ethernet adapter" from the drop-down list. The MAC address will be shown below the drop-down list, by the label "Adapter Address."

Once you have your PC's network adapter MAC address, you must enter it into the "Clone MAC Address" field in the configuration page of your router appliance or wireless gateway. This will look different for every product, and you will have to peruse the Help files or poke around the configuration tabs until you find it. Figure 9.18 shows how it looks in the configuration page of the Linksys WRT54G Wireless-G gateway.

The WRT54G has a *very* nice feature that makes searching for your PC's MAC address unnecessary: If you click on the button labeled "Clone your PC's MAC" the WRT54G will "automagically" go out and query your PC for its network address.

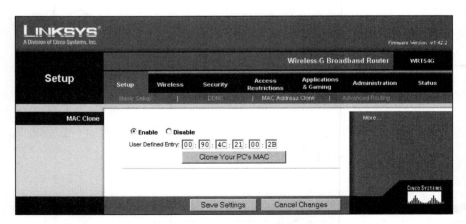

Figure 9.18
Cloning a MAC Address on the WRT54G.

(This assumes, of course, that your PC is connected via CAT 5 cable to the WRT54G!)

For routers and gateways that do not provide that feature, you will have to manually type the PC network adapter's MAC address into the provided field.

Once you've cloned your PC network adapter MAC address into your router or gateway, power everything down (including the cable modem) and power it up again. This time, when the cable system asks the router or gateway for its MAC address, it will respond with the MAC address you entered into the Clone MAC Address field. If you entered it correctly, the problem will be solved, and the cable system will let your network connect to the Internet.

The Weirdness of Networking

I hate to say it, but networking can be a pretty freaky thing. If you spend enough time fooling with networks, and mix enough technologies, things will happen that defy easy analysis and troubleshooting. This is why you *must* keep on studying, and learn networking as deeply as you can find the time and intestinal fortitude to do. Even the experts encounter problems that they never entirely understand. Sometimes swapping out a component (router, switch, access point) will fix things, even if the swapped-out component tests good in all testable ways.

95% of networking problems respond well to calm thought, analysis, cold systematic testing, and reliance on good notes. The other 5% will make you nuts. Be ready.

Testing Your Throughput

I can tell you roughly what data throughput to expect across your wireless links, but you don't have to take my word for it—and shouldn't. Measuring your actual, real-world throughput is easily done, and excellent free software tools are available to do the measuring for you. My hands-down favorite is QCheck, created by NetIQ Software and now distributed by Ixia. You can obtain the software without charge from Ixia's Web site:

www.ixiacom.com/products/qcheck/index.php

You have to fill out a slightly nosy questionnaire to be allowed to do the download, but the company doesn't misuse the information, and the utility itself is more than worth it.

There's a little more to using QCheck than simply installing it and running it. QCheck tests throughput between two nodes on a network. (A node is just network jargon for one connected entity on the network somewhere.) The mechanism that QCheck uses requires that there be two ends to the link being tested. These "ends" are separate pieces of software that NetIQ calls *endpoints*. When you install QCheck on your primary computer, an endpoint is installed on that computer at the same time. But to check connections between your main computer and other computers on your network, an endpoint must be installed on each computer. Endpoints are available for virtually every operating system in use today, for all flavors of Windows, for the Mac and most Unix variants, and even for ancient and mostly forgotten operating systems like IBM's excellent if mishandled OS/2. You can download endpoints free of charge from Ixia's Web site. Download and install an endpoint for each machine on your network. (Of course, if all your computers are running the same operating system, you only need to download the endpoint installer file once.)

QCheck itself is a simple, elegant utility with only a few controls (see Figure 9.19). You can select the network protocol to be tested, and for our purposes, you need to check TCP. You can choose one of several tests to perform, and the one of interest here is Throughput.

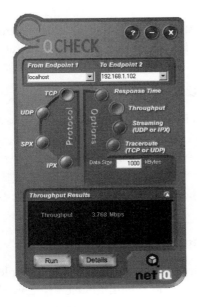

Figure 9.19
The Qcheck Utility.

Set the data size option to 1,000 kilobytes. The larger your test file is, the more accurate the results will be. 1,000 kilobytes is as large as QCheck allows.

The only tricky part is setting the endpoints for the throughput test. You can actually test throughput between *any* two computers on your network, whether they're connected wirelessly or through a cable. One end does not have to be the computer on which the QCheck utility is installed. The computer on which QCheck itself is running is called "localhost," and if one end of your test link is localhost, that should be selected as Endpoint 1.

For Endpoint 2, you need to enter the IP address of the computer acting as that endpoint. Determining the IP address for a particular computer is done in different ways for different operating systems. The best way to do it, however, is by looking at your router appliance's DHCP clients table. Each client was given a unique local IP address, and this is the address that you should use. The client's table lists the hostname alongside the IP address, so you'll know which computer belongs to what IP address.

For the tests to yield accurate results, *no one else should be using the network at all.* Period. If you're testing at a small office, do your testing after hours and make sure everyone's gone home. At home, put all the computers in the house temporarily off limits. Make sure the kids don't have any peer-to-peer file shares going on. Nothing should be moving across the network when you test throughput.

Once you have an IP address (or "localhost") selected for the two ends of the link that you wish to test, make sure the network is idle, and click Run. A test with a 1000-kilobyte test file will take several seconds to run. When finished, the results will appear in green in the results window. For a given link, the same test will not always return precisely the same results, so run ten or fifteen tests and take an average.

I've run a lot of these tests on several networks, and here are some generalizations I can make to help you evaluate your own results:

- When *both* endpoints must communicate through the *same* access point, your throughput will be a little over half what it is when only one endpoint communicates through the access point. For example, a single Wireless-B access point has only 11 Mbps total bandwidth, and all computers connecting through that access point must share that bandwidth (see Figure 9.20).

- For Wireless-B links in which only one endpoint passes through the access point, 90% of the readings I've taken fall between 4.5 and 5.5 Mbps with WEP disabled, and 3.5 and 4.5 Mbps with WEP enabled. Wireless-G throughput is harder to generalize about because there are two ways to

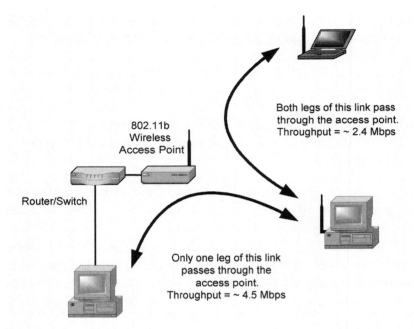

802.11b
Wireless
Access Point

Both legs of this link pass
through the access point.
Throughput = ~ 2.4 Mbps

Router/Switch

Only one leg of this link
passes through the
access point.
Throughput = ~ 4.5 Mbps

Figure 9.20
Testing Throughput.

configure the network (G-only vs. mixed) and many possible bit rates depending on the distance between nodes and intervening obstructions. In most
ordinary circumstances, look for 15-20 Mbps for a link in G-only networks. If
both endpoints are connecting through the same access point or gateway,
you'll get about half of that.

- The manufacturer and model of access point and client adapter will affect
  throughput. Some devices are simply slower than others, probably due to
  differences in the efficiency of the firmware and in the speed of the embedded
  processor.

- Using WEP or WPA will generally reduce your throughput by between 15%
  and 25%. (Occasionally you'll see a performance hit of as little as 5%.) There
  are no free lunches, and security, being a compute-intensive function, will cost
  you cycles. Nonetheless, this is a *bad* reason not to enable security.

The difference between bit rate and throughput also applies to wired links. If any part of your network connects two computers through a cable, test throughput for that link for comparison. It won't be 10 Mbps for 10 Base-T, nor will it be 100 Mbps for 100 Base-T. There is network protocol overhead (though not always encryption overhead) on all types of networks.

Ready To Secure

At this point, you should have a working network. It isn't a secure network yet, and this is a bad spot to stop work, pop the cork from the champagne, and celebrate. Wi-Fi security is arguably the strangest and trickiest of all facets of wireless networking, and I've devoted an entire section of this book—Chapters 11 through 15—to the subject of security. Please read Part III through completely, and then set up the best security technology that your equipment supports.

Older gear will probably support Wired Equivalent Privacy (WEP) only. Newer gear will support both WEP and the newer—and much better—Wi-Fi Protected Access (WPA.) Either way, it's cheap insurance, not against some nasty attacks from mysterious hackers out in the wilds of the global Internet, but from your neighbors' heavily networked kids, or that weird-looking guy sitting in a car out in front of your house with a laptop.

Knowledge is power. Know your network, know your enemy, know your options—and someone else will take the hits, not you.

Wi-Fi Warriors on the Road

There was a time (and not so long ago) when staying connected on the road was such a nightmare that I didn't even bother. Before heading off on a business trip I just put my email on "vacation hold" (Vacation! Hah!) and sorted out the ensuing mess when I got home.

I'm not sure why, but hotels were very slow to understand the value of Internet connections for business travelers. Part of it has to do with the fact that "hospitality" is a low-margin business, and existing hotels are difficult and expensive to retrofit with network connections in every room. Even swapping in phones that provide extra jacks for laptop dialup modems costs enough so that it took forever to happen.

I've stayed in a thin handful of brand-new (and high-cost) hotels with RJ45 Ethernet connections in every room (including one in Koln, Germany with a head-on view of the Dom) but the bright spot in business travel for Wi-Fi users is the hotel, airport, and coffee shop wireless hotspot. Wi-Fi has been a serious winner for people on the road, and this chapter will let you know how it works and how you can take advantage of wireless connections away from home.

Wireless Wandering

There have been public places you can go to use the Internet for some years; typically public libraries and retail establishments called *Internet cafès*, where there are carrels containing connected computers, and you pay by the hour. We've had Internet cafès in our larger cities for some time now, and in places where they existed, business travelers and tourists have made excellent use of them. Internet cafès have never been much of a phenomenon here in the U.S. because they were pretty sparsely distributed, and you could never count on there being a networked cafè at or near any given business destination. (Internet cafès have always been a much bigger deal in Europe and Asia than the U.S.)

A fair amount of capital is required to equip an Internet cafè, and that's the key reason they never caught on, especially since Internet access (if not necessarily *broadband* Internet access) has been ubiquitous in U.S. homes for some years. By comparison, establishing a Wi-Fi hotspot takes very little capital. The wireless gear is cheap. The customers bring their own computers, and there are no cables. Because the customers don't get anywhere near the establishment's equipment, theft and damage are not risks.

Wi-Fi connectivity can be a godsend for road warriors who find themselves "between connections" with laptops or PDAs in their briefcases and work to do. The cost is generally reasonable ($3 to $10 per hour) and the connections are typically much faster than a hotel dialup—sometimes hundreds of times faster. The only downside is that you typically have to "do a transaction" at the counter to use the network. It would be fabulous if someone could "aggregate" hotspots into a network under a single billing system, so you could use any network hotspot without having to tender cash or a credit card every time you stop at a cafè and want to log in.

In the past two or three years, a number of such hotspot networks have appeared, and they have grown spectacularly in recent months. These days, it's a rare city or major airport without a public hotspot or two—or two dozen—falling under the jurisdiction of one or more of those major hotspot networks.

Wi-Fi has not brought us to network nirvana yet, but we're at least halfway there. Here are some points to keep in mind for networking on the road:

- No one place is available on the Web where you can find a list of all commercial or community public hotspots. Hotspot directories exist, but they are almost laughably incomplete. If you plan to use Wi-Fi on the road you should be prepared to do some considerable searching. If you travel a lot to predictable destinations (for example, if you swing through Minneapolis, Chicago, Indianapolis, and St. Louis on a regular basis) you should be prepared to keep your own list and update it based on your own research.

- No single billing system is available for all or even most commercial public hotspots. There are at least four major networks—along with a host of smaller, often local ones—and you have to establish an account separately with each network to use its hotspots without doing manual transactions. Still, four is better than four thousand.

- Billing plans for commercial public hotspots vary widely and in what may seem peculiar ways. One plan may favor logging in quickly for an hour and then logging out again; another may favor logging in for several hours in a hotel room for continuous work. You can reduce your costs by studying the various hotspot network plans closely and matching a plan to the ways you typically use Internet connections. I'll discuss this in more detail later in this chapter.

- In my recent travels, I've found that hotel management often knows very little about how their own Internet connection systems work, and if the system doesn't work for some reason, they can't simply send someone up to fix it. (This is especially true of "no frills" hotels.) Therefore, I suggest you locate a backup connection site nearby, even if your chosen hotel claims to have high-speed Internet connections available.

- Business travelers (and anyone else) can use public community hotspots without any charge at all. The trick lies in finding them, and perhaps living with their bandwidth limitations. For simple things like reading email, this isn't an issue. If you are sending or receiving large files, it is *definitely* an issue.

- Public library policies for Internet connections are all over the map. Some libraries charge non-cardholders. Political restrictions on access to minors have made libraries reluctant to install Wi-Fi hotspots, because when users bring their own computers it's hard to monitor what they're doing. Many library computers do not have floppy drives or other removable media, due to political pressure from copyright lobbies fearful of people using public access systems to trade music and movie files. None of this is the libraries' fault, but it makes them poor choices if you can find public access elsewhere.

- Irrespective of how infatuated you become with Wi-Fi, pack a CAT 5 patch cable when you travel. At significant numbers of new hotels, management has opted for wired rather than wireless access, and it's infuriating to have to stare at an Ethernet jack without having a cable to connect to it!

- As a general rule, assume that both commercial and community hotspots have no encryption, via Wired Equivalent Privacy or anything else. This means that the guy at the next table may be sipping a latte while sniffing your packets on his laptop. Plan and work with that in mind. If your workplace has the ability to implement some sort of virtual private network (VPN) that would be the best thing to do.

- Finally, pay attention to what hotspot you're connecting to. Depending on how your Wi-Fi client adapter and supporting software is configured, your laptop may associate with the wrong hotspot if more than one is available when you turn it on. In a dense urban area, you may be within range of several access points from your seat at the sidewalk table of a coffee shop. Access points in the offices above the shop or even across the street may not have encryption enabled, and it's possible to connect to the wrong access point by accident. A connection utility like Boingo's is very useful for specifying precisely what access point you want to connect to. I'll cover more on this later.

Let's talk a little more about some of these points.

Finding Public Hotspots

The biggest single problem for road warriors seeking wireless connectivity on the road is just finding the hotspots. Nothing like the Yellow Pages exists for Wi-Fi hotspots, though there are bits and pieces of such a directory scattered around the Net. You'll have to dig to find the hotspots you need.

What I do, and what most frequent Wi-Fi travelers do, is keep a personal directory of hotspots in the cities I travel to. Few people, even constant travelers, travel to random destinations. Most people find themselves in a mere handful of places, and return to that same short list of places on a regular basis. Sales people, for example, have territories and major accounts, and visit those accounts on a scheduled basis. You may find yourself in Chicago five times a year, and in Boise... never.

Each of the major commercial hotspot networks keeps a Web-based database of all their locations online. These lists are worth some study, but I find them infuriating, for this reason: When you're in an unfamiliar city and want to find the nearest hotspot, you can't just crank up Internet Explorer or Netscape and go looking for one. You're not connected yet. Web-based directories of any kind are worthless when you need them the most.

Here are some highly fragmentary directories of hotspots on the Web. I've listed a few in Table 10.1, with a 1-5 star rating of how useful I consider each one. My favorite is JIWire, which has more information about more hotspots (including maps, pricing information, and provider data) than any other site. It also includes listings of hotels with *wired* Internet access, which is a fine idea—*how* you get online matters much less than simply getting there. JIWire also has a feature called "JIWire to go," which is a branded version of AvantGo's hotspot database. This is similar to Boingo in that it is an installable offline database of hotspots. Unfortunately, it only installs on PDAs and smart phones, rather than laptops. It is free, and thus worth a look if you use your PDA or smart phone to connect to the Internet on the road.

Table 10.1   Online Hotspot Directories.

Site Name	URL	Stars
JiWire	www.jiwire.com/	*****
Wi-FiHotspotList.com	www.wi-fihotspotlist.com/	****
Wi-Fi 41	www.wifi411.com/	****
Wi-Fi Free Spot	www.wififreespot.com/	***
Hotspot-Locations.com	www.hotspot-locations.com/	***
Open Hotspots Network	www.openhotspots.net/	**
Wi-Find	www.wi-find.com/	**

Because all of these directories are actually database lookups, you can't just print them out or copy them into a separate document with cut and paste. And like the directories of their member hotspots posted by hotspot aggregator networks, they're inaccessible just when you need to find a hotspot to connect from. Since all the sites listed in Table 10.1 are free sites, I find it a little odd that none have chosen to package their databases into a simple standalone database browser and allow them to be installed on laptop hard drives, where they would be of much more use.

The well-known AAA hotel directory now has an indicator for "high-speed Internet access" in their listings. Be aware that these listings are not always accurate. If you're calling ahead to reserve, it only takes a few seconds to ask if high-speed Internet is available. Asking more detailed questions (even something simple like, "Is it wireless?") is usually futile, and when you get to a hotel and want to connect, you're usually on your own. (Bring that CAT 5 cable!)

Most road warriors belong to one or more (usually more) of the "frequent traveler" programs offered by the major hotel chains. These programs give you discounts, frequent flyer miles with affiliated airlines, or other perks for staying at the chain's properties. I make heavy use of these programs, which means that I end up staying at the same short list of hotels in the short list of cities I visit frequently. This makes it easier to create a list of useful hotspots, since I really want something close to the hotel where I'm staying. (This assumes that the hotel itself has no high-speed Internet access.)

Locating free community hotspots is often difficult in the extreme because for the most part they are not promoted and are known generally through word-of-mouth (or "word-of-Net" these days.) Remarkably enough, the excellent Boingo connection utility includes free community hotspots in its directory, right along with Boingo's own hotspots. It just doesn't include all of them.

Finally, if you're stuck somewhere without a public hotspot within striking distance, you may be tempted to crank up something like Boingo's connection utility, locate some hapless person or business's unprotected Wi-Fi access point, and connect through that. Yes, it's easy. But double yes, it's fraudulent, and in most interpretations of current law, illegal. I find it bitterly amusing sometimes that the same people who fret endlessly about attacks from drive-by hackers will knowingly and willingly *become* one if a legal Net connection doesn't come easily to hand. Keep your sense of personal honor. Don't intrude on other peoples' networks and steal bandwidth.

Hotspot Networks and Aggregators

As I define them, *hotspot networks* are groups of hotspots owned and operated by a single company, like T-Mobile Hotspot. A *hotspot aggregator* is a company that provides back-end billing services for hotspots owned and operated by other people. Boingo Wireless falls into this category. From your perspective as a traveler, the distinction is mostly academic. When I say "hotspot networks" here I'm referring to both.

The idea is simple: By setting up one account you get access to any hotspot in that network. The accounts work like a lot of things in the e-commerce world: You give the network your credit card information, and they debit your card either monthly or when you sign into a hotspot, depending on what sort of payment plan you select.

The downside, of course, is that no one network currently dominates the hotspot business, and to get easy access to the bulk of American hotspots you'd have to have accounts with five or six different networks. I myself have accounts with two, and depending on your circumstances you may need accounts with three or four. Much depends on how much travel you do, and (more important) where you go, since the major networks' hotspots are *not* evenly distributed around the country.

All but one of the networks that I've tried employ captive portals for their logon machinery. (I explained captive portals in some detail in Chapter 5.) Basically, when you turn on your laptop and open a Web browser in a hotel or café with a hotspot, your browser will intercept your first URL request (typically that of your browser "home page," like Google or MSN) and take you to the network's login screen. That's where you type in your user ID and password, after which the portal opens and you can access anything you normally would on the Internet.

The exception to this is Boingo, which distributes a separate connection utility that you install on your laptop. When you turn on your laptop near a Boingo hotspot, the connection utility handles the login process. It remembers your user ID and password, and establishes the connection without further input on your part.

Connection Costs and Plans

Each network has its own pricing plans, and when you create an account with one of the networks, you must choose one of their pricing plans. The plans fall into two categories:

- "Pay as you go" plans don't charge your credit card until you actually log into a hotspot. When you log in, you pay either by the connection or by the hour.

- Subscription plans charge your credit card regularly (usually monthly) for either a set number of hours/connections or unlimited access.

By setting up a monthly subscription your per-hour charges are less than pay-as-you-go, but unless you travel enough to make sufficient use of a network's hotspots, you may actually pay *more* per hour for the connect time that you actually use. My analysis hasn't shown that I would benefit from a monthly subscription, so my own use of the two networks at which I have accounts has been strictly pay-as-you-go.

My intuition is that careful planning could make a monthly subscription worthwhile—if you travel frequently to the same cities and stay in the same places when you do. The only way to know is to look at your travel history and see if one of the networks supports all your favorite haunts.

Prices are definitely dropping in the face of increased competition. Almost from the beginning of the commercial hotspot era I predicted that eventually retailers of various kinds would offer hotspots without charge as a means of gaining an edge on their competitors. This is finally coming to pass in a reasonably big way. In mid-November 2002, Schlotzky's Deli announced their Deli Cool Cloud Network, which will consist of no-charge hotspots at selected Schlotzky's sites. In late 2003, Panera Bread announced that it will be rolling out free Wi-Fi hotspots in all of their new locations and some of their existing locations. As more of these "free commercial" hotspots go online, more pressure will be placed on pricey hotspot providers like Wayport and T-Mobile. After retailers hosting paid hotspots have a couple of years' worth of financials in front of them to gauge the ROI of having paid hotspots on site, I think a lot of them will "go free." We'll just have to watch and see.

The Shape of Your Work

One of the striking differences among the ways that the major hotspot networks have structured their pricing plans is the emphasis on "connections" versus "minutes." The older and larger networks (especially those like T-Mobile, which is owned by a cell phone company) charge by the minute, so it's easy to calculate an hourly cost for being connected.

Some of the newer networks charge by the connection rather than by the hour or minute. A connection is usually defined as a time-limited relationship with a single hotspot. Boingo, for example, charges $7.95 for a connection to a single hotspot, and a connection can last as long as 24 hours. You can log into and out of that hotspot as often as you like during the duration of the connection without incurring additional charges. The definition of a connection varies widely among the networks. Wayport defines a "hotel connection" as the time falling between the time you first connect to a hotel's hotspot and the next hotel checkout time.

What this means is that the shape of your work while on the road may dictate what network and what plan you choose. If all you do is log in for five minutes twice a day to send and receive email, any network may do. If you tend to gather information during a working day and process it during the evening (and if that processing includes Web research or sending and receiving large files) it may pay to choose a network offering a plan charging by the connection.

It's complicated. Pay attention to the fine print.

Major Hotspot Networks

For the remainder of this chapter, I'll describe the major hotspot networks and summarize their pricing plans. For those networks that act as aggregators of independently owned hotspots, I also include information on how the aggregator companies set up relationships with independent hotspot owners and share revenues with them. If you're the owner of a bookstore, coffee shop, health club, or other upscale hangout, take a look at the numbers and do a few back-of-the-envelope calculations. It's not riches, but it's what entrepreneurs call "free money"—meaning you have to do virtually nothing to earn it, once the system has been set up and debugged.

Against this must be weighed the growing competitive influence of free hotspots fielded by retailers and charged as a cost of attracting customers. National chains Schlotzky's Deli and Panera Bread are the leaders here, and I suspect other big chains will follow their lead over the next three years. Ultimately, there may be little or no money in providing hotspots, and prospective bandwidth entrepreneurs must keep that in mind.

Boingo

Boingo: **www.boingo.com**

Making the Wi-Fi bandwidth transaction as close to effortless as possible is what Boingo Wireless was founded to do. If you have an account set up with Boingo, you can open your laptop at any Boingo partner hotspot, launch the Boingo connection utility, and you're in. The utility knows your user ID and password, and handles the transaction through the partner hotspot. It then opens the connection to the Internet. This happens in a couple of seconds and does not require any password entry or other attention from you.

The Boingo connection utility is a free download, and you don't have to have a Boingo account to install and run it. Some people have used it as a "stumbling" utility, something like Netstumbler, since it senses the presence of nearby Wi-Fi hotspots and presents a list of hotspots to which you can connect. Unlike NetStumbler, Boingo will connect your computer to any unencrypted hotspot. Nominally this is to provide equal access to the free community hotspots here and there around the country, but the open secret is that Boingo doesn't attempt to determine if a hotspot is truly free and open. (Boingo also has the ability to store Wired Equivalent Privacy keys, so if you are party to a WEP-protected hotspot you can still connect using the Boingo utility.)

The true brilliance in the Boingo idea is this: The Boingo connection utility carries within it an *off-line* directory of Boingo partner hotspots, which is searchable by state, city, zip code, or type of hotspot (airport, cafè, health club, convention center, and so on). The directory is updated periodically as Boingo recruits new hotspots as partners. You don't need to be online to search the directory. See Figure 10.1 for an example of the Boingo utility at work.

Boingo will list free-access community networks as partners on its directory, which is actually pretty amazing in my view. The built-in directory utility does not require you to be online to find a Boingo hotspot, which is spectacularly useful. After all, when you want to find a hotspot to allow you to go up on the Web, it's kind of silly to expect you to go up on the Web to read the hotspot directory.

Rates and Plans

At press time, Boingo offers two different plans for accessing Boingo partner hotspots:

- "Boingo-As-You-Go" provides you with connectivity at any Boingo partner hotspot for $7.95 for a single 24-hour "connect day." You can disconnect and reconnect to that same hotspot during that single 24-hour day without

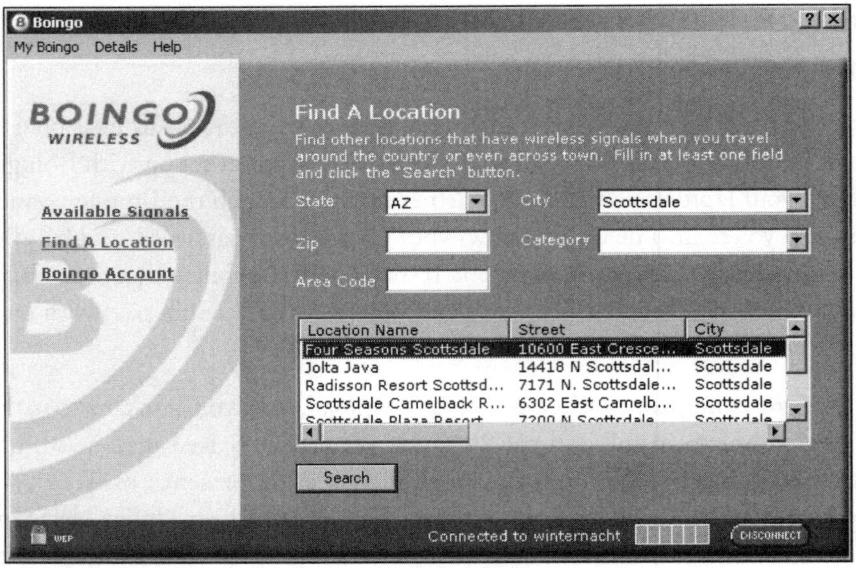

Figure 10.1
The Boingo Off-Line Hotspot Directory Search Screen.

additional cost. No monthly or recurring charges; you pay by the day that you use the system.

- "Boingo Unlimited" gives you unlimited connect time at any Boingo partner hotspot for $21.95 a month for the first year. After the first year, the monthly rate rises to $39.95 per month.

> A "connect day" is a 24-hour period at **one** Boingo partner hotspot. In other words, if you connect at a hotel after breakfast for an hour to read your email, then hop a cab to the airport, then connect to another Boingo partner at the airport, you'll be charged for a second connect day, even though both connections were begun and ended within a single 24-hour period.

For people who do a lot of online work while on the road, this is actually a whole new price point. Most Internet cafés charge $5 to $8 per hour; with Boingo, you can spend all evening holed up in your Wi-Fi equipped hotel room, working a broad-band connection for $8 a *day*.

Compatibility

At this writing the Boingo connection utility comes in two versions. One works under Windows 98 Second Edition, Windows ME, Windows 2000, and Windows XP. (Note well that this excludes Windows 95 and the original Windows 98.) A separate version is available for PocketPC 2002 and 2003.

The list of supported Wi-Fi cards is impressive, especially for Windows XP. However, with installable drivers, most common Wi-Fi client cards will work, and I've tested it with both the Orinoco Gold and the Cisco Aironet PCM-340. There is currently no Macintosh or Linux support.

The Boingo "Hot Spot in a Box" Partner Program

Most Boingo partners establish a relationship with Boingo through individual negotiation, but there is a "canned" program for retailers who want to do as little fooling with computer gear as possible. The "Hot Spot in a Box" program consists of a Columbis high-end Wireless-B access point, and captive portal software for authenticating the user and controlling the connection. The retailer provides a dedicated PC and a broadband connection to the Internet. Boingo Wireless shares revenues with the retailer based on connect days. The current rate is $1 per connect day. That doesn't sound like a great deal on the surface, but recall that gross revenue for a connect day is typically $5, and 20% is a reasonable royalty for a service sold and billed elsewhere and requiring little effort on the part of the retailer.

Additionally, there is a $20 bounty for each new Boingo Wireless user who signs up for an account for at least sixty days, based on a hotspot owner's referral.

T-Mobile

T-Mobile: **www.t-mobile.com/hotspot/**

T-Mobile is a cell-phone company that has gotten into commercial hotspot implementation in a very big way. If you've ever cranked up your laptop at a Starbuck's and connected to the Internet, you've made the acquaintance of T-Mobile. True, if you used the very earliest Starbuck's Wi-Fi connections, they were operated by the now-defunct MobileStar. They're all T-Mobile now, since the T-Mobile's parent company, Deutsche Telekomm, acquired MobileStar's assets in October 2001.

T-Mobile probably has more hotspots than any single provider network (not counting network aggregators like Boingo), and at this writing they list over 4,000. Although originally a bicoastal phenomenon, T-Mobile has now expanded its hotspot coverage to all but a handful of states. (If you're in Montana, Wyoming, West Virginia, or—surprisingly—Vermont, you're still out of luck.)

T-Mobile handles billing, customer service, and user authentication through a captive portal application that manages the hotspot. Logging into a T-Mobile hotspot is done by launching a Web browser within the hotspot and issuing a request for any URL. (The automatic "home page" request that occurs when you launch most browsers accomplishes this with no additional typing.) The URL request is redirected to the portal entry page, where you have to manually enter account and password data. There is no client connection utility *a la* Boingo.

Rates and Plans

T-Mobile offers subscription, prepaid, and pay-as-you-go pricing plans. In a departure from its earlier pricing plans, there are no longer any data transfer limits. Here is what the plans look like in the spring of 2004:

- T-Mobile's "pay-as-you-go" metered service runs $6.00 for the first hour, with additional minutes running $.10 per minute. They no longer offer the option to buy 15-minute segments. There are no data transfer limits, as there were in earlier pricing plans.

- Annual national subscription service (that is, service that is billed annually) runs $29.95 per month, for service at any T-Mobile site in the U.S. There is a 12-month commitment required for that pricing, with a $200 early termination fee beyond the first thirty days of service. No data transfer limits apply.

- Monthly national subscription service (service billed monthly without an annual commitment) runs $39.99 per month, for use at any T-Mobile location anywhere in the U.S. No data transfer limits apply.

- The prepaid "DayPass" plan gives you 24 contiguous hours of service at any U.S. T-Mobile site for $9.99. The 24-hour period begins the first time you log in. If unused, DayPass arrangements expire 120 days from the date of purchase.

Be sure you compare this plan matrix with those of Wayport, Boingo, and SurfHere, which I summarize elsewhere in this chapter. T-Mobile has clearly seen the effects of competition in the Wi-Fi hotspot arena: Its plans are much simpler and less expensive than they were in 2002.

 Keep in mind that you can also "do a transaction" with a credit card through the T-Mobile captive portal software at any T-Mobile hotspot. Just connect to the portal and launch a Web browser—the portal will take it from there and guide you through the transaction.

T-Mobile deploys and owns its hotspots (in cooperation with premises management) and does not currently have a hotspot owner/partner program.

SurfHere by Toshiba

SurfHere: **www.csd.toshiba.com/cgi-bin/tais/hs/hs_home.jsp**

Toshiba's SurfHere hotspot network is relatively new as I write this, but it has a lot of promise and will be a force in the industry once it rolls out nationally. Toshiba has targeted several large national chains of retailers for its service—and some of those national chains are not the first place you'd look for wireless access. Here is a list of some of its larger partner chains:

- Circle K Convenience Stores

- The UPS Store

- McDonald's

- Barnes & Noble

Not all sites in all these partner chains currently have wireless services installed and available. Barnes & Noble, for example, is still testing the service in 13 stores in the greater Atlanta area, and the McDonald's sites are all in several large cities, including Chicago, San Francisco, New York, Portland, Seattle, and Boise. Assuming that the business model works for the chains doing the testing, the expectation is that they will roll out the service nationally.

To use a SurfHere location, you can either establish an account centrally with SurfHere, which provides access to any SurfHere site, or do a transaction individually at a SurfHere site. Pricing at retail sites is not standardized; retailers can adjust pricing or do promotional deals (wireless access bundled "free" with a meal, for example) if they choose. Toshiba offers several different pricing plans for account-based users who sign up on the SurfHere Web site:

- $4.95 for one hour

- $5.95 for two hours

- $7.95 for one day

- $19.95 for one week

- $39.95 for one month

Toshiba has been extremely aggressive in deploying hotspots in their first year of operation, and if they continue with their plan, there will be relatively inexpensive wireless access in virtually all American urban areas. Toshiba is heavily marketing the service to students in conjunction with McDonald's, which in my view is a stroke of genius.

Toshiba does not have a standardized plan for retailers who wish to implement their own hotspots on the SurfHere network; contact them through their Web site for details.

Wayport

Wayport: **www.wayport.net**

One of the earliest providers of fast Internet connections in public places is Wayport. Since 1996 they have provided T-1 class wired access through Category 5 cables in hotel guest rooms and meeting rooms, and airport kiosks under the Laptop Lane brand. More recently they have begun deploying Wi-Fi hotspots in hotel lobbies and airport common spaces, and now have over 450 hotspots around the country, including nine at major airports.

Wayport uses a captive portal to authenticate users and manage billing, and it works identically for both their wired and wireless connections: You boot a Wi-Fi equipped laptop (or plug the Cat 5 cable into the Ethernet port of a wireless-less laptop), open a Web browser and issue a URL request for any URL. The request is redirected to the portal entry page. (Most people have a "home page" that loads automatically on browser startup, and that's enough to take you to the portal entry page. Unless your browser loads with a blank screen, you don't actually have to type a URL request.) You type your user ID and password into the portal form, and after authentication, the portal opens to the Internet at large.

Rates and Plans

Wayport has focused on airport and hotel locations almost exclusively, but is pursuing a pilot program at certain McDonald's restaurants in four states. (See their Web site for a location map.) Registered Wayport users can pay by the connection, on a monthly plan, or monthly on an annual contract:

- A single hotel connection is typically $9.95, though that may vary depending on Wayport's arrangement with a given hotel. A hotel connection lasts from the time the connection is established until the next hotel checkout time. In other words, for a hotel with a checkout time of 11:30 A.M., if you check in and connect at 7 P.M., your connection is paid until 11:30 the following day. Or if you don't connect until after breakfast, at 8:00 A.M., your connection is good only until 11:30. (Check in and connect early!) A hotel connection may be charged either to your hotel room or directly to your credit card. Note that where Wi-Fi access is available in common areas (conference rooms, lobby, etc.) it is billed separately from access in guest rooms. Guest room access is usually via wired Ethernet wall jack.

- A single airport connection costs $6.95, and lasts from the time you connect until midnight local time.

- A month-to-month subscription costs $49.95 per month for unlimited connection at any Wayport hotspot. (Hotel common areas are excluded.)

- On an annual contract, the monthly subscription fee is $29.95 for one year, minimum. (Hotel meeting rooms are excluded.)

- Wayport also offers prepaid connection cards for discounts on connections at certain classes of Wayport sites. Cards may be purchased to provide three connections for $8, eight connections for $50, and twenty connections for $100. The definition of "connection" varies depending on where the cards are used. For airports and hotels, the definition is as listed above. In McDonald's restaurants, a connection is two hours in length. The cards are eligible for discounts on connections at Laptop Lane, but are not considered "prepaid" for Laptop Lane use.

Wayport deploys its own hotspots (in cooperation with hotel and airport management) and does not currently have a hotspot owner/partner program.

The Problem of the Speckled Axe

How secure can you make a Wi-Fi network? Well, consider Benjamin Franklin's Parable of the Speckled Axe:

A boy found an axe in the woods, lying in the dirt. Its edge was still sharp and true, but the iron head was heavily pitted with rust. The boy took the axe to his father and asked his father to grind it bright and new-looking again.

"I'll do the grinding," said his father, "if you turn the stone."

So they went out to the shed, and while the boy pumped the grindstone's treadle, his father held the axe head hard against the stone, and began to grind away the pits of rust. After a few minutes the boy's father paused, held the axe up for his son to see, and asked him if it was done. There was much bright metal now, but the pits amidst the brightness could still be seen. The boy shook his head and asked his father to continue.

So it went for most of an hour, with the boy breaking a sweat turning the stone, and the sparks flying steadily from the axehead. After an hour or so, the boy signaled for his father to stop. The axe looked much better, though the deepest pits were still visible.

"Father, on thinking it over just now, I believe I like a speckled axe best."

Network security, be it wireless or wired, is a speckled axe. No matter how hard you work at security, a network cannot be made *completely* secure. A totally secure network should be theoretically possible, but because of the human factor (i.e., the fact that humans often act like idiots) technology alone isn't enough. Anyone who has managed a department in a mid-sized company or taught third grade (similar challenges in a lot of respects) will immediately understand the human factor. Technology, by comparison, is a snap.

So let that be one of your fundamental assumptions as you consider the whole issue of network security: *There are no secure networks.* The best you can do is minimize your chances of taking a hit. The good news is that this is easier than people in the press have made it sound. Wi-Fi security has gotten some *very* bad press from otherwise good writers who simply don't understand either Wi-Fi or security, and prefer a provocative story to a thoughtful, well-researched one.

In this first short chapter on the topic I hope to give you some guidance on how to think about computer security generally, so you can evaluate your own position intelligently. The gist of the process is balancing trust and risk, which can't really happen until you understand both.

A Matter of Trust

Any security system requires two kinds of trust: trusting technology and trusting people. Not just other people, either. It often requires trusting *yourself* to follow your own procedures, which isn't always easy when time is short and the swamp isn't cooperating with your efforts to drain it. If either the technology or the people violate that trust, security weakens, and if the bad guys learn of that weakness (and understand how to exploit it) the security system will fail.

Trusting technology is problematic for several reasons:

- We don't always sufficiently understand the details of the technology we are called upon to trust, which makes it hard to fulfill our part of security's bargain.

- We often attempt to use technology for purposes it was never designed to fulfill, because it's cheaper or easier (or both) than buying or building technology appropriate to the challenge at hand.

- Technology always contains flaws that even the experts (and its own creators) don't know are there until someone finds them.

- Technology advances, and new technology regularly appears that renders old technology ineffective (whether or not it has serious flaws) and thus unworthy of trust.

- Even if subverting a trusted technology is initially hard and requires an expert, technology can automate any difficult process so that anyone can do it. In other words, breaking a trusted technology only has to be done *once*.

Trusting people is problematic for different but equally important reasons:

- People don't always do what they're told, even when it's in their interest and they know what to do and have done it for a long time.

- People are not always given sufficient information and/or training in how to do what they must do to participate in a secure system.

- People sometimes tell lies about their own loyalties and agendas, and betray trust that has been granted to them.

Let's talk about these points in greater detail, because you know that's where the devil always hides.

Understanding Technology

Knowing whether and how much and in what ways to trust a technology requires an understanding of that technology to some extent. I'm reminded of the old joke about the person who responds with wide-eyed surprise at the news that his checking account is overdrawn: "But that's impossible! I still have checks in my checkbook!" Not too clear on the concept, we say with a grin. But be honest: How clear are you on the concept of network operation, much less network security? And more to the point, how clear on the concept do you have to be?

To use technology without being a hazard, you have the responsibility of understanding it to the extent that you mitigate the chance of being a hazard. There's a well-traveled urban legend about a newly retired man who finally achieves his dream of buying a 40-foot Winnebago RV so he can spend a year on the road seeing the country. Half an hour into his first trek down the Interstate, he pushes the cruise control button and heads back into the RV's kitchen to make himself a cup of coffee. Seconds later, the RV goes off the highway and into the ditch. In some versions of the legend, he sues Winnebago for not telling him that the cruise control wasn't the same as an automatic pilot. (In reality, he would be unlikely to survive such an adventure. Darwin knew what he was talking about.)

This story is a howler because we all know that only a knucklehead would assume that cruise controls can steer a vehicle. Faced with a computer full of complicated and obscure mechanisms, however, how confident are you that you understand what's a hazard and what isn't? Working a computer (especially a networked computer) and driving a car both require a certain amount of study and practice. You don't have to be a degreed expert to understand the hazards that networking carries with it. You must, however, make the effort to learn what the hazards are and what you must do to avoid them. Trusting the machine too much is worse than not trusting it at all.

The easiest way to do this is by reading books (like you're doing right now) and talking to smart people who have been down that road before you. I also recommend the short night courses in computer operation that you'll find at community colleges, public libraries, and senior centers.

However you do it, do it. Be as clear on the critical computing concepts as you can, so you know what parts of the system you can trust, and how much.

A Micrometer Is Not a C-Clamp

I was in high school when I heard the story (possibly but not inevitably an urban legend) of the student in machine shop who needed a couple of small C-clamps to hold two pieces of metal together while he drilled them. The C-clamp drawer was empty, so he went to the micrometer drawer and pulled out two micrometers, which he then used as clamps, at least until the instructor saw him. (I admit that if you've never used a micrometer this won't make sense at all; if you have, well, it's *very* funny. See Figure 11.1 to better understand how the two tools differ.)

Micrometers are not C-clamps, even though they're shaped a little like C-clamps and a naïve person might assume that in a pinch they might serve as C-clamps. However, if you trust a micrometer to do the job of a C-clamp, you run the risk of having your lashup fly apart on the drill press, scattering chunks of metal and micrometers in all directions. You can't trust a micrometer to do a C-clamp's job, and it's not the micrometer's fault when it fails.

This problem infects the Wi-Fi world, where a relatively simple security mechanism called Wired Equivalent Privacy (WEP) is often trusted to do many things it was never intended to do. Big portions of the Wi-Fi security drawer are not only

Figure 11.1
C-Clamps and Micrometers.

empty but until very recently were simply *missing*—so because WEP is at least present, people expect it to do everything.

 This problem can be ameliorated a little by ameliorating the first problem: Know your technology at least well enough to know what problem it was intended to solve, and don't expect it to solve other problems just because it's handy.

Crickets and Termites

All software has bugs. Some are obvious—I call these crickets. Even when you don't see them, you *hear* them. Some are very hard to detect and don't surface for years. I call these termites. Just as Carol and I tune out the crickets living outside our bedroom window when we turn in for the night, most people work around the obvious bugs in their software. Windows crashes, you reboot. I'm very careful typing the letter "A," because some knucklehead years ago defined the control sequence "Control-A" as "select everything in the current document," and the Ctrl key is right next to the A key. One clumsy finger can bridge them and press them both. Select the whole document, and the next key you type destroys it. (Try it! At least, try it if you have an "Undo" option in your menu.)

The innocuous nature of crickets can make us a little blasé about bugs in general, so when the termites surface in a piece of software, we don't always pay attention. There is a whole class of network security bugs in modern software that have been with us for many years, and mostly ignored. These "buffer overflow" bugs come from careless use of programming languages like C. They are common because they usually don't cause problems—and also (if you'll allow me an opinion) because programmers are rarely fired for writing buggy code, and software companies can't be sued for selling it. Unfortunately, what we took to be crickets became termites once hackers discovered that overflowing certain buffers on purpose could give them control of the entire computer.

Eek! Who'd have thought it? (Alas, one can't spray for careless programmers the way one can for termites.)

Several years after the Wi-Fi standard was first implemented, a family of really obnoxious bugs was discovered in Wi-Fi's poor beleaguered security mechanism, WEP. Suddenly, WEP couldn't be trusted anymore. With tens of millions of Wi-Fi access points out there, fixing bugs in WEP isn't easy. A brand-new security technology called Wi-Fi Protected Access (WPA) was created to "fix" WEP by replacing it entirely. WPA is now being delivered in many Wireless-G products, and I'll have more to say about it in the next few chapters. Will there be bugs in WPA? Of course. Will these be crickets or termites? We won't know until WPA is deployed broadly enough for network security experts to get a sense for its reliability. And until that time, trusting Wi-Fi security will remain a slightly touchy proposition.

Unplanned Obsolescence

Back in the Middle Ages, smiths got better and better in working with iron until they could coat an entire knight with it. The knights thought this made them invulnerable to enemy arrows. It did—and then the enemy invented crossbows and (later) muskets. With enough iron on them to stop bolts and musket balls, the knights couldn't move—so much for armor.

The very process of technology is one of continual improvement. Hardware and software doesn't spring fully formed from the brows of inventors. Ideas grow and are improved over time. What this means, however, is that any given technological moment (remember the 486? Lotus 1-2-3?) will be transcended—and replaced—by the next. This is especially true of computer security. A computer system or network may be considered "secure" because it takes a long time for someone to break into it. A long time—*today*. Next week, heh—all bets are off.

There is a way of breaking into a computer or a network called a "brute force attack." (I'll talk about it in detail later in this book.) Without getting too technical right here, it basically means trying passwords one after another until one works. When it takes a 486-33 eighteen months to mount a brute-force attack against a network, you can forgive someone for considering that network secure. However, a modern Pentium 4 running at 2.1 GHz can try a lot more passwords in a lot less time, and might break the same network in five hours. Now it's not so secure.

Being able to trust a security system last year says nothing about being able to trust it next year. The job of securing a computer or a network—or anything else—is never "done."

The Futility of Secrets

The history of DVD copy protection contains an important lesson. The movie industry thought it had an unbreakable system for preventing DVDs sold in, say, England from working on players in the United States or in other parts of the world. (This was done to facilitate price fixing, which was slow to dawn on some governments—duhh!—until very recently, and has already been outlawed in some countries, like New Zealand.) CSS (Content Scrambling System) was good—from the standpoint of an amateur computer user. Not one person in a million could have broken the system.

However, one person in a million *could*—and did. What happened next was so obvious that you wonder why the movie people didn't think of it: The guy who broke CSS wrote a little program called DeCSS that could be run on any computer to get past the CSS technology. He then posted DeCSS on the Web, where millions of people who weren't smart enough to create DeCSS themselves could download it. In a matter of days, millions of not-so-smart people were happily breaking the CSS system in seconds.

The problem with CSS is simply that to do its job (and be trusted by the movie people) its inner workings had to remain a secret. Ferreting out that secret took some brilliance and some work. However, once one smart person had broken the technology, other technology was used to automate the process, so that breaking CSS no longer required any brilliance or any work at all.

Trusting a system because the details of its operation are a secret (something called "security through obscurity") is futile. People who don't understand computer security often assume that all security mechanisms must be shrouded in secrecy, and that as soon as anyone learns how they work, they fail. This isn't true. All security systems of any value at all must withstand attack *even by people who know exactly how they work*. Such systems are harder to design, but they're designed all the time, and their creators generally publish their details of operation and encourage others to try and break them. (Unexpected flaws often turn up this way, and are then fixed.)

Of course, there are things like passwords that must be kept secret. That's not what I'm talking about. CSS only worked because the *methods* it used (mostly how it manipulated data read from the DVD itself) were a secret. Passwords weren't even involved.

Working Dumb

The first of the people problems that compromise trust in a security system is easily the most important: People do stupid things even when they know they're stupid, and may have done the corresponding smart things for some time. They do stupid things even while understanding that working stupidly goes against their own interests. As Schiller said long ago, *Against stupidity the gods themselves contend in vain.*

Backing up your data is probably the best example. The necessity of backing up your computer files is an oft-repeated mantra that goes back to the dawn of computer time. And yet everybody (myself included) has lost data here and there because backups were seriously out of date or nonexistent.

Dumb passwords are another. Is your main (or only) password your dog's name? (And is your dog named "Max?" Everybody else's dog is!) Is that password written on a sticky note and tacked to the side of your monitor?

Unlike computers (which follow our instructions precisely, even if we sometimes craft those instructions badly), people can choose not to do what they know needs to be done, and most of the computer security problems in small-systems (like those of a home network or a small office network) are of this type. In a sense, we trust our computer systems to make up for our own stupidity. Actually, it amazes me that our computers do as good a job as they do of protecting us from ourselves. That's a brittle sort of protection, however, in that when it fails, it fails badly—often spectacularly.

As Woody Allen recognized, 80% of success in life is just showing up. As I'll say elsewhere (and often) in this book, well over half of the trick of Wi-Fi security is *just turning it on.* Once you have WEP or especially WPA enabled, they provide reasonably strong protection, at least in part because so many other people have been stupid and left security turned off. The bad guys thus seek out the "low-hanging fruit"—those countless networks with no protection at all—and pass your network by.

Lots of very smart people can teach you some very simple techniques for protecting your data and your network. None of that matters at all if you don't put that wisdom to use!

Ignorance Is Expensive

Of course, there is stupidity and then there is ignorance. In our drive for productivity, we sometimes short the requirement of telling people how to work smart and why. This is more of a problem in business networks—certainly when it's your *own* butt on the line, you have substantial incentive to be careful and follow security procedures on your home network. But if other people work for you, don't underestimate the importance of training. It takes time, and time is valuable, but the downside when training is omitted can be huge.

Some people think that security techniques are obvious. Possibly—to a person used to being wary, or a seasoned manager with years of looking after people and systems. Ordinary people, especially non-technical non-managers, tend to be trusting and not suspicious, especially about technology. This came to the forefront some time back in the Wi-Fi industry, when junior staffers at large corporations were discovered to be buying newly-cheap Wi-Fi access points and plugging them into the corporate network inside their cubicles. They did this so that they could take their laptops and work in the lunchroom or even (egad) in the washroom. The guilty parties were not working stupidly, because they didn't understand the nature of Wi-Fi operations nor the inner workings of the corporate LAN. They didn't catch on to the (non-obvious) truth that they were opening a door to the corporate network *inside the company firewall*, and making it available to any nutcase sitting in the company parking lot with a laptop.

I find it astonishing to hear from friends of mine in corporate America that many companies still don't have any policy on wireless networking, or heaven knows any program to teach staffers about the risks inherent in wireless networking. When it's so easy and cheap to poke holes in a corporate LAN, companies must teach their people why it shouldn't happen without planning and proper security technology.

Ignorance is expensive, especially if (as in many large companies) you have something to lose thereby.

Don't Forget Original Sin

Good and honest people tend to assume that all other people are equally good and honest. When such people plan systems of any kind, they often fail (as my friend Michael Covington puts it) to take "Original Sin" into account. By this he means that inside all people is a touch of the scoundrel, some more than others. There are no angels here on Earth.

The Internet was originally designed by university people, who were basically good people working in a chummy environment of similar people. They valued openness and accessibility. They neglected to take into account the fact that as the Internet expanded to touch more and more lives, it would inevitably be subverted by people not as good and honest as the Internet's creators.

This is why we have such a problem with spam email. The Internet email protocols were crafted by people who never imagined that those protocols would be abused by scammers and pornographers and other human debris. The Internet email protocols don't have any place to put any means of verifying a sender's identity nor a message's authenticity. And now we're stuck with them (and scams, and spam, and porn) and may be for many years to come.

A certain carefully measured amount of suspicion is valuable in creating and using any security system. Insiders like employees have varying degrees of honesty and loyalty to the company. If you trust them without any way of gauging them, you leave a hole in your system. New employees may not warrant immediate trust with money or sensitive data. But even long-time employees can turn on an organization, and so the organization should spend a little time studying how its ways of working can be subverted by both insiders and outsiders. New systems should always be designed under the assumption that they will be subverted, with built-in measures to minimize such subversion, at least insofar as it can be anticipated. Not all subversion can be anticipated. Much of it can, and what can be anticipated should.

Of course, extremes of suspicion become paranoia and are counterproductive. Like a lot of things, it's a delicate balance. A little suspicion can work wonders. Original Sin remains in all of us.

Balancing Risk and Trust in a Complicated World

I didn't say all that to scare you off computer security. After reading about the problems inherent in computer security, a lot of people panic, and decide to trust *nothing*. That's not the proper response.

Inherent in any relationship of trust is some risk that trust will be broken. That's what trust is about, really: If the relationship were unbreakable, it wouldn't be one of trust. So trust must be balanced by a realistic understanding of the risks involved in any relationship of trust. Trusting technology involves risk. Trusting people involves risk. How much risk? That depends on the technology, the people, and the situation.

Balancing risk and trust is the process of gauging how *likely* it is for trust to fail in a given situation. Not all situations are equally likely. Yes, bad guys can get into your network and into your computers, and in an absolute sense, you can't stop them. This sounds grim, but it's also not "real." There is always some *possibility* of hackers getting into your computers and your network, irrespective of how much trust you put into your security measures. If the likelihood of a successful hacker attack is low, you can stop worrying—especially if you back up your data frequently.

So how likely are hacker attacks? How effective are the countermeasures you can put into place? What are the risks in using a wireless network?

Answering those questions will take a whole additional chapter, in order to put trust and risk into a Wi-Fi context. Read on.

What Hackers Can Do and How You Can Thwart Them

Networking is *inherently* insecure, since it involves connecting machines to other machines, and trusting both the software and the operators associated with those other machines.

You can take certain steps to make a network more secure. The first steps are easy, but the more steps you take, the harder and more expensive it gets to take further steps. You'll never get all the pits ground out of your speckled axe head, and at some point you simply have to make a decision that your network is as secure as you really need it to be, given who you are and what your network contains.

To make that decision, you need to have a reasonable grasp of the threats involved in having a network. And the best place to start is with our mythic enemy, the hacker.

The Hacker Pyramid

The hacker community (like a lot of communities) is a pyramid. At the tip are the real hackers: Guys (almost always male) who know a tremendous amount about computers and networks and expend a great deal of effort staying ahead of the technological curve. Below the tip, as the skill levels decrease, the numbers increase. Toward the bottom are the wannabe hackers who like the glamour and the gritty reputation but don't know enough to be dangerous. They are legion. Real hackers dismiss them as "script kiddies," usually teens who use the most primitive tools to work minor (and easily blocked) exploits. The term "script kiddies" comes from the fact that these people rip off pre-written scripts that hackers have previously developed to do their hacking. This is why they often go after the weakest fish who are still susceptible to older network attacks.

There was a time when the term "hacker" was a badge of honor, of sorts, worn by people who really knew their stuff and could work miracles with it. (The term was originally applied a century ago to expert horsemen who could make a horse do whatever they wanted, and do it with grace and style.) When every machine was an island (as they were before the days of pervasive networking), there wasn't a great deal that a hacker could do to get into other machines. But as networking became possible for personal computers in the early to mid-1980s, the ethics challenged in the hacker community began to create what are now called "hacker exploits." The most common of these are worms and Trojan horses that were distributed on disk or by way of computer bulletin board downloads.

Black Hats and White Hats

The opening of the Internet to the general public (instead of the privileged few at universities and large corporations) in the early 1990s coincided with the blackening of the term "hacker." Without any added security technology, breaking into machines connected to the Internet is almost absurdly easy, and the "black hat" hackers grew in numbers and skill with the expansion of the Internet.

There are people who think of themselves as "white hats" (usually without the appended—but assumed—term "hacker") who study networking and hacker exploits to guard against the black hats. Most of the network security technology we have today would not have happened without the work of the white hats, some of whom (admittedly) got their start as black hats.

And there are always a few hats hanging around whose color seems to be a shade of dirty gray.

The Network Mafia

The genuine black hat hackers are a little like the Mafia. Just as the Mafia don't go around shooting up randomly selected people for the sheer hell of it, the most skillful hackers are the ones with the clearest agendas. These agendas are either criminal or political. Unless you piss them off or have something they want, hackers are unlikely to come after you personally. (You may, however, get caught up in an automated mass exploit like a denial of service attack; more on that later.)

The criminal agendas involve stealing data or information: credit card numbers and phone card numbers, or (more rarely) corporate information, trade secrets, and human resources information for purposes of identity theft.

Political agendas are more common: On August 28, 2002, the Recording Industry of America's Web site was creatively defaced by a crew of hackers who objected to the RIAA's hamhanded and overly broad efforts to protect music CDs. The RIAA home page was edited in various ways. Among other things, a link was added, with the text "Where can I find information on giant monkeys?" and the URL of RIAA chief Hilary Rosen's biography page. (I hate to say it, but I consider that really funny.)

What Hackers Can Do

The press is fond of saying that there are a multitude of different kinds of hacker exploits, but in truth there are only a few different kinds of things that hackers can accomplish:

1. They can connect to your computer without your knowledge or permission, in order to vandalize your machine or steal data or bandwidth.

2. Even without connecting to your computer, they can "sniff" your network traffic to obtain passwords, credit card numbers, or other useful information.

3. They can hijack your machine by planting a Trojan Horse program on it.

4. If you're running a server of some kind, they can mount a "denial of service" attack against your server.

Nearly all hacker exploits fall into one of these four categories, which I'll treat separately. Note that viruses are not, strictly speaking, a hacker phenomenon, though many people think of them that way.

Unauthorized Connection

The whole idea of the Internet is to connect machines with one another across distances that can be global. The challenge of Internet security is to prevent such connections when they're not wanted, and limit the scope of the connections that are permitted.

If a hacker manages to connect to your home network, he can read what's on your hard drives and copy out any files he might deem interesting, or possibly plant Trojan horse programs (more on which below) without your knowledge. Simple vandalism is also possible, but the thrill of nuking files or formatting other people's hard drives wears off quickly and isn't done very often.

If you have a Wi-Fi network in place without any security, a "drive-by" hacker can easily use your Internet connection to surf the Web or check email, which may be annoying but isn't directly damaging. However, drive-by hackers who use your Internet connection are often trying to engage in *IP impersonation*, which is a species of identity theft. IP impersonation means that they do obnoxious or illegal things through your Internet connection, like sending spam email or transmitting kiddie porn. If the authorities trace this activity back to its source, surprise! It looks like the perpetrator was *you*. This is in fact your greatest risk as a Wi-Fi network owner, and I'll describe the problem in detail later on. (You'll be pleased to know that it's pretty easy to prevent.)

Network Traffic Sniffing

"Packet sniffing" is something like a network wiretap. A packet sniffer utility watches traffic going through a network without disrupting it, recording some or all of that traffic in a log file, so the hacker can examine it at leisure. (Traffic over networks is broken into chunks called *packets*, hence the term.

On a wired network, there is the not-inconsiderable challenge of installing a packet sniffer utility on one of the networked machines. However, Wi-Fi is based on radio, which opens up a universe of new possibilities for packet sniffers. Radio waves are not confined to the inside of a cable, and anywhere your Wi-Fi radio signals go, a packet sniffer program can passively monitor them with no one the wiser. A drive-by hacker can park within the field boundaries of your Wi-Fi access point and undetectably sniff packets on a laptop using a free utility like AirSnort or Kismet. Such a hacker doesn't even have to drive: A Linux-based PDA like the Zaurus can run AirSnort in the hacker's pocket or briefcase while he's visiting your company's offices. Once AirSnort logs enough packets, it can reverse-engineer passwords and render your Wi-Fi security mechanism useless.

Packet sniffing is a hazard at its most serious when your Wi-Fi signal extends to places over which you have no knowledge or control. If your office is on the seventh floor of an office building, people in an office directly atop yours on the eighth floor (or below it, on the sixth) can very likely receive your Wi-Fi radio signal, and sniff packets *without any way for you to know that they're sniffing*. If you live in a neighborhood where the houses are set very close to one another, the teenagers next door may be able to break your WEP encryption with AirSnort at their leisure, using a Linux machine on their desk and an unseen gain antenna aimed at your house…right through their bedroom wall! (Wood frame construction is mostly transparent to microwaves like those used in Wi-Fi gear, and gain antennas can compensate to a great extent for the fraction of your signal absorbed by wood and plaster.)

Packet sniffing in a Wi-Fi environment is the most difficult of hacker exploits to prevent. Your best defense is enabling either Wired Equivalent Privacy or better still (if your Wi-Fi hardware supports it) Wi-Fi Protected Access. WEP, while not the perfect defense, is far better than the press has made it out to be. WPA is much stronger, though hardly unbreakable. Again, I'll present much more on this in following chapters.

Hijacking Via Trojan Horse

Perhaps the most diabolical hacker exploit is the "remote access" *Trojan horse*, which is a program that, when run on your computer, opens up a "back door" onto the Internet, through which a hacker can obtain complete control over your machine. A computer under the control of such a Trojan horse has been *hijacked*, or "jacked" as techie insiders usually say. The most famous Trojan horse is called Back Orifice, though there are quite a few others, and they all work more or less the same way.

A Trojan horse program can be installed on your system in various ways. A virus coming into your machine on an email attachment can install a Trojan horse. (Remember that a Trojan horse is *not* the same thing as a virus!) You can unwittingly install a Trojan horse program yourself by downloading a seemingly innocuous program (like a game or animation of some kind) in which the Trojan horse has been deliberately hidden. A hacker who manages to connect to your machine from the Internet can install a Trojan horse manually. If your network defenses are weak or nonexistent, a script kiddie can run an idiot-level script that will install Trojan horse programs automatically on any machine it can get into.

What Trojan horse programs actually do varies widely. Most of them take no action of their own other than simply opening back doors to the Internet, through which a hacker can take control of your machine. Some are "zombie" or "drone" programs designed to launch denial of service (DoS) attacks on other systems, usually Web sites. In a DoS attack, a hacker or group of hackers secretly installs a Trojan horse program on a large number of machines. The silent army of zombie programs then waits patiently for a signal to come in from their installers over the Internet, at which time they wake up and begin sending a flood of nonsense packets or connection requests at a specific target. The target machine or server is soon overwhelmed and crashes or must be shut down.

A different twist on the Trojan horse concept became common in 2003, during which time many Trojan programs appeared, with the mission of planting *open proxies* on infected machines. These Trojans were delivered by viruses sent as email attachments, designed to trick people into opening—and thus running—them on their PCs. An open proxy is a sort of network redirection machine, which is most often used to send spam email. Spammers (who are often the hackers who plant the open proxies) use the proxies to send email messages by the tens of millions. By virtue of the way the proxy works, it becomes very difficult to determine where the spam actually originated. By early 2004, network experts estimated that as much as 40% of all spam was sent through open proxies.

 There are many security utilities that watch for Trojan horse programs, including Norton Anti-Virus and the Zone Alarm Pro firewall. A good firewall will also help by blocking the eventual attempt to access the Trojan horse from the Internet.

The "low-hanging fruit effect" works to your advantage here. There are so many "easy" machines connected to the Internet that no hacker is going to sweat and strain to plant a Trojan on *your* machine, if something like Zone Alarm Pro makes it difficult. (And it does!)

Recruiting machines for Trojan horses is done automatically. Hackers use scripts (simple programs) to probe tens of thousands or millions of machines for vulnerabilities. These vulnerabilities fall into several classes. One vulnerability exists when a Trojan horse program is already present on your machine, either planted earlier by a hacker or installed by a virus-infected program, an email attachment, or a program that isn't quite what it appears to be. My firewall logs and blocks dozens of probes every day for Trojan systems like Back Orifice. Another vulnerability is the availability of a protocol like FTP, which would allow a hacker or a script to upload a Trojan and install it on your computer.

All of this has to be done quickly, because to launch a Denial of Service attack, it has to be done many thousands of times. If your machine doesn't respond instantly to a probe, the script passes you by. On the Internet, there's always another sucker right next door.

Denial of Service Attacks

You can also be on the receiving end of a DoS attack, especially if you're running a Web server or some other service that is available over the Internet. Once the attack begins, there's not much you can do but shut your machine down (and, ideally, disconnect from the Internet) until the attack passes. DoS attacks don't usually damage your data, but simply make it impossible for legitimate users to connect to your machine.

Fortunately, residential networks and small office networks are almost never targeted for DoS attacks, because such networks rarely host publicly accessible servers. This is a risk so small that you might as well ignore it.

IP Impersonation

Of all the various attacks that hackers can mount against home office and small office wireless networks, the most important by far is something I call *IP impersonation*. Unlike the risk of someone mounting a denial of service attack against your system (which is extremely small), the risk of IP impersonation is significant, if not (yet) great.

IP impersonation is a species of identity theft. An intruder connecting to the Internet through your wireless access point is basically impersonating you, and if that intruder's possibly illegal actions are traced back (using the IP address of your Internet connection), it will appear as though you were the one doing the lawbreaking. *Not* good.

Accessing the Internet is *not* anonymous. You are identifiable by your IP address. (See Chapter 3 for more on IP addresses and how they work.) Your Internet Service Provider (ISP) assigns you an IP address (usually automatically, through a DHCP server) and keeps it in a database. Anything you would ordinarily do on the Internet (send email, post a file to a newsgroup, access a peer-to-peer file-sharing network) can be associated with your IP address, and if you do something illegal on the Internet and Somebody Notices, you can be tracked down through your IP address.

Most people intuitively understand this, even when they can't explain all the arcana of IP addressing. What a lot of people *don't* understand is that all machines on a small office or home office (SOHO) LAN that share the same Internet connection also share the same IP address. (See the topic "Internet Connection Sharing" in Chapter 3 for the technical details.) And what almost *nobody* seems to understand is that when someone parks in front of your house and accesses your wide-open wireless access point to get onto the Internet, that someone is also sharing your IP address.

What everybody seems to fear from hackers these days is getting their machines hijacked or vandalized, with wiped-out hard drive and lost files. That happens, of course, but not as often as the media would like you to believe. Vandalism appeals to a certain brand of disaffected teenager, but there's no money in it and it loses its novelty after awhile. On the other hand, being able to access the Internet using someone else's IP address can be a paying proposition, and a dangerous one—for you.

Covert Wi-Fi Spamming

Internet service providers generally prohibit the transmission of spam email from their customer accounts. When someone reports spam coming from such an account, most ISPs shut that account down immediately. This is why so much spam comes from email addresses like kjtqvw@hotmail.com. Spammers understand that these are single-use addresses that will probably be shut down within 24 hours, and simply pump out the spam until the ISP acts. Especially on a broadband connection, you can send a *lot* of spam in 24 hours!

So imagine a spammer with a laptop sitting in front of your house, or perhaps in a parking lot down the street with an innocuous gain antenna on the roof of their car. They connect to your network, run a spam email program, and suddenly tens of thousands of emails per hour begin flowing onto the Internet, through *your* connection, associated with *your* IP address. You probably won't even notice that it happened, if a wily spammer does it at two in the morning when you and your family are asleep and your PCs and Internet connection are idle. You won't notice, that is, until your ISP cuts off your Internet service for spamming the next day.

Spamming, while supremely annoying, is not illegal (as much as most of us would like it to be, sigh). But suppose some devious person wants to upload pirated videos to a newsgroup—or, worse, kiddie porn? If that person connects to the Net on your IP and transmits illegal files, from the standpoint of law enforcement, it's you doing the transmitting, unless you can prove otherwise. (Proving that you didn't do something is notoriously difficult, especially in the slippery world of cyberspace.)

Transmitting illegal files has already happened, and it will certainly happen more frequently in the future. Not long ago, the next-door neighbor of an AT&T Broadband customer began transmitting pirated videos to associates in the middle of the night through the hapless customer's Wi-Fi network and AT&T Broadband Internet connection. The video's copyright owners tracked down the customer using his IP address, and the real culprit was caught using network logging software that showed the unwelcome connection when it happened again.

That wouldn't work quite as well in a drive-by situation because the culprit is usually gone before you notice that anything's afoot. The whole point I'm making is that you can be held responsible for things done by other people through your Internet connection. This is the #1 reason that you should enable the security mechanism on your wireless access point or wireless gateway, and take the several other easy security steps outlined in the next chapter. IP impersonation is relatively easy to stop, especially the drive-by kind, where the impersonator has little or no time to break through even minimal security measures. Don't leave yourself wide-open, as statistics gathered by wardrivers (see Chapter 19) show that almost *65%* of Wi-Fi users do.

What Measures You Should Take

Most network security advice applies whether you have a Wi-Fi network or not. Wi-Fi introduces some specific complications into the network security equation, but you should take general network security precautions first:

1. Install a virus detector, and update it regularly. I've used Norton Anti Virus (NAV) for a good many years, and the only times I've ever been stung by a virus were the times I had turned NAV off for various arcane reasons (all of them connected with low-level systems programming) and forgot to turn it back on again.

2. Make regular backups and keep them in a safe place. I'm continually amazed at the number of people who ignore this stone-age advice. I keep a monthly backup of all my data files in our safe deposit box, and perform a daily backup on any files I work on during the course of the day.

3. Put a firewall in place. Most routers and wireless gateways intended for the small office/home office (SOHO) market include a Network Address Translation (NAT) hardware firewall that works very well—but doesn't do everything. To prevent certain hacker exploits and annoying nuisances like pop-under ads, you should also install a separate software firewall program, such as Zone Alarm Pro. Note well that firewalls protect you from attacks coming in from the Internet. They do *nothing* to prevent attacks that come in through your wireless access point!

4. Be careful about opening email attachments and installing software from unknown parties. NAV will catch a lot, but it must already know what to look for, and if you happen upon a newly released Trojan horse, NAV may miss it.

Adding Wi-Fi specific measures is actually very simple:

1. Turn on your access point or gateway's security mechanism. This will be either Wired Equivalent Privacy (WEP) or Wi-Fi Protected Access (WPA). Nearly all Wi-Fi gear manufactured before late 2003 will support WEP only. All

Wi-Fi access points and client adapters support either WEP or WPA, but all arrive in their pretty boxes with all security turned off. (A few brave Wi-Fi vendors will admit that they do this to keep their technical support calls to a minimum.) If you don't turn it on, it won't help you at all. The press has made much of the fact that WEP can be cracked using packet sniffing utilities, but it's not as quick to accomplish—nor as easy—as non-technical reporters have made it out to be. And WPA is much, *much* harder to break—though it's too new to know for certain whether there are any undiscovered holes in it.

2. Change the default Service Set Identifier (SSID). All access points come with a default SSID. Linksys's default is "linksys"; Cisco's is "tsunami." Changing it doesn't really help protect your system except in a peculiar way: Hackers often assume that people who don't change the SSID have been lax in other ways, and may consider your network "low-hanging fruit." Don't give away too much information in your SSID. Wardrivers often see SSIDs like "The Dorkman Family Network" and "Cloofre Realty, Inc." Why tempt somebody looking for clueless families and businesses? Choose a jumble of letters and numbers, or a weird word like "tatterdemalion" that says nothing about who you are and what you do.

3. Don't use obvious passwords. Avoid your initials, the names of your kids or dogs, the make of your car, your birth year, or other guessable things. There is an obvious tension between rememberability and guessability. The passwords most resistant to cracking are truly random jumbles of characters, but "vanity plate" sequences like "2GOOD2B4GOT10" are almost as good, and much harder to forget.

4. I differ strongly with most of my fellow Wi-Fi advice-givers in one way: If you enable WEP or WPA, you don't really need MAC address filtering. MAC address filtering is almost worthless, and should only be used if for some reason you have client adapters that can't communicate with your access point when WEP is enabled. (And if you can't get your adapters to talk to your access point over WEP, you need new adapters...or a new access point.) I'll speak more of MAC address filtering in Chapter 14.

5. Other security measures mentioned frequently in the press, like turning off your SSID beacon, aren't of much use if you have WEP enabled. Utilities like Kismet can find your access point whether its beacon is on or not. Don't bother.

To this regimen you can add some fairly simple "physical" security measures that will help grind a few more pits out of security's speckled axe:

1. Use removable media for your sensitive data, and pop the media out of the machine any time you're not in front of the machine working on it. I use Zip 250 cartridges for all my data. The only stuff I really keep on my hard drive is installed software. If your data isn't on the machine when a hacker or a Trojan horse strikes, it won't be damaged or stolen!

2. Turn your broadband modem (cable or DSL) off when nobody's using it. Attacks by Drive-By-Hackers often occur in the middle of the night when there's nobody using the machines on your network and thus nobody to notice all the blinking data LEDs on your router. If your broadband modem is powered down, hackers can't use your Internet connection to commit IP impersonation.

3. Turn your computer off when no one's using it. If your computer is powered down, hackers can't break into it. Besides, you may be surprised at how much it costs in electricity to keep a modern, fast PC powered up 24/7. Read point 4 before you choose to do this, however.

4. Points 2 and 3 having been said, leave your wireless access point and (if possible) your client adapters *powered up* if you use Wired Equivalent Privacy. There is a very technical but important glitch in WEP encryption: Many Wi-Fi devices reset their sequence of initialization vectors (IVs) when they initialize on power-up. (Don't fret if this means nothing to you just now.) This is bad engineering for reasons I will explain in Chapter 13, when I discuss in more detail how WEP fails. Most client adapters draw their power from the computer to which they are attached and power down when the computer does, and thus there's nothing you can do about them. However, you can and should put your access point on a separate outlet or power bar from the rest of your system, and leave it on all the time. Note well: This point does not apply if you're using WPA!

Life is rarely simple. Points 3 and 4 are to some extent in tension with one another. Leaving your computers and access point on all the time reduces the hacker threat from duplicate IV values, but if hackers do break in, your computer is on and can be compromised. If you use WEP security rather than WPA, my rule of thumb is this:

- If your network is at your business location, keep your computers and Wi-Fi devices powered up all the time, but power-down your broadband modem after business hours to prevent IP impersonation and incursions from outside via the Internet. Make sure you implement frequent backups and physical security for your data.

- If your network is at your home, power down your computers and broadband modem every night, but keep your access point powered up if possible. As long as your broadband modem is off, there's not much that a drive-by hacker will likely want from your network, especially if there are a lot of unsecured networks nearby.

Some progress is being made: Proxim's Orinoco line of access points and client adapters filter out weak IV values, and you can upgrade the firmware of older units to allow them that same enhancement as new-off-the-line Orinoco gear. The Wi-Fi Alliance is now certifying Wi-Fi gear for the Wi-Fi Protected Access standard. This mostly applies to newer gear, particularly Wireless-G. Older Wireless-B gear probably does not have the internal compute power to handle WPA, and with Wireless-G now stealing the show in the Wi-Fi world, it's unclear whether vendors will bother to certify new Wireless-B gear for WPA. Even if you don't need the additional throughput, WPA is an excellent excuse to re-equip your network with Wireless-G equipment. Still, WEP is not nearly as bad as the press has made it out to be, and in the next two chapters I will cover both WEP and WPA.

The Good News and the Bad News

That's the big picture on security. The bad news is that it's impossible to make a networked computer completely secure, and it's difficult to make a Wi-Fi equipped network even middling secure. The Department of Defense has issued a directive to the military, essentially advising them not to use wireless networks. They have a lot to lose, as do banks, big corporations, and organizations like the RIAA with hordes of enemies in the hacker community.

On the other hand, the risks to you as a home office worker or small business owner are much less, largely because the really expert hackers up at the tip of the hacker pyramid don't have any reason to go after you. Protecting yourself against the great mass of script kiddies and drive-by-hackers isn't difficult and should be done as soon as you install your wireless network. The next three chapters will allow you to do this without losing a lot of hair.

WEP (Wired Equivalent Privacy)

Were it not for the security issue, there'd be a *whole* lot less to say about Wi-Fi. Wires make for reasonable security: Unless you can physically access the wires (and thus tap into them) a wired network is much, much more secure, at least from outsiders. (Subversion from legitimate insiders is a whole different question.)

Radio waves change everything. People sitting out in the street can "listen" to your Wi-Fi network with packet sniffers, and if your network is wide-open and unprotected, they can connect to your network and use it without your knowledge or permission. Maybe they just want to surf the Web on somebody else's nickel—or maybe they're looking for an opportunity to commit IP impersonation, during which they may commit a crime or do other obnoxious things while making it look like the perpetrator is *you*.

When the original 802.11 standards were being designed in the 1990s, Wired Equivalent Privacy (WEP) was developed to protect against such problems. As you've no doubt heard, WEP is flawed, and can be cracked by hackers using free tools like AirSnort. The press on WEP has been mostly bad, but the truth is much more complex. WEP is far more useful than people make it sound, and if your Wi-Fi gear is too old to be upgraded to support Wi-Fi Protected Access (see Chapter 14), WEP is about all you may be able to do to protect your Wi-Fi network.

WEP is a program that runs in your access point's firmware, as well as in the firmware of all client adapters that connect to your access point. All Wi-Fi compliant hardware devices *must* have WEP available in a compatible form. Some manufacturers have extended WEP to make it more secure, but those extensions are not standardized, and if you use the extensions you may not be able to make hardware from different vendors intercommunicate. Be aware that the WEP standard defines *only* 64-bit encryption. The very common 128-bit encryption feature is a WEP extension and may not work identically on equipment from different vendors! (I'll have more to say on these misleading bit-length encryption numbers later on. As usual, all is not what it seems.)

What WEP Does—and Does Not Do

As I said in Chapter 11, a micrometer is not a C clamp, and vise versa. Many of the "problems" with WEP stem from people expecting it to be things it was never intended to be. WEP has one mission: *To keep outsiders from connecting to a wireless network or monitoring traffic on that network.* That's it! WEP was not designed to be anything more than that. Most pointedly:

• WEP is *not* an end-to-end encryption mechanism. It provides the same degree of privacy afforded by sending unencrypted traffic through a network cable, hence the phrase "wired equivalent" in its name. With some work and some stealth, hackers can tap into a wired network. With some work and some stealth, hackers can tap into a Wi-Fi network too.

• WEP does *not* distribute or manage encryption keys. Key distribution must be done manually, outside of the 802.11 specification. This is certainly a burden, but it's not WEP's fault. The more recent Wi-Fi Protected Access (WPA) standard fixes this, with a new protocol called Temporal Key Integrity. The IEEE 802.11i task group standard will bring the fix back into the context of a true 802.11 family standard, but that standard is still (at this writing) incomplete.

• WEP does *not* hide traffic sent by one legitimate user of a wireless network from other legitimate users of the same network. Using common packet sniffer utilities, one user can eavesdrop freely on all the others. Don't be appalled; legitimate users of wired networks can pull the same trick!

• WEP does *not* authenticate users except by checking encryption keys. WEP's assumption is that a user with a valid encryption key is a legitimate user. WEP does not check any sort of user ID, password, or hardware MAC address. Someday this authentication task will be done by 802.1X systems via portions of the Wi-Fi Protected Access technology and the still-evolving 802.11i task group standard. For now, it's not done at all. (MAC Address Filtering is a separate Wi-Fi feature that some consider a primitive form of authentication. It is not part of WEP at all, and as I'll explain later, this feature is not an especially useful one.)

How WEP Works

WEP protects data moving across a wireless network by encrypting the traffic that passes between wireless access points and client adapters like PCMCIA cards inserted into laptops or PDAs, and PCI cards inside desktop machines. Once WEP is operating, an outsider with a wireless packet sniffer will see packets full of jumbled and apparently random numbers and letters.

The encryption algorithm WEP uses is a "stream cipher" called RC4, which was developed by RSA Security quite a few years ago. RC4 was chosen because it's fairly simple and fast-running. Using RC4 slows down a network much less than a more complex algorithm would. Explaining the WEP encryption mechanism step-by-step, while interesting, is not very useful if all you want to do is *use* it—and explaining it *well* would take more space than I can give it in this book. If you're curious, dial up this Web document:

www.isaac.cs.berkeley.edu/isaac/mobicom.pdf

This explanation is extremely technical but it's the best one I've seen online so far of how WEP works and how hackers break it. A less technical presentation (actually, a PowerPoint slide set) is available at the following Web site: www.cacr.math.uwaterloo.ca/conferences/2001/isw-eighth/slides/slides/Borisov.ppt

From a *user's* standpoint, WEP's operation is fairly simple:

- The user generates four different encryption keys. For the standard 64-bit encryption that all Wi-Fi devices understand, each key is a 10-digit "hexadecimal" (base 16) value. You can create a key by picking ten random hex digits out of the air. A hex digit may be any number from 0 to 9, plus the letters A to F. A key looks something like this: 916C5B77AF. Many modern access points include a utility that will generate these four keys for you, from a *passphrase*, which is a sequence of letters or words like "stoddlemerry" or "hoodle the infrey." On a given adapter, the same passphrase will always generate the same four keys. Note that some products will only generate a single key from a passphrase, rather than four.

- The user then distributes the four keys (or a single key, if only one key is required for a given network installation) to all client adapters that will connect to the access point. This process—*key distribution*—is a crucial issue in Wi-Fi security. It may require typing in forty hex digits with absolute accuracy—uggh!—but it can often be done by typing in the same passphrase into a utility running on all your client machines. Different models work in different ways. Linksys hardware, for example, allows you to use a passphrase. Much early hardware from Cisco and Agere required manual entry of all keys. Most modern hardware uses a passphrase-driven key generator. The difficulties of key distribution are to a great extent resolved by the Wireless Protected Access (WPA) standard and, reasonably soon, the IEEE task group 802.11i.

- Once your access point and all client adapters belonging to your network have all required keys, you can enable WEP, and at that point all traffic between the access point and the client adapters will be encrypted.

- Nothing more needs to be done until such time as you decide to change keys. It's a good idea to do this now and then; weekly, if possible but monthly is okay.

I've written a detailed description of how to enable WEP in Chapter 15.

How WEP Fails

In very simple terms, WEP does its encryption by XORing (combining) a block of "cleartext" (unencrypted data) with a string of pseudorandom numbers the same length as the block of cleartext, usually 1,500 bytes. This string of pseudorandom numbers is called a *keystream*. The block of data is called a *frame*. Frames are embedded in packets and then transmitted over the air. It is absolutely vital that a different keystream be used to encrypt each frame. If a network cracker manages to sniff two packets whose frames are encrypted with the same keystream, cracking the secret key becomes easier. In fact, the more packets are recorded with the same keystream, the easier cracking the secret key becomes. So essentially each bit of data that goes out is combined with a bunch of random junk to prevent someone from knowing what is actually in the data. Since the junk changes with each piece of data, the hacker can't (easily) separate the "wheat from the chaff" and thus your communications are safer.

The problem is this: The pseudorandom numbers that go into the keystream are generated with a 24-bit random number seed (a seed is an initial value that the computer uses to generate "random" numbers) called an *initialization vector* (IV).

This IV value is transmitted with every encrypted frame, *in the clear* and unencrypted. So a hacker can look at two encrypted frames and know whether or not they were encrypted with the same IV.

Nominally, each frame transmitted is encrypted with a different IV. The problem is, *there are only 16,777,216 different IV values.* That may sound like a lot, but when you have a Wi-Fi network capable of slinging data at 11 megabits per second, you can exhaust all possible IV values in about six hours if the network is in continuous, saturated use. At that point, most current Wi-Fi hardware resets the IV value to zero and begins again, so a second set of 16,777,216 frames begins to move through the air, providing a patient hacker with a full second set of frames encrypted with the same IV. After another six hours a third set begins with the same IV, and so on. In a little over a day's time, enough frames can be recorded by a hacker to allow the calculation of the secret key used to encrypt all those frames. (It takes between 15 and 25 *billion* bytes of data, sometimes more, to do the crack in a reasonable amount of time. Sometimes it takes less, due to "weak" IV values. More on that a little later.)

The good news is that this is for a network that is *constantly* moving data, at the maximum bit rate, without pause, for an entire day. Some corporate Wi-Fi networks may be used as heavily as that. Most small office and home office networks are not, or anywhere even close. A home office network with two or three users might pass so little data that it would take *months* to gather enough encrypted data to do the crack.

Most hackers aren't especially patient, and in truth what you have on your machine probably isn't worth that kind of effort to them (see Chapter 12). This means that for all its flaws, WEP is strong protection for lightly used networks. As I explained earlier, security isn't necessarily fool proof, but may be thought of as a wall built high enough to discourage all but the most determined intruders. The time it takes to hack into Wi-Fi networks on which WEP is enabled is what will keep you secure.

Weak Initialization Vector (IV) Values

The bad news is that there is a complication: Weak IVs. By an extremely arcane mathematical quirk, about 2% of those 16,777,216 IV values turn traitor: They "leak" a little information about the data that they encrypt. Each frame's IV value is included with the frame, and in the clear. The IV is *not* encrypted! This allows password cracker utilities like AirSnort to watch for weak IV values, and it gathers packets encrypted using weak IVs until it has enough to do the crack. This can shorten the time it takes to crack WEP radically, to as little as an hour or two for a heavily used network, or perhaps a week or ten days for a lightly used home network. The time required depends completely on how often weak IVs turn up in the stream of packets passing between access points and clients.

And how often a weak IV will turn up in a transmission is almost impossible to predict. Weak IV values are not distributed evenly throughout the full range of possible IV values, and if an access point is using IVs sequentially it may use several in quick succession, and then no more for a long time. If an access point pulls IV values at random, all bets are off. You just can't tell.

Published research indicates that it takes between 60 and 256 frames of data encrypted with a weak IV to crack WEP. Weak IVs are sparse enough in the total space of 16 million IVs so that about 5 million frames must be gathered to have enough weak IVs to do the crack. Of course, a hacker can get lucky and gather weak IVs more quickly than that; it's just impossible to tell. For corporate networks in constant use, that can be as little as an hour, though usually longer. For sparsely used home networks, it could still take weeks at the *very* least. So if you notice a guy sitting across from your house in a car that hasn't moved for two days, with a newly grown beard, and a crate full of Power Bars... worry.

Getting rid of weak IVs entirely would at least solve this particular problem. Some Wi-Fi hardware vendors have begun to filter out weak IV values inside access points and client adapters before they're used to encrypt frames. Orinoco, as best I know, was the first product line to incorporate *weak IV filtering*. Others are working on it, and fairly soon weak IV filtering will be *de rigueur* in the Wi-Fi world. Even if you have older Wi-Fi gear, you may be able to add weak IV filtering yourself by performing a firmware update. Check with your Wi-Fi manufacturer's Web site to see if firmware updates are available for your equipment, and if so, download and install the updates.

There are other peculiar glitches that can make cracking WEP easier. Re-initializing some client adapters causes the IV sequence to reset to 0. (This is the *only* reason I can think of for leaving your Wi-Fi hardware powered up all the time.) If the adapter is initialized regularly, low-value IVs will be used more frequently than high-value IVs, and the chances of a listening hacker gathering sufficient packets encrypted with the same IV increases. Certain random IV generation systems fall prey to the "birthday paradox," which indicates that randomly generated numbers will turn up duplicates more rapidly than simply iterating through the full sequence in order.

The "birthday paradox" is a statistical anomaly that can be stated this way: If you have 20 people in a room (say, at a dinner party) the chances that two of them have the same birthday is about 40%. "By inspection" this seems peculiarly high (and you can try it yourself at your next dinner party) but the math has been proven. There are more possible IVs than possible birthdays, of course, so the chances are not as bad as that, but they are still bad enough so that pulling IVs randomly is not the best way to operate.

Unfortunately, I've found that most Wi-Fi manufacturers don't talk about how their firmware works. (Some manufacturers, to be fair, buy their firmware from the chip foundries that supply their Wi-Fi chipsets, or from software houses like KarlNet, and thus don't even *know* how it works!) To find out how your access point chooses IV values probably requires that you do some packet sniffing and analyze the sequence of IVs by which your data is encrypted under WEP. If you're savvy with Linux and have a Linux machine available to you, install AirSnort, learn how to interpret the data it provides, and see what your own risks are. This takes a good deal of skill and isn't for everybody, obviously, but the very best defense you can mount against the black hats is to become a white hat yourself.

Defeating AirSnort with Key Rotation

There's a pretty effective fix for AirSnort-style attacks on WEP: If you change your encryption keys before 16,777,216 frames pass over your system, duplicate IV values don't matter. (This depends, of course, on how IV values are chosen on your hardware, which is difficult to determine. If your hardware issues IVs randomly, duplicates will turn up more quickly than if IVs are issued sequentially.) Similarly, if you change your encryption keys before significant numbers of weak IV values are used, the attack will fail. It's only when duplicate or weak IV values and the *same* encryption key pair up that the attack is possible. Change the keys, and the hacker has to begin recording frames again, from scratch. This is why it's important to change your WEP encryption keys on a regular basis. Changing keys weekly is *very* strong protection for a lightly used home network. Changing them monthly is reasonably good, unless certain members of your family are constantly downloading MP3 audio or DVD video files through their Wi-Fi links. (Are they? It might be a good time to check.)

For large corporate networks that pass a lot of data, the picture is not as good. Key distribution is a difficult and time-consuming process for networks that have a lot of wireless adapters. Changing keys daily would be strong protection, but that would involve running around to every Wi-Fi client adapter on the network every morning to manually re-enter a new set of keys. Some companies are actually doing that, but it's a lot of man-hours to spend.

Automatic key update is one of the "key" features (sorry) of both the Wi-Fi Protected Access (WPA) standard and the (further out) IEEE 802.11i task group draft standard. Automatic key update is part of a larger technology called Temporal Key Integrity Protocol (TKIP) that both WPA and 802.11i implement. Once manufacturers incorporate WPA or 802.11i features into their hardware, WEP becomes a *much* stronger security system. Automatic key update will generate new WEP encryption keys automatically at a preset interval (and if the machine does all the work, it can be done every couple of hours) and transmit them in encrypted form to all connected client machines, which then switch to the new keys automatically. The new keys are encrypted by the old keys, so if new keys are sent out fairly often, even once a day, WEP becomes almost uncrackable by utilities like AirSnort.

Of course, the AirSnort attack is not the only way to attack WEP. It's just the quickest. There's another way that you should be aware of, though it's not as much of a threat.

Brute-Force Attacks

The two methods to break a password or key-protected system are:

1. Exploit some weakness in the method used to encrypt the data. WEP has a serious flaw in its encryption algorithm, and this well-known "RC4" flaw is behind utilities like AirSnort and WEPCrack.

2. Start with a dictionary of common passwords, and throw passwords at the system until you find one that works. Such dictionaries have been compiled by hacker groups around the world and can be found on the Web without a great deal of searching. (I discovered with some amusement that my last name "Duntemann"—is in a password dictionary assembled by hackers in Germany. Needless to say, I'm not using my last name as a password, and I often wonder who is!)

The second method tries passwords or key strings until one works. Because of something called "social engineering" (which basically means taking advantage of other people's stupidity) a dictionary-based brute-force attack can work very quickly—*if* you used the name of your dog or one of your kids or a big city or something common and easily guessed.

A brute-force attack on WEP isn't quite that easy. WEP doesn't actually use a password made out of letters and numbers. WEP uses purely numeric key values that are actually strings of hexadecimal (base 16) digits. Some manufacturers of Wi-Fi gear use a "key generator" to generate a hexadecimal key value from a textual word or phrase like "Minneapolis" or "gotta boogie all night long." But the key itself is a simple number.

Theoretically, with a number you start at zero and count up (or start at the maximum value and count down) trying keys sequentially until one works. It's possible to eliminate some values through arcane cryptographic analysis, but what's left are still a great many keys to try.

 The kicker for brute-force attacks on WEP, however, is the unavoidable time it takes to try a key. "Guessing" doesn't have to go through the entire challenge-response conversation used by WEP, but each guess requires calculations that take a small but still significant amount of time.

Security expert Tim Newsham actually wrote a brute-force WEP attack utility, and found that a brute force attack on standard 40/64 bit WEP would take about 210 days on a typical Pentium system—and calculated that a brute-force attack on the more secure 104/128 bit WEP would take, well, longer than the remaining lifetime of our universe (10^{19} years!).

Brute force attacks generally do not pick keys at random. There are a few shortcuts, and all of them are based on the sort of "social engineering" that I mentioned earlier. Most savvy hackers begin a brute force attack with WEP keys generated from a dictionary of common passwords. To forestall this sort of attack you should not use common words or any word or phrase somehow guessable from your name or business. (That is, avoid using your spouse's name, your children's names, your dog or cat's name, the type of car you drive, things like that.) The best passphrases for WEP key generators are "vanity plate" sequences like 1tallcool1forme2nite or i1thelottery2day that are easily remember-able but not guessable. Random strings of characters are better but not very easy to remember. Do your best, and always remember the low-hanging fruit effect.

To sum up: *Unless you're stupid and use an easily-guessable key*, a brute force attack on standard 64-bit WEP could take several months, and is thus possible but not practical. For 128-bit WEP, brute force is simply impossible. In practical terms, even the 64-bit brute-force crack is academic, because an AirSnort-style crack could be done much more quickly in almost every case. Once the Wi-Fi Protected Access standard is implemented broadly by manufacturers, Wi-Fi gear will support the temporal key integrity protocol (TKIP), which updates WEP keys automatically at defined intervals through encrypted transfers. When this happens, AirSnort-type attacks become *much* more difficult, and brute force attacks become basically impossible—because the keys would change long before a brute force attack would have the time to succeed. I'll describe WPA in detail in Chapter 14.

How Many Bits, and Does It Matter?

Let's talk a little bit about bits and Wi-Fi security. All is not what it seems. You'll see in product documentation and advertisements that most Wi-Fi gear has 64-bit and 128-bit encryption built-in. (Some newer products are being shipped with 256-bit encryption as well.) The numbers specify the length of the encryption key. You can choose which encryption key length to use. More is better, right?

Well, in WEP's case, no. Or maybe. And the numbers they advertise are a "little white lie," as well.

The underlying 802.11 Wi-Fi standard requires support for WEP encryption. The required key length for WEP is 40 bits. This value was chosen because, for a long time, manufacturers could not export products to other countries if they contained any kind of encryption with a key length longer than 40 bits. This little bit of idiocy assumed that only Americans knew anything about encryption, and that if we didn't export more powerful encryption systems, our enemies couldn't get them.

Things like that make you wonder about the sanity of the people ostensibly running our country. People in other countries know as much about encryption as we do, especially since our government cannot (due to the First Amendment) prevent American cryptographers from talking about and publishing discussions of crypto-graphic techniques globally.

But sense has finally prevailed, and the 40-bit encryption limitation has gone away. This has allowed manufacturers to extend standard WEP for longer key lengths. The most popular extension uses a 104-bit key. An even newer extension uses a 232-bit key. If these numbers are unfamiliar to you, grab your calculator and add 24 to each of the numbers 40, 108, and 232. I'll save you the work: It's 64, 128, and 256.

What manufacturers do in their literature and documentation is add the 24 bits of the initialization vector (IV) mentioned earlier to the key length. This is borderline dishon-est for a couple of reasons. The IV is *not* part of the key. It's really a seed for a random number generator. More bits in the IV would not give you "better" random numbers, so adding the IV to the key length makes a key sound more secure than it really is.

What is true is that for a brute-force attack, the more bits in your encryption key, the more secure your encryption system is. And in a brute-force attack, the difficulty of breaking a key goes up stratospherically as the key length increases. A 128-bit key is *not* twice as good as a 64-bit key. It's much, *much* better, although cryptography is subtle enough that I don't want to say (as some do) that the difficulty of breaking the key doubles with every added bit.

So we come down to my earlier rhetorical question: Is 128-bit WEP more secure than 64-bit WEP? The best I can answer right now is, "It's hard to say." If all hackers could do was mount a brute-force attack, then yes, clearly—nay,—*spectacularly*. But attacks on the RC4 encryption algorithm used by WEP are not as mathematically predictable. Key length does matter. The ugly question is, "How much?"

The AirSnort documentation states that it takes 115 packets encrypted with weak IV values per key byte to break a WEP key. (They refer to such packets as "interesting packets." Indeed.) This would mean 5 x 115 = 575 "interesting" packets to break a 64-bit WEP key, because as I explained earlier, a "64-bit" WEP key is actually 5 bytes—40 bits—long. It's not possible to predict how quickly AirSnort can gather 575 "interesting" packets, because weak IV values are not evenly distributed across the 16,777,216 total possible IV values, and different Wi-Fi products choose IV values in different ways. 128-bit WEP systems have 13-byte long keys, which would mean 13 x 115 = 1,495 interesting packets. That's two and a half times more "interesting" packets to be gathered—but does it takes two and a half times longer to gather them?

That simply can't be predicted, but one can be forgiven for assuming that it would. What I have found striking in talking to people who have mounted AirSnort attacks on their own networks is how often AirSnort simply can't perform the crack, no matter how many "interesting" packets it gathers, and no one knows why. Attacks like those made possible by AirSnort aren't mathematically definable. 128-bit or 256-bit WEP are probably more secure than 64-bit WEP, but no one can say how much more. There are just too many variables, and too many things that even the experts don't fully understand.

So let's come back down to Earth: *The important thing is just turning WEP on.*

64 bits is as strong as the Wi-Fi *standard* gets right now, and 64-bit encryption is the key length that all Wi-Fi gear understands. Using the 128-bit or 256-bit WEP extensions provides (somewhat) better security, assuming that all of your various Wi-Fi gadgets understand 128-bit or 256-bit WEP identically. Not all do. This is why I strongly recommend that if you don't already have a Wi-Fi network set up, *buy all your gear from the same manufacturer.* That way you can be sure that the longer key lengths will work across all the links you set up.

Because so many people leave their networks wide open, turning WEP on will make most hackers go "next door" and leave you alone. Your WEP-enabled network is much more resistant to cracking because lazy hackers have so many easy pickings to choose from. (This is what I mean by the "Low-Hanging Fruit Effect.") Unless you're being individually targeted for some reason (and that's very unlikely) you're safer because you're smart and other people are dumb. Like I said, peculiar, but completely real—and as best I can tell, unlikely to change any time soon.

Newer Gear, Better Security

If your Wi-Fi equipment was manufactured before the fall of 2003, WEP is probably the only security technology available to you. However, newer gear (especially for the Wireless-G standard) can provide you with much better protection against intruders. The new Wi-Fi Protected Access (WPA) technology slams the door on certain WEP attacks, like the infamous RC4 attack, and virtually all brute-force attacks that don't involve easily guessable passwords.

If you don't already have a Wi-Fi network, I advise shopping around for gear that supports WPA, regardless of whether it costs a few more dollars. Even if you already have a small home network consisting of an access point or wireless gateway and two or three client adapters, an equipment upgrade costing as little as $250 could strongly immunize you against hacker attacks.

The important issue is using gear that supports WPA. In the next chapter, I'll explain what WPA is and how it works, and in Chapter 15, I'll explain how to enable both WEP and WPA encryption, so that you can use whichever system is available on your network. Remember that the security technology you have is *far* less important than just turning it on!

WPA and the Future of Wi-Fi Security

O n August 21, 2001, a team of three researchers at AT&T Labs fired a shot heard round the Wi-Fi world. Adam Stubblefield, John Ioannidis, and Aviel D. Rubin had used a theoretical attack on the well-known RC4 cipher to recover a password from a wireless network protected by Wired Equivalent Privacy (WEP). The theoretical attack had been published earlier that year by cryptography scholars Scott Fluhrer, Itsik Mantin, and Adi Shamir, but Stubblefield's team was the first to actually use it to break WEP security.

If you're interested in seeing those two seminal papers, they are available on the Web at:

www.drizzle.com/~aboba/IEEE/rc4_ksaproc.pdf
www.cs.rice.edu/~astubble/wep/wep_attack.pdf

The press went nuts. Suddenly, the wireless emperor had literally no clothes, and all network secrets were laid bare. Corporations that had been considering a Wi-Fi component to their networks froze those plans in their tracks, and many that had already installed the equipment simply pulled the plug.

It was *not* the best day for what many in the technology industry had proclaimed a brilliant IEEE standard.

So what happened? Very simply: The IEEE had allowed a team of electrical engineers and computer programmers to define a cryptographic system, without involving anyone who might credibly be considered an expert on cryptographic data security. The 802.11 standard had been ratified and published, and then implemented in products by the millions, without any sort of review by experts in cryptography.

Within a few months, "password recovery" utilities began to appear and be distributed on the Internet, and WEP went fully into eclipse. As I explained earlier in Chapter 13, the panic over WEP was more than a little ironic, given that at that time in history, about 80% of installed wireless networks didn't even turn WEP on. (Proof that we humans learn only slowly is offered by the fact that come January 2004, that number had fallen to a mere 60%.)

The IEEE shrugged and convened a new task group to do the job over, this time correctly. Its 802.11i team began to design (this time with the help of expert cryptographers) a new security technology for wireless networking. They said (with completely straight faces) that they *might* be done by 2004.

In the meantime, consumers and more daring (or perhaps heedless) corporations kept buying and installing Wi-Fi access points and client adapters. The benefits for many outweighed the risks, and during the tech implosion of the early 00's, wireless networking was one of the few technologies keeping the tech industry afloat. The Wi-Fi Alliance (which, after all, had coined the name "Wi-Fi" and helped promote it to the status of a major technology) saw its baby blackened by the bad press over WEP, and felt that some sort of action was necessary. Out of that conviction came Wi-Fi Protected Access (WPA).

WPA: A Modest Proposal

The core problem facing the Wi-Fi Alliance is that the IEEE's 802.11i standard was too much—and too far off in the future. In creating the specs for WPA, two fundamental issues floated to the top of the stack:

- A solution to WEP's problems had to be implementable ASAP—the industry could not wait until 2004 or (more likely) 2005 for the publication and broad implementation of the 802.11i specification.

- A solution to WEP's problems had to be designed so that existing hardware could use it. Millions upon millions of Wi-Fi access points, gateways, and clients were being used daily. They were not going away, and to avoid remaining part of the problem, they had to become part of the solution.

The WPA specification was published in late 2002. The very first products implementing WPA appeared in June 2003, though it was almost 2004 before WPA was implemented broadly throughout the industry. (Still, as standards implementation goes, this was a three-minute mile.) As for 802.11i, it is still not complete at this writing, though optimists still believe it will be ratified and published by the IEEE during the fourth quarter of 2004, and appear broadly in Wi-Fi products by early 2005.

What WPA Does

WPA addresses every known issue with WEP. These can be listed briefly, but don't feel bad if some of these technical issues seem obscure to you. I described WEP's issues in detail in Chapter 13, and won't explain them again at length here.

- *WPA enlarges the standard WEP key from 40 to 128 bits.* This makes brute force attacks *on the key* basically impossible—such an attack would take longer than the remaining life of the observable universe. However, a "dictionary attack" on a WPA pre-shared key passphrase can succeed if you make the passphrase too short. I'll discuss this in more detail a little later.

- *WPA changes keys on a regular basis, automatically—and under the cloak of encryption.* Basically, every so often (you can choose the interval) WPA encrypts a new key with the existing key and sends the new key out to all members of the network. This happens often enough so that intruders cannot gather enough packets to reverse-engineer the key as is possible in WEP.

- *WPA doubles the size of the initialization vector, from 24 to 48 bits.* This means that there are now 281 *trillion* different IV values, rather than WEP's paltry 17 million. Under WPA, a network can pass 281 trillion packets before the pool of unique IVs is exhausted—and that would take well over a thousand years, even on the busiest Wireless-G network.

- *WPA changes keys often enough so that it is impossible for an intruder ever to gather sufficient "interesting" packets to reverse-engineer a key.* "Weak IVs" are an inherent problem with the underlying RC4 cypher (which WPA uses; why is something I'll explain later in this chapter).

- *WPA adds mutual authentication to Wi-Fi security.* WEP did not support authentication at all, except by default, in that a client with the correct key was assumed to be permitted to access the network. WPA authentication, moreover, is *mutual* authentication, in which the access point authenticates itself to the client, just as the client authenticates itself to the access point. This mutual authentication prevents something called the "man in the middle" attack, in which a rogue access point set up by an intruder pretends to be the real access point, and when a client connects to it, network information can be stolen by the intruder.

- *WPA includes a way of detecting whether packets have been tampered with while en route to the access point or gateway.* This technology is called the *Message Integrity Code*, or MIC—colloquially referred to as "Michael."

- *WPA operates as much as possible so that the eventual upgrade to 802.11i can be done with as little difficulty and disruption as possible.* How true this is remains to be seen—we won't know until we actually have the completed 802.11i spec in hand.

- *WPA is designed to be equally usable in both the home office/small office (SOHO) market and in enterprise corporate markets with centrally managed networks.* More on this later in this chapter.

What WPA Does *Not* Do

With all that said, there have been some grumbles about weaknesses inherent in the WPA concept rather than its algorithms. There are three major ones:

- *WPA will shut down an access point or gateway for a period of time as a safety measure if more than 2 packets are seen as failing the MIC test within sixty seconds.* This makes good sense, since there would then be cause to believe that an attacker was attempting to break into the network. However, it also allows an attacker to mount a Denial of Service (DoS) attack against the network by deliberately corrupting packets to force WPA to shut the access point or gateway down. This would deny access to legitimate users of the network.

- *The security of WPA depends heavily on the length of the passphrase that generates the pre-shared key.* Short passphrases generate crackable keys. Longer keys (close to the maximum length of 63 characters) generate keys that cannot be cracked. I will explain this problem in detail later in this chapter.

- *Nothing in WPA forces the end user to turn it on.* The default for Wi-Fi hardware will still be for all encryption to be disabled. Nothing in WPA allows for the delivery of equipment with encryption turned on by default. This is more a human problem than a technical one, but the upshot is still the same: Over half of all Wi-Fi networks will continue to be installed without any protection whatsoever, WPA or no WPA.

*The first problem is **extremely** unlikely to be an issue for home office and small office users, as I explained in Chapter 12. DoS attacks are virtually always mounted against large and visible servers and networks owned by large corporations. The second and third problems, on the other hand, falls square in the lap of small office and home network users, like you. Short passphrases put your network at risk, and, more to the point, **WPA will not do you any good if you don't turn it on.** Unfortunately, turning it on is a more complex business than it is with WEP, at least for now, at the dawn of WPA time. I'll explain how to enable WPA security in the next chapter. In the meantime, let's talk about how WPA does what it does.*

How WPA Works

Like WEP, WPA is a relatively complicated mechanism based on some pretty arcane networking protocols and subtle math. I'm not going to go into those protocols or the math in detail here. I want you to know how to *use* WPA, not implement it or debug it. Getting in deeper would only confuse those of you who simply want a secure network and are happy to think of it as a black box.

Big WPA and Little WPA

The designers of WPA recognized that not all networks are alike, and that big, centrally managed networks have radically different needs from those of small office and home office (SOHO) networks. WPA was designed to deal effectively with both big and small networks, but it works in very different ways when dealing with each.

On a large, centrally managed network, WPA handles authentication and key exchange through a RADIUS server. RADIUS is a server program that centrally manages network authentication and encryption key distribution.

For an access point to associate a client with the network, the access point must first ask the RADIUS server for permission—that's what "authentication" is. This authentication can be handled in a great many ways, all of which are embraced by a framework called *802.1X*, which is really a specification for what sorts of things must happen, in what order. 802.1X doesn't say which specific tools or protocols must be used. It can be thought of as a set of rules for putting an authentication and key management system in place. In a huge corporate network scattered across multiple campuses, an 802.1X authentication system can be diabolically complex and take months to implement and debug. I'm not going to explain "big" network WPA any further in this book, and you really don't need to know what RADIUS or 802.1X really are or how they work.

Small Networks and the Pre-Shared Key (PSK)

For a SOHO network with a single access point, the 802.1X framework is still used, but there is no RADIUS server, and so the complexity of the system is radically reduced. Authentication is done from the access point or wireless gateway. With no RADIUS server to distribute keys, a SOHO network owner must manually distribute a single key to the access point and all the client adapters, so that all the Wi-Fi hardware on the network has the key stored in memory before WPA is enabled. In WPA jargon, this is called a *pre-shared key* (PSK). In Chapter 15, I'll explain how to enable WPA on a SOHO network, using a pre-shared key.

"Manually distributing a key" is just what it sounds like: You walk around to every device on the network and type a key into each Wi-Fi device that you have, access points and clients both. (This is precisely how you do it with WEP.) Most devices do not allow you to enter the key directly. The key is a random-looking 32-digit hexadecimal number, and typing it accurately several times in a row would be difficult. (Apple's AirPort product line is the only one I know of allowing direct entry of WPA keys.) Instead, you type a *passphrase* into a key generator, and the key generator creates a key out of the passphrase. In this it's like a lot of WEP equipment, which has long generated WEP keys from a typed-in word or phrase. If you use Linksys equipment, the notion of a passphrase will be completely familiar to you from its WEP implementation.

The pre-shared key is only the first key of many. After you turn WPA on, the pre-shared key is used to generate a series of subsequent keys, which are automatically distributed to all client adapters on the network after a pre-set interval. I'll have more to say about this shortly.

Getting into the Network

From a height, this is what happens when a station (in other words, a computer equipped with a WPA-capable client adapter) wants to join a WPA-protected network:

1. The station's *supplicant* (a piece of software that handles WPA housekeeping at the operating system level) requests permission to associate with the network's access point.

2. The supplicant and the access point ask one another some questions to determine what level of functionality each is capable of. Some access points

are backed up by elaborate 802.1X-compliant RADIUS authentication servers. In the SOHO world, access points work alone, with no software outside what's in their embedded firmware.

3. Based on what the supplicant and access point now know about one another, the access point authenticates the supplicant, and vise versa. This simply means that the access point determines in some way (negotiated in the previous step) that the supplicant is authorized to join the network. At the same time, the access point indicates somehow to the supplicant that it is in fact the network that the supplicant wants to join, and not a disguised network cracker trying to impersonate the network to steal keys—the infamous "man in the middle" attack. In a big, centrally managed network, this mutual authentication may involve a lot of negotiation with a server running the RADIUS utility. In a SOHO network with no centralized authentication system, all the AP may require is that the client have the pre-shared key, and all the client may require is that its pre-shared key be accepted by the AP.

4. Once the client is authenticated, the supplicant and the access point accomplish *key exchange*. This is a four-way handshake accomplished under cover of encryption, and it establishes the keys that will be used to encrypt and thus secure the wireless connection between the client and the AP. On a big network, the keys come from the central RADIUS server using protocols like EAPOL that are allowed under the 802.1X framework. On a SOHO network, the keys are derived from the pre-shared key that was manually distributed earlier.

At that point, the client is on the network, and all traffic between access point and client is conducted under encryption.

The Temporal Key Integrity Protocol (TKIP)

One of the major problems with WEP is that the encryption keys stay the same for a long time. (In fact, many folks never change them after setting them initially.) A patient intruder could then passively monitor packets until enough packets had been gathered to reverse-engineer the WEP encryption keys by one of the two weaknesses in the underlying RC4 cypher used by WEP. Both weaknesses require that a lot of packets be gathered under the *same* encryption key—sometimes many gigabytes' worth of packets. (This is why WEP is quite secure for lightly used networks: It might take a year to gather enough packets to crack WEP, and few intruders are *that* patient!)

If the network owner changes the WEP keys before enough packets have been gathered by the intruder to crack the key, the intruder has to start again, from scratch. The idea behind WPA's Temporal Key Integrity Protocol (TKIP) is to automatically change the keys on a regular basis, after a pre-defined interval. If this *group key renewal interval* is adjusted appropriately for the volume of traffic passing over the network, an intruder can never gather enough packets to crack encryption before the keys change again.

The group key renewal interval can be set at the access point or wireless gateway. (I'll show you how in Chapter 15.) Most access points and gateways default to an interval of 3,600 seconds (one hour), which is fine for SOHO networks. If the access point or gateway is constantly moving packets, shortening the interval to 15 minutes (900 seconds) is probably a good idea. Key renewal takes a few seconds, so you don't want to do it every minute—and you don't have to. Even when the network is running completely saturated, no intruder can gather enough packets in ten or fifteen minutes to compromise the underlying RC4 cipher.

It's true that the RC4 cipher inside WPA is the same RC4 cipher used inside WEP, and it's the weakness of RC4 that allows WEP to be cracked. The question then arises: Why does WPA still use the RC4 cipher at all? The answer is simple: RC4 is simple and quick to implement, and doesn't take a lot of cycles or memory when it runs. The embedded processors inside client adapters and access points can run RC4 without slowing the network down very much. Other ciphers are available, and in fact you can use at least one of them in WPA instead of RC4. The AES (Advanced Encryption Standard) provides a cipher that is *much* harder to crack than RC4. However, it takes considerably more CPU power and memory to run. Some network administrators might decide that the additional overhead of AES is worth the far stronger encryption that AES represents. That's up to them. My point here is that for SOHO networks, TKIP plugs the holes that RC4 adds to both WEP and WPA.

 Implemented and managed correctly, WPA is extremely strong security for SOHO networks, and easily strong enough to meet most needs at corporate and university installations. (For medical, financial, or military/intelligence applications, additional layers of encryption are a good idea.) Even if it's appropriate for your own network, however, you may not in fact be able to use WPA at all, and the hardware vendors are in a shameful state of denial over this. There are some gotchas. Let's talk about those next.

The Legacy Hardware Problem

The Wi-Fi Alliance designed the WPA standard very deliberately to allow it to be incorporated into "legacy" devices (in other words, gear that you've already bought and installed) through a simple firmware update. That was the original idea. Things are never as simple as that.

There are several legacy problems involving adding WPA functionality to existing Wi-Fi networks:

- Hardware vendors must provide the firmware updates that implement WPA. If the vendor of your hardware refuses or fails to do this, you can't upgrade your network to WPA. Firmware is copyrighted and owned by the vendor. No one else can legally do the upgrade but them. (There are a couple of exceptions, in which vendors have used open source code in their firmware, but as yet no third party has created WPA updates using this code.)

- If even *one* of your client adapters cannot be upgraded to WPA, your entire network remains as vulnerable as it was under WEP. Vendors are very cagey about admitting this, but a single WEP-protected client adapter will drag a WPA-protected access point or gateway down to its own level of vulnerability. If you can't update all of them and won't replace WPA-incompatible gear, don't even bother with WPA. (That said, I will explain a dodge later in this chapter that will allow you to keep older, non-WPA gear on the network by adding a second access point to support WEP connections—keeping in mind that any clients connecting under WEP do not benefit from the added security of WPA.)

- Some older hardware may be incapable of supporting WPA at all, even with its vendor's best intentions. WPA is more compute-intensive than WEP, and early Wireless-B gear may simply not have the internal memory nor the compute power to support WPA.

- There have been reports of a number of weird software problems associated with early WPA firmware upgrades. Even if you download and apply the firmware upgrade for a particular access point, gateway, or client adapter, there's a greater-than-zero chance that it won't work, and a significant chance that it won't be compatible with other vendors' WPA upgrades. Guys, this is *software* we're talking about here…and you know how software is.

Some of the problems with WPA are simply due to the fact that WPA was defined in some haste and released with considerable urgency. Hardware vendors are desperate to do something to counteract the bad word-of-mouth associated with WEP, so they worked quickly, with the predictable results that they created some bugs in the process.

Upgrade Triage

The first products to support WPA were not existing Wireless-B products, but the brand-new (and much faster) Wireless-G products. WPA is in fact a superb reason to upgrade your network to Wireless-G, but in truth there's no technological connection between WPA and Wireless-G. Wireless-B should be able to support WPA just as well.

Why, then, have so few Wireless-B products been upgraded to support WPA?

Vendors have pleaded triage: They have only so many engineers and so much time, so they have concentrated on the parts of their product line that have been in greatest demand, which are (unsurprisingly) those using Wireless-G. Some vendors have stated outright that their early Wireless-B products don't have the muscle to support WPA, even though that support was one of the WPA standard's original goals.

 Many cynics are suggesting that Wi-Fi vendors are holding back WPA upgrades of wireless-B gear to prompt users to buy brand-new, WPA-equipped Wireless-G equipment. Again, if this is true, we have no way to be sure. But at this writing, only a microscopic handful of Wireless-B client adapters have been updated to support WPA. All the real action has been with Wireless-G.

The Supplicant Problem

The weirdest and most outrageous stumbling block between you and WPA may be the simple fact that *your Wi-Fi vendor may not have sold you the whole package.* In other words, not everything you need to run WPA is necessarily there in the box. This is true even with brand-new, WPA-certified Wi-Fi gear. This is a little tricky to explain, so follow along closely.

In order for WPA to work, Wi-Fi client adapters must use a piece of software called a *supplicant.* The supplicant "asks permission" of the access point or gateway to join the network, hence the term. It's unclear to me why the supplicant module isn't part of the client adapter driver, but at this point in time, supplicants are installed as parts of the operating system.

Since WPA is still very new, few operating systems are delivered with a supplicant installed. Microsoft offers a free downloadable upgrade of Windows XP that installs a WPA supplicant. They do not, however, provide a supplicant upgrade for Windows 98SE, NT, or Windows 2000. The kicker is that Wi-Fi client adapter vendors don't provide one either. What this means can be summarized this way:

- If you're using Windows XP, you can download and install Microsoft's free supplicant upgrade and you'll be good to go with WPA.

- If you're using Mac OS/X, the 10.3 release ("Panther") includes full WPA support, including a supplicant. If you're using a prior release, you'll have to upgrade. Note that Panther is a *really* good release, and if you're not using it already you're missing out!

- If you're using any other operating system (including Windows 98SE, Windows 2000, or Linux) you may have to buy a commercial supplicant product to make WPA work at all.

I know of two commercial supplicant products that support non-XP operating systems:

- Funk Software's Odyssey Client ($50; for 2000/98/ME/PocketPC): **www.funk.com/radius/wlan/wlan_c_radius.asp**

- Meetinghouse Data's Aegis Client ($40; for NT/2000/98/ME/PocketPC/ Linux): **www.mtghouse.com/products/client/index.shtml**

Both are high-quality products and work well. Both have a free, time-limited evaluation mode that you can download from the vendor sites to make sure the product works on your network—but after a certain period of time, you must pay for it or it will cease to work.

In addition to the two commercial clients mentioned above, a free client has recently been released: Wireless Security Corporation's WPA Assistant. It supports Windows 2000 only, but it is free, and can be downloaded from this URL:

www.wirelesssecuritycorp.com/wsc/public/WPAAssistant.do

WPA Assistant is "baitware" for the company's more expensive and powerful WSC Guard product, but it installs easily, works quite well for SOHO networks, and is not time-limited. If you're using Windows 2000, I'd say this is your first choice.

Bundles and Punts

Most Wi-Fi hardware vendors are currently punting on the supplicant issue, and stating in the fine print that they are supporting WPA under Windows XP *only*, with the supplicant upgrade installed. This is appalling in my view, but at this writing that's how things are.

A number of vendors are doing the right thing and bundling a supplicant (often the Funk or Meetinghouse product) with their hardware, at no additional charge. The list seems to change on almost a daily basis. In late 2003, D-Link announced that they would be bundling a supplicant with some of their Wireless-G client adapters. Other companies have made mutterings about doing the same, but only D-Link has actually posted a free downloadable supplicant at this writing. (The supplicant only supports some of their products, so check the D-Link Web site before buying a D-Link client adapter for use with WPA.)

Sooner or later, shipping or not shipping a supplicant with a Wi-Fi client will become a serious competitive issue. Until then, it's caveat emptor with a vengeance.

The Passphrase Length Problem

As I described in detail in Chapter 13, Wired Equivalent Privacy (WEP) has two serious flaws that are very difficult to get around:

- A small keyspace (meaning that there are only 16 million or so unique initialization vector values, and a saturated network can work through them all in only a few hours)

- "weak IVs," which are a mathematical consequence of the RC4 cipher used within WEP.

WPA solves both of these problems, and so far, no one has pointed out any new ones specific to WPA.

All of that comes with an extremely big "however":

The strength of pre-shared key (PSK) WPA encryption depends on the length of the initial passphrase that you use. This isn't a flaw in the WPA system, as it was there from the beginning in the small print. Think of it as a rule that is easily broken. What it means is simple, and please take this seriously: *Your PSK passphrase must be at least 40 characters long—and ideally longer—for your network to be adequately secure.*

Using a short word or phrase—like "gazpacho" or "hulahoop"—worked as well as a long one in WEP, because the key-length in WEP was always the same. All that mattered was how "guessable" a passphrase was. The passphrase *length* didn't matter. In other words, under WEP, using your dog's name or your car's make or you kids' names was a serious problem, since these are easily guessable. But if you were using 64-bit encryption under WEP, a guessable phrase like "muffin" (a common dog name) and an un-guessable phrase like "darkels lucky guess" (the kennel name of my late bichon Mr. Byte, and completely unique) both generate the same length key: 64 bits.

WPA works differently. A passphrase in WPA may be anywhere from 8 to 63 characters long. An 8-character long passphrase is thus *allowed*, but it doesn't protect you much from something called an "offline dictionary attack." In an offline dictionary attack, a network cracker monitors some of your encrypted packets and takes them "home" to work on, out of sight and at his leisure. He tries possible passphrases assembled from a custom-made dictionary of likely words until those stolen packets become non-random—meaning that the attack succeeded, and what was encrypted gobbledegook is now "plaintext." This is done by a program capable of trying as many as a hundred passphrases per second, so after a couple of days or maybe as long as a week, a short key will be easily broken.

As in WEP, a passphrase is not the actual encryption key. The actual binary WPA key—a 256-bit number—is created using a process called a "hash." This is a common technique in cryptography, and it is well-known that hashes are subject to dictionary attacks. The longer the initial passphrase, the longer it takes a dictionary attack to succeed. A 63-character passphrase is extremely strong protection, and probably immune to dictionary attacks mounted by ordinary network crackers. An 8-character passphrase, by contrast, offers almost no protection at all.

What this means is that you must create your WPA pre-shared key with some care. It has to be long enough to be strong protection, but should be something you can remember.

My suggestion is to create something with a little internal rhyme and rhythm. That's why poetry was invented, by the way: To give the oral tradition a mnemonic foundation, so humankind's first literature could be remembered before the invention of writing.

The following passphrases are ridiculous, but your PC won't laugh, and they're long enough to do the job. (I've included some no-nos for some sense of perspective.) Note that these are examples, and you should not use them—I'm sure the crackers will buy this book and add them to their WPA-attack dictionaries!

Gotta sing gotta dance gotta shake these ants from out my pants (63chars; ideal!)

Who's hackin lisp on your old AT while you were out hackin lisp (63 chars; ideal!)

Down along the beach I wandered, nourishing a youth sublime (59 chars; great)

Huffin puffin mcguffin bought a muffin for his stuffin (54 chars; good) mama bought a metakeet that sang in xml (39 chars; so-so)

tommyknockers (13 chars; worthless!)

The third example is actually a line from Tennyson's poem, "Locksley Hall." If you're not good at poetry yourself (even bad poetry) consider choosing a memorable line from someone else's poem.

There are security experts who say that only a completely random string of 63 gibberish characters is acceptably secure, but they're working for banks and the military. A string like that is completely impossible to memorize and must be written down, which makes it a whole lot less secure than something living only inside your head!

 If you're comfortable with geek-speak, there's a highly technical paper on the topic of dictionary attacks against hashing algorithm passphrases at: http://131.155.140.135/~galactus/ remailers/passphrase-faq.html#101

Stay with WEP? Or Upgrade to WPA?

My guess is that most Wireless-B gear will never be upgraded to WPA at all, for whatever reason. In fact, I think many Wireless-B product lines may simply be abandoned in the next two or at most three years. So if you're a current user of Wireless-B Wi-Fi equipment, the question you'll have to ask yourself is this: Are you worried enough about security to dump all your Wireless-B gear and replace it with new Wireless-G gear?

My advice, simply put, is this:

- If you have a lightly used home network, WEP is actually much better protection than the press has made it out to be. (I explained why back in Chapter 13.) Low volume packet traffic and the "low-hanging fruit effect" probably make WEP adequate for what you need.

- However, if your business depends on your network, and especially if your business works in a field where data security is important (say, the financial and especially medical fields) upgrading everything to Wireless-G and selling your old Wireless-B Wi-Fi gear on eBay is probably a good idea.

 The prices of Wireless-G equipment have dropped dramatically in the first part of 2004, and now the price premium over Wireless-B equipment is at most 15% to 20%. Most small businesses with one access point and only a few client adapters can upgrade for less than $500. How much is a good night's sleep worth, anyway?

The "Getting Ready for WPA" Checklist

If you've decided to go with WPA, you may have a fair amount of work to do long before you attempt to set up a WPA-protected network. Actually making WPA work once all the hardware and software are in place is fairly easy. Getting to "ready"is in fact the hard part. Here's a checklist of what you have to do to be ready:

- *Replace your access point or gateway if it cannot support WPA.* Not all APs and wireless gateways support WPA; most older ones do not. Check with the product vendor to see if a firmware upgrade allows WPA functionality. Beware of subtle differences in hardware release levels. For example, the popular Linksys BEFW11S4 Wireless-B wireless gateway comes in four release levels, and only the most recent (V4.0; first released in April, 2003) can be upgraded to support WPA. If you have an older BEFW11S4, you're out of luck and must replace it to run WPA.

- *Replace any client adapters that can't support WPA.* Make sure all client adapters on your network are in fact upgradeable to WPA-readiness. This requires doing some Web research and possibly a tech support call or email to the client adapter vendor. If one of your clients can't be upgraded to support WPA, you must replace it with one that can. This may involve a driver update, a firmware update, or both. The whole network must use WPA, or you should stay with WEP. There is no genuine "mixed mode" for Wi-Fi security.

- *Upgrade the OS.* Bring your operating system up to the latest service pack and upgrade level. For WPA to work smoothly under Windows XP, you need to let XP's automatic update system have its way and apply all updates not already present. This may take a few hours, especially over a dialup Internet connection, but it has to be done nonetheless. Bring Windows 2000 up to Service Pack 4, and your Mac to OS/X 10.3.

- *Obtain a WPA supplicant for your OS.* This is a piece of software that implements the OS part of WPA. I predict that it will eventually be shipped in the box with all client adapters, but for the moment that's not the case. For Windows XP, getting it is free and easy; I'll show you how shortly. For Windows 2000, it can be free or it can cost money. For Windows 9x, it will cost money. I don't, in fact, recommend WPA at all if you're using Win9x.

- *Upgrade the firmware in your access point or gateway.* If your AP or wireless gateway doesn't already support WPA, it will definitely require a firmware upgrade, as there are no drivers to upgrade. Upgrading firmware is easier than it used to be, and if you're careful there's little risk involved. *Follow the instructions from the hardware vendor*. If you're not technically inclined, get some help from someone who is.

- *Upgrade the firmware and/or drivers on all your client adapters*. Some client adapters can be made WPA-ready with only a driver update. Others require a firmware update, or both. You have to find out by researching on the hardware vendor's Web site.

With all that done, you're ready to enable WPA security. I'll explain those steps in the second half of the next chapter. For the rest of this chapter I'll present some tips and advice on getting your equipment ready.

Obtaining a WPA Supplicant

As time goes on, I think that more and more Wi-Fi hardware vendors will ship a WPA supplicant utility with their client adapter products. D-Link has made a supplicant available for download at no charge for some of their newer products, but it is the only company I know of that does so. In the meantime, here are some tips on where to obtain a supplicant program for your hardware and operating system.

Windows XP

Before you do anything, use Windows Update to bring your copy of Windows XP to the latest update level. Once that's done, follow these steps:

1. Go to the Microsoft Web site and search for Microsoft Knowledge Base Article 815485. Read the article closely.

2. Download the software patch from the link toward the end of the article. The patch (which contains the supplicant software) is relatively small (932K) and is an executable file.

3. Download it to a directory somewhere and run it.

4. Reboot. That's all you need to do! XP is then ready to do WPA.

For D-Link Hardware

For some of its client adapters, D-Link makes a copy of the Meetinghouse Data Aegis client available for download, free of charge. At this writing, the list includes:

DWL-G650B1   Wireless-G Cardbus client adapter

DWL-G520 Rev A   Wireless-G PCI client adapter

You can download the supplicant application from the drivers download page for the product in question. If the drivers page for a given client does not have the link under "Applications," that client does not support WPA!

 The downloadable copy of Aegis is tied to the D-Link client adapters and will not work with other hardware.

Windows 2000

You have some choices under Windows 2000. A free supplicant called WPA Assistant is available from Wireless Security Corporation, as mentioned earlier. Commercial supplicant products are available from two vendors, Funk Software and Meetinghouse Data.

Windows NT

The only supplicant I'm aware of to support Windows NT is the Aegis client from Meetinghouse Data.

Windows 98

Although both the Funk Software and Meetinghouse Data commercial supplicants support Windows 98, both took some serious screwing-with to get to work correctly with my WPA network. I had no problems getting the same supplicants to work under Windows 2000, so I can only conclude that a slow, memory-limited Windows 9x system is a marginal candidate for WPA.

Mac OS/X

If you upgrade your Mac to OS/X 10.3 "Panther" you've already got a supplicant. For earlier versions of OS/X, you can use Meetinghouse Data's Aegis client. I know of no supplicants, commercial or otherwise, for MAC OS versions prior to OS/X.

Mixing WEP and WPA in a Single SOHO Network

I know I've said that it's impossible to use both WEP and WPA in a single network. Well, that's not quite true. It's impossible to use both WEP and WPA *in the same access point or wireless gateway.* But if you have older Wireless-B Wi-Fi gear that can't be upgraded to support WPA, there's a dodge that will allow you to have it both ways. Quite simply, you add a second access point to your network, to support your "legacy" Wireless-B equipment.

I've shown how this works schematically in Figure 14.1. The central wireless gateway is a newer model, supporting Wireless-G and WPA. All PCs on the network that can support a WPA-capable Wireless-G client adapter connect to the network through the Wireless-G wireless gateway. Their connections are encrypted with WPA, and are extremely secure.

To support legacy PCs and legacy Wireless-B client adapters, you must add a Wireless-B access point by connecting it to one of the switch ports on the back of the wireless gateway with CAT 5 cable. This access point becomes the point of connection for all legacy client adapters, and it is secured with WEP.

From a security standpoint, this kind of network is a mixed bag: All those clients connecting to a WPA-enabled access point will be strongly protected. All those clients connecting to a WEP-enabled access point will be vulnerable to WEP's various flaws. If the clients connecting through WEP don't pass a lot of packets, you can worry less; WEP's vulnerabilities are proportional to the number of packets moving

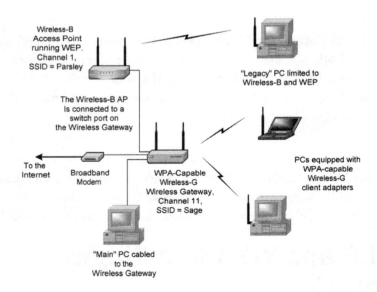

Figure 14.1
A Network Supporting both WEP and WPA.

over the connection per unit time. The more packets passed per second, the more vulnerable the network. It's your call.

Here are some points to keep in mind if this is what you decide to do:

• The Wireless-B access point is configured with a separate SSID from that in the WPA-enabled wireless gateway. This prevents roaming between the two, but there's no way around that.

• The legacy PCs must be configured to use the SSID of the Wireless-B access point.

• The Wireless-B access point is set up to use WEP encryption.

• The Wireless-G wireless gateway and all Wireless-G equipped PCs are set up to use WPA encryption.

• The wireless gateway and access point must be set up on separate, non-overlapping channels. There are only three such channels on the 2.4 GHz Wi-Fi band: 1, 6, and 11. If you have the choice, use 1 and 11, as they are as far apart as it's possible to get in terms of frequency—and thus interference between the access point and the gateway is unlikely. Because the access point must be cabled to the wireless gateway, the two will likely be quite close physically. To avoid interference between the two radio systems, they need to be separated in frequency as widely as possible.

• Put as much physical distance between the Wireless-B access point and the wireless gateway as is practical. Three to five feet should be enough. (Don't stack them atop one another!) In my lab tests, I've set up a system like the one shown in Figure 14.1 with the access point and wireless gateway as little as 24" apart, and everything still worked fine.

When WPA first came out, I set up a system like this to support my newer WPA-capable equipment as well as Carol's slightly cranky old Compaq, which would not work with any WPA-capable client adapter. The system worked fine for the several months we used it, and Carol's PC used the network so little that WEP's vulnerabilities were not an issue.

Looking Ahead to 802.11i

As I hinted at the beginning of this chapter, WPA was a "quick fix" to the RC4 flaw in WEP that I described in Chapter 13. As quick fixes go, it's pretty good, but it looks ahead to the time when the IEEE 802.11i security standard will be finalized and published. WPA was designed to be a proper subset of 802.11i, and the expectation is that equipment compatible with WPA will also be compatible with 802.11i.

For the SOHO market, 802.11i won't provide much that WPA doesn't provide already. Most of 802.11i caters to big, centrally managed networks that require extremely strong encryption, like that provided by AES, the Advanced Encryption Standard. Nonetheless, I think it will be useful to upgrade any gear with the muscle to run full 802.11i when it happens—which may be by the end of 2004 or (more likely) the beginning of 2005. By the time the third edition of this book appears, 802.11i should be implemented, and I'll be here to tell you all about it.

In the meantime, WPA is *extremely* strong protection for SOHO networks—so move on to Chapter 15, where I describe how to enable both WEP and WPA, as appropriate. Use WPA if you can, but if you can't, at least enable WEP. Don't be a low-hanging fruit!

Setting Up WEP and WPA Security

Ninety percent of Wi-Fi security consists of simply turning it on. For a long time, this meant enabling *Wired Equivalent Privacy* (WEP), the security mechanism with a bad rep, as I described in Chapter 13. Faced with blistering press reports on WEP's weakness, some people threw up their hands and said, "If it's so bad, why bother?" (Talk about an excuse!) This may be part of the reason that only 40% of Wi-Fi users enable any security at all, though abject terror at the thought of configuring the device is probably most of it.

Starting in mid-2003, you got a choice—sort of. In addition to WEP, some Wi-Fi equipment now allows the use of the newer, stronger Wi-Fi Protected Access (WPA) technology. Not all Wi-Fi gear supports WPA, and getting to the point where you can enable it can be a hassle—and can cost you $50 that you hadn't expected to spend. Additional, non-standard security features are possible—but they introduce complications, incompatibilities, and additional expense. The most secure among them, like virtual private networks, require access to "the other end of the pipe" (typically a server at one's place of employment) and are not automatically available to just anyone.

If you've been reading chapters in order this far, it may sound pretty grim: WEP is weak, and WPA seems available only to the few who buy new Wireless-G gear and run Windows XP. Take heart. WEP security is not as flimsy as much of the press (few of whom have any technical training and fewer of whom seem to care about their own ignorance) have made it sound. At this writing, WPA is still very new, and by the time you read this, there may be upgrades to existing gear, and new drivers and supplicant software that I haven't heard of yet. Do some research and see what your WPA options are, guided by the pointers that I listed in Chapter 14. You may be pleasantly surprised.

This chapter is about the actual, step-by-step process of enabling either WEP or WPA security on your Wi-Fi network. The details vary widely by manufacturer and product line, and obviously I can't cover every single configuration you might have on your network. Look carefully at the big picture behind the examples I provide, and you should get some useful hints on configuring your own gear.

 If you haven't read Chapters 13 and 14 yet, I think it would be good to do so before you proceed. Those two earlier chapters explain how WEP and WPA work, give you some idea of what you're up against, and may allow the following instructions to make more sense.

A Word on Mac Address Filtering

It's true that WEP and WPA aren't the only Wi-Fi security mechanisms available to you. Many people speak of and recommend a technique called *MAC address filtering* as a secondary measure worth taking, especially if you're using WEP. And while it's true that MAC address filtering doesn't do any harm, it's unclear to me that it does much good.

First of all, what is it? With virtually all Wi-Fi access points, you have the ability to specify a list of computers that are permitted to associate with the access point. Any computer not on the list will be turned away by the access point, and will not be able to join your network, even if it has the WEP or WPA security key. Since every networkable machine has its own unique MAC (Media Access Control) address (as I explain in Chapter 2) you identify machines that are permitted to use your access point by creating a list of those machines' MAC addresses. The name nails it: *MAC addresses allow you control access to your network.*

MAC address filtering sounds great—in fact, it sounds like a terrific way to keep intruders out of your Wi-Fi network, avoiding the significant risk of bandwidth theft and IP impersonation. However, there's a snag: When one of your machines associates with your access point, it transmits its MAC address as "cleartext" (unencrypted) with no attempt to keep others from listening in. A hacker with a packet sniffer program can listen for the transaction by which your laptop (or one of your other machines) associates with your access point, and your laptop's MAC address will be right there for the hacker to see, without any encryption or concealment. The hacker can then use a technique called *spoofing* to apply your laptop's MAC address to his own machine, and immediately pretend to be the legitimate user.

The access point cannot tell the difference between two clients both presenting the same MAC address. Although having two different clients associated with a single access point under the same MAC address is a recipe for confusion, the intruder can request that the access point *de-associate* (in other words, break the connection) with the spoofed MAC address. The intruder can then immediately re-associate, leaving the legitimate user (who is probably non-technical at that level) to wonder what went wrong.

Spoofing kills MAC address filtering stone dead, as far as I'm concerned. Although unique MAC addresses are indeed burned into the hardware of every Ethernet-compatible network adapter (whether wired or wireless) and cannot be changed, *a piece of software can "pretend" to have any MAC address it wants.* (That's what spoofing is all about.) Software can ignore the MAC address of the network adapter it's using and report an entirely fictitious one. This is one of two reasons that MAC address filtering is useless.

The other reason is more significant: Both WEP and WPA encryption provide the same benefit and are *much* more difficult to break. If you use either WEP or WPA, there is no additional benefit that MAC address filtering can give you. Yes, WEP can be broken, but it takes time and effort, and you can thwart WEP attacks by rotating your encryption keys on a regular basis. WPA rotates the keys for you, and strengthens the encryption in other ways as well. The FBI or CIA might be able to break WPA encryption, but if the FBI is after you, well, you have more urgent problems to think about.

MAC address filtering does have uses outside of security, particularly in something called load balancing, in which you have multiple access points serving the same physical area, and need to control how many clients connect to each access point so that they all carry a roughly equal load. I explained this in more detail in Chapter 9.

You'll hear me say this in numerous places in this book: *If you use WPA or WEP, you've gotten virtually all of the security benefit that standard Wi-Fi machinery can give you.* For more security, you'll need to use a virtual private network system or a vendor-specific security solution, both of which cost additional money and may not be available to you unless you work for a company that implements the proper server to be "the other end of the tunnel."

If you do want to enable MAC address filtering, the place to look is in your access point's configuration screens. For example, in the D-Link DWL-900AP+ access point, the screen for entering a list of permitted MAC addresses is shown in Figure 15.1. To get to that particular screen, you must log into the configuration system, click on the Advanced tab, and then click the Filters button in the left margin.

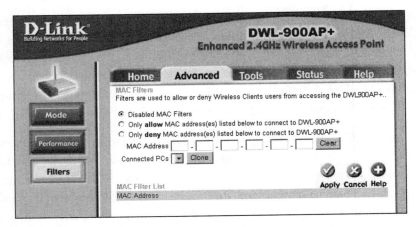

Figure 15.1
The D-Link DWL-900AP+ MAC Address Filtering Screen.

The D-Link DWL-900AP+ is interesting because it allows you to either permit the list of devices to associate with the access point, or forbid the list from associating with the access point. It's far from clear to me how useful it is to have a list of machines forbidden to associate, especially since it's so easy for users to change the MAC address of laptops and other network adapters via spoofing. My guess is that this feature was included as an aid to load balancing, or (in larger company networks) insuring that one department's PCs don't automatically connect to another department's access point.

Explain Twice, Succeed Once!

I'm going to explain setting up security here twice. The first time I'll explain it step-by-step, with all the "whys" and "what this means" in place, but without using any particular system as an example. Then I'll go through it again, with screen shots for the extremely popular LinkSys WRT54G Wireless Gateway and the Orinoco Gold Classic client adapter, but without the background advice and side comments. I'm doing it this way to keep the general principles separate from the details that are specific to a particular make and model of Wi-Fi hardware.

If you have hardware different from what I use in the examples, you'll have to follow along with your manufacturer documentation. If that documentation puzzles you, don't feel bad—virtually all Wi-Fi documentation I've seen so far has been terrible. Read the sequence of steps in the next section first, so that you'll have a sense for what you're actually doing, and why. If you understand that, working through illiterate or outdated documentation will be easier.

The good news is that for WPA, configuration of client adapters is not done from the client adapter management utility that comes with a specific client adapter. On the client side, you configure WPA from the supplicant utility (see Chapter 14) or from the operating system itself. This means that the step-by-step instructions I provide for WPA will not cite specific client adapters and should be applicable to all.

One more thing before we start: This should be obvious and simple common sense, but you must configure both WEP and WPA from the PC connected to your access point or wireless gateway via CAT 5 cable. Trying to configure an access point or gateway over a wireless connection is futile. Turning on WEP at the access point will instantly break any wireless connections to Wi-Fi client adapters—including the one in the machine you might be using. Don't embarrass yourself.

With that caution, let's get to work.

Setting up Security—General Steps

Here are the steps you should first study to understand the general techniques for setting up security:

1. *Make sure your wireless network works without encryption first!*

    Wi-Fi gear arrives on your doorstep with security disabled by default. You should install a new Wi-Fi network fully—and test it thoroughly—before you attempt to enable either WEP or WPA.

2. *Change the Service Set Identifier (SSID) value to something other than the factory default.*

    What you change this identifier to matters less than simply changing it from the defaults. Network crackers will sometimes target a wireless access point that bears a default SSID because they assume that whoever left the default SSID in place will also be careless or simply clueless about passwords and other security measures. It's also wise to use a word or phrase that doesn't carry much information about you or your business. Some guy somewhere may for reasons unclear want to break into a real estate office's network. Therefore, don't use an SSID like "Uberhaus Realty." At the other end of that scale, I've spoken with one security consultant who advises *against* using random character sequences like "i190shl6k2u." Why? That's what consultants always recommend to large corporate clients. A totally random SSID, in his opinion, screams out "Big Organization With Something To Hide."

My advice? Use the name of a plant. Coriander. Hollyhock. Jacaranda. Sunflower. Plants are boring. In my examples in this chapter I'll use "Coriander."

3. *WPA only: Make sure all your client PCs have a supplicant utility installed.*

I explained the need for a WPA supplicant utility in Chapter 14; *please* read that chapter now if you haven't already. For Windows XP it's a free download from Microsoft. For other operating systems you may have to do some hunting, or some purchasing. See Chapter 14 for details and sources. Obtain appropriate supplicants and install them for all client PCs. (The PC connected directly by cable to the access point or wireless gateway does not need one.)

4. *Turn off all machines containing client adapters before you begin.*

This may be an unnecessary step, but I've heard that some access points and wireless gateways get confused if clients are attempting to associate with them while you're setting up security on the access point or gateway. After security is enabled at the access point, you'll power the other machines up one at a time and configure WEP or WPA on their Wi-Fi client adapters to match the security keys you entered at the access point.

5. *Bring up the access point or wireless gateway's configuration screen.*

Virtually all access points and gateways use a Web-based configuration system. In other words, you must run a Web browser on the machine connected via Ethernet CAT5 cable to the access point or gateway. Typically (and you'll have to check your vendor documentation here), you type in a *nonroutable IP address* in its "raw" form, something like this:

http://192.168.1.1

(Your vendor documentation will give you the precise IP address to use.) This should bring up the configuration screen password dialog. Enter your user name and password to log in. You didn't leave those on the defaults did you? If so, change them now!

6. *Select which security technology you intend to use.*

Access points and gateways that support both WEP and WPA will have a configuration option somewhere allowing you to select which of the two you want to use. For WPA, the option you're looking for will be something like "WPA PSK" or "WPA – Pre-Shared Key." For WEP, it will simply say "WEP." Find the "security mode" item in the tabs on your access point or gateway configuration screen and select the appropriate option.

7. *WEP only: Decide what WEP key length you wish to use.*

Most Wi-Fi products will offer you the choice of two or sometimes three WEP key lengths: 64, 128, or (more rarely) 256 bits. Theoretically, the more key length bits, the more secure your Wi-Fi network will be against intruders. However, there is one really big gotcha:

Only the 64-bit key length is fully defined in the Wi-Fi standard. This is a nasty problem that little has been written about. Because encryption using the longer key lengths is not part of the Wi-Fi standard, different manufacturers have used the longer keys in different ways, ways that sometimes make it impossible for Wi-Fi gear from different manufacturers to communicate when using 128 or 256 bit WEP keys. If your access point/gateway and *all* your client adapters are from the same vendor, you can feel safe in using the largest key length that the vendor offers. If not, you'll have to experiment. First test your network using 64-bit keys all the way around. Once it looks like everything works, set up your access point/gateway with 128-bit keys, and then set your client adapters to 128 bits and see what happens. If the client adapters can't communicate at the higher key length, you may have to fall back to 64 bits. If there's *any* doubt in your mind about the compatibility of your Wi-Fi gear, set everything up at 64 bits *first!*

If your network can only operate using 64-bit WEP keys, don't despair. 64-bit WEP is better protection than most writers have indicated, and with all the completely unprotected networks out there, it's much more likely that a cracker will move on to a nearby unprotected network than attempt to crack yours.

8. *Create a passphrase or individual hexadecimal key values, as required.*

For WPA: Create an alphanumeric passphrase longer than 40 characters but no longer than 63 characters. It can contain spaces and punctuation. Make it something easy to remember, like a line of poetry. (I discussed this issue in detail in Chapter 14.)

For WEP: Here we run into an important difference in the way all the various manufacturers implement WEP. The Wi-Fi standard specifies that you need four different keys for WEP. For the standard 64-bit encryption level, these keys are 10-digit *hexadecimal* numbers. Hexadecimal (base 16) numbers use the digits from 0 to 9, and for the values "after" 9 up to 15, the letters A through F. You don't need to know anything more about hexadecimal numbers to turn WEP on. A typical 64-bit WEP key would thus look something like this: 670DF5BA16. If you're using 128-bit WEP, you'll need 26 hex digits instead of 10.

For some client adapters, you need four of these hexadecimal keys. Others will allow you to set up WEP with only one. Some make the other three keys optional. Refer to your product documentation for details.

You can make up hexadecimal WEP keys "from whole cloth" by jotting down four strings of random symbols (0 to 9 and A to F). If your access point has a "key generator" (as Linksys products and many others do) you can type in a more memorable passphrase and the key generator will generate a group of four keys of an appropriate length from that passphrase. Thankfully, most of the newer Wi-Fi access points have built-in key generators. Some of the older ones do not.

To tell what system your access point has, go to the WEP screen or tab and see if there is an entry field marked "password" or "passphrase." If there is, you don't have to manually generate keys. If all you see are entry fields for four keys, get out your pencil and paper and start jotting down four sequences of ten random digits.

9. *Enter the passphrase or hexadecimal key values.*

   For WPA: Once you locate the wireless security screen or tab in your access point or wireless gateway, entering the passphrase is easy. There will be a field for entering a passphrase; enter it *carefully*. (No products that I know of force you to enter a hexadecimal WPA key.) This is more of an issue in WPA than in WEP, because WPA passphrases are quite long, and for best security should be 63 characters in length. The risk is not just typing something incorrectly—the risk is typing something incorrectly while *thinking* that you typed it correctly. Later on, even if you type the passphrase correctly into a client supplicant utility, the client will not connect, and you'll be scratching your head over it. The worst case is with Windows XP, where you can't see what characters you're typing. Type it in slowly and (if you can!) check each character twice.

   For WEP: Once you find the WEP screen or tab, this will be easy. As with WPA, your main concern is to be absolutely sure that the passphrase you enter is the same one you decided to use. In other words, don't misspell your passphrase when typing it in! Most access points do not force you to type a passphrase in a second time for verification, even though that would be a good idea. (Windows XP, which does not echo your passphrase back to you, does force you to enter passphrases twice.) If you type in "lollapaloosa" instead of "lollapalooza" the access point will take you at your word. If you later type "lollapalooza" into the key generators on your client adapters, nothing will work.

This caution goes double if you must enter the hexadecimal WEP key values manually. Write your keys down clearly, then type them in character by character and check each one twice. The keys in all your client adapters must match the keys stored in the access point. Get even one digit wrong and things won't work.

Once everything has been entered, check it character-by-character one last time. Then click either the OK or Apply button (or whatever it is on your particular access point) to store the key values.

10. *Power up your first client computer and enter the keys or pass phrase.*

At this point, your access point/gateway is ready to go. Now you need to get everybody else set up with their security configuration. Power up your first client computer, wait for it to boot, and then bring up its Wi-Fi client management utility or (for WPA) supplicant. The client management utility was installed when you installed the Wi-Fi client adapter; the supplicant you'll have to install separately.

For WEP: Find the WEP configuration screen or tab, and enter the passphrase or hexadecimal keys precisely as you entered them into the access point. The one possible snag you may encounter here is one that I faced long ago: My old Linksys WAP11 access point had a key generator, and the Orinoco Gold PCMCIA card in my laptop did not. So although I easily generated the four keys on the access point by entering a passphrase, I had to enter the four keys manually into the Orinoco Gold's configuration screen. Again, be careful when typing and check what you type twice.

For WPA: Bring up the supplicant software's configuration screen (which is part of the operating system for Windows XP) and enter the passphrase you created in Step #8. Be careful what you type, especially under Windows XP, where you can't see what you're typing.

Theoretically, when you get your passphrase or keys entered correctly and click the OK or Apply button, your client computer should be in (encrypted) communication with your access point.

11. *Test the connection and repeat for any other clients.*

See if your connection still works. If there are shared drives or printers, copy or print a file. See if you can access the Internet through the wireless link. If you can, go to the next client computer and repeat the process until everybody has the keys and WEP or WPA is functioning for all the clients.

Once you've completed all these steps, your wireless network should be completed and functional.

Some Real-World Examples

Now that I've explained the general steps for setting up security, let's go through it with real screens. Because WEP and WPA are configured so differently, I'm actually going to present several separate examples below, each in its own section labeled by security technology and (for WPA) by operating system. Watch the section heads carefully to find an example close to your own situation!

Configuring a Wireless Gateway for WEP (All Operating Systems)

The Linksys BEFW11S4 wireless gateway is perhaps the most popular Wireless-B device in its class. It's easy to configure, and I choose it here as an example of how to set up WEP on a gateway. For WPA, I'll use the newer WRT54G gateway instead, later in this chapter. Note that this example applies for *all* operating systems, because you're configuring the gateway through a Web browser. Here are the steps required:

1. The BEFW11S4's configuration system (as with almost all such products) is Web-based. There's an embedded Web server inside the gateway, and you enter a non-routable IP address into your Web browser to bring it up:

   http://192.168.1.1

   This is the address my own unit uses, and is the default address for the BEFW11S4 as it comes out of the box. The actual address will vary by both manufacturer and product line. Check your product documentation to make sure this is the same address used by yours! Figure 15.2 is a portion of the configuration screen as you'll see it in your Web browser.

2. If you have WEP disabled (as it is by default) the Disable radio button will be checked and the WEP Key Settings button will be grayed out. Once you check Mandatory, the WEP Key Settings button will come to life. Click on it. A child window will appear over the first, and it will look a lot like Figure 15.3.

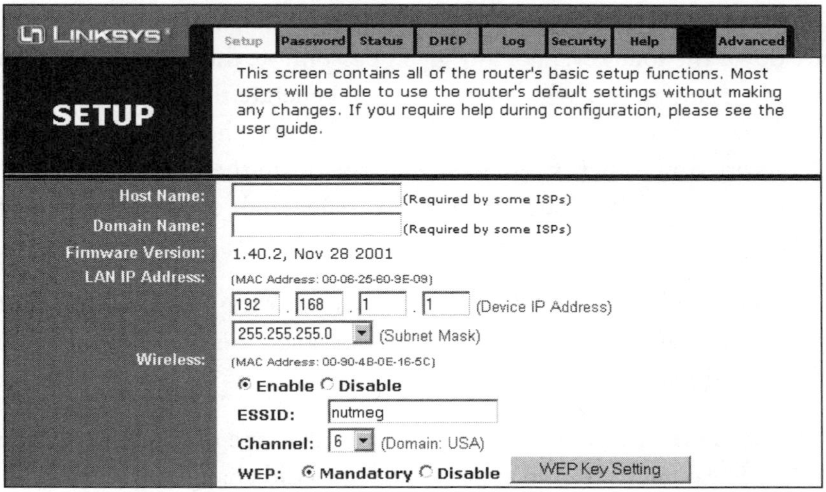

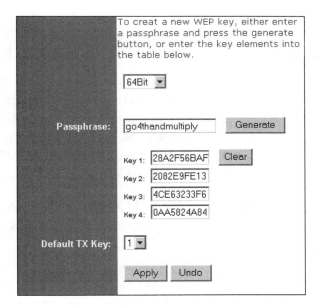

Figure 15.2
The Linksys BEFW11S4 Configuration Screen.

Figure 15.3
The BEFW11S4 WEP Key Settings.

3. The first time you bring it up, the passphrase field will be blank, and the keys will be all zeroes. Type in your chosen passphrase (Let's just say that I recommend *against* using the one shown here!) and click the Generate button. The four key fields will be filled with the generated keys, all in hexadecimal.

If all your Wi-Fi client adapters are from Linksys as well, you don't have to write down the four keys. For any given passphrase, the key generator from the same manufacturer will (almost always) generate the same keys. Key generators are not standard across all manufacturers, however. If your client adapters are from other manufacturers, write down the four keys. Check them digit-by-digit against what's on the screen. One digit off, and the connection will not work.

4. Once your four keys are safely written down, click the Apply button. The child window will clear, and you'll see the message "Settings are successful" with a Continue button.

5. Click Continue. If you didn't change anything on the main configuration screen, you can close your Web browser. If you did change something, click the Apply button at the bottom of the main screen, click Continue, and then close your browser.

That's it! WEP is now operating on your gateway.

Configuring a Wireless Gateway for WPA (All Operating Systems)

Although the latest revision (V4) of the BEFW11S4 can be firmware upgraded to support WPA, the newer WRT54G Wireless-G gateway from Linksys comes WPA-ready right out of the box. In this section I'll show you how to enable WPA on the WRT54G for all operating systems. Later on I'll demonstrate how to enable WPA on your client adapters as well, for both Windows XP and Windows 2000:

1. Like all Linksys access points and gateways, the WRT54G's configuration screen is Web-based, and you bring it up in your Web browser by entering a local IP address:

    http://192.168.1.1

2. Again, the address for your particular AP or gateway may be different; check your product documentation. For the WRT54G, unless you're doing something exotic, everything in the first screen will be configured automatically or left to the defaults. To configure security, click on the Wireless tab, which is the second tab from the left. You'll see the screen shown in Figure 15.4.

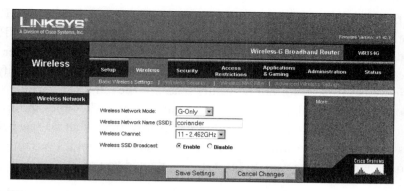

Figure 15.4
The Linksys WRT54G Wireless Tab.

 By the way, if you haven't already changed the SSID from the default ("linksys") this is the time to do it. Ditto the wireless mode. To set up security, however, you're going to have to click on the "Wireless Security" sub-tab. Out of the box, security is disabled, and the only option you'll see at first is Security Mode.

3. The Security Mode field has several options, including WEP and the "big network" RADIUS-based modes. For a SOHO network running with a pre-shared key, you need to select WPA Pre-Shared Key. Pull down the list and select it. The screen will now look a lot like the one shown in Figure 15.5. (Before capturing the screen shown in Figure 15.5, I had already changed the security values to their required values.)

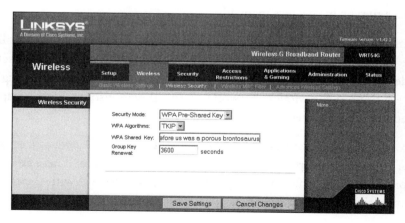

Figure 15.5
The WRT54G Wireless Security Tab.

4. From the pull-down list labeled WPA Algorithm, you need to select TKIP. The other option, AES, is for big, centrally managed networks. Under WPA Shared Key you must enter the WPA passphrase. As explained in Chapter 14, this needs to be more than 40 characters long to provide acceptable security. I'm annoyed at Linksys for not providing space for the full 63 characters without having to scroll; I suspect many people will stop when they think they're filling the field. The full passphrase shown is "then what we saw before us was a porous brontosaurus." It could be longer, I guess, but it's certainly easy to remember! (I grew up on Dr. Seuss—or could you tell?)

5. Unless your network will be carrying lots and lots of data, you can leave the last option, Group Key Renewal, at 3600 seconds. For networks that will be running at full saturation, I recommend reducing this to 900 seconds.

6. Once you have all the options entered, click Save Settings, and you're done. Your WRT54G wireless gateway is now set up to run WPA security.

Configuring Client Adapters for WEP Using Vendor Client Managers (All Operating Systems)

Once your wireless gateway has WEP enabled, you have to enable WEP on all other wireless clients in your network, with the same keys (or passphrase) that you entered into the gateway. If you have Linksys client adapters, the process will be similar, and you can use the same passphrase in the client adapter key generators. Otherwise, you will have to type in the keys manually.

In this section I'll demonstrate how to set up WEP using the client manager utilities that come on CD "in the box" with Wi-Fi client adapters. That's how you set up WEP under Windows 9x and Windows NT/2000. Windows XP is new enough to have built-in support for wireless networking, so I'll demonstrate client setup for XP in a separate section later in this chapter.

For this example, I'm going to use the Orinoco Gold Classic PC card, as it's a good example of those client adapters that do *not* provide key generators. These are growing less common all the time, but you need to know how to deal with them when you encounter them. Here are the steps you need to follow:

1. Run the Orinoco Client Manager, which was installed with the Orinoco Gold Classic card. The main screen is shown in Figure 15.6.

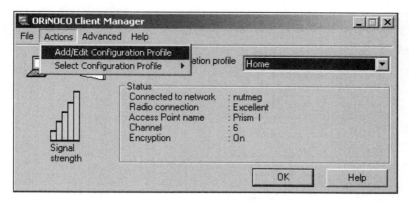

Figure 15.6
The Orinoco Client Manager.

2. Pull down and select the Actions | Add/Edit Configuration Profile menu item. This will bring up a child screen allowing you to select a profile to edit. See Figure 15.7.

3. Make sure the profile that you want to change is shown in the pull-down list. (Here it's called "Home.") Click the Edit button. This will kick off a five-screen wizard, of which the Set Security screen is #3. You move from screen to screen by clicking on the Back and Next buttons at the bottoms of the screens. The Set Security screen is shown in Figure 15.8.

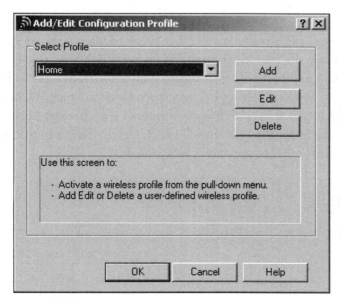

Figure 15.7
Selecting a Profile to Edit.

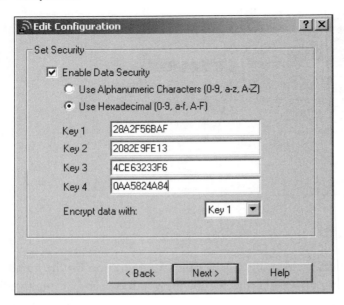

Figure 15.8
The Orinoco Set Security Screen.

To enable security, you must check the Enable Data Security check box, and then enter the four keys. Also make sure you check the Use Hexadecimal check box, for compatibility with other equipment. Orinoco allows the use of alphabetic characters in its keys, which is something most other manufacturers do not support.

4. There is no passphrase support like many other client adapters have, so you'll need to manually enter the four WEP keys. (These were either generated by the wireless gateway's key generator or invented—by you—from scratch. I explained how in the section "Setting Up Security – General Steps.") Check your typing twice. Once you have all four keys entered and checked, click the Next button until you reach the final screen, which has the Finish button at the bottom. Click the Finish button, and you're done!

Make sure you test the new WEP-enabled connection. Once you've finished configuring WEP for your first client PC, do the same for any additional client PCs.

Setting Up WEP Using Windows XP's Built-In Wi-Fi Support

Whenever possible, I prefer to use the client manager utility that comes with a Wi-Fi client adapter to set up its various configuration options, including WEP. Increasingly, Wi-Fi client managers won't install at all under Windows XP. Instead, client adapters vendors are choosing to rely on the built-in Wi-Fi support that XP offers. If you install the drivers for your client adapter under Windows XP and discover that the install CD hasn't also installed a client utility, you can still set up WEP right from Windows XP. It's a little more trouble, but it works just as well.

To set up WEP on a client adapter using XP's built-in client support, follow these steps:

1. Open the Network Connections applet from Control Panel. The applet is shown in Figure 15.9.

2. Your Wi-Fi client adapter should be listed as one of the wireless network connections (most likely the only one) in the main pane. Right-click on it and select Properties. The Properties window will appear. Click the Wireless Networks tab at the top of the window. Make sure that the check box labeled "Use Windows to configure my wireless network settings" is checked.

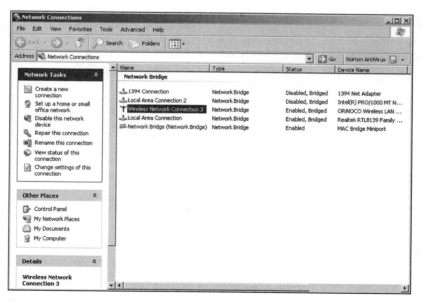

Figure 15.9
The Windows XP Network Connection Applet.

3. On the Wireless Networks tab is a list of available wireless networks, also known as the "site survey." What you see will look something like the screen shown in Figure 15.10. Your network (named by its SSID) should be present in the list of available networks. Other wireless networks may be there as well, if you're close enough to them for your client adapter to pick them up. These would include networks owned by your neighbors or companies in nearby offices.

4. Click on your network in the list of available networks to highlight it, and then click the Configure button. You'll see a window like that in Figure 15.11.

5. Un-check the item labeled "The key is provided for me automatically." For a SOHO network running WEP without central management, you need to enter the key manually. When you un-check the item, the window will change, and the Network Key field will become live (see Figure 15.12).

6. Type in the first of your four network keys. You'll need to type it twice, as the key is not echoed (except as generic dots) when you type it, and Windows needs to be sure that you typed it correctly. If both entry attempts don't match, an error will be displayed and you'll be required to enter the whole key again. In most cases, one key is all you need, but if you are using multiple keys (the

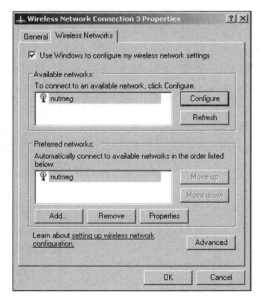

Figure 15.10
The Windows XP Site Survey Window.

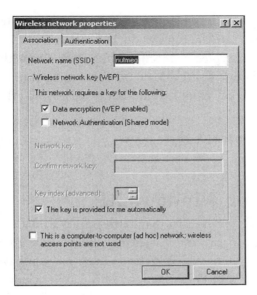

Figure 15.11
The Association Configuration Window.

Wi-Fi standard supports up to four) you enter additional keys by incrementing the Key Index field to the next higher key index and entering subsequent keys.

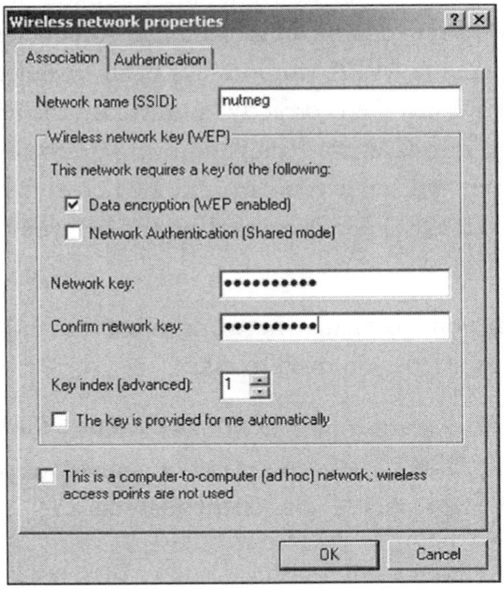

Figure 15.12
Entry of WEP Keys.

7. When you've entered all the keys you'll be using, click OK. It will take a few seconds for Windows XP to negotiate the connection, but within thirty seconds you will either have an encrypted connection or know that something is wrong. If you're reading WEP keys written down on paper, make sure they're correct—typing the wrong key twice isn't any better than typing the right key once!

That's all you need to do to enable WEP for Windows XP, using XP's built-in Wi-Fi support.

Setting Up WPA Under Windows XP

Setting up WPA under Windows XP is even easier than setting up WEP. Windows XP has built-in wireless networking support, and it's getting better as time goes by. That statement comes with a caveat, however: WPA is so new that you have to install a Microsoft-provided patch to have WPA support. This patch includes the necessary supplicant software (see Chapter 14 for more on WPA supplicants) and the user interface allowing WPA client configuration without the use of a client manager utility.

The patch can be downloaded from Microsoft's Web site. Search the Microsoft Knowledge Base for Article 815485. That article contains the instructions for installing the patch, plus a link toward the end for downloading the patch installer program. It's a .EXE file. You simply need to download it to a folder somewhere and run it, then reboot the PC. At that point, WPA support has been installed into Windows XP. If you're unsure that it got installed correctly (admittedly, the updater doesn't give you a lot of feedback) go into Control Panel and bring up the Add or Remove Programs applet. Scroll down and see if you can find a Microsoft Hotfix with the reference number Q815485. If Q815485 is present on the list, your WPA patch is truly installed.

You still need to configure WPA for your particular network, however, and that's what this section is about. Here are the steps you need to take:

1. If you haven't already configured your access point or wireless gateway for WPA, do that now. (I explained how on p. 336.) The access point or gateway of your network *must* be set up for WPA before any of your client adapters are!

2. Open the Network Connections applet from Control Panel. There is a screenshot of this applet in Figure 15.9 (back a few pages) in case you're unfamiliar with it.

3. Locate and select your wireless network client adapter from the list of installed adapters and bridges.

4. Right-click on the client adapter's entry and select Properties from the context menu. Click the Wireless Networks tab at the top of the Properties window.

5. There is a checkbox at the top of the Properties window reading "Use Windows to configure my wireless network settings." That checkbox *must* be checked.

6. On the Wireless Networks tab is a list of wireless networks labeled "Available networks." This is your "site survey." In nearly all cases, you will only see one network listed, and that one will be yours. It's possible that you're close enough to your neighbors to see more than one. If you have multiple Wi-Fi access points or gateways in your own setup, you will see those as well. Figure 15.13 shows a site survey with two networks listed. My WPA gateway is labeled "coriander." The network labeled "cragstan" is a lab network I was using to test new gear.

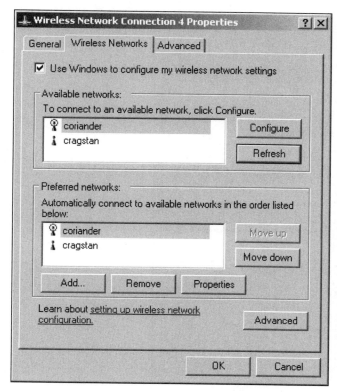

Figure 15.13
The Windows XP Wireless Networks Tab Window.

7. To be sure the site survey is completely current, click the Refresh button to the right of the survey list. The window will gray out while Windows performs the refresh. When it comes back, select your network and click the Configure button.

8. A whole new window will appear, as shown in Figure 15.14. This is the window where you actually set up the WPA parameters for your particular network. First pull down the list labeled Network Authentication and select WPA-PSK.

9. Pull down the list labeled Data Encryption and select TKIP.

10. Below the Data Encryption list are two fields for the entry of your WPA passphrase. Enter it carefully, and then enter it again in the second field to confirm it. This is tricky because Windows echoes your typing as dots instead of readable characters, and you can type a character incorrectly without knowing it. Click OK. If the two fields don't match when you click OK, Windows will display an error and you'll have to type both in again from scratch.

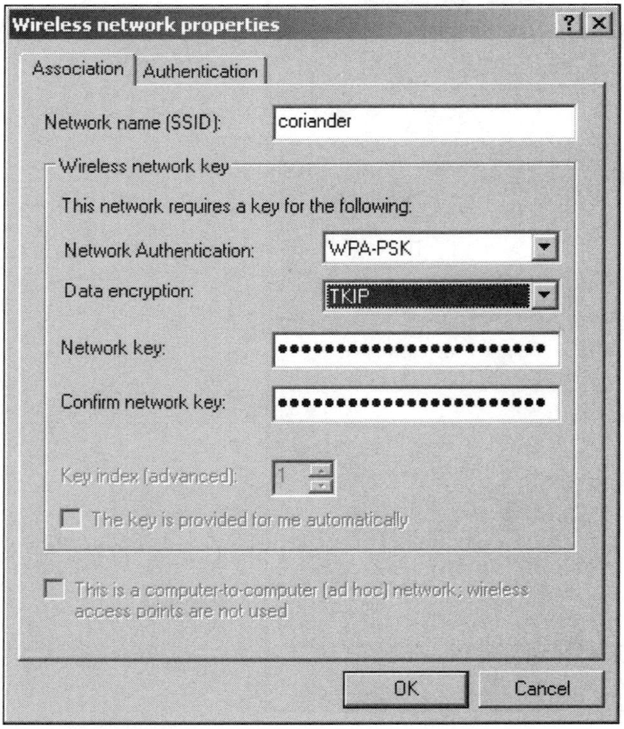

Figure 15.14
Setting WPA's Parameters.

11. Assuming that you typed your passphrase correctly—twice—clicking OK will store the WPA parameters and establish a WPA-secured connection with your access point or wireless gateway. You're in!

Setting up WPA Under Windows 2000

There is no built-in support for WPA in Windows 2000, and no convenient Microsoft patch to add it. You need to acquire a third-party supplicant utility, install it, and configure WPA that way. Thankfully, there is a reliable free supplicant called WPA Assistant, which I mentioned in Chapter 14. Download it from the vendor site and install it:

www.wirelesssecuritycorp.com/wsc/public/WPAAssistant.do

When it's installed, you'll see a small key icon in your Windows taskbar tray in the lower-right hand corner of the screen. Before you connect to your access point or gateway, the key icon will be gray. After you connect, it will turn sky-blue.

Here are the steps to take to configure WPA Assistant so it will connect a Windows 2000 client to your wireless network:

1. Make sure WPA Assistant is installed: Look for the key icon in the tray!

2. Double-click on the key icon. The WPA Assistant configuration window will appear. See Figure 15.15.

3. The window includes a site-survey list of available networks. The site survey includes some useful information, like the type of encryption used by the networks listed. To connect via WPA, your network must indicate "WPA-PSK" as the encryption method. If your network indicates "WEP" instead, you've configured your access point or wireless gateway incorrectly, and you need to go back and correct that. If your network appears there with "WPA-PSK" indicated, select it by clicking on it.

4. Type your WPA passphrase in the field provided. WPA Assistant echoes it in plain text (which is useful for long passphrases) and gives you a count of how many characters you've typed.

5. Once you've entered your passphrase, make sure the checkbox labeled Save Key is checked. If you leave it un-checked, you will have to re-enter your passphrase each time you connect to your network.

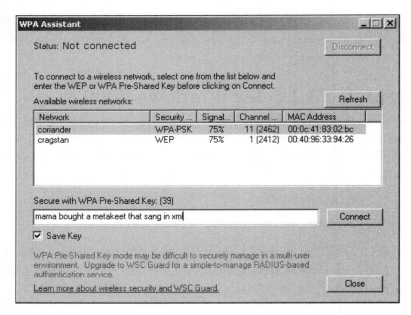

Figure 15.15
The WPA Assistant Configuration Screen.

6. Click the Connect button. If you entered your passphrase correctly, the status line toward the top of the window will change to "Connected to <SSID>" with the SSID of your access point or gateway displayed. The key icon in the taskbar tray will turn blue. You're in!

Final Wi-Fi Security Tips

Once you have WPA or WEP enabled, you've achieved nearly all of the security that a Wi-Fi network can offer. Other measures available to owners of SOHO networks are minor by comparison, but they're worth laying out again:

*   Once WPA or WEP is enabled, you can turn off the SSID Broadcast beacon, and your network will be more difficult to find by drive-by network intruders. Difficult is not the same as impossible, however, and as I've said elsewhere, the really dangerous intruders can find you, beacon or no beacon.

- If your access point or gateway offers you the ability to reduce the transmit power (alas, most do not), try turning down the power to the next lower level, and then see if all of your connected client computers retain their connection at full speed. If they do, you don't need the highest power level—and at lower power, your network will not be accessible from as far beyond your premises. Keep lowering the power until you begin to lose some of your client connections, and then raise it only to the point where all clients connect at the top bitrate for the technology that you're using.

- If you use your Internet connection to connect to servers at your place of employment, inquire at your company's IT department to see if they can provide you with a virtual private network (VPN) connection to the company network through your broadband Internet connection. Configuring a VPN is beyond the scope of a book like this, but if your company can provide one, there are people at your company who can explain how to set it up and make it work. A VPN operating under cover of WEP or WPA is as close to uncrackable security as you're ever likely to have.

- Technology advances. Perhaps you have older gear and have been forced to use WEP rather than WPA. Every now and then, check on the Web site belonging to the manufacturer of your Wi-Fi gear to see if they have begun to offer any firmware/driver upgrades that will provide WPA support for your access point or gateway and client adapters. If such upgrades are ever offered, download them and install them, and move from WEP to WPA. WPA is much stronger protection than WEP, though as I've said many times, for lightly used networks WEP is much better than the press has made it sound.

How About Some Projects?

At this point, you have a network, functioning and (reasonably) secure. Nothing more needs to be done—but if you have a curious mind and are good with tools, there are some refinements to be considered, especially if you have dead spots around your home or office, or other problematic network coverage. Antennas, reflectors, wireless bridges—that's what the rest of this book is all about.

The Tin Can Bandwidth Expander

Sometimes, when you have a location out on the fringes (or even beyond the fringes) of your access point's reach, it takes a gain antenna to connect at the maximum bit rate, or sometimes to connect at all. In this chapter I'll present two hands-on projects that show you how to build gain antennas out of easy-to-find objects such as tin cans and rectangular liquid containers. With each project I'll provide the list of materials you need and the step-by-step construction techniques. You'll be amazed at what you can build in your own garage.

Gain antennas have a sort of spotted reputation in the Wi-Fi business. Some people think that if you're fooling with gain antennas, you're up to no good. Certainly the FCC frowns on them, but as long as you stick within the FCC's effective radiated power limits they're not illegal, and they can be extremely useful in a number of ways, as you'll learn in this chapter.

As I've said in Chapter 8, gain antennas aren't magic. They're basically lenses for radio waves. They take the radio-frequency energy from your access point or client adapter and focus it so that it travels mostly in a single direction rather than in all directions at once. Just as a focused beam of light from a flashlight travels farther than the light radiating in all directions from a lit match, your omnidirectional (all-directions-at-once) radio signal will become a beam, and it will go much farther in a single direction than it does coming out of an omnidirectional antenna. Similarly (though not as obviously) they focus the weak radio signals coming into the antenna from a distant access point or client adapter and make them easier to read.

You can buy some very effective microwave antennas for Wi-Fi use from commercial vendors (see the subtopic "Choosing a Commercial Antenna" in Chapter 8) but for a lot of applications you can simply make your own out of appropriate-sized tin cans. In order to do this project you don't have to be a participant on Discovery Channel's *Monster Garage* but you do need to be reasonably adept with hand tools such as:

- Electric drill

- Combination square and scribe

- Soldering iron

Before you even *think* about building your own gain antenna, you need to read Chapter 8, particularly the subtopic "How Antennas Work." Once you understand the theory behind what you're doing, you can look around and see what other materials may be available to you. Antennas have been made from dryer vent pipe, 3" and 4" copper drain pipe, and even rolls of sheet metal curved into a tube and soldered or riveted together.

The type of antenna you can build from tin cans is called a *waveguide* antenna. The other popular build-it-yourself antenna is called a *Yagi* antenna, and while it's not prohibitively difficult to build your own Yagi, it's certainly a lot more fussy metalwork, and I'm not sure the results are better commensurate with the extra effort required to make one.

Yes, once again, you *can* make a Pringle's can antenna, but virtually any waveguide antenna made of a real tin can will plow a cardboard potato chip can into the proverbial soil.

For B & G, Not A

All of the antennas described in this chapter are for the 2.4 GHz Wi-Fi band. That's the band where both Wireless-B and Wireless-G operate (as well as minority players like 802.11b+ and Super G). The antennas here will function with clients and access points for any technology that uses the 2.4 GHz band. This even includes non-Wi-Fi technologies like Bluetooth and HomeRF, both of which share the 2.4 GHz band with Wi-Fi.

However, this pointedly excludes Wireless-A, which operates at 5GHz. These antennas will not work with Wireless-A for two reasons:

- The frequencies are wrong. You'd have to completely redesign the antennas I describe here to work on the much higher 5 GHz band.

- There are FCC limitations on the use of "add-on" antennas on the 5 GHz band. Some of the Wireless-A channels are in a sub-band for which the FCC forbids detachable antennas. That's why, if you have Wireless-A or multiple-band gear, that the antennas may move but they don't come off. There are some 5 GHz channels for which detachable antennas are legal, but gear for these channels is quite rare and expensive. All of the common, low-price Wireless-A equipment allows you to operate on any Wireless-A channel, including the antenna-restricted ones. Even if you forcibly remove an antenna from such a device, attaching an external antenna is a violation of FCC rules.

What Tin Can Antennas Are For

Tin can antennas do what all gain antennas do: Enable you to throw a Wi-Fi signal farther than with a simpler antenna, or sniff a signal farther. Or both. (Creating a connection at a distance requires both.) You can use tin can antennas as fixed point-to-point antennas to connect two networks in two different buildings (see the network bridge project in Chapter 17) and you can use them as directional sensing antennas for wardriving or warscanning, as I'll explain in Chapter 19.

Probably the most broadly useful application of simple tin-can antennas is as *range extenders*, which allow you to connect to an access point from the fringes of its range. Back when I lived in Arizona, a tin can antenna solved a problem for me that a lot of people have, and probably don't realize how easily it can be fixed.

It was like this: My office, broadband Internet connection, primary computer, and wireless access point were on the second floor of my long, rambling Arizona ranch house. My wife's office was directly below mine. Her computer could connect easily to my access point right through the floor for a full-speed 11 Mbps network connection.

At the opposite corner of the house on the first floor was our living room, where the big TV and comfy couch were. Sometimes in the evenings I did the couch-potato thing and just watched a movie, but there were times when I also wanted to keep an eye on something on the Internet, usually an eBay auction, that requires an occasional glance but not constant attention. I had hoped to do this by parking my Wi-Fi equipped laptop on the coffee table and letting the Wi-Fi machinery do its magic.

Well, it was a bridge slightly too far. If I positioned the laptop just *so*, it would connect—barely. When it connected, I generally got 1 Mbps. Careful tweaking of the laptop would sometimes get me 2 Mbps, depending (oddly enough) on where I was sitting on the couch, or (even more oddly) where on the coffee table I had placed my can of Diet Pepsi Twist. More than 2 Mbps, forget it. The path between the coffee table and my access point was optimal-bad, with a couple of walls (including a dense slump block wall), the microwave oven, a steel spiral stairway, and a cupboard full of tin cans in the way.

Tin cans...hmmm.

I went out in the garage, dumped the wood screws from a twenty-year-old coffee can, did some quick calculator math, drilled the can for a coaxial N connector, soldered a carefully-measured stub of wire into the connector, and bolted it together. I bent a bracket out of a scrap of aluminum sheet metal, and cobbled together a flexible gooseneck base out of pipe fittings, scrap iron, and a gooseneck I had salvaged from a long-defunct (and otherwise missing) microphone stand. It took about two hours, most of which was spent making sure I had the math right. (Figure thrice, measure twice, cut *once*!) I mounted the can on the base, and hauled back into the house. What I had is shown in Figure 16.1. The short length of wire is the pigtail that connects the antenna to the Orinoco Wi-Fi client adapter installed in my laptop.

It looks goofy, but don't judge from appearances: When connected to my laptop via a short pigtail of coaxial cable (see Chapter 8 for more on pigtails and coaxial cable), I was able to connect to my Wi-Fi network from my coffee table at full speed, instantly, without even having to do any fussy pointing. I just twisted the gooseneck so that the can was aimed generally up and toward my second-floor office, and I was in, at 11 Mbps. I had hoped to connect at 5.5 Mbps, which would have given me full advantage of my broadband connection, which sometimes gave me 2 Mbps on downloads. I wasn't expecting 11 Mbps!

The Tin Can Bandwidth Expander, Mark I, was both ugly and larger than it needed to be. I've made several more, striving for something a little prettier and somewhat more compact. My best is shown in Figure 16.2. The Mark III uses a smaller can and a nicer base, which had once been a Fifties gooseneck desk lamp. I bought it on eBay for $6.95. I was the only bidder, and there were literally dozens of crufty old gooseneck lamps to choose from.

Not all my experiments were equally successful. (That's why I call them "experiments.") Mark II was a 9" length of 2 $\frac{1}{2}$" brass tubing with a printed circuit board disk soldered over one end, and it was a little narrow to work well at 2.4 GHz. It

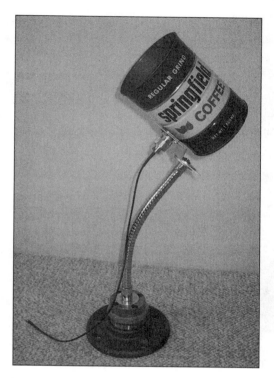

Figure 16.1
The Duntemann Tin Can Bandwidth Expander, Mark I.

mimicked Mark VI, which used a 2 $^{7}/_{8}$" diameter tennis ball can. Both failed units taught me that the physics mean business: Do the math and follow what it tells you!

Checking Internet auctions from the living room couch wasn't the only use I ever made of these gadgets. I also used Mark I from outside the house, to allow me to connect to the Internet from a small table beside my large Newtonian telescope out in the back of my large lot. I used it from the garage, where my workshop was, even though that's a long, metal-strewn path that didn't always let me connect at full speed.

 Wi-Fi experts will understand that the tin can expander works as well as it does in part because your typical PCMCIA card client adapter's antenna is wretched beyond hope, so almost anything would be an improvement. However, the tin can antenna is a nice compromise between effectiveness and complexity. A parabolic dish would have more reach, obviously—but if you don't need that much gain, why bother?

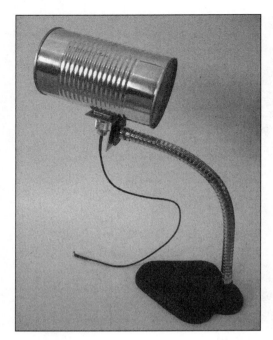

Figure 16.2
The Duntemann Tin Can Bandwidth Expander, Mark III.

Admittedly, I'm a machine-tool hobbyist, amateur radio operator, and electronics technician of long standing (30 years plus now, sigh) but there really isn't much to it. If there are parts of your house that you can't reach with your laptop or other client adapter with a connector for an external antenna, consider putting one together.

Project #1: Building the Bandwidth Expander

The simplest bandwidth expander consists of the following:

• One tin can

• A type N female coaxial connector

• Less than 2" of #12 copper wire

The tin can might be the most difficult part to locate. (See the following section.) You can obtain the other two parts at your local hardware store or a chain home improvement store such as Home Depot.

The work required to build the project involves:

- A little math (but don't worry because I'll walk you through the calculations)

- A little measurement

- Some minor handywork with an electric drill and a soldering iron

I'll provide very detailed instructions for how to build one. After that, well, the field is ripe for experimentation. I encourage you to study up on the theory and try different things, and at the end of this chapter I'll point out some of the possibilities that you can pursue.

Choosing Your Can

In an ideal world, you could just order the precise length of metal cylinder (ideally silver-plated copper or brass) at the precise diameter your calculations specify, say, 93 millimeters. Doubtless there is somebody somewhere in the world who will sell you tubing like that, but if you have to ask what it costs, you can't afford it.

We'll be using a tin can instead. So we have to get a little creative, see what's out there, and then decide what available sizes fit within the constraints of the RF physics that govern waveguide operation. You can think of this like creating sculpture out of found objects.

Diameter is the key. For any given frequency, the diameter of a useful circular waveguide is constrained by a minimum and a maximum value. Within these two bounds, your waveguide will conduct Radio Frequency (RF) energy at the given frequency (for us, within a band centered on 2.45 GHz) with the least loss of power on transmit and signal on receive.

These two bounds define the waveguide diameter limits within which a single wave *propagation mode* (called TM11) predominates at a given frequency. Above and below the bounds, other propagation modes begin to operate as well, and the lossiness of the waveguide increases.

If the notion of a "propagation mode" is meaningless to you, don't sweat it. Having a complete understanding of waveguide physics isn't necessary to make a good waveguide antenna, but the physics are very cool nonetheless, and I encourage you to read up on it. (The best treatment I've seen is in the ARRL UHF/Microwave Experimenter's Manual, Chapter 5.)

So what are the bounds for our frequency, which is 2.45 GHz? (2.45 GHz is roughly the center of the band of frequencies used by Wi-Fi gear.) The lower diameter limit in centimeters is defined by the "free space" wavelength at 2.45 GHz divided by 1.706. The wavelength there is 12.25 cm:

$$\frac{12.25\ cm}{1.706} = 73mm$$

The higher diameter limit is defined by the wavelength divided by 1.3065:

$$\frac{12.25\ cm}{1.3065} = 94mm$$

There's our bounds: 73 mm on the low side, and 94 mm on the high side. Explaining where the two constants 1.706 and 1.3065 come from is more than I can tackle in this book, but they're consequences of the geometry of circular waveguides. You'll have to trust me on it—or go read the *ARRL UHF/Microwave Experimenter's Manual.*

So... do we aim down the middle and pick a can with a diameter of about 85 mm? (This would be convenient, as by total coincidence that's one of the commonest can sizes in your local supermarket!) Not necessarily, unless you can find an 85 mm can that's long enough. The problem is that the efficiency of a circular waveguide doesn't peak halfway between the bounds. It's mostly flat inside the bounds, and decreases (with increased lossiness) in both directions outside the bounds.

Furthermore, this increase of lossiness outside the bounds is not symmetrical. It goes up *much* more quickly as your waveguide gets smaller than as it gets larger. In fact, going outside the bounds on the large side doesn't lose you all that much for the first fifteen or twenty percent.

Another advantage of choosing your waveguide on the larger end is that the position of the probe (the quarter-wave spike that transfers RF energy between the waveguide and your coax pigtail) is much less critical there, so small errors in drilling for the N connector won't make as much difference.

The Ideal Can

If you could choose your size arbitrarily, it would be 94 mm. I'm not sure about Europe, but in the U.S. I've found nothing at that size. I'm already laughing at the thought of thousands of Wi-Fi users around the world searching the canned food aisle and coffee section of supermarkets with ruler in hand seeking the perfect can. I measured enough to say that cans in the U.S. tend to be in one three sizes: 3", 4", and 4 $^3/_{16}$", which in metric terms are 87, 100, and 105 mm, respectively.

Of these three, only the 87 mm can is inside our diameter bounds. Can we use the others? Yes. This isn't like crossing the streams in *Ghostbusters*—in fact, a 100 mm waveguide will work fine for Wi-Fi, and that's the size I recommend, for two purely practical reasons: 4" (100 mm) cans are very common, and the 4" cans that are out there are longer than the 3 3/8" cans. They are long enough, in fact, so that you can use a single tall 4" can (like a 1-pound coffee can) as an effective waveguide antenna. If you decide to use the 3 $^3/_8$" cans, you might have to solder two or three together, end-to-end, which is a lot more work. (I found a 5 $^5/_8$" tall one in that diameter, full of Hunt's Spaghetti Sauce, and used it on Mark III. I don't know how common that size can is, but grab one if you can. The antenna works great, and the sauce is actually pretty good!)

To get yourself some cans, here is what I recommend (this might sound silly and your spouse will probably want to be two aisles over, but it works):

1. Take a pocket tape measure with you to the supermarket.

2. Find something sold in a 4" can that you can force down without choking. If you're a coffee drinker, look for ground coffee in the 1-pound size. (These days, you may only get 12 ounces of coffee in that size can.) That's a relatively tall can (which we want) and virtually all such cans are 4" in diameter. In fact, I consider the 1-pound coffee can the best all-around can for use as a waveguide antenna.

Another possible prospect is the 46-ounce tomato juice can. It's 7" long and 4 $^3/_{16}$" diameter (about 105 mm). The greater length gives you a little more gain, which compensates for the slightly greater loss inherent in its diameter. The other problem with tomato juice cans is that they have fairly pronounced corrugations along most of their length. These increase the scattering of RF energy within the can and thus reduce the can's effectiveness as an antenna.

Dinty Moore Beef Stew and various Chef Boy-Ar-Dee glop lunches come in 4" diameter cans, as do various species of canned fruit. They aren't very long cans, so if you drink neither coffee nor tomato juice, (and can't find that variety of Hunt's Spaghetti Sauce) you may have to solder two or three ravioli or peach half cans end-to-end to get sufficient gain to make the work worth the bother. (Soldering cans together requires a hefty soldering iron, a jig to hold the cans together, the right kind of solder, and some practice. Teaching structural soldering is outside the charter of this book. If you're not already an ace, avoid it if you can.)

Don't use a 2-pound coffee can, which at 6" diameter is *way* outside the diameter bounds for a 2.45 GHz waveguide. An antenna performance "shoot-out" published on the Web showed that 2-pound coffee cans do not perform as well as the narrower cans. For more information about this, visit the following Web site:

www.turnpoint.net/wireless/has.html

Ideally, the can should be clean and not dented nor distorted in any dimension. Cans get rough handling and most do not end up as waveguide antennas. Choose a can that hasn't been dropped, dented, or otherwise bent.

You'll need a can of an acceptable size, plus a chassis-mount N-style coaxial connector (see Figure 16.3). The connectors are available from many places. (I order silver-plated ones, but you can do well with the ordinary zinc-plated connectors, which are half the price.) See the vendor list in Appendix A. You'll also need about 2" of #12 copper wire.

The Overall Antenna Design and a Little More Math

A waveguide antenna is basically a cylinder open on only one end, with an N-type coaxial connector fastened into a hole drilled somewhere along the long axis of the cylinder. When you take the food/juice/coffee out of the can, remove one end entirely with a can opener, but leave the other end intact. Take off the label and wash the can thoroughly. If the can opener left any burrs, take a small file and file them down until they're not a threat to your hands. (Burrs won't reduce the electrical effectiveness of the antenna, but they can be razor-sharp.)

Figure 16.4 is a drawing of the finished antenna. The work to be done consists of calculating and measuring the distance from the closed end at which the connector should be mounted, then drilling a hole there for the N connector. After you measure, cut and solder the wire probe to the N connector, you mount it in the hole you drilled.

Figure 16.3
The UG-58 Chassis Mount N Connector.

And that's it!

But before you grab your electric drill, there's some more math to be done. We need to calculate how far from the closed end of the can to drill for the N connector. The distance to measure for is the *guide wavelength* divided by 4.

The guide wavelength is *not* the same as the free-space wavelength. The *free-space wavelength*, as the name implies, is the wavelength of radio energy traveling through free space. The guide wavelength is the distance between successive radio wave peaks and nulls as they impinge on the walls of the physical waveguide.

A waveguide is essentially a pipe for radio waves, but radio waves do not travel in a single straight line down the center of a waveguide. They bounce back and forth off the walls, at an angle, and at any given point along the waveguide the incident waves either cancel or reinforce one another. This canceling and reinforcement creates a pattern of electromagnetic peaks and nulls within the waveguide. The distance between successive peaks (or between successive nulls) is the guide wavelength. It depends upon both the frequency of the radio waves passing through the waveguide, and on the diameter of the waveguide itself.

Understanding this completely isn't necessary to making a good antenna. What you *must* understand is that you have to calculate the guide wavelength for each different can size that you use. The guide wavelength for a 4" can is *not* the same as the guide

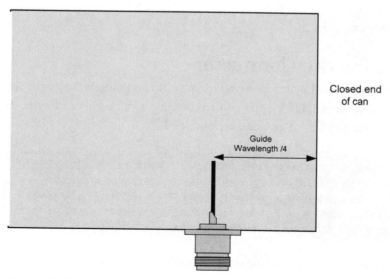

Figure 16.4
The Simplest Tin Can Antenna.

wavelength for a 4 $^3/_{16}$" can. I could give you a pre-calculated table for common can sizes, but if you come up with an odd size piece of can or tubing or pipe, you'll need to crunch the numbers yourself.

The formula isn't hideous. In fact, if you're mathophilic (hah!) it may even look familiar:

$$\lambda_g = \frac{1}{\sqrt{\left(\frac{1}{\lambda_o}\right)^2 - \left(\frac{1}{1.706D}\right)^2}}$$

Here, λ_g represents the guide wavelength, λ_o represents the free-space wavelength, and D represents the waveguide's diameter, all in centimeters. (If you haven't forgotten your junior-year math, you'll see that what we're doing here is using the Pythagorean Theorem to solve for one of the sides of a right triangle—which is key to understanding the physics, but not key to solving the equation! See the *ARRL UHF/Microwave Experimenter's Manual* for the full treatment.)

If you're more a coder than a mathematician, here's the formula expressed in Pascal:

```
GuideWL := 1 / SQRT(SQR(1/FreeSpaceWL) - SQR(1/(1.706*GuideDia)));
```

The three variables are all floating-point types. This should translate without much hassle into most other programming languages. Pop in 12.245 for FreeSpaceWL and the diameter of your can for GuideDia (both in cm) and turn the crank to find the guide wavelength in cm.

Drilling for the Connector

The N connector must be attached one quarter of the guide wavelength from the closed bottom of the can. Divide the guide wavelength value by 4 and write it down. For a 4" can, that will be 4.2 cm, or a hair under 1 $^{11}/_{16}$".

Virtually all tin cans have a bead running around their top and bottom edges. The bottom of the can is inset slightly (usually about 1/8") from the edge of this bead. Measure this inset before you mark, and take the inset length into account when you mark the drill point, by adding the inset to the quarter guide wavelength value. This value will be the distance you measure and mark from the bead edge of the can. Call it the probe offset length. See Figure 16.5.

Set the can on a flat surface, and measure as precisely as possible from the bottom of the can to the probe offset length. Put a dot at that point with a permanent marker.

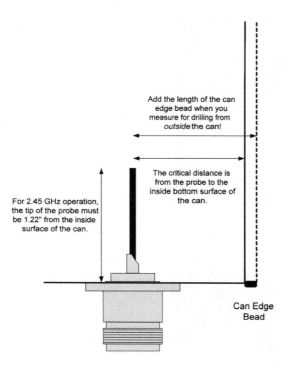

Add the length of the can
edge bead when you
measure for drilling from
outside the can!

The critical distance is
from the probe to the
inside bottom surface of
the can.

For 2.45 GHz operation,
the tip of the probe must
be 1.22" from the inside
surface of the can.

Can Edge
Bead

Figure 16.5
Probe Measurement Cautions.

Drilling into the can for the N connector might be tricky. You want to avoid pushing so hard on the side of the can that you bend the can. The best way to do it is to clamp a short length of 2 x 2 lumber in a vise so that 8" or 10" of wood extends away from the vise. If you have a drill press, you can clamp the 2 x 2 to the drill press plate with C clamps, and then offset the drill press plate as required so that the drill bit can come down on the measured point. What you want is for the wood to support the can as you drill it. See Figure 16.6.

Place the can over the 2 x 2 so that there is wood under the point where you need to drill. With a center punch, tap lightly at the center of your marked point. Then, drill a $1/_8$" pilot hole. The actual size hole you need to drill for the connector depends on the connector—they are not all precisely alike.

The very common and highly standard UG-58/AU 4-hole mount N female connector has a flange diameter of 15/32" (.469") and that's the hole size to drill in the can for that type of connector. The less common bulkhead N connector (see Figure 16.7) is designed to go through a 5/8" hole. The bulkhead connector is a little more expensive but obviates the need to drill the four additional small holes required for the UG-58.

Figure 16.6
Drilling the Can.

If you're using the UG-58 connector, drill the $^{15}/_{32}$" hole, then file the burrs with a rat-tail file. Insert the connector into the hole so that it's snug against the can, then mark through the four flange holes with a felt marker. Punch and drill the holes $^1/_8$". Use 4-40 thread flat-head screws, at least $^3/_8$" long.

A single clean $^5/_8$" hole is all you need for the bulkhead connector.

Making the Probe Assembly

The probe is pretty simple: It's a short length of #12 copper wire soldered into the "solder pot" of the N connector. The #12 wire is the commonest size used in residential construction wiring. You'll need at most about 2", so if you can avoid it, don't buy a whole roll! In fact, if you look around any construction site in the framing stages, you'll probably find little snippets of wire lying around everywhere. Take a few home. The #12 wire is 0.0815" thick, but that's not critical. The #10 wire will do fine, but is less common. The #14 wire is a little thin, and too easily bent.

Figure 16.7
An N Female Bulkhead Connector.

Take about 2" of the wire, remove the plastic insulation, and get it as straight as possible. (Clamping it in a vise for an hour works well.) Solder the wire into the N connector's solder pot, which is the small protrusion opposite the connector end. Get it as close to perpendicular to the connector as you can. This may take a few tries, each of which requires re-melting the solder in the pot around the wire.

The probe length measurement must be reasonably precise. Do your best. The length is dependent *only* on the free-space wavelength, which for Wi-Fi is 2.45 GHz. The diameter of the can doesn't matter, and you can use the same probe in any size can suitable for a waveguide at 2.45 GHz. What you want to measure is from the *inside of the can* to the tip of the wire. Tin can metal varies slightly in thickness, but it hovers around .01" (one one-hundredth of an inch) and you can use that for a working value.

At 2.45 GHz the probe length is 1.22". Since it's easier measuring the probe outside the can than in it, add .01" for the sake of the tin can's thickness, and measure 1.23" from the inside surface of the mounting flange to a point on the wire. Mark and snip it with diagonal pliers. File the snipped end so that it's slightly rounded. Your probe is done. See Figure 16.8.

All that remains is to fasten the probe into the can (as appropriate for the type of N connector that you're using) and the antenna is complete. If you're using a UG-58 connector, make sure you put the heads of the mounting screws inside the can, pointing out. Do *not* put the "long" ends of the screws, with nuts, on the inside!

If possible, avoid drilling additional holes into the can for mounting it. I used small pieces of thin aluminum sheet to create brackets, and drilled a hole to clear the body of the N connector. The bracket is held to the can by the same screws as the N connector. See Figure 16.9 for a close-up photo of the finished tin can antenna, including a mounting bracket I made for it by bending a strip of aluminum in a vise.

Figure 16.8
The Finished Probe.

Figure 16.9
The Finished Mark I Bandwidth Expander.

What you mount the can on is more or less up to you. I chose a gooseneck mount because I had one in my junkbox, but you can mount it on anything that will keep it from moving around once it's been aimed. You can paint it, inside and out (paint on the inside will not reduce its effectiveness) and make it a little less ugly. I left Mark III unpainted because I felt it looked better that way. See Figure 16.10 for a shot of how it looks on my coffee table.

How Long Should a Tin Can Antenna Be?

The types of cans I've mentioned here work very well as waveguide antennas, and longer cans work better than shorter cans. So the question often comes up: How much is too much? Are there limits to the length a waveguide antenna should be?

The diameter of a waveguide antenna is really its critical dimension. Given the same diameter, a tin can antenna may be of various lengths. In general terms, the longer a waveguide antenna is, the greater its gain—and the tighter its beam. There are limits, however, and as a rule of thumb, once you get past a ratio of 3:1 for length to diameter, you reach a point of diminishing returns. 2:1 is probably ideal for the sorts of things we do in the Wi-Fi world at 2.4 GHz.

I did some experimenting with an interesting type of tin can: One in which a bottle of "designer" rum was packaged. If you go to a liquor store and look at the "fancy" products, some will be shipped in a tall tin can. I received such a bottle as a gift some years ago (before the age of Wi-Fi, actually) and kept the can "just in case." The product was Malibu Caribbean White Rum with Coconut. (I do like piña coladas, though not getting caught in the rain.) The can is 11" long and 3 $^5/_8$" in

Figure 16.10
The Tin Can Bandwidth Expander, Mark III, in Use.

diameter. This is a nearly perfect diameter for a circular waveguide antenna—and better still, there are no signal-scattering corrugations along the length of the can. It's smooth metal all the way.

A long antenna means a tighter beam, and a tighter beam means that the antenna is tougher to aim and keep aimed. I installed a probe in the rum can and mounted it on a gooseneck base (see Figure 16.11). The gain was wonderful—but it was miserable to get it pointed correctly by twisting the gooseneck around. The beam was just too narrow to be useful in that application. If you're going to use a 3:1 waveguide antenna like this one, you have to mount it permanently, and give yourself some way to "fine-adjust" the direction in which it's pointed. It would be a very effective antenna for bridging two networks across a few blocks of distance.

If you obtain a rum can (or some other liquor can with the same dimensions) mount the probe exactly 2" from the closed end. To test it out, mount it on a camera tripod so you can steer it smoothly, and test your signal strength from the far reaches of your AP's range. Its "reach" will astonish you—and its touchiness in aiming will make you nuts!

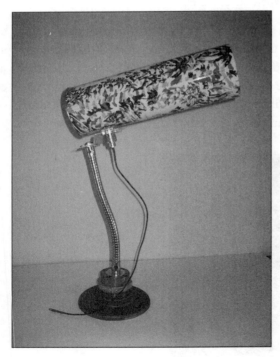

Figure 16.11
A Rum Can Bandwidth Expander.

Project #2: Building a Tetra Brik Bandwidth Expander

Not all waveguides are round in cross section. Rectangular waveguides are very common too, and if there were a metallic container with the right cross-sectional dimensions and proportions, you could build an antenna from it. Such a container exists, and it's called a "Tetra Brik" sanitary liquid container. They're used to hold soup, chai tea, rice milk, and other things like that.

A Tetra Brik is a European-designed layered rectangular package. It has cardboard on the outside, aluminum foil in the middle, and a thin plastic sheet on the inside to keep the soup from attacking the foil. They now come in several sizes, but the ones you're looking for are 65 mm by 95 mm in cross section. (That's 2 $\frac{1}{2}$" × 3 $\frac{3}{4}$".) I've seen them in several lengths, with 165 mm (6 $\frac{1}{2}$") the most common. A 200 mm (8") long Brik is also available, and will net you a little more gain if you can find one. The cross-sectional dimensions are about right for a rectangular waveguide, and the material can be easily cut with a sharp knife.

After seeing people on the Web create waveguide antennas from Tetra Briks, I tried it myself, using a Tetra Brik that had contained Swanson's chicken broth. Mine came together in about twenty minutes without any drilling—using only a Swiss Army knife and a soldering iron. The antenna is small, light, and not easily damaged (see Figure 16.12). It's not quite as effective as a tin can antenna, especially for long distances, but it definitely works in finessing weak spots and dead spots.

Calculating a Tetra Brik Antenna

The calculations you need to make to build a Tetra Brik antenna are similar but not identical to those required for a tin can (circular) waveguide antenna. As with a circular waveguide antenna, you need to calculate the free space wavelength, which I explain in this chapter. The free space wavelength depends only on the channel on which the antenna operates, and it will be the same for both circular and rectangular waveguides. I recommend calculating it for Channel 6, which is the middle of the Wi-Fi band. For channel 6, the free space wavelength will be 12.31 centimeters.

The second calculation is specific to rectangular waveguides, and it's quite easy to do. You need the cutoff wavelength, which is twice the length of the long dimension of the rectangle's cross-section. For the common Swanson's soup box I show here,

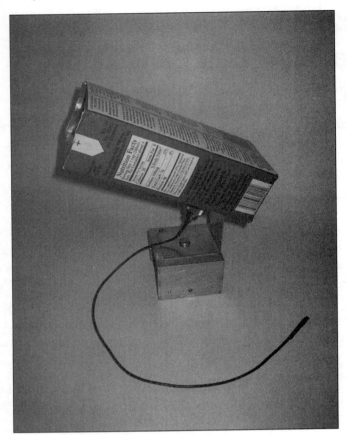

Figure 16.12
A Tetra-Brik Waveguide Antenna.

the rectangular cross section is 65 × 95 millimeters, so the cutoff wavelength is 2 X 95 mm or 190 mm, which is 19 cm.

The third calculation is the Brik's guide wavelength value, and it depends on the first two calculations. The mathematical formula is this:

$$\lambda_g = \frac{1}{\sqrt{\left(\frac{1}{\lambda_o}\right)^2 - \left(\frac{1}{\lambda_c}\right)^2} -}$$

Here, λ_g is the guide wavelength, λ_o is the free-space wavelength, and λ_c is the cutoff wavelength.

If you want to use a computer program to do the calculation, it can be expressed in Pascal this way:

```
GuideWavelenth =
  1 / SQRT(SQR(1/FreeSpaceWavelength) - SQR(1/CutoffWavelength));
```

 Express all values in meters, not centimeters or millimeters. In other words, express 12.31 cm as .1231 meters. If you express everything in meters, the final result will be in meters, and you won't have to fool with decimal points.

Once you calculate the guide wavelength for the Brik you've chosen, divide it by four, and you'll have the probe offset from the closed end of the Brik.

Here are some tips as you build a Brik :

- As with circular waveguide antennas, one end is open, the other end is closed.

- You can use the same probe as with the tin can antennas described earlier in this chapter. The probe's length depends solely on the frequency, not the shape or dimensions of the waveguide.

- Mount the probe centered on one of the 95 mm faces, not on a 65 mm face! (If you have the same Brik I show here, the probe offset is 40 mm from the closed end.)

- This is the real trick: Make sure that there is electrical contact between the probe N-connector's body and the foil lining of the Tetra Brik. The plastic film covers the foil and will normally insulate the probe assembly from the foil. However, if you place "spiny" lock washers under the screw heads holding the probe assembly to the Brik and tighten the screws very tightly, the lock washers' spines will pierce the inner plastic film covering the foil lining, allowing the screws to make contact with the foil. Without that contact, the antenna will not work correctly!

As Figure 16.12 shows, you don't necessarily need a gooseneck base. Once I worked out the correct angle for aiming the antenna from my problematic coffee table, I just bent a scrap of aluminum to that angle and made it the base. (The scrap heat sink at the bottom is just ballast to keep it upright.)

I was actually unaware of Tetra Brik containers before seeing the following Web sites. Note that some of these sites are not in English—open a browser window to Babelfish! (http://babel.altavista.com/)

http://users.skynet.be/chricat/horn/horn-javascript.html (A feed horn calculator.)

http://reseaucitoyen.be/?BoiteDeLait (French)

http://reseaucitoyen.be/?BoiteDeLait2 (French; shows a feed horn on a Brik.)

For further research, calculate and attach a foil-lined horn to the opening of the Tetra Brik, and see how much that improves its performance.

Bad Ideas and Further Research

I've tried a number of things in terms of cheap waveguide antennas. Nothing beats the tin can antenna so far—in fact, even improving on the tin can antenna has been difficult. Theoretically, putting a "horn" on the front of the can will improve its operation. I found a 4" to 6" stove pipe reducer at Home Depot that fit snugly over the outside of a coffee can. It wasn't of quite the right dimensions to be a horn, but it was certainly cheap and easy. See Figure 16.13.

Unfortunately, the horn didn't improve things much, and I don't consider it worthwhile. Attaching a correctly dimensioned horn would doubtless work better,

Figure 16.13
An experimental feed horn on a coffee-can antenna: **not recommended.**

but would take some significant metalwork. If you're good with a tinsnips and pop riveter, and don't mind pushing some numbers, it would be worth a try. Here's a document that will explain how to calculate a proper horn for waveguide antennas:

www.qsl.net/n1bwt/chap2.pdf

PrimeStar TV Dish Antennas

Several people have used tin can antennas as feed points for surplus PrimeStar satellite TV parabolic dish antennas. Such a rig could net you tremendous gain over a "naked" tin can, but even without trying it myself I see some challenges:

- The PrimeStar dishes are *offset antennas*, meaning that microwave signals strike the dish from an angle and exit at an angle. The can antenna feeder thus does not cast a microwave shadow on the disk (which is good) but this makes aiming the antenna, which has a very narrow beam width, difficult and touchy.

- The PrimeStar dishes are "solid" antennas rather than grid or mesh. In other words, they are made of unperforated metal. This gives them a slightly higher gain, but also makes them wind scoops, and heavy. Mounting one will be tricky and must be done in such a way that the wind will not knock it out of its (touchy) alignment.

If you have such an antenna lying around (or know where you can find one) this might be worth some research. The following Web site will get you started:

www.wwc.edu/~frohro/Airport/Primestar/Primestar.html

Other Odd Notions

When I was a kid in the 1950s and early 1960s, I had a aluminum saucer sled. (Remember the wild ride Chevy Chase took on such a sled in *National Lampoon's Christmas Vacation*?) The sled was circular and roughly parabolic in cross section. I've been searching for such a sled for a couple of years and haven't found one yet, but if you find one, I suspect it would make a very nice parabolic dish gain antenna. If you find one, build a short tin can antenna and attach it with aluminum strips so that it's pointed at the concave face of the sled, at the sled's focus point.

Finding that focus point will be tricky. Here's a hint: If the sled is shiny metal, take it out into the bright sunshine and try to focus the sun on a fencepost or some other object, and measure the distance between the bottom of the sled and the bright spot on the post when the spot is at its smallest.

Even if the sled is made of plastic, if it's close enough to a parabola you should be able to cover it with aluminum foil and make it work just as well.

Another thing to look for at garage sales and flea markets would be a large wok. Woks are made of metal but you may need to coat the parabolic surface with foil to reflect enough sunlight to find the focal point, as described above. Once you have the focal point, you can remove the foil, since even if the wok has a Teflon coating, the cooking surface will certainly be metallic and thus will reflect microwaves.

Another source of extremely high gain antennas is the increasingly common cast-off screen-surface satellite dish. These days, satellite technology has improved to the point where a satellite dish (like the PrimeStar dishes mentioned above) are only about three feet in diameter, but ten or twelve years ago, satellite antennas could be six or eight feet in diameter. These are awkward to use and neighbors consider them ugly, but you can often get them for free simply by asking around to see who has one under the weeds in the corner of the backyard.

The easiest way to use such a dish is to literally mount a USB or an Ethernet client adapter at the dish focal point. This isn't the most efficient way to "feed" such an antenna, but the enormous gain of such antennas (which can be as much as 30 dB!) means you can waste a little signal in the cause of expediency. I spoke with a couple of guys who had used a pair of retired satellite dish antennas to bridge a *23-mile* distance with nothing more than a pair of Linksys WUSB11 USB Wireless-B adapters mounted at the dish foci. As you might imagine, pointing a 6-foot parabolic dish is more art than science, but if you have the opportunity, definitely give it a try.

As always, I'm interested in hearing from people who have put Wi-Fi antennas together from unconventional materials.

Bridging Two Networks

I n the previous chapter I showed you how to build two projects to expand your bandwidth. In this chapter we'll take the next step and I'll show you how to build a powerful bridge to span two networks. As you'll learn in this chapter, a bridge is a way to link together two separate access points that are some distance apart. The bridge will essentially create a wireless link between two physically separate networks.

As a project, bridging two networks is fairly ambitious—and describing a bridging system is not as simple as describing how to drill holes in a coffee can. No two wireless bridges are alike. You're going to have to do a fair amount of designing yourself, and you may have to run cables up to high places. You will certainly have to understand, in detail, every part of the wireless bridging system. You can't just blindly copy something off a set of plans.

Before you even think about setting up a Wi-Fi bridge link, be very sure that your knowledge of ordinary Ethernet and TCP/IP networking is as complete as possible. This is a relatively advanced topic. If you're clueless about MAC addresses, subnets, IP addresses, and DHCP servers (to name only a few), you will be lost. Definitely read Chapters 2 and 3 if you haven't already, but in truth, the more you know about networking, the easier it will go.

Understanding Bridges

Wi-Fi access points are pretty versatile, and getting moreso all the time. They were originally designed to be wireless hubs (see Chapter 2 for more about hubs), and the vast majority of home office and small office wireless installations still use them as hubs: Central points to which computers are linked wirelessly as part of connecting them into a small network. Such a setup, with a single access point associated with one or more wireless clients in infrastructure mode, is called a *basic service set*. Probably 95% of all Wi-Fi access points in user hands are operating in infrastructure mode as part of a basic service set.

Some newer access points can also act as Ethernet client adapters (see Chapter 7) which are external Wi-Fi clients linked to a networkable device like a printer or game console via Ethernet cable. Some can also act as *repeaters* to extend the range of a wireless link inside the home, though this service falls outside of the Wi-Fi standard and sometimes requires that all participating access points be of the same manufacturer, or sometimes even of the same model.

Some wireless access points have yet a few more tricks up their sleeves—though those tricks are sometimes *way* up their sleeves and difficult to shake loose. Key among these is the ability of some access points to link two physically separated wired networks via a point-to-point connection, often between buildings, sometimes between locations several miles apart. This ability is called *bridging* or *bridge mode*. Schematically, it looks like the setup in Figure 17.1. The details can vary; what I show here is the simplest take on the idea, and the one that I will describe in detail at the end of this chapter.

With proper setup, good antennas, correct adjustment, and a few prayers to the Wi-Fi gods, this should enable the two networks to pass data seamlessly at up to the maximum throughput that the access points allow. How fast data moves depends (as always) on the technology, the equipment make and model, signal strength, and

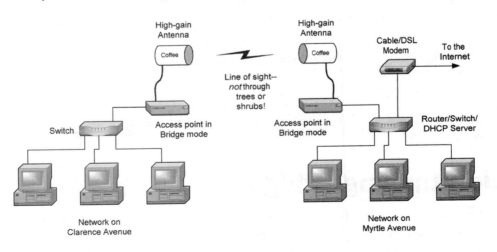

Figure 17.1
A Wi-Fi Bridge Linking Two Networks.

signal quality. The better your signal, the faster those bits will go. For Wireless-B, maximum throughput is about 5 Mbps. Using the AirPlus access points from D-Link, as I'll describe later, can give you throughput as high as 6.5 Mbps, courtesy of Texas Instruments' 802.11b+ chipset. Using Wireless-G, you can get throughput in the 20-22 Mbps range, and with the SuperG enhancement to Wireless-G, you might make it almost to 50 Mbps.

Whatever the throughput of the APs you use in a bridging setup, keep in mind that data will move between the two legs of the bridged network only as fast as the link between the bridging APs. If the two legs of the network are large and have a lot of users, the bridge could prove to be a choke point. Twenty PCs all accessing the Internet through a single Wireless-B link will not be pretty. If you possibly can, use Wireless-G for bridging setups. Wireless-A is not a good candidate, because low-cost Wireless-A APs have non-removable antennas, and the special-purpose Wireless-A bridging units are not cheap.

Bridge Size Matters

When considering a bridge, the first question you need to answer is simple: Can you cross the distance you need to bridge with equipment that you can afford? Several parameters affect the viability of a Wi-Fi network bridge, but the overwhelmingly largest one is distance. I spent the last portion of Chapter 8 discussing the notion of a *link budget*, which is how you determine when your network bridge is too large of a bridge. You should go back and read that section before you work through the project in this chapter to build your own bridge.

Briefly summarizing: You begin with a stated amount of radio power from your bridging access point. You calculate the loss inherent in the path you want to bridge, and add to that any losses in coaxial cables and connectors on each side of the bridge. You must balance that loss to some extent with gain in antennas on both sides of the bridge. It cooks down to this kind of an equation:

Input power (dBm) + total losses (dB) + total gain (dB) = received signal (dBm)

You end up with a received signal figure in dBm, which is the power delivered by the remote antenna to the receiver of the access point on the far side of the bridge. If this received power figure is greater than the sensitivity of the access point's receiver, your bridge will work. If it's less, your bridge will not connect. If it's barely sufficient, your bridge may connect, but the bit rate across the bridge will be low and you will lose packets to noise, fringe ("Fresnel zone") obstructions, reflections, interference, and "unknown causes." Ideally, your received signal figure needs to be 20 dBm above the receiver's sensitivity figure to connect reliably at the top rate that the bridging access points support.

Just to scare you a little bit going in, the path loss across a one-mile path is *104* dB.

This isn't a slam-dunk, whatever else you may have heard.

What You're Up Against

Assuming first of all that the path you've chosen to bridge can in fact be bridged with equipment that you can afford, setting up a wireless link bridging two networks presents you with two separate sets of challenges, one purely physical, the other technological. Some points to ponder:

- Not all access points can be made to operate in bridge mode. Most high-end products do; for example, those from Cisco like the Aironet 340 and 350. On the low end it's spotty, but the Linksys WAP11 and WAP54G, and the D-Link DWL-900AP+ are among the less expensive APs that will bridge. My experiments with wireless gateways like the formidable Linksys BEFW11S4 indicate that they will *not* work in bridge mode.

- In order to bridge, many (perhaps most) older access points will require firmware upgrades. Bridge mode was not a priority when older APs were manufactured. It's not, in fact, a priority now, but most new firmware does support it to a greater or lesser extent.

- Not all Wi-Fi manufacturers implement the details of bridge mode in precisely the same way. Much bitter experience has shown that you have your best chance of making bridging work with access points of the *same* manufacturer, model, and firmware release level. In other words, don't try to put a Cisco on one end and a Linksys on the other. Some wizard somewhere might be able to make this work, but it's a stretch. Get yourself two identical APs, upgrade both their firmware to the same (ideally the current) release level, and use those. Newer AP models are better than older. All Wireless-G access points that I've tried support bridging, and the additional throughput can be *very* handy if the bridged networks have a lot of users.

- Note that when operating in bridge mode, an AP will *not* talk to wireless clients! Bridge mode is a full-time job for an AP. If you want to attach wireless clients to your network on either side of the link, you will need separate APs (on different channels) to do the work.

- How bridge mode is configured varies wildly with AP manufacturer and model. Generally, it's a tab or subscreen on the AP's configuration window, but there are no step-by-step instructions that apply to any arbitrary AP. I can't provide detailed instructions here for all different products, but later in this chapter I will go through configuring a pair of D-Link DWL-900AP+ access points to bridge two LANs. Check with the manufacturer of your access points, cruise the Web... and more important, *be prepared to experiment.* (This used to be called "tearing your hair.")

In general terms, to set up bridge mode you must do the following:

- If the two access points acting as bridge endpoints are called A and B, access point A must be given the Ethernet MAC address of access point B, and access point B must be given the Ethernet MAC address of access point A. In other words, each end of the link must know the Ethernet MAC address of the other end.

- The SSIDs of the two access points must be set to the same value. From the standpoint of the wireless link, the two networks become one network, under a single SSID.

- Both APs must be set to operate on the same channel.

- The "operation mode" parameter must be set to "point-to-point" or "wireless bridge" mode. It's not always the same name; check your AP's documentation or Web site.

The configuration details will vary by manufacturer and model, as will the jargon, the names of the configuration options, and almost everything else.

The physical challenges are significant, if much lower tech. You rarely set up a bridge entirely indoors, though it can be done if you have two networks in two widely separated parts of a (large) home or office space. Working outdoors, and at a distance, and way up in the air somewhere will complicate things. Consider:

- **You can't do it alone.** Have at least one person at each end of the link, and provide some way to communicate, be it cell phones or FRS (Family Radio Service) 2-way radios.

- **You need a very clean line of sight (LOS) path between the two antennas.** Especially avoid trees and shrubs. They contain water and are about as transparent to microwaves as sheet iron. Furthermore, your line of sight can't be "just barely" there. Obstructions near but not across your line of sight will cause losses. The area immediately around your line of sight is called the "Fresnel zone," and you need to keep trees, hills, and buildings out of the Fresnel zone if at all possible.

- **The longer the path, the more gain your antennas will need.** Realistically, you won't get more than a block or two with tin can antennas of the sort I describe in Chapter 16, and to go over a mile you'll need a professionally manufactured yagi array or parabolic dish. To be sure, calculate the path loss and analyze the link budget over the distance your signal must cover, as I describe in Chapter 8.

- **Your access points will need to be up in the air with your antennas, enclosed in weatherproof boxes of some kind.** You can't just pipe your signal up a pole in a long run of coaxial cable. At microwave frequencies, the losses inside a run of coax are crippling.

- **That being understood, you will need to run both Ethernet cabling and power for the access points up to where the antennas and access points are.** Most category 5 Ethernet cable is not rated for use out in the weather, and will need to be inside pipe or conduit. It's possible to use Power over Ethernet (PoE) injectors and taps to run power through unused conductors in your Ethernet cable, but not all access points make it easy. You can do it yourself with some care, but you need to be mindful of voltage drops through the cable. Both D-Link and Linksys now sell PoE adapters compatible with their own Wi-Fi gear, and you should use those if you can.

- **Gain antennas tend to have narrow beam widths.** Aligning the two antennas can be infuriatingly touchy. Make sure you can clamp them down so that they do not wobble or otherwise move, even in a reasonably strong wind, or your link won't stay linked through your first storm.

- **Speaking of storms… make sure your pole and cabling are properly grounded for lightning protection.**

I have seen excellent waterproof gasket boxes at Fry's Electronics. Cheaper still are military surplus ammo cans. Don't use Tupperware food containers! UV makes them brittle, and they will crack and leak after as little as a few weeks out in the sun. Been there. Tried that. (In Arizona!) Antenna poles and clamps can be had at Radio Shack. Go for rigidity, and remember that making the system happen probably requires considerable personal presence (including the use of both hands) right there where the antenna is. Trying to balance on a ladder while aiming a gain antenna is a *really* bad idea. Use a roofer's safety harness and rope if you're working somewhere where a bad fall is even a remote possibility.

The rooftop wireless connection that I had in Arizona used an extremely rigid micro-tower from Rohm, weighted down by concrete blocks and not nailed or screwed or bolted to the roof at all. (Having a flat roof is handy for that sort of thing.) This particular installation was point-to-point fixed wireless rather than Wi-Fi, but the frequencies are roughly the same, and the antenna retained its alignment for more than three years through half a dozen really gnarly windstorms (see Figure 17.2).

Designing a Bridging System

Cooking down my own experience and that of several people I know to a general logistical approach, here is the way to setup your bridge:

- If you've never done a bridge before, or are using unproven Wi-Fi equipment, it's smart to create a "lab lashup" somewhere indoors to prove the configuration out first. Set up two minimal LANs with routers, switches, and laptops or spare desktop machines, even if it's in the same room, and work the bugs out of bridging at the AP level before you go to great effort on the final physical setup, power over Ethernet, etc. It's entirely possible that the two APs you've chosen aren't compatible for some reason, and it's better to find out before you spend hours wedging an AP into a weathertight box and running Ethernet cable up to the roof.

- Once you have the access point configuration nailed, set your antennas up on photo tripods and do a ground-level "dry run" across a parking lot or other unobstructed open space before hoisting the hardware onto the rooftops (see Figure 17.3). Align the antennas, make the software work, and *take good notes*.

Figure 17.2
A Short Tower for Rooftop Antenna Mounts.

- On the ground or on the roof, mount and align the antennas *first*. It's hard enough to make two APs talk in bridge mode without troubleshooting a gain shortfall or intermittent alignment at the same time.

- Once you have the software configuration figured out and are passing packets over the air during your dry run, get the APs into their weathertight boxes and do another ground-level dry run over the same path to make sure everything still works after you button it all up. You want your time up on the roof (or, if worst comes to worst, up on a ladder) as short as possible. A pinched wire or not-quite-connected pigtail can make you crazy, and might force you to bring everything back down to the ground for detailed physical troubleshooting.

- Get your hardware mounted up in the air, and do what you did during your dry run. The hard part here is pointing the antennas down one another's throats, but once you get that done, you should be able to place the APs in bridge mode and be finished.

There is a separate bridging mode called point-to-multipoint, in which one AP can bridge to multiple APs (say, from several different buildings to a central point) but no one I know has ever implemented this, and thus I can provide no useful advice. If you've pulled it off, I'd appreciate a note letting me know how it's gone for you!

Switches, Routers, and DHCP

The wireless bridge will link two physically separated Ethernet networks. However, if the two networks are intended to support the TCP/IP protocols (as they must if you intend to use the Internet and most modern networking software) they really must be configured as a single routable network, under the control of one router, with one DHCP server applying private IP addresses to all connected devices (including the access points) and one Network Address Translation (NAT) server handling intermediation between the private IP addresses used and the routable outside world of the Internet.

I once untangled a bridging scheme for a person I know who couldn't make it work, and it didn't work because he had two routers, one on each end of the link, and both routers were running DHCP servers and handing out private IP addresses in the same range. (If you don't understand IP addressing, routing, and DHCP servers, bail out here and read Chapters 2 and 3 now.)

Both legs of the bridged network must be separately switched or hubbed, but one router can and should handle Internet routing for both. A non-wireless router/ switch combo box like the popular Linksys BEFSR41 can act as a simple switch,

Figure 17.3
An Outdoor Lashup for Bridge Testing.

but you have to disable its DHCP server. To minimize hassle, I recommend using a dedicated switch without router features, like the Linksys EZXS55W. These are tiny, very inexpensive, and require no configuration at all.

All devices requiring IP addresses should be configured to request their IPs from a local DHCP server. This includes both computers and access points, and any other odd network hardware (like dedicated print servers) accessible via TCP/IP. Nearly all modern access points respond out of the box to a specific, preset non-routable IP address (usually in the 192.168.X.X range) but most can be reconfigured to replace the preset address with one from a DHCP server. If you use identical access points and leave both as they are shipped, responding to the *same* preset IP address, you *will* have problems!

One final reminder on IP addresses: You may have problems if the preset configuration screen addresses of your router and your APs are not on the same subnet. This can be a problem when you mix devices from different manufacturers. The preset configuration IP address for the Linksys BEFSR41 router is 192.168.1.1, and the preset configuration IP address for the D-Link DWL-900AP+ is 192.168.0.50. If like most people these days your subnet mask is 255.255.255.0, these are *not* on the same subnet!

I've changed the configuration address of my Linksys BEFSR41 wired router to 192.168.0.1. This is on the same subnet with the D-Link APs and allowed me to log in to the D-Links and change them from a preset configuration address to a dynamic address requested from the Linksys router's DHCP server.

Project #3:
Building a Bridging System

If you've digested all that thoroughly, I'll now run through a bridging configuration that I've used very successfully. It's shown schematically back in Figure 17.1. The two AP's I use are the D-Link DWL-900AP+. I like the 900AP+ (from the D-Link AirPlus product line) as a bridge for the following reasons:

- It's cheap. I've seen them for sale online for as little as $55 each new, and they have gone for as little as $25 used on eBay. With Wireless-G now commonplace, the 802.11b+ technology has little reason for being, and I suspect that D-Link will drop prices even further as time goes on.

- It's physically small and very light.

- It has only one antenna jack, so there's no uncertainty about how to configure the antenna logic for use with a single gain antenna. (You cannot use diversity reception in a wireless bridging setup. If you bridge with dual-antenna APs, you must disable diversity reception and choose the "live" antenna jack for your gain antenna.)

- It can be configured to request an IP address from a DHCP server. By default, the DWL-900AP+ responds to a specific non-routable IP address (currently 192.168.0.50) but it's better to leave all IP assignment to a single DHCP server.

- D-Link sells a relatively inexpensive and compatible pair of power over Ethernet blocks: Injector and tap together should cost no more than $40.

- My pair of DWL-900AP+ units went into bridge mode and bridged without a struggle, once I had everything else set up correctly.

What You'll Need

To duplicate my configuration, here's what you'll need:

- Two D-Link DWL-900AP+ access points. Make sure both are at the same firmware release level. You can check on D-Link's Web site to see that it's the current level.

- One Linksys EZXS55W or some equivalent dedicated switch for the "far" leg of the network. ("Far" here meaning the leg without the Internet connection.)

- One Linksys BEFSR41 router/switch for the "near" leg of the network; that is, the leg with the Internet connection.

- Two gain antennas capable of bridging the required distance.

If the link will be outdoors, you will also need enclosures and supports for both APs, power over Ethernet (PoE) adapters on both ends, plus all associated cabling. A laptop incorporating a Wi-Fi client adapter with an antenna jack is also extremely useful for aiming the antennas.

Setting Up the Bridge

Start by making sure that the "near" leg of the network works completely, before you even connect the DWL-900AP+. This install assumes dynamic IP addressing through DHCP, so be sure your nearside router has its DHCP server enabled and that all nearside machines are getting their IPs and talking to one another and to the Internet. If there is a Wi-Fi access point attached to the nearside network, take note of what channel it's running on, so you can put the DWL-900AP+ APs on a non-conflicting channel.

As I mentioned earlier, I think it makes a lot of sense to perform the initial AP configuration in a lab setup, preferably indoors. Configurations are saved in non-volatile Flash memory, so when you actually hoist the equipment into its final position, all you will have to do is aim the antennas. The bridging APs will be in the proper mode with all their various parameters intact as soon as you power them up.

Configuring the Nearside Network

With the nearside network functioning correctly, follow these steps to configure the nearside network for bridging:

1. Hook up the nearside DWL-900AP+ to a switch port on the nearside router/ switch and apply power.

2. Bring up a browser from one of the computers on the nearside network and enter the non-routable IP URL to access the AP's internal configuration HTTP server. (For the DWL-900AP+ this is currently **http://192.168.0.50**.) If you have trouble with this step, check to see that the router is on the same subnet. I changed my Linksys wired router's base IP address to 192.168.0.1 to eliminate this problem.

3. Log into the D-Link AP's configuration page and go to the Home tab. Click on the Wireless button. Set the SSID and the channel. It's also handy to give the AP a name, so that when you look it up in the router's DHCP client list later on there's no mistaking which client is the nearside bridging AP. (Without giving the AP a name, all you'll see is its MAC address, which looks pretty much like everybody else's MAC address...) Leave WEP disabled for now. Click Apply. The AP will reboot itself, and you'll return to the Home|Wireless page.

4. Click on the Home|LAN button. Select the Dynamic IP Address radio button. This will force the DWL-900AP+ to request an IP from the DHCP server. Once you click Apply, the AP will no longer respond to **http://192.168.0.50**. A time or two when I did this, the AP got confused and its HTTP server hung. If that happens, power the AP down for ten seconds and power it back up.

5. Close the browser. Bring up a new browser window and go to your router's configuration page. Find the DHCP clients table listing. For the Linksys BEFSR41, this is reached by clicking the DHCP Clients Table button on the DHCP tab. The DHCP clients table should list all devices that pulled an IP address from the router's DHCP server. Find the entry for the D-Link AP (this is why I earlier suggested giving it a name) and write down the IP address listed for the D-Link AP. This IP address, embedded in an HTTP URL, will be the new address of the AP's configuration page.

6. Using the D-Link AP's new IP address, log back in to the AP configuration page. Click on the Status tab and write down the AP's Ethernet MAC address. Note that there are two MAC addresses listed: One for Ethernet, and one for wireless. The Ethernet MAC is what you need when you configure the access point on other end of the link.

Configuring the Farside Network

Just as you did with the nearside network, make sure that the farside network is completely functional, and then follow these steps:

1. Hook up the farside DWL-900AP+ to the farside switch and apply power.

2. Bring up a browser window and enter the access point's preset configuration page URL, which currently is **http://192.168.0.50**. Log in. From the Home tab click the Wireless button.

3. Enter a name for the access point, something different from the name of the nearside AP. This is optional, and is done simply to make it easier to tell the two APs apart in the nearside router's DHCP table. Enter the *same* SSID you entered for the nearside AP, and the same channel. If there are already one or more Wi-Fi access points on the farside network, make sure the channel is not one already in use by one of those access points. Leave WEP disabled for now. Click Apply.

4. Click on the Status tab. Write down the Ethernet MAC address for the farside AP. This will have to be entered into the nearside AP's configuration screen to complete the bridge link.

5. Click on the Advanced tab. Click the radio button for Wireless Bridge. In the Remote Bridge MAC field, enter the Ethernet MAC address of the nearside AP. Click Apply.

6. Click on the Home tab, and from the Home tab click the LAN button. Click the Dynamic IP Address radio button, and then click Apply. After this step, the farside AP will no longer respond to the preset configuration page address of **http://192.168.0.50**.

Completing the Bridge Link

At this point, almost everything is configured. What remains is to enter the farside AP's Ethernet MAC address into the nearside AP. Return to the nearside network and follow these steps:

1. Log into the nearside AP's configuration page using the dynamic IP address it pulled from the DHCP server. This address can always be found by inspecting the DHCP clients table in the router.

2. Click on the Advanced tab. Click the radio button for Wireless Bridge, and enter the farside AP's Ethernet MAC address into the Remote Bridge MAC field. Click Apply.

3. Power everything down on both legs of the network and power it up again. If you did everything correctly, the AP and computers on the farside network will use the wireless link to request IP addresses from the nearside router's DHCP server. Your link works!

Troubleshooting the Network Setup

Network configuration is closer to an art than a science, and troubleshooting is easier in a lab setting than up on a roof or a ladder. That's why I powerfully recommend setting up two simple networks in a lab to get the APs configured so that they bridge, long before you install anything in its final position up in the air.

Your first evidence that the bridge is functional will be the presence of the farside AP and the farside computers on the router's DHCP clients table. If *any* farside device is present on the nearside DHCP clients table, your bridge is working! If some devices are not present, check to make sure they're configured to request a dynamic IP via DHCP.

Note that it's possible to assign a local, non-routable IP address to an Ethernet device manually, without pulling it from a DHCP server, and some people prefer to work that way. If you're not using DHCP, try using the ping utility to get a response from one of the devices across the bridge.

If you can't ping any device across the bridge, log into the AP configuration pages and double-check these points, which I've arranged in the order that they're likely to be a problem:

1. The SSID must be the same on both APs.

2. The channel must be the same on both APs.

3. Bridge Mode must be selected on both APs.

4. Each AP must have the Ethernet MAC address of the other AP entered into its Remote Bridge MAC field. Double-check that you entered the MAC addresses correctly. Double-check that you entered the Ethernet, and *not* the wireless, MAC addresses.

5. Check that WEP is not enabled by mistake, either on one side or on both sides with different keys. WEP should ultimately be used, but enabling it is the last thing you should do before calling the bridge complete. Until everything is known to be working correctly, leave WEP disabled.

6. The bridging channel must not be one in use by any other nearby Wi-Fi device. Audit the area near both legs of the network with NetStumbler (See Chapter 19) to see if any other APs are operating on your bridging channel and possibly interfering. If either leg has additional access points, it's best to turn them off while troubleshooting your bridge.

7. Make sure you don't have two (or more) DHCP servers operating. Lots of Ethernet devices now contain DHCP servers, including the DWL-900AP+ access point itself. You should have one router—and one DHCP server—for the linked network. Make sure that any other DHCP servers connected to the network are disabled.

8. If you're using manually entered IP addresses, check for subnet conflicts between the two legs of the network. If you're using DHCP, subnet conflicts should not be an issue, since you're letting the router decide what addresses and subnets everything should use.

9. Check the firmware release levels of both APs to see if they're identical and up to date.

10. Finally, look for "dumb stuff" like detached antennas, yanked power cables, wall warts not plugged in, not-quite-inserted CAT 5 plugs, crossover cables accidentally used where a straight-through cable should be, and so on.

If all your troubleshooting fails, it may be time to call on expert help.

Aiming Your Antennas

Once you've gotten your two APs to bridge in a lab setting, the hard work is done. The only other really tricky thing is aligning your gain antennas across the space your bridge is to cross.

The best way to do this is to temporarily connect an access point *in access point mode* to one antenna, connect a laptop client adapter to the other antenna, and then use NetStumbler's field strength display to sense when the antennas are aimed optimally. You're looking for the best signal figure (the green portion of the line) and lowest noise figure (the red portion). The access point and client adapter used should have similar power output and receiver sensitivity to the APs used in the bridge link.

Some notes on aiming antennas:

• Have somebody on both ends, communicating via cellphone or FRS radio.

• Remember that gain antennas operate in three dimensions, and must be aligned up-and-down as well as side-to-side. Once you get over 10 dB of gain in an antenna, the beam width will likely be just as narrow vertically as horizontally.

• Be realistic about the distances involved. If NetStumbler can't "hear" an AP across the gap you've chosen to bridge, your bridge APs are unlikely to hear one another either. Crossing distances measured in miles is quite a feat, and you're likely to need sizeable parabolic dish antennas to pull it off. *Calculate your link budget first!* (See Chapter 8.)

- Be careful if you're installing antennas in high places. Use a roofer's safety harness if you're more than eight or ten feet from the ground. It's easy to get distracted and forget that you're up on the roof or on a ladder. If you have a laptop with you, it's smart to rig a safety cord of some sort to keep it from making a one-way trip down to the pavement.

- Watch out for power lines. Power lines represent a serious hazard both to you on your ladder and to your AP/antenna setup. Ideally, you should be no closer than 50 feet to a power run.

Enclosures for Bridge APs

I've used two types of enclosures for bridging APs: Commercial plastic gasket boxes and military ammunition cans. Both are watertight and relatively inexpensive. I favor ammo cans because it's often hard to tell how well a plastic box will stand up to sun, wind, rain, and extremes in temperature. Ammo cans are steel and will stand up to almost anything, though they have the downside of being harder to drill. They have spring-loaded lids with rubber gaskets, and when the lid is snapped closed the box is not only watertight but airtight (see Figure 17.4).

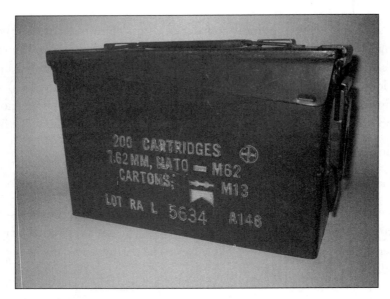

Figure 17.4
A Surplus 30 Caliber Ammo Can.

Military surplus stores often have ammo cans, as do mail order surplus vendors. (See Appendix A for sources.) The cans come in various sizes, and you can't always count on finding any given type in any given store. Look around. The one I've used successfully is the 30 caliber can, which measures 10 $\frac{1}{2}$" × 4" × 7". (This is the type of can shown in Figure 17.4.) The can must be large enough to contain the access point, the power-over-Ethernet tap or other power supply, connecting wires, and some structure to keep everything in place. The 30 caliber size is the smallest ammo can I'm aware of, and it's more than large enough to hold the DWL-900AP+ access point, the power over Ethernet tap, and the various associated cables. The Linksys access points are physically larger, and fitting them into a 30 caliber can with everything else will take considerable care and cleverness.

The cans are quite cheap; I've seen the 30 caliber size go for as little as $4 each, and usually between $5 and $8. Shipping and handling will be more than that!

Here are some tips if you decide to go the ammo can route for an AP enclosure:

- A 30 caliber ammo can will hold a Linksys WAP-11 or WAP54G access point, but it will be tight, and getting the AP, the PoE tap, and the wiring to coexist will be a challenge. If you have a long distance to span and some budget to spend, a Cisco Aironet 350 access point is a good choice for a 30 caliber can, as it's quite compact and puts out 100 mw to boot. Keep in mind that there are larger ammo cans as well, and the 50 caliber size will fit most any access point without a struggle.

- If you're not familiar with ammo cans, take note that the can and the lid come apart nondestructively: Just swing them so that they're 90° to one another and slide the lid to one side. It's *much* easier to drill and work with the lid without the can flopping off of it.

- Make as few holes in the can assembly as possible, and make holes only in the lid. Mount the can on the pole or other support lid-down, using a bracket or $\frac{1}{2}$" pipe floor flange attached to the lid rather than bolt holes through the can itself. This way, all holes will be on the underside of the enclosure, and water will be unlikely to enter the can via gravity.

- Use a double-ended bulkhead female N connector to bring your antenna feed into the can (see Figure 17.5). Your gain antenna cable plugs into the outside end of the connector, and the pigtail to the access point connects to the inside end. Note the rubber O-ring in the photo. The O-ring should be on the outside of the ammo can, and the hex hut on the inside. The O-ring is squeezed between the metal shoulder and the can, and provides a nice weather-tight seal.

Figure 17.5
A Female Bulkhead N Connector.

An Enclosure Example

Figure 17.6 is a photo of a workable 30 caliber ammo can installation for a D-Link DWL-900AP+. There was plenty of room in the can for everything. The can is mounted upside down atop a length of $^1/_2$" water pipe. A $^1/_2$" galvanized pipe floor flange is bolted to the lid of the can with four $^1/_4$"-20 flat-head bolts. A $^5/_8$" hole is drilled through the lid beneath the center of the floor flange. The CAT 5 Ethernet cable, carrying power for the access point, is run up the water pipe and through the $^5/_8$" hole into the can.

A female bulkhead N connector passes through the lid of the can. On the inside of the enclosure, a 19" pigtail connects the access point antenna connector to the N bulkhead connector. Outside the can, the parabolic grid antenna is bolted to the pipe mast close enough to the enclosure that the antenna's built-in pigtail reaches the bulkhead N connector directly, making more connectors and coax (with their

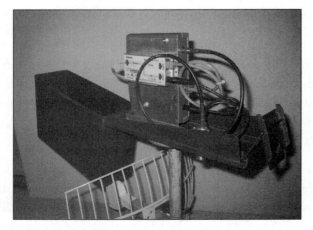

Figure 17.6
The Duntemann Ammo-Can Enclosure, Mark I, with Cover Removed.

attendant losses) unnecessary. Ordinarily I'd like to leave a little more room between the enclosure and the antenna, but in our tests the signal doesn't appear to suffer.

In my ammo can unit I mounted the D-Link AP to a piece of scrap aluminum sheet metal to keep it from rattling around inside the can. There are bolt slots in the base of the DWL-900AP+ that made this easy. Drilling into the AP's case was unnecessary. The sheet metal to which the AP is mounted is in turn bolted to a piece of scrap aluminum angle stock that attaches to the ammo can lid under the hex nuts holding the lid to the pipe floor flange.

The D-Link PoE tap has no holes with which to mount it, so I bent a clip out of scrap sheet metal to hold the tap, and bolted the tap bracket to the vertical sheet metal piece with small machine screws. A closer-in view of the assembly from above is shown in Figure 17.7.

Figure 17.8 shows the assembly up on the roof during final testing, with the can closed and everything running. I had some concerns as to the ability of a setup like this to survive an Arizona summer. D-Link indicates that the DWL-900AP+ is rated for operation from 32° F to 131° F (0°-55° C) but I moved to Colorado before things got hot, and so I'm not sure how well it might have fared. Temperature inside the can is certainly an issue, and if possible, I recommend locating a bridging module like this under an overhang or somewhere else where it will be in shade most of the time. Painting it white would certainly help. An associate asked how an enclosure might be

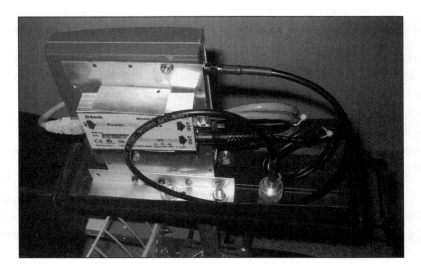

Figure 17.7
Ammo Can Enclosure Interior Closeup.

Figure 17.8
The Enclosed Access Point in Place for Testing.

constructed to allow a bridging AP to survive a Maine winter. As D-Link only rates the DWL-900AP+ down to 32°, I'm far from sure it would survive a Maine *summer*.

Don't forget to weatherproof your enclosure before committing it to the outdoors. (The photos in this chapter show the unit during testing, before final weatherproofing.) A liberal coating of exterior silicone caulk on the face of the floor flange before bolting the flange to the lid of the ammo can is essential, as is tape-wrapping or shrink-wrapping the N connector on the underside the assembly. Do whatever you must to keep water out of the N connector between the enclosure and the antenna; water and microwave transmission do not mix!

An enclosure like this doesn't necessarily have to be used for bridging. If you have to serve a sizeable open area, it can help to put an AP up in the air on a pole, working into an omnidirectional or sector antenna instead of the highly directional antenna used for bridging.

Building a Parabolic Mesh Reflector

In Chapter 16, I described a range booster for Wi-Fi client adapters, made from a tin can and a gooseneck lamp base. It proved extremely useful for getting my laptop connected from the far corners of my rambling Arizona ranch house, and even from inside our detached garage and way out back where my big telescope lives.

My Tin Can Bandwidth Expander got me connected to my access point at full speed, but it was really a fix for a problem with my access point: The shape of its microwave field was nothing even close to the shape of my house. Ideally, I'd like the access point to fill my house with its radio field, but not go outside the walls. This is a vain hope, since radio waves don't respect wood very much, and brick only a little more.

A practical solution for a problem like this is to incorporate a parabolic mesh reflector. As you'll learn in this chapter, this type of reflector can help you improve your Wi-Fi reception in a home or office space that might be a little more complex than a simple house or office. The best part is that you can build a reflector using inexpensive materials from your local hardware store.

Solving Problems with Parabolic Reflectors

When I lived in Arizona I had an access point with an omnidirectional antenna sitting in my upstairs office at one end of my long and crooked house. The full-speed region of the access point's field was going most of the way to my living room couch, but it also extended quite a ways through my walls out into the driveway, where it was of no use (except perhaps to a drive-by hacker). Worse, the kitchen lay between my access point and my living room coffee table, and it cast a "microwave shadow" due to the presence of large metallic things like the refrigerator, microwave oven, and cupboard full of canned goods and utensils. A rough sketch of the shape of the access point's field is shown in Figure 18.1. I've compressed the size of the house and simplified its shape, but the gist is there: The kitchen cast a shadow, leaving a "dent" in the top-bitrate boundaries of the field right where the living room couch was.

Thus the *shape* of the microwave field within our house was almost optimally bad for connecting from the living room. My Tin Can Bandwidth Expander was a "spot fix" for a misshapen microwave field. The real solution would be to reshape the field so that it fit the shape of our house a little better.

I played with a number of things, and the good news is that most of them worked. I put a gain antenna high up on the wall above my access point—and that worked. (The little rubber antennas that come with access points are optimized for low cost, not high effectiveness.) I could connect from the living room without the help of the Tin Can Bandwidth Expander. Unfortunately, it also extended the field another forty feet out past my driveway and as much as I like my neighbors I'm not necessarily into sharing my bandwidth with them nor inviting them to peruse my home network.

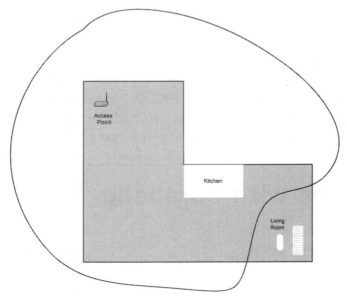

Figure 18.1
The Effect of a Microwave Shadow.

I put a flat piece of sheet metal 18" × 24" behind the access point. This worked too, in that it changed the shape of the field and significantly reduced the extent to which the field excursed behind the access point, out into the driveway. It also changed the shape of the field inside the house, but mostly by moving the dead spots around. Signal strength in the living room came up some, but not radically.

What worked best for me came out of an idea I saw on the Web. A gentleman named Michael Erskine had done some work with parabolic reflectors made of $^1/_4$" mesh hardware cloth, the same stuff you buy at Home Depot by the roll and use to keep the bunnies away from your roses out in the garden. Michael's Web site contains photos of how he used a mesh reflector with a Linksys USB Client Adapter to shape its field and extend its range, and built the whole thing into a tidy and unobtrusive plastic cylinder:

http://osiris.urbanna.net/antenna_designs/projects/template/index.html

Michael's *geistesblitz* provided me with a whole new approach, and eventually yielded a gadget that made the Tin Can Bandwidth Expander obsolete—at least from the living room. (I still found it useful for connecting from out in the garage or in back by my telescope.)

Designing Focused Reflectors

The basic idea is to shape a piece of hardware cloth into a parabolic reflector, and put the antenna of your access point at or close to that focus. The parabola doesn't have to be a parabola of *rotation*—in other words, a parabolic dish—like those used for receiving satellite TV, especially in the old days. (Remember when neighborhood wars were fought over people who wanted to mount 7-foot satellite parabolic dish antennas in their backyards?) It can be nothing more than a flat piece of metal shaped to parabolic form in the horizontal dimension only. The focus of such a parabola is a vertical line, not a point, but if you park a Wi-Fi omnidirectional antenna at that focus line, the reflector will focus incoming microwaves onto that antenna, and focus the microwaves coming off the antenna into a beam.

In case you can't yet see in your mind what I'm talking about, the finished reflector is shown in Figure 18.2, along with a D-Link DWL-900AP+ access point. In the photo, the antenna of the access point is positioned so that it falls precisely at the reflector's linear focus. Microwave energy leaves the access point's omnidirectional rubber antenna in all directions. The energy radiated back toward the reflector bounces back and forward, along with the energy radiated in a forward direction. The parabolic shape of the reflector confines most of the energy coming off the antenna into

Figure 18.2
A Parabolic Mesh Reflector.

a relatively narrow beam. Position the reflector carefully, and you can aim that beam in any direction you choose. I aimed it toward the corner of my living room, down along the long axis of my house, and the field strength there came up radically (see Figure 18.3).

The reflector had reshaped the AP's field to something longer and narrower than its original shape. I discovered that I had created a new dead spot at one corner of the house, but that wasn't a potential work location.

Project #4:
Building a Parabolic Reflector

The easiest material for making a parabolic reflector is galvanized soft iron hardware cloth with a $1/4$" mesh, which can be had in rolls for a couple of dollars at any hardware store or home improvement center. You cut an 8" × 8" or 6" × 6" square with tinsnips, optionally cover the edges with duct tape to cover the sharp points, and then shape it into a parabola.

You can make a reflector like this from any soft metal that keeps its shape when bent. A galvanized iron sheet like that used in heating ducts works well, but it's not as easy to find in small quantities, not as easy to cut with tinsnips (especially *dull*

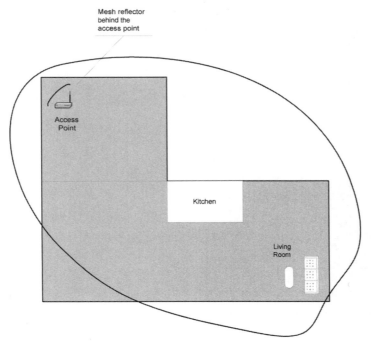

Figure 18.3
Aiming the Beam Into the House.

tinsnips) and its cut edges are *razor* sharp. I also found when I bent a piece of galvanized iron sheet into a parabola, that over a few days' time it tended to flatten out and lose its shape. Hardware cloth is softer iron and keeps its shape better. Also, hardware cloth comes in a roll, and when you cut a piece it will already be curved to within striking distance of the parabolic shape that you want.

On the next page is Figure 18.4, a full-size template for the parabola. The squares are $1/4$" in size. Slap the page down on a copy machine and copy the page onto a sheet of paper. Cut your hardware cloth, tape the edges if you choose, and then shape the hardware cloth until its bottom edge follows the curve on the paper. That's literally all there is to it!

The focus of a parabola of this curvature is just a hair over $1\,1/2$" forward from the center of the curve. For shaping the field of an access point the accuracy of the curve isn't a serious issue, though it should be within $1/8$" or so for best results. Do the best you can, and getting close is almost as good as being bang-on.

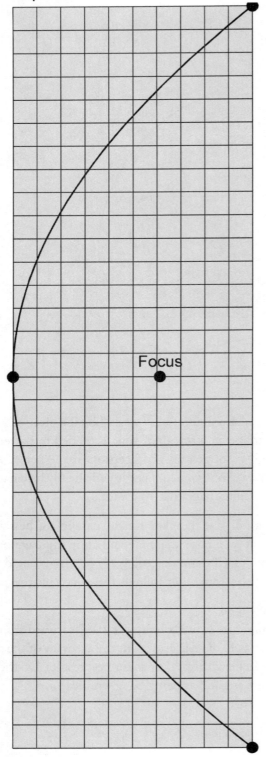

Focus

Figure 18.4
The Parabolic Curve Template.

It's Frequency Independent!

The nicest thing about parabolic mesh reflectors is that they are *not* frequency dependent, unlike the tin can waveguide antennas I described in Chapter 16. You can use a parabolic reflector with any of the Wi-Fi technologies: Wireless-B, Wireless-G, and even Wireless-A. This means that a parabolic reflector can be used with a dual-mode or all-mode access point.

Most people don't realize that the flexible antennas on a Wireless-A access point (or any access point that supports Wireless-A, such as dual or all-mode) cannot be removed. The FCC regulations governing Wi-Fi make that stipulation, and that means that you don't have the option of attaching a gain antenna to any access point that includes Wireless-A support. If Wireless-A is in your Wi-Fi plan, a mesh reflector could be the only tool available to you for extending the reach of your AP.

How Parabolic Reflectors Work

It's useful to have an intuitive grasp of how parabolic reflectors work, especially once you have to adjust one. The geometry of a parabolic reflector brings parallel rays to a single point focus. It works the other way, too: Rays emitted from a single point that strike a parabolic reflector will be reflected in parallel in a single direction (see Figure 18.5).

Most of the times you'll use a parabolic reflector in Wi-Fi work will involve very high gain antennas that need to cross distances measured in miles rather than yards. For that kind of work, you want to create as tight a beam as possible. Placing the microwave source at the focus of the parabolic reflector will create a tight beam, with most of the microwave energy traveling in a single direction.

By moving the microwave source either toward the reflector or away from the reflector, you can make the beam broaden out (as in the center diagram) or converge on itself and then broaden out (as in the bottom diagram). The center and bottom diagrams are mostly equivalent in their effects, in that they create a much broader field sent in generally one direction.

It takes relatively little movement toward or away from the reflector to create a tremendous difference in the shape of the microwave field. Keep that in mind later on, when we discuss adjusting the mesh reflector—which actually involves adjusting the position of an access point's antenna relative to the reflector.

Mounting the Reflector

The mesh reflector concept is simple, and actually making one will probably take you half an hour at worst. The difficulties you'll have will lie in keeping the reflector

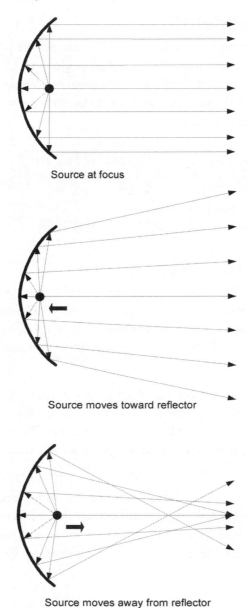

Source at focus

Source moves toward reflector

Source moves away from reflector

Figure 18.5
How Parabolic Reflectors Work.

from moving once you aim it. Aiming it is tricky, not so much in terms of steering the beam as in keeping the dead spots away from important places in your house. (More on aiming the reflector later.) Once you get it set correctly, you don't want a light breeze to knock it over.

I tried a number of different things, but what worked best was actually what I tried first: Attaching the reflector to a sheet of scrap acrylic plastic 8" × 11". That size isn't critical; it was just what came to hand in the scrap box. What you want is something big enough to comfortably hold both the reflector and the access point.

To size the base, put your reflector and curve template down on a piece of paper or cardboard and position your access point so that one of its antennas lies directly above the point marked "Focus" on the template. Then choose a circle or rectangle of plastic or wood (but not metal!) that comfortably embraces the reflector and the access point. The smaller an access point it, the less the body of the device will get in the way. This is yet another reason why I like the D-Link APs: They're quite small and most have only one antenna. The model I used in this project is the DWL-900AP+but almost all the D-Link APs are the same size (5.6" × 4.3" × 1.2") and thus you can swap in the DWL-700AP or the DWL-2100AP without making any other changes.

Dual antennas finesse fading, but fading was not much of a problem at my Arizona house, so giving up dual antennas (and thus diversity reception) was not a big loss. If you use a two-antenna AP, you will have to remove one antenna and then set the AP's configuration screen parameter that governs which antenna is used. You don't want your Wi-Fi signals going out to an empty antenna jack!

 An alternate approach is shown on Michael Erskine's Web site. He created two much smaller mesh reflectors, and cut out central blocks of hard foam plastic with holes drilled in them to support the reflectors. He then fit the reflectors onto the AP or gateway rubber antennas themselves. This may not give you the gain and reach that a single, larger reflector might, but it's a brilliant idea and Michael provides photos and detailed instructions on his site:
http://osiris.urbanna.net/antenna_designs/projects/template/index.html

Figure 18.6 shows a 6" × 6" reflector resting on a paper copy of the curve template. The dark surface is a piece of $\frac{1}{8}$" clear acrylic with its blue protective film still in place. I've omitted the access point so you can see how the curve of the reflector matches the curve on the template. As a general rule of thumb, the more of the printed parabola on the template that your reflector covers, the narrower and longer the field formed by the reflector will be. I made and tested an 8" × 8" reflector, but it did no better a job than the 6" × 6" reflector and made the entire assembly larger and more ungainly.

Once you have things arranged so that they will fit on the base you've chosen, tape the template securely to the base. Using a very small drill bit (1/32" or something

Figure 18.6
The Reflector on the Curve Template.

near to that) drill pairs of holes on either side of the parabolic curve on the template. The holes will allow you to secure the mesh reflector to the base by threading short lengths of copper wire up through the holes and then twisting the ends together by gripping them with a needle-nose pliers. See the photo in Figure 18.7.

I suggest drilling a small hole through the dot marking the focus on the template, just so you don't lose track of where the focus falls when you take the paper pattern away.

Figure 18.7
Tying Down the Mesh Reflector with Wire.

You also need to take into account the CAT 5 data cable and power cable that connect into the back of the access point. One mistake I made in my first mesh reflector assembly was not allowing quite enough room for the cables. I eventually cut a largish hole in the plastic sheet and put four short legs on the assembly so that the CAT 5 cable could be routed below the plastic sheet. The cables eventually became the gnarliest single problem with the whole gadget. The final form of this particular version is shown in Figure 18.8.

As I'll explain shortly, one aspect of adjusting the reflector means adjusting the position of the access point in front of the reflector, and if you're not careful, tension on the cables will disturb the position of the access point and destroy your adjustment. Once you know what position the access point will need to be in, you can use cable clamps or tie-wraps to fix the cables to the base so that they do not pull on the access point and change its adjustment.

Mounting the Access Point

Attaching the access point itself to the reflector base might be a problem. My D-Link and Cisco APs have bolt slots in their bases, to allow attaching them to walls. Many other APs do not have bolt slots, and in those cases you'll just have to get creative. You could try 3M Scotch Double-Sided Foam Mounting Tape but be aware

Figure 18.8
The Complete Reflector Assembly and Access Point.

that this stuff is sticky enough that someday you'll have to scrape it off. You could also use Fun-Tak, which might work very well as well and is much easier to scrape off a surface. Both of these should be easily found at a local office supply store.

To give yourself the most precise control over the shape of the field formed by the mesh reflector, you need to be able to move the AP's antenna along a short line that runs from immediately behind the parabola's focus to immediately in front of the focus. (Look back to Figure 18.5 to see why.) Moving the antenna from side to side changes the direction of the field more than its shape, and you can do that by moving the assembly as a whole.

I found a pair of round-head brass 6-32 machine screws that fit snugly into the DWL-900AP+ bolt slots. See Figure 18.9 to get an idea of how the screws fit into the bolt slots. Round-head screws are best; the flatter head "binder" screws will rattle around and come loose very easily. I then cut a pair of slots in the Plexiglas base allowing the AP to slide forward or back but not side to side. This is best done by drawing short lines with a permanent marker and then drilling a series of holes side by side, finally smoothing out the holes into slots with a small file. Make sure the slots run perpendicular to the mesh reflector and not at an angle. The idea is to be able to move the AP's antenna along a line running from behind the focus point to in front of it.

Figure 18.9
Machine Screws in the AP Bolt Slots.

After positioning the AP on the Plexiglas, put washers and hex nuts on the machine screws but leave yourself some slack to allow the AP to slide forward and back during adjustment. The initial position should put the antenna as close as possible to the reflector's focal point.

Adjusting the Mesh Reflector

Adjusting the Tin Can Bandwidth Expander is easy, because it's designed to work on the client side. You aim it while watching your signal strength change on a client application display like that of Netstumbler. With a mesh reflector behind your access point, you're still forced to monitor signal strength at the client end of a connection, but you're adjusting something that may be at the other end of your home or office. Having some help is useful—especially if you're within earshot. ("A little bit to the left!") If earshot fails (or if hollering across the length of your home or office is a non-starter) a pair of cell phones or Family Radio Service (FRS) walkie-talkies is extremely useful.

In adjusting the mesh reflector, it's better to think of what you're doing as changing the shape of the field rather than creating some kind of beam. A 6" square of hardware cloth isn't big enough to create a very tight beam, and that's not necessarily what you want anyway. In my case, I wanted to change the shape of the access point's field from something roughly circular to something roughly elliptical, with the ellipse's long axis running down the diagonal dimension of my house.

I say "roughly" with some emphasis. Radiation patterns from antennas are not simple circles or ellipses, but more significantly, the environment within which the antenna operates changes the shape of the pattern radically. The structure and materials of your home or office have a powerful effect on where the field will reach, and how well. For example, my Arizona kitchen and cupboard cast a microwave shadow on my living room. The original field pattern was roughly circular, with a huge "dent" on one side of the circle. (Look back to Figure 18.1.) This dent was the reduction in field strength caused by the presence of the kitchen between my access point and my living room. The whole point in creating the mesh reflector was to fill in that dent as much as possible and improve my ability to connect to my access point from my living room coffee table.

There are actually two aspects to adjustment:

1.   **Adjusting the access point on the reflector's base.** This is a relatively limited adjustment. You want to be able to slide the access point so that its vertical antenna moves on a straight line, perpendicular to the reflector, from a little

behind to a little in front of the precise focal point. The full distance you want to allow for is $\frac{1}{2}$" at most, and in practice it won't be much more than an eighth of an inch either way. Moving the access point from side to side with respect to the reflector gives you very little that moving the entire reflector assembly from side to side does not. This adjustment changes the *shape* of the microwave field, largely in terms of length and width.

2. **Adjusting the entire assembly.** This simply means moving the whole device around on the shelf or desk. This primarily changes the *direction* in which the field is pointed.

I played around with different ways to limit the movement of the AP on the reflector base, but the best one was machine screws in the bolt slots of the DWL-900AP+, moving within $\frac{1}{2}$" slots drilled in the Plexiglas base. This adjustment, unfortunately, is highly dependent on the shape of your access point and what sort of mounting it uses. Without bolt slots it's very difficult to adjust the AP with respect to the focal point. If your AP does not have bolt slots, I recommend somehow fixing it in place at the reflector's focus and performing all your adjustments by moving the assembly as a whole.

Here's how you go about the adjustment.

1. **Sketch out your house or office and print a few copies to draw on.** I use Visio 2000, which has some very nice templates for architectural drawing. (All the technical figures in this book were drawn with Visio 2000.) Visio is a great product and I highly recommend it. If you're on a bit more of a budget you can also try Smart Draw, which is a shareware product that's a bit less costly than Visio. Smart Draw is found at www.smartdraw.com.

2. **Find out where your field reaches, and where your dead spots are, without using the reflector.** This is a standard technique for installing Wi-Fi access points under any circumstances: Walk around with your Wi-Fi equipped laptop or PDA, watching a field strength indicator like the one in Netstumbler (see Chapter 19). Mark weak spots and dead spots on your architectural sketch. If you're really ambitious, choose a particular field strength value and mark a point on your plan anywhere the reading shows that value. If you mark enough of these points, you can draw what amounts to field isoclines on your sketch, and literally show yourself the shape of your field. It won't be a simple shape, and there may be holes like Swiss cheese in the middle of it.

3. **Decide where the field must reach, and where it doesn't have to reach.** Sure, it would be nice to be able to take your laptop anywhere in your home or office and connect at top speed. But unless you have a fairly small home or office, you will have weak spots, and in any substantial space with a lot of internal structure you will have dead spots. Unless you're prepared to install multiple access points with cables connecting them, some triage may be necessary.

4. **Put the reflector in place, and see what you've got.** Aim the reflector assembly in the direction where you need the longest reach for the access point's field. Repeat step 2, checking each location where you need coverage.

5. **Tweak and try for optimal coverage.** This is the hard part. If you find locations with weak signal off to the sides of the field, move the access point closer to the reflector to broaden the field. *Keep the antenna on the reflector axis,* otherwise the field will veer to one side or another. If the field is more than wide enough but not long enough, see if the access point antenna is at the focus. Only at the focus will the field be of maximum length. If the field appears to be pointed in the wrong direction, turn the entire assembly rather than attempt to move the access point with respect to the mesh reflector. Each time you change either the access point's position on the base or the entire assembly's position on its shelf or desk, you'll have to re-check the field to see if the AP's signal reaches where it must. Note that this can be a *very* touchy business. If you're impatient, well, it can drive you crazy!

6. **Try to keep the assembly from moving once it's adjusted.** This means keeping other objects away from it, and more than anything else keeping anything from yanking on the AP's CAT 5 and power cables. If you can somehow mark on the surface of the desk or shelf where the four feet of the assembly rest after adjustment is complete, you can get a head start on readjusting the device if you ever have to move it. Drawing light lines with a pencil around the four feet to mark their position works well, though be careful not to move the assembly in the process.

Final Thoughts

Although I initially created the mesh reflector shown in this chapter to work with an access point, it works well for client adapters too, when the client adapter is a moveable device not tucked inside the body of a computer. I tested the reflector with the LinkSys WUSB-11 USB client adapter, and it worked extremely well, and allowed my laptop to connect at full speed from the problematic corner of the living room.

You may find that over a period of weeks, the mesh reflector loses some of its parabolic shape and tries to return to a more circular curve like the one it had while it was part of a roll of hardware cloth sitting on the shelf at Home Depot. Tying it tightly to the curve on the base will help keep it from deforming too much, but you may have to touch up the curve on the top of the reflector every so often. Keep in mind that doing so may throw off your careful alignment of the device and force you to go through adjusting it again.

Some people think that hardware cloth is ugly, and in truth, the mesh reflector doesn't get high points for style. If you rest the whole thing on a shelf of some sort, you can put non-metallic items in front of it to hide it. On a deep enough shelf you could place a row of paperback books in front of it; books are virtually transparent to microwaves as long as there is no metal foil in their covers.

My wife suggested getting a decorative wicker basket at a craft shop and hiding both access point and a small reflector in the basket under or behind some dried or artificial floral arrangement. For best results (and I haven't tried this myself) make sure the artificial flowers don't contain wire or other metal.

As with any of the gadgets I describe in this book, I always enjoy hearing from people who have built and tried them. Let me know what worked for you and what didn't, and how well. Contact me at:

jduntemann@paraglyphpress.com.

Going Wardriving

Project Chapter

Remember the 1983 film *War Games?* It's about a teenager who creates a "dialer robot" program for his personal computer that dials phone numbers in sequence, listening for the telltale tone of a modem on the other end. He eventually gets into very serious trouble by accessing a nominally intelligent DOD computer with the power to unleash nuclear war. (Giving the computer an outside line was maybe not quite so intelligent.)

The movie *War Games* provided the inspiration for a new term, "wardialing," which was rapidly taken up as a pastime by every teenage goofball who could string BASIC statements together on his VIC-20. (I recall that as the start of the era in which I received five or six phone calls a day with no one on the other end of the line.) The term *wardriving* mutated out of wardialing, and the acronym WAR (Wireless Access Reconnaissance) was distilled after-the-fact from wardriving.

The project I'll present in this chapter will help you put a wardriving rig together and gather data on the state of wireless networking with the best of them. I've written a Web FAQ on wardriving which presents a terse summary of much of the material in this chapter:

www.duntemann.com/wifi/wardrivingfaq.htm

I update it reasonably regularly, so bookmark it and check it periodically.

Introducing Wardriving

Wardriving is a brand new hobby, albeit kind of a loopy one: Driving around town with your laptop and GPS receiver in the back seat, mapping wireless access points (APs) that come into range. It's neither difficult nor particularly expensive, assuming you already have a laptop or PDA capable of accepting a suitable Wi-Fi client adapter card.

It works like this: You run a "stumbler" program on your laptop or PDA. The vast majority of people use a program called NetStumbler (for your Windows laptop) or MiniStumbler (for PocketPC PDAs). Other stumbler software exists, especially for Linux and BSD Unix. You connect a GPS receiver to your computer, configure it to emit NMEA (National Marine Electronics Association) standard positioning data, and feed that data to the computer (see Figure 19.1). The stumbler program listens for Wireless-B and Wireless-G access points, and when it finds one, it notes the current latitude and longitude and logs the position with the SSID and signal strength of the access point being logged, plus a few other odds and ends contained in the access point's beacon broadcast. Note that it doesn't attempt to connect to the networks it logs, nor does it "sniff" the presence of an access point that has disabled its SSID beacon.

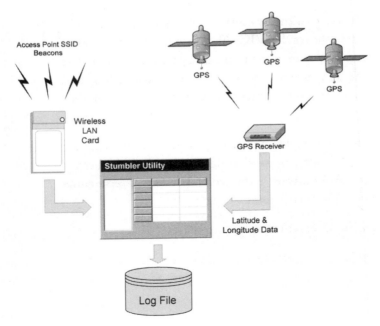

Figure 19.1
The Basic Wardriving Setup.

The log may be written to a file, and some stumbler utilities support the uploading of these log files to a central location, allowing the creation of a map of wireless access points, with each point contributing a spot on the map, defined by its GPS coordinates. This sounds a little scary to some people, but most stumbler utilities list only those bits of data that the access points make available in their broadcast beacon. How legal this is hasn't yet been settled (as I'll discuss in detail a little later) but few think that wardriving *itself* is illegal. What is certainly illegal is breaking into networks, and wardriving's role in *finding* networks puts it in a light gray area in some legal circles.

Taking the Pulse of Wireless Networking

It's certainly fair to ask, *Why wardrive?* Having been a wardriver since early 2002, I'll be the first to say that (like a lot of other hobbies that seem pointless on the surface of it, like stamp collecting) wardriving is simply fun. It has the flavor of a scavenger hunt about it: How many nodes can you collect in how few miles? What's the most wirelessly connected part of town? There's always an element of surprise: Sometimes the shabbiest looking industrial area will be discovered to be a hotbed of Wi-Fi activity. You just never know.

And that's the key fact leading to wardriving's real value: *It provides a way to gauge the growth of the wireless networking industry by direct inspection.* Research companies have for years attempted to hang numbers on the growth of PC sales, printer sales, digital camera sales, and items like that by gathering numbers from manufacturers, interviewing consumers, and doing a lot of extrapolating from far too few data points. How much you can trust such numbers usually depends on who's paying for the research and what you're prepared to believe. With Wi-Fi, you don't have to take anybody's word for it—you can go out there and see for yourself.

An example: When I lived in Arizona, I traveled to a meeting at our VP of Sales' house on a monthly basis. It was a longish trip, but I always took the same route, and I always took my wardriving rig. After each meeting I came home and compared my latest NetStumbler log file to the ones that came before. It was fascinating to see the number of stations increase monthly, sometimes by 15% or 20%. A few stations would disappear between meetings, but most of them remained, and the new ones, predictably, were newbie-clueless and didn't enable WEP.

It was fascinating to watch the month-by-month Wi-Fi growth at a Phoenix high school along the way, which added one or two access points every time I went by.

You can take the pulse of the Wi-Fi industry in your area by defining a "standard wardrive" for yourself, and taking the drive on a regular basis, weekly or monthly, keeping logs as you go. I'll show you how to do this later in this chapter.

Warmemes

I suppose it's only really "wardriving" if you're in a car. People carrying a PDA with a Wi-Fi adapter can *warwalk* around downtown sniffing for networks. (This is actually the preferred way to do it in superdense surroundings like London, Paris, New York, and Washington, DC.) People standing on the balcony of a highrise apartment can use a high-gain directive antenna (like the legendary Pringle's can antenna or—much better—a genuine tin can antenna like the one I describe in Chapter 16) to *warscan* nearby buildings for wireless access points. People in small planes have reported logging beacons while *warflying* at thousands of feet above a city. *Warbiking* is easy and fairly common. No one has yet reported *warswimming* or *warskating* to my knowledge…but it's probably only a matter of time.

And as for warmemes, let's discuss the reigning champ next.

Warchalking

As I explained in Chapter 10, there is no single directory that lists all public hotspots; in fact, there's no single directory that even comes close. So knowing where public hotspots are (and among public hotspots, the non-commercial community hotspots most of all) is a serious problem. Wardriving is certainly one way to locate hotspots, but as I'll explain later in conjunction with the NetStumbler utility, just detecting a hotspot tells you nothing about its private/public status.

Sometimes a high-tech problem has a decidedly low-tech solution. Londoner Matt Jones probably didn't expect to become a legend from an idea that he first published in mid-2002. He and some friends had been warwalking in downtown London, cataloging wireless networks, and thought it would be useful to be able to put a physical marking (say, on a wall or a sidewalk) to indicate to other wireless users that a public access point was nearby.

Matt's idea was to create a 21st century version of the Depression-era secret symbols used by hobos to communicate key facts about the marked locale to other hobos. Perhaps the best-known hobo symbol is a sketch of a smiling cat, indicating that a kind-hearted woman lived in the house bearing the symbol. Other symbols indicated vicious dogs, places where one could hear a sermon and get fed, doctors who would treat a patient without charging, places where the water was not drinkable, and so on.

Twenty-first century wireless hobos ("wibos" as another related warmeme puts it) don't need to know quite such a long list of things. A node is either there or it isn't, and a node that exists is either open or closed, or perhaps open to those who know the WEP password.

So there's really only three necessary symbols, as summarized by the "warchalking card" that Matt Jones published first on his own site, and later at— **www.warchalking.org**.

The card is shown in Figure 19.2.

Even after a couple of years, warchalking remains a downtown London thing, mostly, though news reports regularly give excitable accounts of "secret" warchalking symbols turning up all over the world. I myself have never seen a warchalking symbol anywhere in my travels within the United States. I was amazed, however, at how quickly and completely it became a *global* meme, reported everywhere on the Web and in print media, irrespective of its obvious drawbacks, like being arrested for defacing private or public property. (There are laws in most cities against graffiti.)

What I suspect the warchalkers are hoping is that the symbols will be adopted as a *de facto* standard by the growing number of wireless Internet providers, especially in the cores of large cities. So instead of forcing wibos to draw the symbols on the

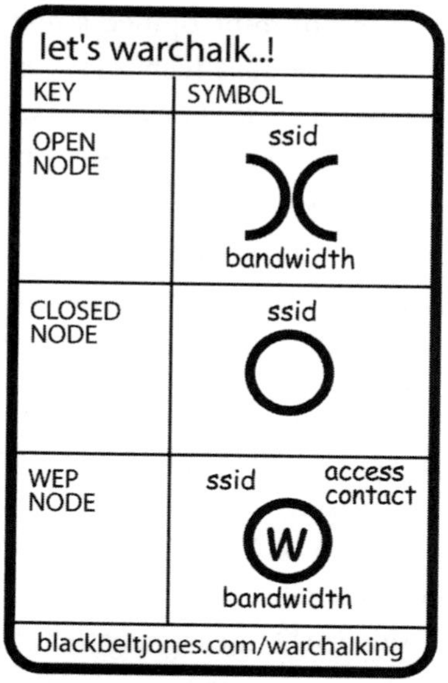

Figure 19.2
The Warchalking Quick Reference Card.

sidewalk with chalk (chalk? Do you know what a mess it is to carry around *chalk*?) wireless node providers would display a card with an appropriate symbol in their windows where prospective customers could see it. This would actually be extremely useful; for example, some of the Starbucks coffee shops in the larger cities now have a fee-based wireless Internet system, but the Starbucks shops in my city do not. Being able to tell at a glance would be useful to people anxious to log into the Net while on the road, as I frequently am. In early 2003, Schlotzky's Deli announced that they would actually have their managers warchalk outside those Schlotzky's restaurants implementing their new Deli Cool Cloud Network of free and open Wi-Fi hotspots. So Matt's vision may in fact become reality.

On the other hand, the usefulness of the "closed node" symbol is open to question.

I think what made warchalking a meme is its mythic allusion to hobo life, with the connotation of freedom and setting your own agenda. Wireless networking is definitely in its delicious early life, cherished by its enthusiasts and mostly unsuspected by the world at large, even by the uninformed who buy wireless access points and cards and use them without understanding what they're doing. Sooner or later, all that will pass away (think of the very clubby insider's Internet before the public was admitted in the early 1990s) and Wi-Fi will become… ordinary. Enjoy it (as I do!) while it's still mythic!

Legality and Ethics

The legality of wardriving is untested. A lawyer friend of mine opined a few years ago that the law will never catch up with technology because technology evolves much faster than law. Keep in mind here the crucial difference between "laws" and "law." Laws may be made by any legislative governmental body; but *law* is the cumulative body of precedent that comes from years (sometimes decades, or even centuries) of court cases, legal opinion, and numerous individual laws that interact in nonobvious ways. Laws may happen overnight, but law does not, and in that fact lies a great deal of peril for things that evolve as quickly as computer technology.

The mainstream press, when they've covered wardriving at all, typically declare it to be of a piece with cracking networks or even terrorism. (Anything that somebody doesn't like these days, alas, tends to be called "terrorism.") The truth depends entirely on how you wardrive. Consider what NetStumbler or MiniStumbler do: They poll for beacons, then listen for the SSID beacon of a wireless access point (AP) and report various items included in the beacon, like the SSID, the signal strength, and (if a GPS receiver is integrated with the system) the AP's longitude and latitude.

Is this hacking? No. Consider: *The AP is broadcasting its SSID in a continuous beacon.* In other words, it *wants* people to know that it exists—that's what "broadcast" means.

Furthermore, all APs offer their owners the option of turning off the beacon, so that the SSID is no longer broadcast. Once the SSID broadcast is turned off, NetStumbler and MiniStumbler have no way to know that the AP is there, and will not report its presence, even if its radio signals are received by the wireless card.

That's the NetStumbler family of utilities, of course, and there are others. The Kismet utility for Linux goes a great deal further, and will detect a wireless network whether or not its beacon is enabled. It can place compatible wireless cards (currently cards based on Intersil's Prism chipset) into RF monitoring mode, which means it will detect and attempt to interpret any Wireless-B radio signal received at the card's antenna. It can sniff packets (that is, capture them nondestructively) and record them, and can even attempt to reverse-engineer Wired Equivalent Privacy (WEP) passwords because of the well-known flaws in the WEP cryptographic algorithm. (I discuss these flaws in some detail in Chapter 13.)

This definitely sounds like network hacking, but whether it is or not depends on who you are and whose network you're listening to. Kismet was intended to be used by network administrators who are auditing or troubleshooting. If you're doing a security audit of your own network (or the network of someone who hires you to do it) it's your job. If it's not your network and nobody told you to do it, well, that's hacking. This is true for the other wired or wireless network auditing tools and password-recovery utilities like AirSnort and Ethereal as well.

Nearly all wardrivers use NetStumbler or MiniStumbler, and one of the reasons is that these programs don't have the machinery to do anything but detect an access point by its broadcast SSID and record its presence. Using tools like these is ethically much "cleaner" than using something with more intrusive powers. NetStumbler by itself cannot crack a network. Of course, once an AP has been found with NetStumbler, other tools can be used to break into it—if it needs "breaking into" at all. The vast majority of APs found by NetStumbler have *no security whatsoever*, and are "wide open." (This is no exaggeration. In my two years of wardriving, I've logged data proving that *at the very most* 30% to 35% of access points have WEP enabled!)

That being the case, my fellow wardrivers and I adhere to a relatively strict code of ethics that can be cooked down to the following:

• Don't look

• Don't touch

• Don't play through

In other words, 1) don't examine the contents of a network; 2) don't add, delete, or change anything on the network; and 3) don't even use the network's Internet connection for Web surfing, email, chat, FTP, or anything else. Somebody else paid for the bandwidth, and if you don't have permission to use it, you're stealing it.

Basically, unless you have permission, *don't connect*.

The seriousness with which this code of conduct is held becomes obvious every so often on the NetStumbler forums (more on which a little later) when an overenthusiastic newbie who isn't too clear on the concept gets on a forum and asks how to connect to stumbled APs—or, worse, brags about what he did after he connected. The subsequent ass-chewings are quick, thorough, and merciless. (Do it more than once and the NetStumbler moderators will ban you for good. They are *very* serious about where they stand regarding hacking into other people's networks!) I won't be so naïve as to state that wardrivers never connect to somebody else's AP, but it's pretty clear that that's not the primary intent, and the guys who do it don't talk about it when they do.

Some emerging trends make the picture even fuzzier. More and more coffee shops and restaurants in major metro areas are installing WLANs with broadband connections to the Internet, as are some hotels, bookstores, and other profit-making enterprises. Many of these connections are fee-based (like those at Starbucks), while some are free (like those at Schlotzy's Deli and Panera Bread) and not password protected at all. So…is it legal to lean out your window with a high-gain Yagi antenna aimed at the Schlotzky's three blocks down and read your email through their unprotected public wireless connection? Probably. Is it ethical? No. But what if you ate lunch down there earlier this afternoon, and stop by for coffee frequently on the way to the subway station? Yup, it gets fuzzier and fuzzier.

I read a news item about a competing coffee shop chain that deliberately tries to rent storefronts within two hundred feet of new Starbucks shops so that their customers can mooch the Starbucks wireless connection—clearly unethical and possibly legally actionable, but unless the competing shop promotes this as a "feature" (rather than simply relying on the inevitable word-of-mouth) the path to legal redress is still very muddy. The fact that customers pay for the Starbucks connection makes it fuzzier still. You're paying for their bandwidth—but do you have to be on their premises to use what you pay for? Yikes!

There's a final consideration on which the whole issue of wardriving's legality may ultimately depend. My lawyer friend (who is not a technologist) asked why so many Wi-Fi APs are "wide open." The reason, of course (as I've described in Part 3 concerning Wi-Fi security) is that APs *default* to wide open, and when unsophisticated home users take them out of the box and plug them in, that's how they come up, and without further configuration they stay wide open. "So," said my lawyer friend, "most of those people with wide-open networks don't even *know* that they're wide open."

True. And *that* may become a problem. If the user of a Wi-Fi AP has the "reasonable expectation" of privacy when he or she sets up a WLAN, a court could rule that detecting that WLAN is an actionable violation of privacy. It sounds dumb, but this is how it evolved for analog cell phone traffic, and the courts seem to be leaning in that same direction for all sorts of data communications issues. The court case may not come this year or the next, but eventually this question will be tested, and nobody knows how it will be resolved. My guess is that the manufacturers of the wireless APs will take the hits if any hits are to be taken, but all current and future wardrivers need to keep alert for developments on the legal front.

Project #5: Building a Wardriving System

Before I turn you loose on the road, here's a checklist of what you'll need to pull together your wardriving rig:

- **A laptop or PDA.** Wardriving is a facet of mobile computing, so you'll need a machine you can move around.

- **A "stumbler" utility compatible with your mobile computer.** There are several, but the very best is Marius Milner's Network Stumbler for Windows and PocketPC, which almost everyone calls NetStumbler. (The PocketPC version is called MiniStumbler.) Others include Kismet for Linux and dstumbler for BSD Unix. Not all stumbler utilities work with all operating systems, or all Wi-Fi client adapters. You'll have to read the fine print later in this chapter, and check with the stumbler utility Web sites for compatibility information.

- **A GPS receiver capable of NMEA-format output through a serial port (Optional).** Note that "serial port" is not the same as USB. NetStumbler has limited USB support, as I'll explain later.

- **An external antenna for your Wi-Fi client adapter (Optional).** The built-in antennas on PCMCIA card client adapters are uniformly hideous. Almost any external antenna will increase your access point capture by 50%.

That's the essentials. Once you have logged some access points ("nodes" or "stations" as people often call them) on a wardriving run, you can plot them on maps using various utilities like WiGLE and Stumbverter. I'll explain more about this in Chapter 20.

NetStumbler

It's officially called "Network Stumbler" but no one (except its author) ever really calls it that. NetStumbler (as we all say) is a completely free application for 32-bit Windows, running under XP, 9x, ME, and 2000. (It has not been tested on Windows NT.) It was written and is being actively maintained by Marius Milner, and it is a remarkably useful thing—even if you never go out wardriving. It has a full-screen high-resolution field strength display, which I use for testing and adjusting antennas, plotting access point field coverage, and so on.

The key issue in using NetStumbler is whether it will in fact work with your Wi-Fi client adapter. Not all client cards are supported, though Marius adds support for additional products on a regular basis. I can't quote a list here, as it would be obsolete almost immediately. You need to download the NetStumbler package and peruse the readme.html file that comes with it to see what cards are currently supported. NetStumbler was originally written to support the Hermes Wi-Fi chipset, and most (but not all) Hermes-based client cards will work. Support for the industry-leader Prism chipset is at this writing still a little thin—but there appears to be better support than Marius describes in the readme.html file. I was able to make NetStumbler recognize my Cisco Aironet 340 client adapter under Windows 2000 by downloading and installing the latest drivers from Cisco, even though Cisco clients are supposedly unsupported. Certainly you'll do best if you run Windows XP, which contains better support for Wi-Fi than any other version of Windows.

If you don't already have a Wi-Fi client adapter for your laptop, your safe choice would be one of Proxim's (originally Lucent's) Orinoco Classic PC cards. All of these work with NetStumbler, and I have used an Orinoco Gold Classic card with NetStumbler since I first discovered wardriving. The great advantage of the Orinoco cards is their external antenna connector, which most Wi-Fi PCMCIA client cards do not have. An external antenna is pretty important in wardriving; more on this later.

Using the NetStumbler Forums

If you're serious about taking up wardriving you should join the NetStumbler forums at **www.netstumbler.com** before you begin. Most of the current wardriving gurus hang out on the forums and answer questions, though neophytes should spend a few hours reading the FAQs and threads on the forum before asking simple and obvious questions. It's ever so easy to sound like a goof and you should do your best not to. There's a pretty good search feature on the forums site, and if you are considering a particular piece of Wi-Fi hardware or antenna, or GPS receiver, you can often find commentary and helpful tips on using the device by typing its name into the search field.

Like most sites of this type, you'll need to register (which is free) to access the forums. The custom is to operate under an assumed name, though not everyone does. Yes, the site isn't organized as well as it might be, but since it's all volunteer labor, complaining about this is gauche in the extreme. It's a fun site. Poke around. You almost can't avoid learning something.

Many of the most obvious questions about installing and using NetStumbler will be answered later in this chapter, so stay tuned.

Installing and Configuring NetStumbler

Download NetStumbler from the "Downloads" page of NetStumbler.com:

www.netstumbler.com/

The file is a self-extracting installer suite; just run the .EXE and follow instructions. The default values will get you going. About all you have to explicitly configure is the COM port on which NetStumbler can find your GPS receiver. (More on this later, when I discuss GPS receivers.)

In addition to the wealth of information on the official NetStumbler site (especially the forums) NetStumbler author Marius Milner has his own site, which is organized as a blog, on which he periodically posts some news pertinent to his ongoing NetStumbler development:

www.stumbler.net/

Using NetStumbler

The most important thing about running NetStumbler is preparing your mobile system to pay attention to access points other than your own. If you've used your laptop at home or at the office, you've almost certainly configured it (probably through setting up profiles) to associate with a particular SSID at home and at the office. I can't speak for all makes and models of Wi-Fi client adapters, but all the clients I've used with NetStumbler will ignore all SSIDs but the ones it is configured to associate with. There is good reason for this, as you'll discover when you wardrive in a dense office district and literally dozens of access points may be within range. You don't want your laptop to guess which AP to associate with—there lies only trouble. Hence your profile instructs your wireless card to look for and associate with only *your* APs. This makes wardriving impossible. Your AP will be the only AP found.

What you must do, then, is create a separate profile for stumbling. This profile must have only one defining characteristic: *It must leave the SSID field blank.* (This field is called "Network Name" on some profile editors, including that of the popular Orinoco PCMCIA cards.) You should also un-check the Enable Data Security option, so that WEP is not enabled. This may or may not be an issue, depending on the firmware in your particular client card, but it's a good idea in any event.

With a "stumbling" profile created, you simply select that profile and run NetStumbler before you roar out of your driveway.

When you click the Scan button in the toolbar, NetStumbler will begin scanning for APs. By default, NetStumbler will honk every time it senses and logs an access point. Other than that, it will sit quietly (ideally on your *back* seat, where you won't be tempted to be watching the display when you should be watching traffic!) and need no further attention from you. Running NetStumbler is no more difficult than that. The interesting stuff appears when you get back home and inspect your log to see what you've discovered.

NetStumbler's Main Display

NetStumbler is in effect a special-purpose database manager, with Wi-Fi machinery to discover, format, and add new records to the database. Although this isn't immediately obvious from the display, it adds a new record to the log every time the signal strength reading of an in-range access point changes. So if you're sitting at a light, or creeping past an office building full of access points in bad traffic, NetStumbler will be busily adding a record to the log every several seconds or so for each AP within range. This is one reason that NetStumbler's log files are as large as they are. On the other hand, if you're tooling down the road at 35 miles an hour, you may get only one record logged for the more distant and barely-reachable APs.

A screen shot of NetStumbler in action is shown in Figure 19.3 Let me run down the numerous display fields that NetStumbler shows on its main screen, from left to right. (Not all are shown in the screen shot—they won't fit on the screen all at once.)

1. At the left margin is a small circle. When an AP is within range, this circle will be colored: Green for good signal strength; yellow for so-so signal strength, and red for barely reachable. When an AP moves out of range, the circle goes to gray. If WEP is enabled, there will be a small padlock icon inside the circle.

2. The **MAC Address** field of the stumbled AP. This is the address that the AP is configured to send out with its beacon frame. By default it is the AP's "real" MAC address, but most APs allow an arbitrary address to be entered in its place. Keep this in mind if you attempt to do statistical analysis on AP manufacturers by

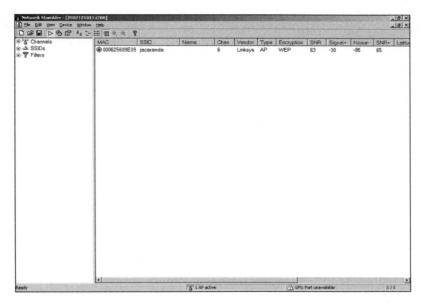

Figure 19.3
NetStumbler's Main Display.

inspecting the MAC address. (MAC addresses are issued in blocks which are manufacturer-specific, so theoretically you can determine the manufacturer of an AP by looking at the first several digits of its MAC address.)

3. The **SSID** field shows the SSID of the stumbled AP.

4. The **Name** field will almost always be blank. Some APs allow an administrator to give the AP a descriptive name, which acts as an alias for the AP's MAC address. If NetStumbler can determine the name of the stumbled AP, it will place that name in the Name field. (Note that the name is *not* related to the SSID!) Few people give their APs names, and for some reason, NetStumbler cannot always discern the name of a stumbled AP (which is the fault of the AP, not NetStumbler!) so you won't see text in this field very often.

5. The **Channel** field indicates what channel or channels the AP was operating on during the time it was within range of NetStumbler. This will virtually always be a single number, but if an AP's channel changes while it's in range, NetStumbler will add a new record to its log and display both channels. Some newer chipsets (most notably the Whitecap chipset) support a feature called "channel agility," which allows the AP to change channels if it encounters interference on its operating channel. It's hard to prove, but I suspect that any AP showing multiple channels in NetStumbler's display supports channel agility somehow.

6. The **Vendor** field shows the name of the AP's manufacturer, if NetStumbler can determine it. Note that this is *not* the same as the name of the chipset!

7. The **Type** field indicates what mode the AP is operating in. It will be "AP" for infrastructure mode, or "Peer" for stations operating in ad-hoc mode.

8. The **Encryption** field will show "WEP" if WEP is enabled. It will otherwise be blank. I suspect that a future release of NetStumbler will show "WPA" if an AP is logged with WPA enabled. The current release of NetStumbler (0.3.30) predates WPA.

9. The **SNR** field will show the *current* signal-to-noise ratio, but only while the stumbled station is within range. If you only inspect the log after you're back home, this field will be blank for all stations. The SNR changes almost constantly as you move into and out of an AP's range, and this field is intended to be a "snapshot" of how an AP is coming in *now*. For the best reading obtained while in range, see the SNR+ field.

10. The **Signal+** field indicates the *best* signal strength reading obtained by NetStumbler while the AP was in range.

11. The **Noise-** field shows the "best" (lowest) noise reading obtained by NetStumbler while the AP was in range. It's "Noise-" because less noise is better, so the lowest reading received is what is reported in this field.

12. The **SNR+** field shows the best signal-to-noise (SNR) reading obtained while the AP was in range.

13. The **Latitude** field shows the latitude reported by the GPS receiver (if you have one attached to your mobile machine) when the AP came into range.

14. The **Longitude** field shows the longitude reported by the GPS receiver (if present) when the AP came into range.

15. The **First Seen** field is the local time that the AP first came into range of NetStumbler.

16. The **Last Seen** field is the local time that the AP last went out of range of NetStumbler. Note that an AP can "come and go" while you drive past it, as buildings or other obstructions interfere with the signal path. The Last Seen time is the last time that NetStumbler lost track of the AP during the time that particular log was open.

17. The **Signal** field shows the *current* signal strength reading. As with the SNR field further back on the list, this field will be blank except when the AP is within range. The best reading reported in this field while the AP is in range is reported in the Signal+ field.

18. The **Noise** field shows the current noise reading. As with the Noise- field further back on the list, this field will be blank except when the AP is within Netstumbler's range. The best (that is, the lowest) noise reading taken while the AP is within range is reported in the Noise- field.

19. The **Flags** field reports several technical parameters gleaned from the AP beacon. These definitely represent "advanced topic" wardriving, and I'll explain them in detail in the next chapter on NetStumbler's log files.

20. The **Beacon Interval** field reports the beacon interval, in milliseconds, of the stumbled AP. This is the frequency at which the AP broadcasts its beacon frame. The default value is almost always 100 ms (milliseconds) but it can be changed, and you will occasionally see other (usually shorter) values.

Yes, the fields could be in a more intuitive order. Don't "read in" significance to the order of the display fields. There is none. I would prefer that all the signal strength readings be grouped together, but that's just the way the software works.

Something to keep in mind as you examine your NetStumbler logs at the end of a long day of wardriving: The GPS coordinates listed for access points are not the coordinates of the access point—they are your coordinates, where you were located when NetStumbler first picked up the access point. This should be obvious on reflection, but it's an easy enough thing to forget. Furthermore, the precision of GPS these days (now that the GPS signals are now longer dithered to reduce their precision) is sufficient that a distance of as little as 100 feet will be significant most of the time. You'll see this with striking clarity if you plot your stumbled APs on a high-resolution city map with Stumbverter and MapPoint (see Chapter 20): Plotted APs seem to fall almost exclusively on street alignments. (This effect is especially vivid in anally rectilinear cities like Chicago.) This is simply because GPS was following your car and not the APs that you find.

NetStumbler Views and Filters

NetStumbler has two primary views and seven built-in filters that allow you to do certain simple "canned" database queries on your logs of stumbled APs. These are found in the views tree on the left of the main display screen, under the Filters node. If you click on one of the filters, the display will change to include only those stations meeting that filter's criteria. To show the full list after selecting a filter, click on the root Filters node, and you'll see them all.

There are two primary views of NetStumbler's logged data:

1. The **Channels** view separates stumbled APs by the channels they were on. If a single AP was present on more than one channel, it will be seen in all channel views where it was logged during the time it was within NetStumbler's range.

2. The **SSIDs** view lists each separate AP by its SSID. Although this is middling uncommon, if you encounter an ESS (a network with multiple access points) and come into range or more than one of its APs, each AP will be listed separately under the same SSID. (In an ESS, all access points that belong to the same network will have the same SSID.) You can tell the APs apart because each will have a unique MAC address.

There are seven filters in the version current at this writing (version 0.3.30), which I'll quickly describe here:

1. The **Encryption Off** filter shows the stumbled APs for which WEP was not enabled.

2. The **Encryption On** filter shows the stumbled APs for which WEP was enabled.

3. The **ESS (AP)** filter shows the APs operating in infrastructure mode. This means all those APs for which the Type field holds the value "AP." This will be virtually all of them; in two years I've stumbled only three or four ad-hoc stations other than the times I've set up an ad-hoc network at home.

4. The **IBSS (Peer)** filter shows APs operating in ad-hoc mode. Again, these will be vanishingly few.

5. The **CF-Pollable** filter shows those APs that have their CF-Pollable bits set. This bit is in the Flags field, as I'll explain in more detail in the next chapter. The CF (Coordination Function) bits support a feature allowing a station to request that it be told when other stations are quiet and it's safe to transmit. A station that can "hear" its access point cannot necessary hear all the other stations associated with that access point, so the Coordination Function helps keep the various stations from transmitting at the same time and interfering with one another. This feature isn't seen often, and is usually used by larger networks incorporating higher-end access points.

6. The **Short Preamble** filter shows those APs that have their Short Preamble bits set. This bit, like the CF-Pollable bit, is in the Flags field, as I'll explain in the next chapter. Some access points support a feature allowing certain types

of data (like Voice over IP and streaming media) to be sent using a "short preamble" on their frames to boost throughput and improve the quality of the transmission. (Digitized voice and media are much more sensitive to variations in the rate of transmission than "pure" digital data.) More and more APs will be seen using short preambles once the IEEE 802.11e task group completes and publishes its "Quality of Service" specification. For now, they're still pretty scarce, and are usually Cisco products.

7. The **Default SSID** filter shows those APs that are using the default SSID values with which their manufacturer ships them. These include "linksys" for Linksys products, "tsunami" for Cisco Aironet products, "Wireless" for Netgear products, and "default" for several others, including D-Link and Acer. Table 19.1 lists all the default SSIDs of which I am aware.

Table 19.1 Default SSIDs by Manufacturer

Manufacturer	Default SSIDs
Acer	default
Cisco Aironet	tsunami
Compaq	Compaq
D-Link	WLAN, default
Linksys	linksys
Netgear	Wireless
SMC	WLAN
Symbol	101

The Signal Strength Display

One of the very best features of NetStumbler is its signal strength and noise display. This is practically a full-screen graph of the signal strength and noise performance of a particular AP, updated roughly once per second, and scrolling to the right over time. You can display the graph for any stumbled AP by expanding either the Channels node or SSIDs node to display individual APs, and then click on the AP you want to monitor (see Figure 19.4).

If the AP is still in range, you can watch the signal and noise values march toward the right as new readings are taken. If an AP is no longer in range, you can see the graph for all readings that were taken while the AP was in range. For most APs gathered during a wardriving run from a moving vehicle, this will be a relatively short sequence of readings. If you're auditing your own AP, looking for dead spots and weak spots, you may have a great many readings. Once there are more readings

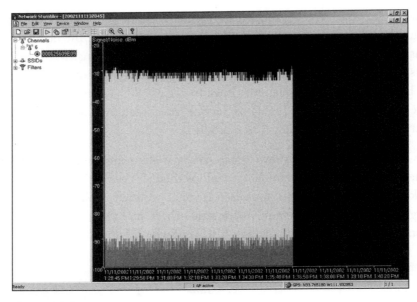

Figure 19.4
NetStumbler's Signal Strength and Noise Display.

than will fit across your display, a scroll bar at the bottom allows you to scroll through the full run of readings.

NetStumbler automatically adjusts the vertical display scale so that the readings are always displayed over most of the vertical range, allowing you to take maximum advantage of the precision inherent in the readings.

Even if you never go out wardriving at all, NetStumbler's field strength display can be extremely useful for determining the reach and the flaws of your access point's coverage. Just run NetStumbler at your home or office location, display the field strength screen for your access point, and walk around. You'll see very quickly where the field is weak or dead.

At this writing, the current release (version 0.3.30) has a selectable audio feedback feature that plays musical notes as the signal-to-noise ratio goes up and down. As the ratio goes up, so does the tone of the musical note. As the ratio goes down, so does the tone. It's off by default, but you can turn it on from the View|Options|MIDI option. I'm still of two minds about how useful this is, but it has been of some help when I'm outside in bright sunlight and my laptop display is hard to read. I can hear myself heading into a deadspot by rapidly descending tones, and then when the music stops completely I know I'm out of range of my AP.

*If you find you enjoy NetStumbler and intend to make wardriving a regular activity, consider making a donation to the author, Marius Milner. You can do this through PayPal (**www.paypal.com**) by sending something (I suggest $10) to **mariusm@pacbell.net**.*

GPS

You don't need a GPS receiver to wardrive with NetStumbler, especially if you're just gathering statistics about Wi-Fi adoption growth and aren't going to plot maps or otherwise correlate the results to geographical locations. NetStumbler, however, will add GPS-discerned coordinates to its log files if a GPS receiver is available. With those GPS coordinates present, you can plot access points on maps using several methods, and get a bird's eye view of where the Wi-Fi clusters and deserts are.

NetStumbler's GPS requirements are straightforward:

• It understands NMEA-formatted GPS data.

• It requires that this GPS data be available at a serial port.

The National Marine Electronics Association (NMEA) has defined a data format for data received from GPS satellites. Other formats exist, but the NMEA 0183 format is a strong standard, and virtually all GPS receivers can emit it. (Still, you should check for NMEA 0183 compatibility before putting out money for a GPS receiver.)

The issue of a serial port is a little slippery. By "serial port" I mean a COM port, not a USB port. True, USB (Universal Serial Bus) is a serial technology, but it uses an entirely different driver architecture under Windows, and USB ports are not accessible through the COM1-COM4 (or however many) serial devices available through Windows.

As often, there is an out: I use a USB-based GPS receiver with NetStumbler, even though at this writing NetStumbler is only beginning to have built-in USB support. The trick is that my GPS receiver comes with an installable driver that "maps" the USB port to one of the standard COM serial ports that Windows understands. The receiver plugs into the physical USB port, but the data comes in (and NetStumbler grabs it) from one of the COM ports.

This is good, for a reason that seems trivial on the surface but matters a lot in the practical world: USB devices can draw their electrical power (up to half an amp!) right from the USB port. This eliminates a power cable in the car, when I already have too many wires lying around between the seats.

But that's a decision I leave up to you. Any GPS receiver that emits NMEA 0183 formatted data and can be read from a serial port will work with NetStumbler. Whatever GPS receiver you choose, you must tell NetStumbler what port to listen to for NMEA 0183 data. This is done by selecting View|Options and clicking the GPS tab. The screen is shown in Figure 19.5.

Newer versions of NetStumbler also support the Garmin protocols (both text and binary) and TripMate. Older versions (prior to August 2002) support only NMEA.

The GPS device I use is an obscure receiver called the Holux GM-210 (see Figure 19.6). It's tiny, self-contained, waterproof, and magnetic. It sticks to the roof of my car, with a single thin wire coming in the window. If WAAS (Wide Area Augmentation System) is available in your area, it will automatically use the WAAS signals to refine the accuracy of the coordinates it emits. It comes with two selectable cables, allowing it to plug into either a USB port or a conventional DB-9 serial port. It worked perfectly the first time, configured easily, and has never given me any trouble.

The Holux GM-210 is much easier to find in Europe than in the US. Here are some sources:

www.semsons.com   **US**

www.holux-uk.com   **UK**

www.dsh2000.com   **BeNeLux**

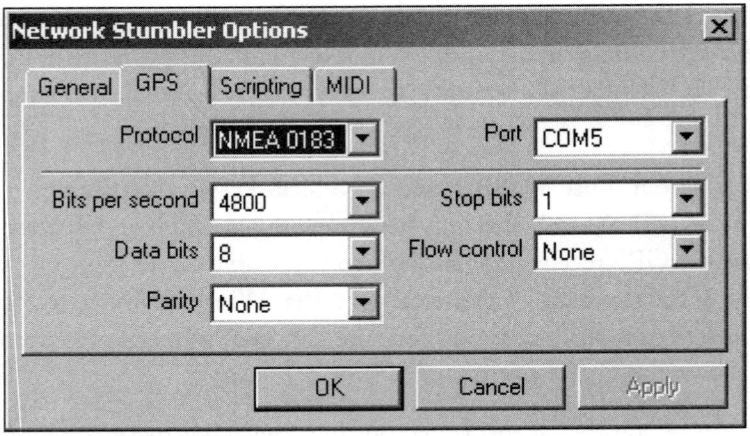

Figure 19.5
The NetStumbler GPS Configuration Tab.

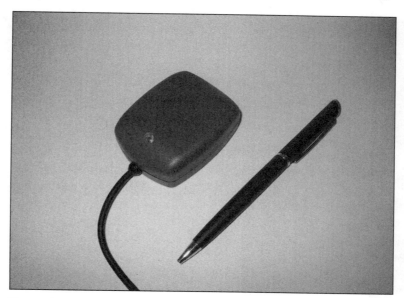

Figure 19.6
The Holux GM-210 GPS Receiver.

External Antennas

NetStumbler does not require an external antenna. You can wardrive with the antenna built into your Wi-Fi PCMCIA client adapter. However, those "bulge" antennas are totally miserable, and if you're serious about wardriving you should consider getting a client card with an external antenna connector and a matching antenna. You'll pick up a great many more access points with a better antenna, ideally one mounted outside your vehicle.

The antenna I use and recommend is the 5 dbi mag-mount omnidirectional mobile antenna from Fleeman, Anderson, & Bird (FAB) (see Figure 19.7). Its magnetic base sticks to the roof of your vehicle, and the signal is brought in through nine feet of low-loss coaxial cable terminated in a female N connector. You will need a suitable (short) pigtail to connect the N female connector to the connector on your client card. These are also available from FAB. (I cover this and other types of commercial antennas in Chapter 8.)

Admittedly, the total investment for an antenna of this type (including the pigtail) is almost $100. Less expensive things that I've tried include hanging a cheap blade antenna from a suction cup on the inside of one of my car's windows. This works far better than the built-in antenna on the client card, but nowhere near as well as an omnidirectional antenna on the roof of the vehicle. It also allows me to keep the windows rolled up, which matters in rainy cities like Chicago.

Figure 19.7
The FAB 5 dBi Magnetic Mount Omnidirectional Antenna.

Effective Wardriving

Once you've got everything set up and working, plan your drive and do it. Here are some tips that come out of my experience so far:

- Although it's fun just driving around randomly to see what you can find, I think it's even more fun to define a "standard wardrive" and do the run on a regular basis (weekly or monthly) to see how the installed Wi-Fi base along that route changes over time. The easy way to do this is just use your daily commute, if it takes you through enough city to get a decent station count.

- The consensus seems to be that the optimum speed for wardriving is 35 MPH. NetStumbler needs at least a little time to work, and access points on the fringes of reception are not within range for very long. Hurtle past at 75 MPH and you will definitely miss some of the weak ones.

- Stick to surface streets as much as possible. On expressways you're generally going very quickly (except maybe on your morning or evening commutes) but more significantly, you're farther away from the buildings where the APs are and will miss more of them.

- This should go without saying, but be careful not to pay so much attention to what's coming into your laptop that you get into a crackup. The best thing to do (I know it's hard) is to leave your laptop in the back seat so you won't be tempted to look at it. It will honk every time a new station is detected, so you'll have some audible indication of your progress.

One thing I've done on several occasions is "wardrive" from the back seat of a taxi. This allowed me to watch the show and not worry about driving. I use a blade antenna suction cupped to the cab window. The cabbies usually don't ask what's going on—they probably think I'm some kind of government spook!

The Autoconnect Problem

Not a few wardrivers have reported something disconcerting: While out wardriving, they discovered that their laptops were *automatically* connecting to unprotected APs. This is important for two reasons:

1. It's technically illegal to connect to someone else's network without their permission, even if you don't *deliberately* connect.

2. With some client adapters, after autoconnecting the adapter places the SSID of the autoconnected AP in the SSID field, after which the adapter will not report the presence of any AP with a different SSID. Autoconnect even *once*, and you won't see any more APs for the rest of your drive.

Most people notice the autoconnect problem when they stop for a red light within the field of a nearby unprotected AP. After fifteen or twenty seconds, their laptops report connecting to the network. (If your laptop is in the front seat—not really a good idea—you may see a "talk balloon" appear over the taskbar tray icon.) During a wardrive, you're constantly moving and aren't in the AP field long enough for the laptop to hook up with the AP. Only when you stop at a light (or when traffic is moving at a crawl) does it tend to happen. Of course, if everybody had WEP on, this wouldn't be an issue, but...when is Hell scheduled to freeze over?

Under the hood, here's what's happening: If you have your laptop configured to request IP address information from the local DHCP server, some adapters will request an IP address from any network they can see, even if the AP's SSID doesn't match the blank or "ANY" SSID in the wardriving profile. Doing a DHCP transaction takes a certain amount of time, but if more than fifteen or twenty seconds goes by, most DHCP servers will hand out an address, and *boom!* You're on the network, whether you want to be or not.

The only foolproof way to prevent autoconnect is to disable the TCP/IP protocol on the Wi-Fi client adapter you're using to wardrive. Without TCP/IP, the client adapter has nothing to connect with. However, it will still report the presence of an AP through Netstumbler.

Here's how: Bring up the properties window for the Wi-Fi client adapter you're using for stumbling. Find "Internet Protocol (TCP/IP)" in the list of installed components. To its left will be a check box. Un-check the box, and click OK. Then reboot the computer. Your client card will still be enabled, but it can't use TCP/IP and thus cannot connect to any network.

Not all client adapters seem as willing to autoconnect as others, and the reasons for the difference is obscure. I think it might pay to disable TCP/IP before wardriving even if you haven't observed your stumbling rig doing an autoconnect. Quite apart from the risk of accidentally making an illegal connection, some adapters will suck in the connected SSID and cease reporting other APs.

Admittedly, disabling and re-enabling network protocols is a nuisance. One suggestion I have is to shop for an older laptop on the used market, and configure it strictly as your wardriving machine. 1997-era laptops running Windows 95 can be had for as little as $150, and they will run NetStumbler without any trouble. Upgrading to Windows 98SE is a good idea, as long as the processor is faster than 100 MHz. Once you have NetStumbler installed, disable all networking protocols, and you're good to go. As for getting NetStumbler's log files off the machine in the absence of network protocols, find a copy of LapLink and use the serial port!

If You Get Pulled Over While Wardriving...

If you do a lot of wardriving, it's likely that eventually you'll be pulled over by a police officer, if not for wardriving then for driving erratically, or cruising slowly up and down the streets of a residential neighborhood. So what should you do in that event?

First of all, *cooperate fully with the officer who pulls you over*. Stay calm, be polite, and don't act like you're smuggling dope or have an open container under the seat. Let the officer lead the conversation, and answer his/her questions honestly. Don't assume the officer knows nothing about wardriving. This might have been true in 2001, but it's not true anymore.

What I've heard is that nearly all such encounters are due to bad driving, not some suspicion of "hacking" or "terrorism." The police are pragmatists and have more than enough to do simply enforcing traffic laws; officers on the beat are unlikely to be looking for ill-defined threats to national security. You're much more likely to be pulled over if you have a laptop on the passenger's seat and you're constantly trying to watch what's going on—and thus weaving all around the road like a drunk. I suggest leaving your laptop on the back seat. Wardriving really isn't interactive. Your stumbling utility logs stations automatically and doesn't require any input from you while it's working. (It will honk audibly to let you know it's working, and that should be all the feedback you need.) Don't let it be a distraction that gets you into a crackup.

Also, there are laws in some states that prohibit watching screens like TVs and computers while you're driving. You can definitely get a ticket if you're pulled over in those states and are found to have a working laptop in the front seat somewhere, and the ticket has nothing to do with wardriving *per se*.

Even if you keep your laptop in the back seat, try to turn off video if you wardrive at night, so as not to have the interior of your car awash in a bluish glow. The police are always watching for weird stuff going on in their turf. That's their job. Try not to stand out. (I do all my wardriving during the day.)

I have heard that you're less likely to be seen with suspicion if you're a licensed amateur radio operator with ham radio plates on your car. The police are familiar with ham radio, and seeing cars full of weird electronics is just part of the ham radio template. Also, radio hams have traditionally assisted the police in local emergencies like tornadoes and floods, and the police respect amateur radio. This doesn't excuse bad driving, but it may deflect suspicion from your cables and laptop.

Even if you're a networking consultant or IT staffer and have multiple legal uses for packet sniffers and password crackers, I suggest not having such tools installed on the computer you use for wardriving. It's very unlikely that you will be taken to the station and have your laptop looked at, but against that possibility, don't fill the machine up with network utilities, MP3s, or porn. Dicey stuff suggests dicey behavior. Keep your nose (and your laptop) clean!

Crank 'Er Up!

That's nearly all of what you need to know to get started. Once you've logged a certain number of stations with NetStumbler, it's useful to know how to interpret the files that it generates. That's what I'll be talking about in Chapter 20.

NetStumbler's Log Files

If you consider wardriving fun—but *only* fun, a sort of cruisin' for the oughties—then this chapter won't interest you much. The scavenger hunt feel of wardriving is often satisfying enough. But as I mentioned in the previous chapter, wardriving tells you something about the state of wireless networking, first in your own community, and then (if you connect to the larger community of wardrivers nationally and even globally) in the world at large. Over the two years that I've been wardriving, I've watched the number of access points grow rapidly along my "standard wardrives," first in the greater Phoenix metropolitan area, and more recently around Colorado Springs, and I tracked the proportion of "clueless" Wi-Fi users: those who leave the default SSID in place and fail to enable Wi-Fi security. (Conclusion: It's appallingly high!)

I've seen reports from elsewhere in the country indicating that where wardriving has gotten TV coverage, suddenly the percentage of people enabling WEP jumps by 10 or 15 percentage points. So let it not be said that wardriving is "hacking" or, God help us, terrorism. At the very least, it's technology market intelligence. At best, it's a reality check for network security, and encouragement to use the security features that Wi-Fi offers.

To make the best use of the intelligence that wardriving gathers about wireless networking, you're going to have to become familiar with NetStumbler's log files. The data gathered by NetStumbler is fairly sophisticated technically, and in this chapter I'll explain how to generate the text files you'll need to analyze the data, and how to interpret the data in the files. Toward the end of this chapter, I'll also show you how to generate maps on which stumbled stations are plotted, using the free Stumbverter utility.

NetStumbler's Native Data Files

What you have in your hands at the end of a wardrive is a log file of all the stations detected by NetStumbler while you were out driving around. My description of log file data gets pretty technical in spots, so you can skip anything that seems outside your interests. Not all of it is equally useful. Most of what's in the log is pretty obvious, but I want to be as complete as possible, since I haven't seen the whole thing documented in any one place.

For its logs, NetStumbler generates binary files with a .NS1 extension. Netstumbler's author Marius Milner has not documented the binary format of the .NS1 file, which is ok, since I think we'd all prefer that he be adding features to NetStumbler. (He may also prefer that we not write software that manipulates .NS1 files directly, so that he can change the format as NetStumbler evolves without breaking other people's code.) The .NS1 files can be merged together, or loaded back into NetStumbler for examination by selecting File|Open and entering the file name, but there isn't anything else you can do with them directly. To somehow process the data that you collect on a wardrive, you must export a log file to a text file, as I'll explain shortly.

Merging Netstumbler Log Files

NetStumbler's .NS1 log files can be merged together very easily. The File|Merge option opens a file selection dialog, and the file that you select will be merged with the active file in NetStumbler. This can be useful if you want to gather the results of several trips into a single file covering a week's or a month's wardriving, or from several people canvassing a metropolitan area on a cooperative basis.

You can begin by creating a new, empty file with the File|New option, or the New button in the button bar. One caveat: Unless you've un-checked the "New document starts scanning" option on the General tab of the Options dialog, you'll add your own access point to the new file if the AP is within range. Turning off scanning by clicking the Scanning button won't prevent this. Once you have a new file, you can add existing files to it by selecting each in turn from the File|Merge dialog. Once you've added everything that needs adding, you can save the new file out under an appropriate name.

Exporting to Text

To export to a text file, select File|Export and choose from the three options:

- Summary: Each stumbled station is one text record.

- Text: Each different signal strength reading on each station is a separate record. These are *much* larger files.

- Wi-Scan: Similar to the Text format, but saves files for the Wi-Scan utility written by Pete Shipley, who basically invented wardriving as we know it. This format omits certain items present in the other export formats.

In each case, give the file a name with a .txt extension. NetStumbler does not provide the .txt extension automatically.

The exported text records (each line being considered a record) are tab-delimited. Each field within a record is separated from the next field by a tab character.

The Text File Field Structure

For the most part, each text record corresponds to a line on the NetStumbler display, so this description repeats the description of the display to some extent. Here is a summary of the fields output by NetStumbler 0.3.30, in order from the left column:

1. Latitude of the GPS receiver when NetStumbler detected the station, in degrees.

2. Longitude of the GPS receiver when NetStumbler detected the station, in degrees.

3. SSID of the station, enclosed in parentheses.

4. Type: The mode in which the stumbled station was operating. "BBS" = infrastructure mode. "Ad-hoc" = ad hoc mode. The "BBS" may be a bug; Marius may have intended to use "BSS" here, as BSS is IEEE jargon for a station operating in infrastructure mode.

5. BSSID: The MAC address of the station, enclosed in parentheses. "BSSID" is jargon for "MAC address."

6. The time that the station was logged, in GMT (Greenwich Mean Time).

7. The signal-noise ratio, signal reading, and noise reading, given as three numbers enclosed in square brackets.

8. Name: The AP's descriptive name, if it can be determined. This field is usually blank. NetStumbler cannot always determine an AP's name, even if the AP has one. (Most do not.)

9. The Flag bits. I'll discuss these bit fields later in this chapter.

10. The channel bits. This indicates the channel or channels on which the stumbled station was detected during the time it was in range of NetStumbler. It's a hexadecimal value, which I'll relate to channel numbers below.

11. The beacon interval at which the stumbled station is sending beacon frames, in milliseconds. I've never seen this with a nonzero value in an exported text file, even though it displays correctly on the main NetStumbler display. I can only assume that there's a bug in the export code.

The Name field exists to show an access point's descriptive name. Keep in mind that in an Extended Service Set (ESS) there may be several access points with the same SSID. The SSID is the name of the *network*, not the access point! (Since the vast majority of small office and home office networks have only a single AP, this can easily be misunderstood.) Most APs allow administrators to assign a descriptive name, which acts as a more-easily-remembered alias for the AP's MAC address. Curiously, the name of my Cisco Aironet 340 AP is not reported by NetStumbler, and I really don't know why. This is probably a chipset- or firmware-specific problem. If you have any insights, please let me know.

Note: You won't see the Signal+, Noise-, and SNR+ fields in the exported files. These fields exist only on the main NetStumbler display, and are calculated internally every second or so from the multiple signal strength readings taken on each stumbled AP while it remains in range. To duplicate the Signal+, Noise-, and SNR+ fields, you would have begin with the "big" text file, and examine all the Signal, Noise, and SNR readings taken for a given AP. (Each reading has a separate exported text record, and if you spend any significant time within range of a single AP, there may be hundreds for that AP.) From these readings you would determine the highest signal reading, lowest noise reading, and best SNR for that AP.

If you're looking at an exported summary text file, the Signal, Noise, and SNR fields are the overall best reading taken while the AP was within range.

The Flag Bits

The Flag bits are a 16-bit block of information returned by the client card. Each bit in the lower 8 bits of the Flag bits has a distinct meaning, some of which are defined in the IEEE 802.11 specification, in section 7.3.1.4.

Until very recently, the higher 8 bits of Flags were considered "reserved," and were always seen as 0 in NetStumbler's log files. With the release of Wireless-G, one of those reserved bits started coming back with a "1" value. NetStumbler does not interpret the Flags bits, but simply reports them as it sees them. Although I've seen no formal announcement from any Wi-Fi vendor, my tests indicate that this bit, when set to 1, always indicates an AP capable of supporting Wireless-G. This includes G-only APs as well as units that also support Wireless-B or Wireless-A in the same physical device.

Interpreting the Flag bits requires a little knowledge of both hexadecimal and binary numbers. Alas, if you're completely clueless about hex and binary numbers I'll have to send you elsewhere, since I don't have the room to explain them in detail here. I cover it thoroughly in my book *Assembly Language Step By Step* (John Wiley & Sons, 2000: ISBN 0-471-37523-3). Hex numbers are in base 16, and use the letters A to F to indicate the values 10 to 15.

Let's look at an example. Figure 20.1 shows how the 12 significant flag bits are defined.

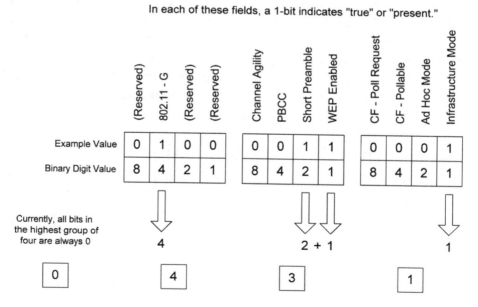

Thus, what you'll see in the NetStumbler display for Flags is "0431"

Figure 20.1
NetStumbler's Flag Bits.

Each bit in the Flag bits maps to a feature or condition inside the access point. A 1-bit means that the corresponding feature or condition is enabled, present, or true, however that makes sense in context. Each bit also has a binary value of 1, 2, 4, or 8. The 12 defined bits of the Flag bits field are divided into three four-bit hexadecimal digits. Within each of those digits, the binary values of any 1-bits are added together to yield a value for the hex digit.

In the example shown in Figure 20.1, four bits are set:

- Infrastructure mode

- WEP enabled

- Short Preamble

- 802.11g

The binary value of the Infrastructure mode bit is 1, and it's the only bit set in the lowest digit. Thus, the lowest digit has a value of 1. In the next highest digit, WEP Enabled and Short Preamble are both set. The WEP Enabled bit has a binary value of 1. The Short Preamble bit has a binary value of 2. Adding 2 and 1 gives us the hexadecimal value of the digit, which is 3. In the next highest digit, there is only one defined value: 802.11g. The other three bits in that digit are still "reserved" and will always show up as 0, at least until the IEEE defines some new use for them. (The 802.11n standard may present a different value—we'll have to wait and see!) The value of the 802.11g bit is 4, which becomes the value of the highest significant digit. Because the very highest digit is not used and is always set to zero, the value you would see in a NetStumbler log file is 0431.

Interpreting the Flag Bits Value

Pulling apart a value from the log file means going in reverse, in a sense: You have to look at a hexadecimal digit and find out which of the values 1, 2, 4, or 8 are "inside" it. Table 20.1 shows what bits are present in all 16 possible values for a hexadecimal digit.

Table 20.1 Hexadecimal Values and Their Equivalents Bit Patterns.

Hexadecimal Value	Bit Pattern
0	0000
1	0001
2	0010
3	0011
4	0100
5	0101
6	0110
7	0111
8	1000
9	1001
A (10)	1010
B (11)	1011
C (12)	1100
D (13)	1101
E (14)	1110
F (15)	1111

The way to use Table 20.1 is to look down the left column for the digit you see in the Flag bits field in a NetStumbler log file, then go over to the right column to find the bits that it represents. Compare those bits to the named bit fields shown in Figure 20.1, to see which bit fields correspond to the 1-bits in the digit.

I suppose I should let you dope out the common ones for practice, but hexadecimal is not everybody's taste. (I'm an assembly language programmer and it's in my blood.) So Table 20.2 shows the commonest Flag bits values and their meanings.

Table 20.2 Common Flag Bits Values.

Value	Meaning
0001	AP is in infrastructure more; WEP is off
0002	AP is in ad-hoc mode; WEP is off
0011	AP is in infrastructure mode; WEP is on
0031	AP is in infrastructure mode; WEP is on; AP is using short preambles
0051	AP is in infrastructure mode; WEP is on; AP is using PBCC

If you see a "4" instead of a zero in the second column from the left, that means that the AP in question is capable of 802.11g operation. This doesn't mean that it is currently operating in 802.11g mode, only that it has that capability. For example, the value "0411" means that the AP is capable of 802.11g operation, and that it is currently in infrastructure mode with WEP enabled.

The presence of the 802.11g bit doesn't change the meaning of any of the other bits, though I have yet to see the 802.11g bit and the PBCC bit both set in the same AP—the two bits represent two different technologies, and thus are mutually exclusive. Also, you may someday see a letter from A-F in one of the digits. (I have yet to see one, in two years and thousands of stumbled APs!) Remember that the digits are hexadecimal, and if you add the 8 bit and the 4 bit, you get a "C" value. If an AP were to have Channel Agility enabled, plus Short Preambles and WEP, you would see a B digit. (Do you understand why? Hint: Add 8, 2, and 1 and express the sum in hexadecimal!)

What the Flag Bits Mean

That's how the encoding of the Flag bits works. Some of what the Flag bits do is pretty obvious. Most is obscure. This gets pretty technical, so I'll be brief.

- Channel Agility is an extension to the 802.11b standard that allows a station to change channels automatically if it detects interference on the channel it's using. ShareWave's Whitecap technology, which represents an extended 802.11b system, uses channel agility. Cisco's Aironet line has something similar but not interoperable. Channel Agility is part of the larger "quality of service" issue being addressed in the IEEE task group 802.11e, and when 802.11e is adopted, we will have a standard for channel agility. I rarely see this bit set; my guess it will be set for any access point that uses channel agility, probably through the Whitecap chipset.

- PBCC means *Packet Binary Convolutional Code*, which is an encoding scheme allowing higher bit rates in 802.11b transmissions. As best I know, PBCC is currently used only by access points incorporating the Texas Instruments chip set that implements a proprietary extension to the 802.11b standard. This is called 802.11b+ and is used by a number of products from several vendors, including D-Link's AirPlus product line. (I discuss this in greater detail in Chapter 4.) The DWL-900AP+ access point uses PBCC to boost its *theoretical* bit rate (when communicating with other 802.11b+ devices) to 22 MBps. (In "real life," throughput on the DWL-900AP+ doesn't get anywhere close!) If you find a station with the PBCC bit set, you are most likely seeing an 802.11b+ access point. My tests show that the DWL-900AP+ does set this bit.

- The Short Preamble bit refers to a feature in the 802.11b standard's physical layer. Each frame begins with a block of bits called the *preamble*. There is a long preamble format that all 802.11b compliant devices are required to support. A second, shorter form of the preamble is optional, and can be used to improve link throughput when the functionality of the long preamble isn't required. (Streaming video and voice over IP are two instances when a short preamble can be used to good effect.) Short preambles are the default condition on some access points, including the Cisco Aironet 340. Most of the APs I see with this bit set are Cisco units.

- When the WEP Enabled bit is set to 1, that means the station has enabled WEP.

- The CF-Poll Request and CF-Pollable bits are part of something called the *coordination function* (CF) that not all access points fully implement, though it is an element of the 802.11 standard. CF is about wireless Ethernet collision detection, and comes into play when a Wi-Fi client can hear its access point but not the other clients associated with that same access point. The client can request that its AP tell it when it's "clear to send," that is, when all the other clients are quiet and won't interfere. Explaining this fully here would be a handful, but I don't consider it especially useful knowledge for stumbling anyway. See section 7.3.1.4 of the IEEE 802.11 standards document for details. My guess is you'll see these bits set in business networks with lots of clients rather than home networks. I see them in about 2% of stumbled nodes.

- When the Ad Hoc Mode bit is set to 1, the station is operating in ad-hoc mode.

- When the Infrastructure Mode bit is set, the station is operating in infrastructure mode. The Ad-Hoc Mode and Infrastructure Mode bits are mutually exclusive and you will never see both set simultaneously on the same AP.

The Channel Bits

The channel bits are a 16-bit data block, in which each Wi-Fi channel has an associated bit. This might seem an odd way to express a channel number, but it allows NetStumbler to store multiple channels for a single access point. It's possible (though fairly rare) for a station to change its operating channel while it's in range of NetStumbler. (This may become much more common once the IEEE 802.11e task group is adopted, since 802.11e standardizes "channel agility," which is the ability of an access point to duck interference by moving on its own initiative to another channel.) If that happens, NetStumbler displays all channels on which it detected that station during the time it was in range. It stores multiple channels in the log file by raising the appropriate bit for each channel.

Table 20.3 summarizes the common values for the channel bits, when only one channel was detecting while the station was in range. Ninety-nine percent of the time, you'll see only these channel bits values in a log file.

Table 20.3   The Channel Bit Values.

Channel	Channel Bits Field Value
1	0002
2	0004
3	0008
4	0010
5	0020
6	0040
7	0080
8	0100
9	0200
10	0400
11	0800

Note from the table that the value 0001 is invalid and can never appear, as that bit corresponds to no channel. Any other value not in the table indicates multiple channels.

As an example of multiple channels, consider Figure 20.2. Let's posit that an access point jumps through the channels 1, 6, 8, and 11 while in range of NetStumbler. (Once "channel agility" is made a part of the greater 802.11 standard, this will become a commonplace.) NetStumbler stores a bit in the channel bits field for each of those four channels. This is shown in the "Example" line in the figure. Each group of four bits corresponds to one hexadecimal digit in the channel bits value.

More to the point, each digit in a hex number is represented by four binary bits. A 16-bit quantity like the channel bits, therefore, can be represented in four hex digits. Figure 20.2 separates the 16 bits of the channel bits field into four groups of four bits. Each bit in its group stands for a value of 1, 2, 4, or 8. Within each groups, the values of any "set" bits (bits with a 1 value) are added together to give you the value for the associated hex digit.

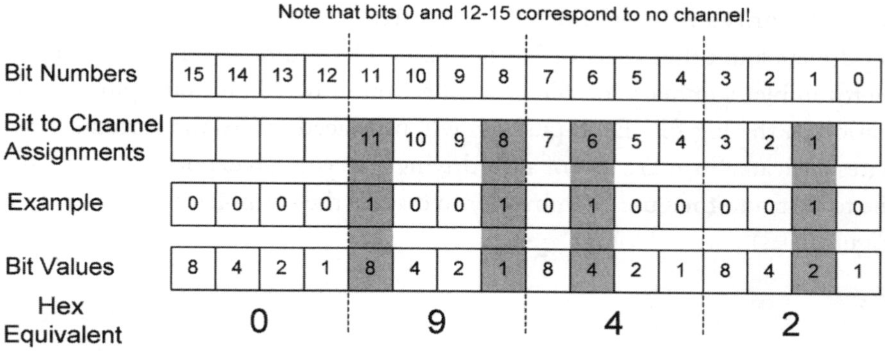

Note that bits 0 and 12-15 correspond to no channel!

Bit Numbers	15	14	13	12	11	10	9	8	7	6	5	4	3	2	1	0
Bit to Channel Assignments					11	10	9	8	7	6	5	4	3	2	1	
Example	0	0	0	0	1	0	0	1	0	1	0	0	0	0	1	0
Bit Values	8	4	2	1	8	4	2	1	8	4	2	1	8	4	2	1
Hex Equivalent	0				9				4				2			

Figure 20.2
The Channel Bits for Channels 1, 6, 8, and 11.

The bit for channel 8 has a value of 1. The bit for channel 11 has a value of 8. Adding 8 and 1 gives you 9, the value of the hex digit for that group of channel bits. If channel 9's bit were also set, you'd have to add 1 + 2 + 8, for a total of 11—which is the hex digit B.

That's how channel bits are formed. You can "reverse engineer" a given channel bits value by separating it into its four hex digits, and then looking for the values 1, 2, 4, or 8 within each hex digit. A 3 digit would contain 1 and 2; a 6 digit would contain 2 and 4. Work upward in the figure to find the channel bits associated with each value of 1, 2, 4, or 8 you find inside a hex digit.

Note that the first hex digit is *always* 0, or something is wrong. No channels correspond to bits 12 through 15.

Mapping Stumbled Stations with MapPoint and Stumbverter

I'm an enthusiastic user of Microsoft's MapPoint product. It's a little like a road atlas that knows your location and follows it. Carol and I run it on my laptop while traveling to verify our location: It displays a map with a symbol in the middle indicating where you are.

MapPoint has another, little-known trick: It contains a map server, and a properly-written program can request maps from the MapPoint server and use them to display specific map-based information.

Sonar Security's Michael Puchol has written just such a program, specifically for wardrivers and other users of NetStumbler. His Stumbverter utility will convert a NetStumbler summary log file to a collection of MapPoint pushpins, one for each station in the log file. Each pushpin will be placed where the stored GPS coordinates indicate. So at the end of a wardriving run, you can export the drive's summary file to text, and then use Stumbverter to display the stumbled stations on a map (see Figure 20.3).

 Stumbverter requires that Microsoft MapPoint be installed on the system for it to run, as it makes heavy use of the MapPoint server. Stumbverter is MapPoint version-specific. The current version (1.5) works only with MapPoint 2004. If you have MapPoint 2002, you will have to hunt around for Stumbverter Beta 5 or earlier, as the author no longer distributes earlier versions.

Stumbverter is free (though donations are welcome, and can be sent through PayPal) and installs conventionally after downloading from Sonar Security's Web site:

www.sonar-security.com

Using Stumbverter

Stumbverter does not read the native .ns1 files created by NetStumbler. Before attempting to convert a NetStumbler log file you must export a log file to a summary

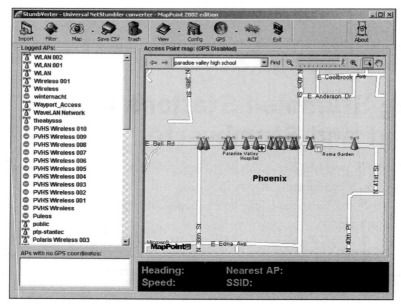

Figure 20.3
A Stumbverter Map with Stations.

text file using NetStumbler's File|Export|Summary option. Once you have your summary log file in .txt format, follow these steps:

1. You must first load or create a MapPoint .ptm map file. These can be created in MapPoint itself, or you can create a new map from within Stumbverter. Loading a map is done by selecting the Map|Load option and navigating to the .ptm file you wish to load. Creating a new map file is done by selecting either the Map|Create New North America or Map|Create New Europe options.

2. Your exported summary text file can then be loaded into Stumbverter by clicking the Import button and navigating to the summary file.

3. When the import is complete, there will be a list of stations in the left pane, and the map with stations plotted in the main pane.

The map does not automatically zoom to the imported pushpins. You have to manually zoom to the pushpins by right clicking the little station pushpin symbol and selecting "Zoom to."

Stumbverter does not have the ability to print a map. To print a map on which you've plotted stumbled stations, you must save the current map to a .ptm file, then run MapPoint, load the .ptm map file, and print from within MapPoint.

It's probably worth a reminder as you look at your maps that the positions plotted on the map are your positions when NetStumbler detected the station, *not* the station's position!

If you have a GPS receiver and install Stumbverter (as well as MapPoint) on your laptop, you can cruise around with your position displayed on the map. Your directional heading and speed will be displayed in Stumbverter's lower pane, along with the SSID of the nearest plotted access point.

Cut the Cables and Go!

At this point you should be well-equipped to make good use of the various Wi-Fi technologies, and should have learned enough about the state of the art today to follow it as it evolves. (You'll need to do that following at a dead run to stay ahead of it all!)

What do I think are the most important points to watch in the future? Here are some highlights:

- *The IEEE 802.11n draft standard.* 200 Kbps bitrates, woo-hoo! The non-standard Super G enhancement to Wireless-G may be superceded by 802.11n once it's completed and published, so be careful about taking a deep position on Super G. Look for 802.11n in mid-late 2005 or very early 2006.

- *Free hotspots replacing commercial hotspots.* Following the example of Schlotzky's Deli and Panera Bread (as well as the occasional discount hotel and Dairy Queen) I think we'll see more and more businesses use free Wi-Fi hotspots as bait to attract more customers and give them a competitive edge.

- *Low-power Wi-Fi adapters for PDAs.* New, small (probably in the SDIO form factor) Wi-Fi client adapters with extremely aggressive power management (and possible shorter range as a result) will make Wi-Fi practical from a PDA without draining the battery in an hour or forcing the use of bulky sleds or backpacks.

- *Wi-Max technology for rural broadband.* While not in the Wi-Fi family, the related 802.16 standard will help bring broadband Internet to remote and sparsely-developed areas. Although nominally a point-to-point technology, I suspect a future Wi-Max enhancement will allow portable computers to connect through Wi-Max anywhere the field extends. Farm country tomorrow, Central Park the day after. Sooner or later we'll be wireless…everywhere!

If you've got the wireless bug, keep on eye on these items in particular—and check into my Wi-Fi Web page from time to time:

http://www.duntemann.com/wifi/index.htm

Got a hot Wi-Fi tip or interesting wireless story? Worked up a cool Wi-Fi antenna or other gadget? Contact me at:

jduntemann@paraglyphpress.com

Good luck. Have fun. Wires are just *so* twentieth-century!

Appendix A: Directory of Suppliers

Alltronics

PO Box 730
Morgan Hill, CA 95038-0730
408-847-0033
408-847-0133
ejohnson@alltronics.com
www.alltronics.com

I mourn the passing of Alltronics' Zanker Road retail store (a wonderland of peculiar surplus electronic and mechanical parts, where I spent a lot of time and money in the late 1980s) but their paper and online catalogs are still worth seeing. I cite them here because they carry a large variety of microwave-compatible coaxial connectors, including SMA, TNC, and most varieties of N connectors. They do not, unfortunately, carry any of the reverse polarity connectors. They have a $15 minimum order and a secure Web site.

CDW NetComm

200 N. Milwaukee Avenue
Vernon Hills, IL 60061
888-465-4239
www.cdw.com

CDW NetComm used to be called DataComm Warehouse before the Micro Warehouse Group was purchased by CDW in late 2003. The firm carries a good selection of Wi-Fi and wired network hardware, routers, switches, hubs, tools, network cabling (including CAT 5 patch and crossover cables) uninterruptible power supplies, software, and various networking exotica.

Fleeman, Anderson, & Bird

7143 State Road 54, #228
New Port Richey, FL 34653-6104
727-853-0256
727-841-7110 FAX
sales@fab-corp.com
www.fab-corp.com

FAB is probably the best single source of Wi-Fi antennas, connectors, and cables going. They carry pigtails in various lengths, with N male connectors on one end and all the major (peculiar) Wi-Fi RF connectors on the other. They carry many antennas for Wi-Fi work, including a mini mag-mount vertical for netstumbling, ceiling antennas for cube-farm installations, and outdoor antennas for point-to-point work, up to a 24 dBi parabolic. Loose reverse-polarity connectors are available, as well as low-loss microwave coax by the roll or by the foot. They sell the Orinoco Gold Classic Wi-Fi PC card, which has an external antenna jack and works with NetStumbler. There is a $10 minimum shipping charge, and goods may be ordered through a secure Web site.

RAM Electronics

7980 National Highway
Pennsauken, NJ 08110
888-726-2440 Order Line
856-488-9196 FAX
sales@ramelectronics.net
www.ramelectronics.net

RAM has just about every type of network and communications cable I've ever heard of, including USB 2.0, FireWire, and CAT 5 patch and crossover cables. They also sell switches, hubs, network interface controllers, and lots of other products that connect things, from audio and video up to Gigabit Ethernet.

RF Parts

435 S. Pacific Street
San Marcos, CA 92069
800-737-2787 Order Line
760-744-0750
760-744-1943 FAX
888-744-1943 Toll-Free FAX
rfp@rfparts.com
www.rfparts.com

I've ordered amateur radio parts from RF Parts for almost 20 years now, and they've been completely reliable all these years. They carry a nearly complete selection of coaxial cable and microwave coaxial connectors, including all the reverse-polarity varieties, and the elusive RMC-6010-B. They have a $25 minimum order.

Appendix B: FCC Regulations Governing Wi-Fi

W<sup>i-Fi is governed by rules embodied in Federal law, in a document people refer to informally as "Part 15." Technically, this document is "Part 15 of Title 47 of the Code of Federal Regulations," and it's the rules and regulations imposed by the Federal Communications Commission (FCC) on unlicensed use of the radio spectrum. Devices that fall under Part 15's jurisdiction include microwave ovens, shortwave diathermy medical devices, cordless phones, low-power "walkie talkie" 2-way radios, and of course, 802.11 wireless networking gear.

What I want to do here is walk you through some of the jargon, regulations, and issues that you may have to confront as Wi-Fi users. The burden of following the rules mostly falls on equipment manufacturers, *unless* you begin setting up high-gain antenna systems or in some other way boost the effective power of your Wi-Fi signals. And even if you follow Part 15's rules to the letter, there may be issues involving interference, both to your network and from your network, which may not be easy to understand, much less solve. Knowing where you stand in terms of government regulations may prove helpful in working out difficulties as a citizen in the greater Wi-Fi community.

Part 15 itself is an immense body of government legalese, and until you have some practice reading government regulations, it's hard to pick out the portions of the law that apply to ordinary Wi-Fi operations. In this topic I'll summarize the most significant points. One thing to keep in mind is that if you use Wi-Fi equipment unmodified and as it was intended to be used, there's almost nothing in the law that you need to know. It's the technical enthusiast who works with antennas and broad-ranging, outdoor installations who has to keep certain restrictions and limits in mind.

Power Limits

The power limits that the FCC sets on Wi-Fi gear are easy to state, but maybe not quite so easy to understand. The total equivalent isotropically radiated power (EIRP) coming off of a Wi-Fi antenna is, in most cases, limited to four watts. (And we all understand EIRP, right? Right.) If your antenna has high gain, your EIRP could be over the FCC's limits and illegal even if the microwave power measured going into the antenna were well below the legal limits. A gain antenna effectively "boosts" signal power by focusing the radiation in certain directions at the expense of others.

EIRP is the power that you would have to apply to an isotropic antenna to get a signal equivalent to what is radiated from a real-world setup being evaluated. An isotropic antenna is one that radiates equally in all directions, including up and down. (I speak more of isotropic antennas and antenna gain in Chapter 8.) An isotropic antenna is a mathematical abstraction. It exists to provide a sort of "base point" for calculating antenna gain. In figuring EIRP, both the power coming from the actual transmitter and the antenna doing the radiating must be taken into account. It sounds forbidding, but if you use commercial antennas it's really not that hard, because all commercial antennas come with a measured antenna gain figure.

In the fine print of Part 15, the FCC states that the transmitter output power of a piece of Wi-Fi gear is limited to 30 dBm (1 watt) when connected to an antenna with a gain of 6 dBi. (I discuss dBm and dBi in detail in Chapter 8.) If you calculate the EIRP by adding the transmitter dBm figure to the antenna gain, you get 36 dBm, which is equivalent to 3.98 watts—close enough to four watts to call it there.

If your Wi-Fi adapter puts out 1 watt (which is something I've never actually seen!) and you want to use an antenna with *more* than 6 dBi gain, you must reduce the transmitter power so as to keep the EIRP at 4 watts (36 dBm) or under.

In truth, most Wi-Fi access points and client adapters put out 35 to 50 milliwatts tops, and it takes a bodacious amount of antenna gain to turn 35 mw of transmitter power into 4 watts EIRP. To see just how much, convert 35 mw to 15 dBm, subtract that from 4 watts, or 36 dBm, to give you 21 dBi of necessary antenna gain. That's a *big* antenna! (Of course, you can buy monster 24 dBi parabolic antennas for under $100 these days, so getting in trouble is possible, and won't even cost you that much.)

If you're constructing your own gain antennas, it's a little trickier, as measuring the actual gain of an antenna in dBi requires expensive lab gear and fairly controlled conditions. However, if you're using standard access points and client adapters putting out 100 mw or less, a tin can antenna or simple 5-element shotgun Yagi will not get you anywhere near four watts EIRP. You would need 16-18 dBi gain to take 100 mw to the limit. For 35 mw (which is what most access points put out) you would need more antenna gain, to the tune of 18 to 20 dBi, and making an antenna like that in the garage out of junk takes real skill.

Interference with Other Users

The sections of Part 15 that deal with interference are tricky enough to understand. The real problem, as I see it, lies in understanding how interference problems can be resolved within the Part 15 framework. There's a lot of misunderstanding about things like who has priority in the band and who doesn't, and even legal experts can be mistaken in their interpretation of FCC rules. I am neither a government bureaucrat nor a lawyer, and so my interpretation may be flawed as well. What I write here is for general orientation only. If you feel you have a true "legal situation" regarding Wi-Fi or another service in conflict with a Wi-Fi installation, get legal counsel—ideally, counsel with some experience in FCC regulations and communications law generally. This might be a lawyer who represents local radio or broadcast TV stations, for example. A local legal referral service may be helpful, as this is a rather arcane legal specialty.

The big picture with Part 15 is fairly simple: Part 15 devices (including your Wi-Fi installation) must not cause harmful interference to others, and must gracefully accept interference received from others. This seemingly contradictory philosophy reflects (in legalese) the inevitable truth that interference is going to happen. We must try our best to avoid it, but when it happens, *we have no legal basis to fight it.*

This sounds grim, but it's not... at least, not yet. (More on which later.)

Keep in mind that "harmful interference" as the FCC defines it does not mean deliberate jamming. That's a Federal crime, though it's difficult to prove. "Harmful interference" means interference from devices that are legally certified to operate and are just doing their ordinary jobs correctly.

As I hope I made clear in Chapter 1, the 2.40 to 2.47 GHz stretch of the electromagnetic spectrum is not only "the Wi-Fi band." Wi-Fi technologies are a *very* recent addition to an already-substantial crowd of users in that region of radio space. It is also sobering to note that virtually all of those earlier users have a better legal claim on the spectrum space than Wi-Fi does.

It's useful to take a look at some of the other users of the band and see what the problems might be.

- *Part 18: Industrial, scientific, and medical RF devices.* These are things like microwave ovens, induction heaters, medical diathermy machines, jewelry cleaners, and medical diagnostic equipment. They use RF (radio frequency) energy for things other than communication; mostly heating, sometimes imaging. The FCC has pretty tight standards on such gear, and unless you're right on top of a business using machinery of this type, it's unlikely to be an issue. That's good, because there's very little to be done about it. Part 18 ISM devices are primary in the band, and even if they interfere with you, that's in a legal sense their right. Users of Part 18 devices have no control over their frequency or power output. Many ISM device users may not even understand what their machines are doing nor that they have any "radio" component at all. If you have an apartment over a business that uses Part 18 gear, well, consider a move to Wireless-A gear operating at 5 GHz.

- *Part 97: Amateur Radio.* There is an Amateur Radio allocation from 2390 to 2450 MHz. There is some fine print about the amateur radio service being primary on some frequencies and secondary on others, but the kicker is that Part 15 devices (which include Wi-Fi networking gear) are secondary to *all licensed services using the same frequencies.* So if a ham radio station interferes with your network, you have no legal recourse and will have to accept that interference gracefully. On the other hand, ham radio ops have a lot more mobility on the bands, in that ham radio transmitters are allowed to move around within a band and are not tied to one frequency. So with a little diplomacy you may be able to persuade nearby ham operators to slide up or down away from the Wi-Fi channel on which you're operating. The very best diplomacy is to become a ham radio operator yourself. Apart from diplomacy, you'll have access to one of the brightest bunches of guys in the technology arena, and you'll learn something in the process. I've been a ham radio op for thirty years now, and the good news is that amateur radio use of 2.4 GHz is very thin, and almost no factory-made gear is sold for those frequencies. What gear is used on 2.4 GHz is hand-made or modified from some other service. Thus the guys who do use the band are *extremely* sharp technically, and may be able to work with you if approached gracefully. (They'll be much more inclined to do so if you're also a licensed amateur!)

- *Part 80 and Part 87: Maritime and Aviation Radar.* Aircraft and watercraft are allowed to use radar devices on broad stretches of frequencies from 470 MHz, past 2.4 GHz and all the way up to 10.5 GHz. There's not much to be done about this, but the interference is likely to be transient (as ships pass by or planes fly over) and your Wi-Fi signals are so weak as to not even be on their radar.

- *Part 90: Public Safety Radio.* Part 90 radio communication devices operate from 2.45 to 2.835 GHz. Use of the band may be on a licensed or unlicensed basis, under parameters that I do not fully understand. Police and fire departments are the main users, along with rescue services and other odds and ends. Legally, they are considered licensed and have priority on the frequencies that they use. Unless you're next door to a police station or fire department Part 90 is unlikely to be a problem. Part 90 frequencies do not overlap the entire Wi-Fi band, so if you're asked by a public safety agency to move your network, you can take it to one of the channels (1 to 6) below 2.45 GHz.

- *Part 74: Electronic News Gathering (ENG).* Mobile TV news crews operate vans with their own high-gain parabolic antennas on retractable masts. You've probably seen these vans running around town or parked with their antennas cranked up in front of baseball games or major crime scenes. There is an ENG allocation from 2.45 to 2.4835 GHz. Because they're mobile and running at higher power levels you're unlikely to interfere with them. That's good, because they're a licensed service and have a claim on the band that you don't. If they interfere with you, well, you have to just wait it out—but by the nature of the beast, the interference is unlikely to last very long. As with Part 90, the overlap with Wi-Fi is not complete, and you can move to a lower channel (6 or under) if it becomes a problem.

That's the short list of people who have a better claim on the band that you and I and our Wi-Fi networks share. (There are some others but those are the ones you're most likely to encounter.) It sounds grimmer than it is. Most licensed sources of interference are mobile, and will come and go and won't be a problem for long. The exceptions are Part 18 machinery and public safety base stations. You can dodge Part 74 and Part 90 base station users by moving down to channels 1 to 6. Interference from Part 18 devices you may have to live with, or else move to Wireless-A.

As for amateur radio operators, well, they have frequency mobility options that you don't, and their use of the band is still fairly thin. Join them, don't fight them—especially since a lot of ham radio people are also avid users of Wi-Fi gear. My sense is that many (perhaps most) computer enthusiasts who are also ham radio ops avoid using the 13 cm band (as they call it) to avoid interfering with their *own* networks. This is your saving grace. Take it gladly.

Interference from Other Wi-Fi Users

Your biggest single problem in terms of interference is likely to be *other nearby Wi-Fi networks*. Such interference is almost inevitable, and your legal recourse is close to nil.

If you live in an apartment building or condo complex, your problems may well be intense, if not now then in coming years, as Wi-Fi use moves from sparse to ubiquitous. Your neighbors may have no idea how to change their access point channels, and they may not feel inclined to let you tinker with their networking machinery.

If you suspect interference from a neighbor's Wi-Fi network, download the NetStumbler utility (see Chapters 19 and 20) and determine what channels your neighbors are using. See what signals are strongest, and try to identify a channel as far removed in frequency from the strongest nearby access points as you can manage, and move there. (See Figure 1.3 for a frequency chart of 2.4 GHz Wi-Fi channels, which embraces both Wireless-B and Wireless-G.) If you're on good terms with your neighbors, it's possible to work with them to limit the excursion of both your and their signals, possibly by placing a flat or curved mesh reflector (see Chapter 18) behind their access points or yours. (Try yours first to see if that helps. It's easier tweaking your own system.)

If things seem hopeless, you can switch to Wireless-A equipment, which is shorter-range and more suited for use in an apartment or condo than in a largish house. (It is unaffected by interference from Wireless-B or Wireless-G equipment, and users of the 5 GHz spectrum where Wireless-A operates are much fewer and farther between.)

One very new Wi-Fi technology has the potential to be a *big* problem among closely-spaced networks: Super-G. This speed-enhanced version of Wireless-G is fixed on channels 5 and 6 of the 2.4 GHz Wi-Fi band, and it gets its high speed (108 Mbps!) by using channels 5 and 6 simultaneously. If you're close to a Super-G network, your only option is to move your own network to either channel 1 or channel 11, and pray. The signal of a Super-G network is quite broad, and if you're close enough to a Super-G access point, it may seem like it occupies the entire Wi-Fi band. The first fix to try is putting all possible distance between your access point and the nearby Super-G access point. Putting some metal mesh or sheet metal between your access point and the Super-G access point is another thing to try—take a look at the mesh reflectors that I describe in Chapter 18. If that doesn't work, you may need to go to Wireless-A.

Other Part 15 devices are occasionally a problem, including cordless phones and microwave ovens. The one I'm really worried about is still too new to weigh the interference threat: Bluetooth. This supposedly ultra-short-range "personal area network" technology isn't quite as short-range as some claim, and it works on many of the same frequencies as Wi-Fi. I'm not convinced that Bluetooth is as useful as claimed, and I recommend against using both Bluetooth devices and Wi-Fi devices in the same computer installation, at least until we know more about how well the two technologies coexist. Bluetooth and Wi-Fi are both Part 15 devices and are on equal legal footing in terms of using the band, but that doesn't help when your connection locks up.

In summary: According to Part 15, you and I and others in Wi-Fi land *have no legal standing against other users of the Wi-Fi frequencies*. Finesse, technical flexibility (that is, learning how to change your access point's channel), and diplomacy are your only weapons. Use them. Complaints to the FCC and lawsuits will get you nowhere.

Appendix C: Finding Your TCP/IP Configuration Data

If you're installing your first home network but already have a broadband Internet connection, the computer connected to your broadband cable or DSL modem is already configured to connect to the Internet. To do so, it had to be configured for certain parameters, according to the requirements of your Internet Service Provider (ISP). These parameters were (hopefully!) given to you in a small booklet or piece of paper. On the other hand, if someone else installed your broadband Internet connection for you, the configuration may never have been written down.

The first parameter is "big picture:" Are your configuration parameters provided *dynamically*, from your ISP's remote DHCP server, or are they *static*? Static means that the several parameters have specific, unchanging values that must be entered manually.

If the answer is "dynamically," there's the whole answer, and nothing more need be looked for. (It's very easy to use DHCP, and almost all modern Internet connections do.) If the answer is "static," you'll need to find the values for your

- IP address

- Subnet mask

- Default gateway

- DNS server address or (more likely) your 2 or 3 DNS server addresses

You can, of course, call your ISP and ask for them again. On the other hand, if your agreement requires that you pay extra for each additional computer in the house, doing so is an invitation for them to hike your monthly bill. It's possible to determine what your configuration is by looking at configuration screens on the computer that is currently connected to your broadband modem, and that's what this appendix is about. Displaying these screens is a different procedure in Windows XP, Windows 2000, and Windows 98, so I'll explain it separately for all three.

Once you obtain these configuration values, they need to be entered into the configuration screen of your router appliance or wireless gateway, as I explain in Chapter 9.

Windows XP and 2000

The screens where configuration information can be found look the same on both Windows XP and Windows 2000. Getting to those screens is done a little differently on each Windows version, however.

Windows 2000: Click the Start button, and scroll up to Settings, then across to Network and Dial-up Connections. Select "Local Area Connection" from the Network and Dial-up Connections menu. The status window for your network adapter will appear. Click on the Properties button in the window. The "Local Area Connection Properties" window will appear. In the central pane you'll see a list of network protocols. Scroll down to the Internet Protocol (TCP/IP) entry. With that entry highlighted, click Properties.

Windows XP: Click the Start button, and from the Start menu click **Control Panel**. From the control panel browser, double click **Network Connections**. The Network Connections applet window will appear. Each of the network adapters installed on your computer will be listed below the heading "LAN or High-Speed Internet." You will probably only have one (some computers have several; my own has four!) but make sure that you highlight the adapter to which your broadband modem is connected. (Hint: If you have several adapters listed, see if only one is enabled, and choose that one.) Right-click on your network adapter and select **Properties** from the context menu. In the **Local Area Network Connection** properties window that appears, highlight Internet Protocol (TCP/IP) and click the Properties button.

The properties window that appears (for either Windows version) tells the whole story. Figure C.1 shows two such properties windows side by side. What you'll have on your computer should resemble one or the other. On the left is the properties window for dynamic configuration. Not much there: Just two radio button selections indicating that those values are set automatically. On the right is a properties

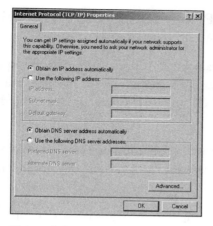
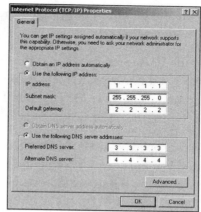

Figure C.1
Dynamic (Left) and Static (Right) TCP/IP Properties.

window indicating static configuration. The values for the addresses are artificial, though I can't guarantee that somebody somewhere isn't using them. The point is that real values are present in those fields, and that the fields are not grayed out. Copy them down carefully, or (better still) take and print a screen shot of the window. All the values you'll need are right there in that single window.

Windows 95, 98, and ME

Unfortunately, Windows 9x (which is built on an entirely different operating system "chassis" than Windows 2000 and XP) does not make its network configuration data quite as easy to find, because it doesn't display it all in one tidy window. Here's how to show it:

Click the Start button. Scroll up to the **Settings** item and across to **Control Panel**. From the list of Control Panel applets that appears, double click on **Network**. The Network applet displays a list of both hardware adapters and protocols, which can be confusing. What you need to find is the TCP/IP protocol for the network adapter through which your PC is connected to the Internet. Look for something that looks like this:

TCP/IP -> DazzleCom 100-Base T Network Card

Again, there may be multiple adapters listed, but only one is likely to be enabled, and if only one is enabled, that's the one you want. Highlight the appropriate line and click the Properties button. The **TCP/IP Properties** window for that adapter will appear. It's a tabbed window with seven different tabs, and the information you want is present on three of those tabs: the **IP Address** tab, the **Gateway** tab, and the **DNS Configuration** tab.

Look at the **IP Address** tab first. If the **Obtain an IP Address Automatically** option is selected, you know your Internet connection is configured for dynamic address configuration using your ISP's remote DHCP server. If this is the case, you don't need to look at the other two tabs.

However, if **Specify an IP Address** is selected, your configuration information is static, and you must copy information from (or take screen shots of) all three tabs. Figure C.2 shows the three tabs side by side.

That's all there is to it. Fortunately, static configuration is now quite rare for home office broadband Internet connections, and you will almost certainly have to do nothing more than select "Obtain Address Information Automatically" in the proper place in your router appliance or wireless gateway. This is explained in Chapter 9.

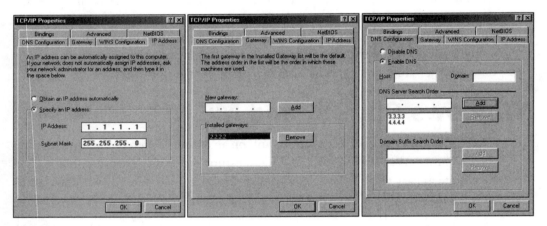

Figure C.2
Windows 98's TCP/IP Configuration Tabs.

Encyclopedia of 802.11 Standards

802.11

Wireless networking has been around for some time. The University of Hawaii pioneered the wireless LAN idea with an experiment called ALOHANET way back in 1971. ALOHANET was an expensive, big-iron system solving a serious problem—trading data among university sites scattered across four islands—but the principles are the same as those that govern data-trading between the machine in your den and the one in your kids' rooms. Sun Microsystems created a prescient hand-held mini-tablet computer called the Star 7 in 1992, which included 900 MHz wireless networking, but it never made it to market.

The first wireless LAN technology I ever saw was a 900 MHz UHF ISM band WaveLAN system, which was demonstrated at a COMDEX trade show in 1994. The demo consisted of a laptop with a PCMCIA card (physically identical to today's Wi-Fi PCMCIA cards) networked to a PC about ten feet away. The data rate was 1.6 Mbps, which seemed mighty fast at the time.

The WaveLAN system worked, and worked well. It was expensive, but the people who needed it needed it bad, and WaveLAN and numerous systems like it became a small and little-known sliver of the networking industry, mostly used by high-priced consultants to create proprietary solutions to specific problems, usually for big corporations. Everybody had a different scheme for bundling data into packets and spinning it off into the airwaves, and nobody's scheme talked to anybody else's scheme. That was the way all the vendors in that era wanted it; their customers had money and were willing to spend lots of it, so there was bottom-line value in keeping them captive to a proprietary system.

In 1997, the Institute of Electrical and Electronic Engineers (IEEE) released their 802.11 standard for wireless networking, and everything changed.

The Magic of (IEEE) Numbers

The IEEE is a large and influential body of engineers that does a great many things, but what they do that matters most (in my view) is develop and establish technology standards. Standards are important because they enlarge markets, and make it possible for technologies manufactured by different vendors to interoperate and communicate with one another. This is especially important in the area of computer communications, in which the whole idea is to get the machinery talking.

The IEEE has been doing this for a long time, and in many areas, some of them pretty far removed from computing. The process, however, happens in pretty much the same way: The IEEE establishes a "working group" to pursue a particular standards issue. The group meets and hashes out the issue, sometimes for several years, and eventually creates a document that defines or modifies a standard. The document is then sent out to interested IEEE members for a mail vote. Based on the results of that balloting, the document is either sent back for further work or is adopted as a new (or modified) standard.

Working groups are given numbers. When a working group is tasked with modifying an existing standard that already has a number, the group is given a new number that has either additional digits or else letters appended to the existing standard number.

The 802 Standard

The mother of all IEEE networking standards is the 802 standard, which was under discussion for most of ten years. This standard, which was finally adopted in 1990, governed the lowest level of networking functions: Physical and link control. (These are the bottom two layers of the Open Systems Interconnection model for networking. If you're reasonably technically inclined, the OSI model is worth some study, as it is enormously useful in keeping the countless network standards and mechanisms separated and correctly related. Unfortunately, it's a big subject, and I cannot cover it in detail in this book.)

The overall networking standard was numbered 802. Different standard areas within the greater 802 standard were given decimal qualifiers. The original Ethernet protocol invented by Xerox in the early 1970s was refined slightly and given the number 802.3

when it was standardized as part of the 802 definition. The Token Ring networking technology introduced by IBM in the mid-1980s was given the number 802.5.

In the mid-1990s, the IEEE created a working group to develop a standard for wireless networking. The working group was given the number 802.11 (which is the eleventh working group under the 802 standard, *not* a refinement of 802.1) and it was adopted in 1997.

The original 802.11 standard specified a frequency of 2.4 GHz with available data rates of 1 and 2 megabits per second (Mbps). 802.11 products were marketed almost immediately, but were slow to be accepted, at least in part because the data rates were so slow. 802.3 wired Ethernet technology had gone from 10-Base-T (10 Mbps) to 100-Base-T (100 Mbps) at about the same time, and 2 Mbps looked pretty grim by comparison. Furthermore, radio hardware that could work effectively at 2.4 GHz frequencies was still pretty expensive at that time. The end result was that 802.11 networking did not exactly set the world on fire. The IEEE almost immediately created several task groups to begin work on improving 802.11, especially in the area of data rate.

The fire came in 1999, when the 802.11b amendment to 802.11 was accepted and published. 802.11b was formerly known as "802.11 High Rate" because it added 5.5 Mbps and 11 Mbps data rates to the existing 1 and 2 Mbps rates. 802.11b was the right spec at the right time, and most manufacturers who had been selling 802.11 hardware wasted no time updating their products to adhere to the new 802.11b standard. Although still fairly expensive (I paid $1200 for an 802.11b access point in early 2000) the higher bit rates were enough to put 802.11b wireless networking on the radar screens of large and mid-sized companies that could afford it.

High prices kept 802.11b networking out of the hands of ordinary consumers until 2000, when Apple's AirPort wireless networking system took prices down into consumer territory. After that, it was *le deluge*, especially once an industry consortium called the Wireless Ethernet Compatibility Alliance (WECA) created the Wi-Fi compatibility testing program. (WECA later changed its name to the Wi-Fi Alliance.) At this writing wireless access points can be had for under $100, and client adapters for as little as $50.

802.11b remains the most significant 802.11 standard, but others have now been released and still more are in process. 802.11a products reached the market late in 2001, with still-faster bit rates (though much higher prices), and 802.11g products are now mainstream and cheap. (Note that the letters are assigned when a task group is *formed*, not when the eventual standard is finalized and adopted. The 802.11a and

802.11b task groups were formed at the same time, but the 802.11b folks had a less difficult job to do and finished first.)

Some 802.11 task groups are addressing only specific features of 802.11 networking, like encryption. Not all letters in the "alphabet soup" are full upgrades to the 802.11 idea.

Competing wireless network technologies are out there, but none have the same sense of destiny that 802.11 has. A technology called HomeRF hit the market early in 2000, and although slower than Wi-Fi, it was at its introduction much cheaper, and has arguably better security and built-in machinery for handling telephone calls. (In a sense, HomeRF merges wireless LANs and cordless phones.) However, HomeRF never achieved what 802.11 achieved: The magic of an IEEE standards designation.

The IEEE imprimatur, with its respect among major industry hardware vendors, is what makes the magic happen. Unless or until a directly competing technology gets that imprimatur, I don't see anything knocking 802.11 from its leadership position in wireless networking.

Individual explanations of all the significant "alphabet soup" extensions to 802.11 follow this topic.

802.11a (AKA "Wireless-A")

When the 802.11 standard was finalized in 1997, it was clear that the initial standard's 2 Mbps data rates were lower than the market was likely to accept. Very soon thereafter, the IEEE created two task groups to define faster refinements to 802.11 wireless networking. The 802.11a and 802.11b task groups were formed at almost the same time, but the 802.11a concept was more ambitious, and even though both 802.11a and 802.11b were finalized in 1999, it took more than a year longer for 802.11a hardware to reach the market. Indeed, the 802.11a equipment market was just beginning to hit critical mass in late 2002.

The reasons are not hard to explain. 802.11b was intended to be backwards-compatible with the initial 802.11 standard. It uses the same frequency band and much technology in common with 802.11. Companies with existing 802.11 products were able to upgrade their products quickly to 802.11b. 802.11a, on the other hand, was a radical rethinking of the 802.11 idea, especially at the lowest, physical layer of data transfer, where the radio waves and modulation schemes happen.

802.11a completely re-makes the network physical layer. It operates in the 5 GHz portion of the radio spectrum, literally more than twice the frequency of 802.11. Radio technology at 5 GHz is only distantly related to radio technology at 2.4 GHz. The parts and assembly techniques used are incompatible.

Perhaps even more radical differences lie in the frequency management and modulation schemes used by the two standards. *Frequency management* is a scheme for controlling where in the frequency spectrum a radio's signal exists at any given moment. *Modulation* is a scheme for imposing data on the radio signal. 802.11 uses two different *spread spectrum* techniques for frequency management, Frequency Hopping Spread Spectrum (FHSS) and Direct Sequence Spread Spectrum (DSSS). A different modulation scheme is used in 802.11 for each of the two supported bit rates. 802.11b improves a little on DSSS to boost its bit rate to 11 Mbps.

802.11a systems, by contrast, use a frequency management system with the intimidating name Orthogonal Division Frequency Multiplexing (ODFM). ODFM allows eight different bit rates, from 6 Mbps to 54 Mbps, by using five different modulation schemes. An 802.11a connection will use the highest data speed possible given current conditions between the two 802.11a devices. This speed is chosen automatically.

It's not necessary for you to digest or remember the heavy tech here, so much as the fact that 802.11a and 802.11b are radically different in how they work, so much so that there is zero compatibility between the two. The importance difference between them is that 802.11a gives you *speed*. 54 Mbps is major, almost five times what 802.11b can develop under the best of circumstances.

The bad news (as always) is that "circumstances" do matter. The range of 802.11a wireless networking is significantly shorter than 802.11b. This has less to do with the frequencies used (as many have said) than the simple fact that high bit rates don't "travel" as well over radio waves as lower bit rates do, power levels being equal. The quality of a high bit rate signal degrades faster with distance than a low bit rate signal. With more bits flying through the air per unit time, even minuscule noise pulses can corrupt a packet and force a resend. The quality of radio reception (in terms of signal to noise ratio) is better closer to the receiver, so the closer you are to the receiver, the higher a data rate is possible. In part it's engineering, of course, but a lot of the problem is simple physics.

The practical consequences are that as you move an 802.11a client adapter farther from an 802.11a access point, the bit rate used will drop. On the fringes of reception, don't expect much more than the lowest rate of 6 Mbps. You'll get your best rates when the clients are in the same room with the access point, without any obstructions between the two. (Think of a conference room with an access point on the wall and everybody tapping away on wireless-equipped laptops at the main conference table.) Put any walls in the way, and 54 Mbps will drop to a lower rate. How much lower depends on the distance and the construction of the wall, and as always in fluky things like radio work, Your Mileage Will Vary.

It probably doesn't matter to small office and home office people, but 802.11a is still strictly an American phenomenon. (Don't expect your laptop to talk to European access points with an 802.11a PC card stuck in it.) European governments have not set aside precisely the same spectrum space at 5 GHz as our American FCC has, and there is already a high-speed European wireless LAN standard called HIPERLAN/2. The IEEE has a couple of task groups working on ironing out differences between 802.11a and HIPERLAN/2 (as well as a few other non-US wireless protocols) so European and American high-rate wireless LAN hardware can interoperate at 5 GHz. This is being addressed in task groups 802.11h and 802.11j. See those topics for more information.

On the upside, interference from other devices is much less of a problem with 802.11a. The 5 GHz band it uses is part of the National Information Infrastructure program (remember the Information Superhighway?) and it does not have to share radio space with cordless phones, microwave ovens, jewelry cleaners, induction welders, and Bluetooth smart gadgetry.

Costs on 802.11a hardware have always been higher than 802.11b—generally at least twice as much. These high costs—and the widespread perception of 802.11a as very short-range—have kept it from winning very much market share. The appearance of low-cost 802.11g gear in late 2003 pretty much sealed the fate of 802.11a to obscurity, and my expectation is that 802.11a will slowly drift into the shadows and be mostly out of production by 2006.

802.11b (AKA "Wireless-B")

The vast majority of wireless network activity happening around the world today operates under the 802.11b standard, which many now prefer to call Wireless-B. The original 1997 802.11 standard called for two data rates—1 and 2 Mbps. This was par for that time (pre-802.11 wireless products like the original WaveLAN operated at similar speeds) but far below the 10 or increasingly 100 Mbps that wired Ethernet networks were achieving.

The IEEE created the 802.11b task group to develop a faster but still backwards-compatible enhancement to 802.11. The final standard was approved and published in 1999, and the first products appeared on the market soon after. The IEEE simultaneously created a separate task group to develop a much faster wireless system that was *not* required to be backwards compatible. This was 802.11a, and because both the standards work and creation of actual products took longer than 802.11b, "a" trailed "b" by almost two years. (I discuss the differences between 802.11a and 802.11b at greater length in the 802.11a topic.)

802.11b added two additional data rates of 5.5 and 11 Mbps. At its best, 802.11b was thus on par with the common and inexpensive 10-Base-T Ethernet system. 802.11b hardware could still communicate with most older 802.11 hardware, though at the slower 802.11 data rates.

When implementing the original 802.11 standard, manufacturers could choose either of two frequency management schemes: Frequency Hopping Spread Spectrum (FHSS) or Direct Sequence Spread Spectrum (DSSS). The two schemes are similar, and both grew out of original ideas patented in the 1940s by (of all people) actress Hedy Lamarr and a composer and player piano hobbyist named George Antheil. FHSS was cheaper to implement, but DSSS allowed higher data rates, so DSSS quickly pushed FHSS into the status of a historical footnote. The 802.11b spec calls for the use of DSSS alone, except at the lowest bit rates—and that's simply an option; modern Wi-Fi gear neither generates nor understands FHSS, even at the lower bit rates. DSSS does it all for 802.11b. This means that 802.11b gear is for the most part *not* backward compatible with 1997-vintage 802.11 equipment running FHSS.

802.11b networks, like the original 802.11 networks, operate in the unlicensed 2.4 GHz Industrial Scientific and Medical (ISM) band. As the name of the band implies, 802.11b networks must share spectrum space in the band with all manner of gadgetry including microwave ovens, industrial heating machines, medical monitoring equipment, cordless telephones, and (more recently) Bluetooth-equipped computers and peripherals. Spread-spectrum techniques reduce the effects of interference, but it's possible that running the microwave oven will cause your Wi-Fi network to drop packets. Reports from my contacts indicate that interference is rarely a problem, and defining when it becomes a problem is a fluky business. I have both a microwave oven and a 2.4 GHz cordless phone system in my home, and it has never become an issue in almost four years of Wi-Fi experience.

After 802.11g equipment hit the mass market in late 2003, 802.11b began its long, slow decline to obsolescence. 802.11g provides five times the bit rate at almost the same cost, and supports the newer Wi-Fi Protected Access security technology as well. It will take some years but by 2008 I think that 802.11b will take its place in history, pushed out by 802.11g and the even faster 802.11n.

802.11c

The original 802.11 specification indicated that 802.11 gear could connect two distinct wired networks across a wireless link. (Imagine separate LANs in your home and in your detached garage, with data running between the two LANs over a wireless connection.) This is called *bridging* or *bridge mode*, and most of the newer access points can do it, with some persuasion.

The original specification was none too clear on how bridging was to be accomplished with 802.11 gear, so the IEEE assembled a task group to define it clearly. This group wrote the 802.11c specification for wireless bridging, which is complete and implemented by all but the least expensive access points. Older access points that support upgradeable firmware can often be upgraded to support bridging with 802.11c compliant firmware.

Bridging is used most often by colleges and business campuses with networks in multiple but nearby buildings. Friends and relatives living within line of sight of one another have also used bridging to connect networks in their various locations. Bridging requires fixed-position gain antennas, weatherproofed access points mounted on poles, power feeds to operate the access points, and a certain considerable amount of fooling around to make it all work. Incompatibilities between access points are the start—but not the end—of your problems! See Chapter 17 for detailed advice on creating a wireless bridge of your own.

802.11d

The thorny problem of getting wireless networking to interoperate throughout the developed world was the point of IEEE task group 802.11d. The United States, Japan, and most of Europe had regulations on frequency and bandwidth that more or less harmonized; the 802.11d group basically clarified the rules for manufacturers who wished to extend their markets to several other countries with different regulations. The work of this group is complete and has been adopted as part of the larger 802.11 standard. It's not of much interest, however, unless you're a manufacturer looking to sell wireless gear in places like Israel or Korea.

802.11e

Sending a file over a network connection is a little like a Star Trek transporter system: You break the file down into a great many small packets of data, and transmit those packets individually to the other end of the connection. There, the packets are reassembled into the full file.

It doesn't matter what order the packets are sent in, nor that they arrive all at the same time or at the same rate or in the same order. It simply matters that they all arrive intact. If they're all present, the system can reassemble the packets into the complete file.

In sending other sorts of data over a network connection, things like the order that packets are sent and received and the rate at which they arrive *do* matter. Voice and streamed audio or video can be seriously distorted if packets turn up out of order, or if they "bunch up" or "space out" and do not arrive at a consistent rate. Nothing in the original 802.11 specification addressed what they call "quality of service" (QoS) for data transmission, and that was the primary goal of IEEE task group 802.11e.

There are mechanisms for ensuring QoS in wired network, but for various arcane technical reasons these mechanisms cannot be used in 802.11 wireless networks. The 802.11e group is working on various enhancements to 802.11 to improve QoS, and the intent is that existing Wi-Fi gear will be able to take advantage of these improvements via firmware upgrades. The group is still working at this writing, with approval and publication not expected until mid-2004 or after.

802.11f

Most wireless networks in small offices and home offices have only a single wireless Access Point. With only one access point, a wireless network is called a Basic Service Set (BSS). For networks that must cover areas larger than a single access point can reach, multiple access points may be connected (via cable) to form an Extended Service Set (ESS). Although the concept of an ESS is part of the original 802.11 specification, certain details of how an ESS operates are lacking.

Key among these are the details of roaming. It is often useful to allow a person to carry a laptop or PDA around in a large building or area served by an ESS without losing a connection to the network when moving from the range of one access point into the range of another. In a manner similar to the familiar cellular phone network, the access points must "hand off" a connected user to adjacent access points when a user leaves the range of the first access point.

Roaming requires that the access points present in an ESS communicate with one another. Defining what data the access points must share about roaming clients and how the data is shared is the mission of the 802.11f standard, which will create the Inter-Access Point Protocol (IAPP). Many of the higher-end access points have supported roaming for some time, but lacking this IAPP standard, manufacturers have had to devise their own roaming machinery, and most such proprietary systems do not work well (or at all) with access points from other vendors. The appearance of 802.11f changes this, and makes standardization for roaming possible. If you're going to implement an ESS and support roaming, check with your equipment vendors to see if 802.11f compliance is available in new products or firmware/driver upgrades, The 802.11f task group published the final version of the standard in October 2003, and products incorporating the standard are beginning to come on the market. Because it is a feature most desired by corporations and large organizations with multi-building office campuses, you're most likely to see 802.11f compliance in high-end, enterprise-level access points. It's quite likely that consumer-level access points and wireless gateways will never fully implement IAPP.

802.11g (AKA "Wireless-G")

802.11b hardware has been with us since 1999, and its maximum 11 Mbps data rate is looking smaller and smaller all the time. "Gigabit Ethernet" (sometimes called 1000-Base-T) is starting to appear in new computers and network interface controllers, providing a *billion* bits per second through the network, rather than 802.11b's measly 11 million. People have long been demanding faster bit rates—the question is how to get there. 802.11a hardware provides a faster maximum bit rate of 54 Mbps, but it's not backward compatible with 802.11b, and moving to 802.11a requires that you replace *all* of your wireless hardware before *any* of it will work at faster speeds. Costs of 802.11a gear being several times that of 802.11b gear, few have elected to take that road to a faster wireless network.

In the fall of 2000, the IEEE created a task group called 802.11g to devise a faster version of 802.11b, while preserving backward compatibility with 802.11b within the 2.4 GHz band. An 802.11g client will communicate with 802.11b access points, though at the lower bit rate supported by 802.11b. When communicating with other 802.11g devices, an 802.11g device will communicate at up to 54 Mbps—almost five times the speed of 802.11b.

The 802.11g standard was finally released—after much wrangling and arguing among semiconductor industry powers—in July 2003. Interestingly, many of the Wi-Fi industry leaders "jumped the gun" toward the middle of 2003, and released "draft-G" equipment based on early drafts of the 802.11g standard. This early equipment worked well with other units of its own kind, but there were often incompatibilities between draft-G units from different manufacturers. After the final draft of the standard was published, manufacturers of draft-G gear worked out firmware upgrades for their products to bring draft-G equipment up to full 802.11g compliance. Be careful: If you buy 802.11g equipment on the used market, check for firmware level and see if any upgrades are available from the manufacturer. Draft-G equipment is not guaranteed to work correctly with true standard 802.11g gear!

The price point on 802.11g equipment is surprisingly low, only 10% to 15% more than comparable 802.11b equipment—and less than half the cost of 802.11a, which works at the same speed and has a shorter range. This has led to its immense popularity, and my suspicion is that over time, 802.11g will replace both 802.11b and 802.11a.

802.11h

The 802.11d task group worked on harmonizing 5 GHz frequency allocation among America, Europe, and Japan. Although its work is completed and considered successful, that task group didn't get the whole job done. Task group 802.11h was formed to address some additional radio frequency regulatory issues governing 5 GHz wireless networks. In particular, most European nations require that wireless network hardware operating at 5 GHz have two features called Transmission Power Control (TPC) and Dynamic Frequency Selection (DFS). These are both present in the European HIPERLAN/2 specification, and the goal of 802.11h is to extend the definition of the 802.11 physical layer (the radio technology layer) to embrace those features of HIPERLAN/2 that government regulations require in Europe and other places where HIPERLAN/2 is used.

The 802.11h draft is still in play as I write this, but it is getting close to completion, and should be ratified by mid-2004. Additional, non-technical delays in implementation are expected because European governments and standards agencies have to ratify 802.11h as well. Products are not expected until third quarter 2004, pending ratification both here and in Europe.

802.11i

Wireless Equivalent Privacy (WEP) was broken in August 2001 by a team at AT&T Labs, based on work published earlier that same month by Scott Fluhrer, Itsik Mantin, and Adi Shamir. (The paper by Fluhrer, Mantin, and Shamir was actually about a flaw in the cryptographic algorithm used by WEP and was not itself an attack on WEP.) Ever since then, security has been the Big Honking Problem with wireless networking.

Earlier, in March of 2001, the IEEE formed the 802.11i task group to attempt to standardize security in wireless LANs. This was prior to the cracking of WEP, but many thought even before the crack that WEP was at best a bare minimum security technology. For example, WEP does nothing to prevent the several legitimate clients connected to a wireless network from monitoring one another's traffic. WEP protects only against outsiders who have not yet connected. The same key is used to encrypt all traffic coming into or going out of a single access point, so all connected clients must have the same key—hence there is no privacy at all among the clients.

Concerns like this led to the task group's creation, but as yet nothing has been approved, though drafts have been circulating since early 2003. The general approach to 802.11 security has two layers: 802.1X authentication and a WEP fix called Temporal Key Integrity (TKI).

802.1X Authentication

A good part of the 802.11i task group's mission is to seamlessly incorporate support for 802.1X authentication into the greater 802.11 standard. Although the callouts are confusingly similar, 802.1X is *not* a part of the 802.11 standard. The IEEE 802.1 standard is separate from 802.11, and specifies general management mechanisms for both wired and wireless networks. The 802.1X sub-standard lays out an authentication framework that defines a challenge-response method of determining whether a client is authorized to associate with an access point. The standard additionally provides a way for the client to determine if the access point is in fact "real" and not a hacker emulating an access point as a security attack called "the man in the middle."

One of the challenges in using 802.1X authentication is that it requires a fair amount of centralized administration, including an authentication server program running somewhere on the network to which the access point is connected. In a corporate LAN this isn't a problem. In a home office or small office environment, however, it could be a showstopper, so provisions are being made for simplifying 802.1X to allow implementation of 802.11i security in Wi-Fi gear targeted at the SOHO market. We can look at *Wi-Fi Protected Access* (WPA) as a preview of how this will probably work. (See Chapters 14 and 15 for more on WPA.)

Nor is 802.1X authentication completely hack-proof. A peculiar attack called "session hijacking" was published by University of Maryland researchers William Arbaugh and Arunesh Mishra in February 2002. The attack is difficult to describe briefly, but it involves "race conditions" in timing between the authentication server and the wireless access points that use it. Unless the timing of establishing and breaking associations with wireless clients is *exquisitely* managed, hackers can break in and hijack a session with neither the client nor the access point (and thus the authentication server) realizing that anything is amiss.

This problem is a timing problem, and is due to the fact that 802.1X authentication is currently "stateless." A fix has been proposed that will make 802.1X a "state machine" and eliminate the session hijacking attack.

Key Management with TKI

One of the things that WEP lacks is effective automatic key management. Because keys are set manually and changed only when the network administrator decides to change them (again, manually) WEP keys do not change very often. This is especially true in larger organizations where there are many users and lots of laptops floating around, not always in places where they can be easily found. When a given key is used for too long, it becomes vulnerable to cracking, because the ability to crack a key depends on the number of packets intercepted that had been encrypted using that key. If a hacker with a packet sniffer utility intercepts a large enough number of packets encrypted with the same key, utilities like AirSnort or Kismet can crack the key.

In lightly used networks (like those used in home offices) it takes a *long* time to gather enough packets to crack WEP; in some cases many months. (This is why WEP is relatively secure for home network use, contrary to conventional wisdom.) But in heavily used corporate networks where an access point is basically moving packets continuously, without pause, an AirSnort attack can succeed in as little as five hours.

The whole idea of intelligent key management is to link renewal of keys to the volume of packets sent through a given wireless access point. If the keys are changed before enough traffic moves through the access point to allow an AirSnort attack, the attack is foiled and AirSnort has to begin packet sniffing again from scratch. There is a performance burden inherent in replacing keys frequently, but the hope of TKI is to renew a wireless network's keys just often enough to prevent a packet-gathering sniffer attack. Ongoing research will refine our understanding of how often keys will need to be changed, but at the moment it looks like every 10,000 packets or so.

TKI also adds an additional security touch by encrypting something called the initialization vector, which makes AirSnort-type attacks even more difficult.

Once the TKI mechanism is fully defined and the 802.11i standard approved, access point and client adapter firmware will have to be upgraded for TKI to work—but TKI would appear to be our best near-term bet for fixing the gaping hole in WEP-based Wi-Fi security.

Ultimately, WEP will have to be abandoned entirely. There are far more secure wireless network encryption systems on the drawing boards. WEP's eventual heir is likely to be the Wireless Robust Authentication Protocol (WRAP), which is based on the extremely secure AES encryption mechanism. As WRAP will be completely incompatible with WEP, it will probably require a whole new generation of wireless hardware, and is still a long way off.

802.11i is still being actively debated, and it's unlikely that firmware upgrades or new products will appear before mid to late-2004—perhaps later. In the meantime, the Wi-Fi Alliance has developed tests for a subset of 802.11i that can be implemented in firmware without changes to existing Wi-Fi certified hardware. Wi-Fi Protected Access (WPA) was released in completed form in the fall of 2002. The Wi-Fi Alliance feared that a tidal wave of bad publicity on Wi-Fi security would damage the acceptance of Wi-Fi in corporate IT shops. (These were not groundless fears!) WPA-compliant devices became available in mid-2003, and are now common, especially among 802.11g access points, gateways, and client adapters. Manufacturers have been slower to upgrade older gear, at least in part because the internal processors are slower and memory more limited.

There is no guarantee that full 802.11i compliance will be something that can be added to current (and especially older) Wi-Fi gear with only a firmware or driver upgrade. My hunch is that 802.11i will be implemented initially on new-design, high-price enterprise-class Wi-Fi gear only, and consumer-class gear may be limited to incorporating the 802.11i subset WPA. This is not necessarily a tragedy; WPA is extremely strong protection for SOHO networks, and probably more than strong enough for corporate networks that do not traffic in financial, medical, or military information.

802.11j

The very new IEEE 802.11j task group has begun to work out some details of the media access control and physical layers for 5 GHz wireless networking so that the American 802.11a standard and the European and Japanese HIPERLAN/2 standard may coexist and eventually converge. Unless you're a manufacturer looking to develop gear to operate at 5 GHz worldwide, there's not much of interest here. Regulatory issues (see 802.11h) must be solved before anything will come of this effort.

802.11k

This 802.11 task group addresses the Quality of Service (QoS) issue in terms of providing feedback from the radio layer of a piece of 802.11 wireless gear, indicating the quality of the link and how well things are getting through. There's no standard way of providing such feedback, so it's difficult to get different pieces of 802.11 hardware to "agree" on how good or bad a connection really is—and thus how to improve the connection or simply live with what it has. 802.11k will dovetail with the 802.11e standard to provide a coordinated system for ensuring quality of service over an 802.11 wireless link. This is a highly technical matter, and a final solution remains far downstream.

802.11l

For some reason, the IEEE chose not to use the letter "l" as a standards qualifier in its 802.11 program, perhaps because it looks too much like the letter "i" and the digit "1". Whatever the reason, there is no "802.11l" task group.

802.11m

In mid-2003, the IEEE convened a task group to do a little housekeeping on the greater 802.11 standard. The 802.11m task group will be looking over the previous amendments to the 802.11 standard and out of that study will create a summary document to reflect "the state of 802.11" on its publication. Note well that this is not a technical task group, and no new 802.11 functionality will be defined in its eventual document. The final publication date of this document is unknown, but will probably not occur until early 2005.

802.11n

Now that the 802.11g standard has been approved and is taking over the Wi-Fi market, much of the current excitement among future projects centers around 802.11n. This task group, which was convened in September 2003, is chartered with raising the throughput—not simply the bitrate—of 802.11 wireless networking to 100 Mbps. This certainly means raising the bit rate to a breathtaking 250 Mbps or beyond, which is a daunting technical challenge.

It's also a change in custom for 802.11 wireless networking, which has always focused on the bitrate as the defining characteristic of a networking technology. This has led to a gap in expectations (and some end-user disappointment) when implementing a "54 Mbps network" only to find that data moves over the network no faster than 20 or 22 Mbps. For the 802.11n group, the speed of the technology will be defined as its throughput, and the bitrate will become a footnote, raised to whatever level necessary to achieve the technology's throughput goals. The hope is that 802.11n will be marketed as a "100 Mbps" networking technology, even if its bitrate is as high as 250 Mbps.

Because the task group is so new, crisp details on the technology are rare. One requirement is that the standard not be irrevocably tied to a particular frequency band. Another is that it must be implementable on the NII bands at 5 GHz, which is a far less crowded frequency than 2.4 GHz. The IEEE has asked the FCC to consider opening up entirely new bands to 802.11 family wireless networking, and currently the 802.11n proposal is the only heifer in this particular pen.

The IEEE is cooperating with the Wi-Fi Alliance during the development of the 802.11n standard, so that Wi-Fi compliance testing will be ready to implement almost as soon as the standard is completed and published. As soon as "Wireless-N" gear hits the market, the Wi-Fi compliance logo will be ready to put on the box, avoiding all the "draft-G" incompatibilities that plagued early 802.11g gear.

When will this happen? The IEEE set an unusually tight schedule for the completion of 802.11n—by the end of 2005—which would be at least a year faster than a new technology task group typically completes its work. I'm not willing to guess whether or not they'll make this schedule, but the promise of 100 Mbps throughputs are making many industry mouths water, especially in connection with home automation and home media distribution.

The existence of an IEEE 100 Mbps networking task group may put the brakes on acceptance of proprietary high-throughput technologies like Atheros' Super G, which achieves 50 Mbps throughput by using two 2.4 GHz channels simultaneously. Texas Instruments' 802.11b+ technology, which boosted bit rates from 11 Mbps to 22 Mbps, did fairly well until 802.11g burst on the scene, and it is now increasingly irrelevant.

Keep your eyes open. It's going to be an interesting couple of years.

802.11x

You'll see this term now and then, in the press and on the Internet. 802.11x is *not* an IEEE task group! (At this writing, they're only up to the letter "n.") What people mean by "802.11x" is "all the 802.11 wireless networking standards." In other words, when they say, "802.11x security is easily crackable," they mean that the 802.11a, 802.11b and 802.11g wireless standards are all prey to the same weaknesses in their security features.

Also, please don't confuse the term "802.11x" with the security standard "802.1X." (Nobody said this would be easy, right?)

Index